Money, Morals, and Politics

Money, Morals, and Politics

MASSACHUSETTS IN THE AGE
OF THE BOSTON ASSOCIATES

William F. Hartford

Northeastern University Press
BOSTON

Northeastern University Press

Library of Congress Cataloging-in-Publication Data
Hartford, William F., 1949–
Money, morals, and politics : Massachusetts in the age of the Boston
Associates / William F. Hartford.
p. cm.
Includes bibliographical references and index.
ISBN 1-55553-489-9 (cloth : alk. paper)
1. Whig Party (Boston, Mass.). 2. Boston Associates. 3. Elite (Social
sciences)—Massachusetts—History—19th century. 4. Massachusetts—Politics
and government—1775–1865. I. Title.
JK2334.B7 H37 2001
974.4'6103—dc21   2001041021

Composed in Caslon by BookComp, Inc., Grand Rapids,
Michigan. Printed and bounded by Thomson-Shore, Inc., Dexter,
Michigan. The paper is Writer's Offset, an acid-free stock.

MANUFACTURED IN THE UNITED STATES OF AMERICA

05   04   03   02   01   5   4   3   2   1

Contents

Acknowledgments

$\mathcal{A}$S WITH ALL HISTORICAL STUDIES, this work would not have been possible without the aid of numerous institutions and individuals. Acknowledgment of these debts must begin with the librarians and archivists who helped me gather the data on which the book is based. I am especially grateful to staff members at the W. E. B. DuBois Library, University of Massachusetts at Amherst; Microtext Department and Department of Rare Books and Manuscripts at the Boston Public Library; American Antiquarian Society, Worcester, Massachusetts; Houghton Library, Harvard University; and the Massachusetts Historical Society. For permission to quote from their manuscripts, I would like to thank the following institutions: Boston Public Library/Rare Books Department, Courtesy of the Trustees; American Antiquarian Society; Manuscripts and Archives Division, New York Public Library, Astor, Lenox and Tilden Foundations; Schlesinger Library, Radcliffe Institute, Harvard University; Houghton Library, Harvard University; and the Massachusetts Historical Society.

Among scholars in the field, my greatest debt is to Bruce Laurie, who has been a source of inspiration and guidance for almost two decades. In putting together this study, I benefited as much from Bruce's current work on the antebellum middling classes as I did from his careful reading of the manuscript. Another former teacher, Leonard Richards, brought his keen editorial skills and vast knowledge of antislavery politics to bear on the book's central chapters, saving me from several blunders and helping me to restructure what had been a particularly confusing section of the work. I would also like to thank Ronald Story for helping me to sort out my thoughts on elite philanthropy. I should further note that anyone who chooses to write about nearly any era of Massachusetts history must walk in some very big footsteps. This is especially so for the early national and antebellum periods, and I want to express my gratitude to the many scholars whose contributions made my trek much easier than it otherwise would have been.

At Northeastern University Press, John Winegartner provided editorial assistance. Ann Twombly of Northeastern and Fred Thompson of Book Production Resources guided the study through production. I am also grateful to Yvonne Ramsey for her careful and thorough copyediting of the manuscript. Closer to home, my sister, Kathleen Vermette, stepped in at a critical moment and retyped the study. Lastly, I must thank my parents, Francis and Julia Hartford. Without their continuing support, my days as an active historian would have come to an end some time ago.

Introduction

A GROUP OF WEALTHY FAMILIES bound together by marriage and financial interest, the Boston Associates controlled extensive elements of the antebellum Massachusetts economy. As leading figures in the Whig Party, they also dominated state politics. Although they remained a powerful force in Bay State economic life long afterward, by 1860 their political authority had been sharply curtailed. A major aim of this work is to show how this occurred. I am by no means the first historian to do so. Indeed, Kinley J. Brauer stated one of the study's main themes when he wrote that the Associates' rule "lasted only through their own generation: born of an economic revolution, they succumbed to a moral revolution."[1]

What sets this study apart from those of Brauer and other students of Boston's elite is that it also asks, How did the Associates and their Federalist forebears maintain their political authority for so long? To some scholars of the period, the question scarcely needs asking. Citing Thomas Jefferson's remark that Bay Staters had a "traditionary reverence for certain families, which has rendered the offices of government nearly hereditary," one historian has written that the Associates "wielded power with unassuming ease, as had the Adamses or Otises before them." This is not the place to contest Jefferson's grounds for making such an observation. It is enough to note that—during the postrevolutionary era at least—his comment would have been news to the commonwealth's independent-minded voters as well as the families who were the supposed beneficiaries of that "traditionary reverence." Although Massachusetts Federalists and their Whig successors did enjoy periods of relatively uncontested rule, such periods rarely lasted long. To maintain their dominance, party leaders knew better than anyone that they could not rely on family reputation. Rather, they had to do what all aspirants to political power in democratic societies have done to secure and preserve that power: fashion a compelling appeal that attracted support from broad elements of the electorate. In the case of Bay State Whigs, it is particularly important that one understands the bases of that appeal, because the Whigs' later retreat from fundamental principles explains much about the party's demise.[2]

My examination of those principles and the role they played in the rise and decline of Massachusetts Whiggery rests on two conceptual foundations: class and region. As the people who created Lowell and other manufacturing centers, the Associates contributed much to the formation of an industrial working class in nineteenth-century New England. The significance of this development receives some attention in the pages that follow. Of much greater consequence for our story is their relations with another social grouping that contemporaries referred to as the "middling interest" or the "middling classes." These were the politically active shopkeepers, farmers, lesser professionals, and master artisans who throughout the antebellum period continued to account for a large proportion of the region's production and exchange. No party that failed to enlist their backing or that of the mechanics with whom they generally had close ties could expect to control state government, and given the acute sensitivity of these people to elite condescension, upper-class Bostonians could hardly take their support for granted. When they finally lost that support, their days as a political ruling class were numbered.[3]

Though less important than the foregoing, intraclass relations also had an effect on the Associates' political fortunes. As the economic basis of elite power shifted from commerce to manufacturing after the War of 1812, the conflicting interests of merchants and mill owners temporarily obstructed efforts to fashion a coherent and compelling political appeal in the wake of Federalism's demise. Although these differences were quickly resolved, a later conflict proved far more damaging. This struggle pitted the Associates against a group of younger subelites who had not yet achieved full elite status. Disgusted by elite backtracking on the slavery issue, these Conscience Whigs subjected their elders' conduct to pitiless attack, in the process shattering the moral authority undergirding elite rule. No less important, their rebellion took place at a time when age and physical debility were beginning to thin the Associates' ranks. The subelites' abandonment of Whiggery made the filling of political vacancies a much more difficult task than anyone had anticipated.

What made the Conscience Whig insurgency so destructive was that it struck at the very roots of elite hegemony. Forged during periods of sectional crisis, the Federalist and Whig appeals combined a spirited defense of regional economic interests with a bold assertion of regional values. So long as the Associates could maintain a credible pose as defenders of New England civilization, there was little likelihood that they would lose the middling-class support needed to control state government. By midcentury, their halting and equivocal response to a series of events, beginning with the annexation of Texas in the mid-1840s, had given rise to a much different image: that of a morally vacuous aristocracy more concerned about promoting its own interests than protecting the commonwealth from the aggressions of a malevolent slave power. As these perceptions spread, it was only a matter of time before the Associates' adversaries established a new political order in Massachusetts.

My account of these developments begins at the turn of the century. With the rise of Jeffersonian democracy and the Virginian's election to the presidency in 1800, Massachusetts Federalism seemed destined for an early end. Distrustful of the middling classes and committed to a rigidly hierarchical view of social relations, the Federalist Party's old-school leaders had nothing but contempt for the popular electioneering techniques of the new era. Yet, their gradual withdrawal from active politics did not signal the death of Federalism. Rather, it gave the party new life by creating openings for a group of young Federalists more willing to adapt to the demands of political combat in an age of mass democracy. The economic distress and political turmoil caused by Jefferson's embargo and the War of 1812 provided these younger men with a golden opportunity. Making the most of it, they crafted a political appeal that established a sound basis for elite rule by linking merchant fortunes to those of regional farmers and mechanics, and by depicting Federalism as a bulwark against the economic assaults of an envious slaveholding aristocracy. Their achievement not only enabled the party to retain control of state government into the 1820s but, more important for our story, it furnished an ideological framework that a proto-Whig manufacturing elite later refashioned to suit its needs during the nullification crisis of the early 1830s. How it managed this feat is the subject of Chapter 2.

For all the attractions of Whig ideology, elite rule did not go unchallenged. Where the Associates proclaimed that all Bay Staters would benefit from the spread of manufacturing, others asked how people forced to work twelve-hour days in a textile mill could conceivably better their condition. Small in number and with limited resources, the labor radicals who raised such questions never seriously threatened elite dominance. Their critique was nevertheless important. On one level, demands for legislation mandating a ten-hour workday fueled political insurgencies in Lowell and other mill towns. More generally, labor activists focused attention on the costs of an industrializing process that had losers as well as winners. What they had to say and how the Associates justified their own activities are examined in Chapter 3.

Whereas the radical critique exposed weaknesses in the Whig doctrine of social interdependence, increasing concern about slavery-related issues tested elite commitment to the defense of regional interests and values. As Chapter 4 shows, the Associates' response left much to be desired. In the 1830s, their heavy-handed treatment of William Lloyd Garrison and his followers—which prompted criticism from within the Associates' own ranks—did more to facilitate rather than check the spread of antislavery sentiment. A decade later, when the Tyler administration's efforts to annex Texas heightened fears of slave power aggression, their unwillingness to exhaust all avenues of opposition led discontented subelites to question whether they could be trusted to place principle before profit. Apart from shared doubts about elite constancy on the slavery issue, these younger men had various reasons for rejecting the Associates' political leadership. Chapter 5 looks at the diverse factors that influenced three of them: Charles Francis Adams, Theodore Parker, and Horace Mann.

By midcentury, Bay State Whiggery was in serious trouble. The Compromise of 1850 added to party woes by creating a division between Websterite forces willing to make any concessions to reduce intersectional discord and party regionalists committed to preserving Whiggery's reputation as a champion of free labor and New England civilization. Meanwhile, a coalition of Free Soilers and Democrats captured state government in the 1850 and 1851 elections. Although the Whig Party rebounded from these setbacks, it did so mainly because of coalition factionalism. Still divided and still led by an economic elite that no longer possessed the moral authority needed to command popular respect, Massachusetts Whigs were unprepared to meet the challenges presented by the Kansas-Nebraska Act. With the Know-Nothing insurrection of 1854, an era of upper-class rule that stretched back to the Federalist period came to an end. These developments are examined in Chapters 6 and 7.

CHAPTER ONE

Forging a Popular Conservatism

*I*N THE EARLY 1800S, Bay State Federalism and the system of elite rule that it sustained seemed fated for an early end. As one party leader lamented in a letter written shortly after Jefferson's overwhelming victory in the 1804 election: "We appear to be changing very fast, & the little Federalism that is left, will soon be no more. We may rise to something else, but not to that." On one level, this writer's foreboding proved premature. It would be another two decades before the "party of good principles" passed from the scene in Massachusetts, where as late as 1823 it still controlled the governorship. But his broader point was well taken. Though Federalism did "rise to something else," it was not the same party it had once been. To prevent the early demise many predicted, party bosses had to abandon an older elitism and create an electoral style more congruent with the popular politics of the era.[1]

Important parts of the story have been told before, most notably by David Hackett Fischer, whose study of early-nineteenth-century party development provided an able account of the organizational innovations adopted by beleaguered Federalist leaders. Our account here focuses on ideology and class relations, beginning with an examination of the traditional social views that obstructed Federalism's adaptation to the new political world created by the rise of Jeffersonianism. It then goes on to relate how Jefferson's embargo and "Mr. Madison's War" furnished a propitious set of circumstances that enabled Bay State Federalists to secure the backing of a heretofore resentful "middling interest" and forge a popular conservatism capable of maintaining elite rule.[2]

The story's main actors fall into three groups of Federalists, identified by Fischer: a group of old-schoolers who viewed popular politics with disdain and largely withdrew from active participation in party affairs after Jefferson's triumph in 1800; a transitional group deeply imbued with old-school principles and biases but still too young and energetic to remain content hurling abuse from the sidelines; and an ambitious band of young Federalists who were all too ready to accommodate the new order as they set about doing whatever was necessary to establish their political relevance. Though such ideal types are never perfect, Fischer's categories remain extremely useful and will be employed here to distinguish among major tendencies within Federalism.[3]

The most distinctive feature of old-school Federalism was its uncompromising adherence to a hierarchical view of sociopolitical relations in which the masses deferred to their wealthier and more learned superiors. Believing inequality to be part of the natural order of things, old-schoolers peered out upon a two-class society comprising "the better sort of people" and "the lower sort." One group had a responsibility to rule, the other to obey. And so long as each acted accordingly, peace, prosperity, and happiness could be had by all.[4]

It was no coincidence that many of the most prominent old-schoolers hailed originally from the North Shore port towns of Essex County, where early seafaring experiences left a lasting mark. "The habit of the quarter-deck," Thomas Wentworth Higginson once wrote, "went all through Massachusetts Federalism." An even more important factor in shaping the old-schoolers' view of social relations was the networks of dependency that leading shipowners established in these locales. In postrevolutionary Salem, Newburyport, and other maritime communities, sailmakers, cordwainers, shipwrights, stevedores, common seamen, and a host of other occupational groups relied on wealthy merchants for their livelihood. In turn, merchants expected dependent mechanics and laborers to follow their lead on political matters. As late as 1816, Salem Republican William Bentley complained of Federalist threats to withhold employment from any seaman or dockworker who cast a ballot for the party of Jefferson.[5]

Outside the port towns, economic power was generally more diffuse. In rural inland communities, most farmers and craftsmen operated independent household enterprises, and wage labor occupied a less prominent place in productive activities. Yet even here, substantial merchants and landowners could exact some measure of deference from subsistence farmers and small tradesmen by providing debt relief and various favors. After departing his ancestral home in Essex County, George Cabot found life in late-eighteenth-century Brookline more than agreeable. "The swinish multitude are occasionally noisy," Cabot said of his neighbors, "but a sop from the cook or a pail from the dairy-woman never fails to quiet them. More humane than those of Paris, they are satisfied with milk instead of blood. Accordingly, we go on harmoniously together; I support their table, and they support mine."[6]

Had all the world been Brookline, Bay State Federalists would have been a happy lot indeed. Unfortunately for them, it was not. One source of unease was the ambitious mechanic, farmer, or small trader who was discontent with his current social position. The old-schoolers did not condemn social mobility per se, for many of them had experienced substantial mobility in their own lives. Having come of age during the chaotic years of the American Revolution, when older patterns of wealth and authority were thrown into question, they had seized their opportunities and made the most of them. They also demonstrated a willingness to promote the advancement of bright young men of good principles but modest fortune such as Fisher Ames, who drew criticism in his first electoral contest for being the son of a mere almanac writer, and who perhaps best stated the Federalist position on social mobility in an 1801 essay: "All cannot be rich, but all have a right to make the attempt; and when some have fully succeeded, and others partially, and others not at all, the several states in which they then find themselves become their condition in life; and whatever the rights of that condition may be, they are to be faithfully secured by the laws and government."[7]

The problem was that many of those who failed to succeed refused to accept their fate. To the old-schoolers, these disappointed social climbers constituted the most dangerous group in the community because of the pivotal role they played in the social dynamics of revolution. Eager to attribute their lack of success to others, George Cabot explained, "the desperate adventurers who are uneasy with their present condition know that the poor we have always with us, and that these, with many of the ignorant, are easily formed into a revolutionary corps in every country." At such moments, Cabot added, reason was unavailing, for "jealousy of the rich is a passion in the poor, which can always be appealed to with success on every question, and instead of an answer to every argument."[8]

Cabot's fears, which old-schoolers generally shared, reveal much about the Federalist response to events of the 1790s. They help explain why Federalists came to view the French Revolution with such alarm, and why they saw a similar threat in Jeffersonianism. When old-schoolers condemned Republicans as Jacobins, they were not simply engaging in partisan rhetoric, but expressing deeply ingrained apprehensions about a political creed that gave unchecked rein to the aspirations of ambitious men. Moreover, recent history provided a frightening example of what happened when those aspirations went unsatisfied. Many old-schoolers believed Shays'

Rebellion had resulted from the actions of just such people—people who, in Stephen Higginson's words, "have too high a taste for luxury and dissipation, to sit down contented in their proper line, when they see others possessed of much more property than themselves."[9]

In Salem, William Bentley later observed, "the Republicans are the middle class & the Federalists, the top & bottom." Although Bentley oversimplified, the statement did reflect a basic truth: there was little room in Federalist social ideology for the middling interest. To be sure, old-school criticism focused on those who sought the unattainable and refused to accept the result. But such fine distinctions were never easy to convey, given the elitist tone of most old-school social pronouncements. This was especially so during the economic boom of the mid- to late 1790s when, said Theodore Sedgwick, "The rage for acquiring property by other means than industry and economy was not confined to towns but extended to almost every neighborhood in the country." Federalists paid a heavy price for these attitudes, as their political adversaries took advantage of their inability to address the middling interest without condescension. Among rank-and-file Republicans, Henry Adams shrewdly commented, "dislike of Federalists was a social rather than political feeling, for Federalist manners seemed to them a willful impertinence."[10]

Old-schoolers might have found the middling interest a little easier to bear had they been able to rely fully on members of their own class. But there were problems here as well. One was the politician who craved popular applause. Ardent proponents of government by the rich, the wise, and the good, Federalists had little patience with wealthy political leaders who—to them at least—appeared neither wise nor good. When confronted with a public figure of this sort, old-schoolers felt they had a duty to expose the man's shortcomings.[11]

In postrevolutionary Massachusetts, John Hancock best exemplified the problem. To old-schoolers, the flamboyant Hancock was a ridiculous figure who had more money than sense, and Stephen Higginson assumed the responsibility of letting people know why this was so. Writing under the pseudonym "Laco," Higginson penned a series of newspaper articles that presented a savage indictment of Hancock's political career. As a member of the Continental Congress, Higginson wrote, Hancock had been a veritable model of indecisiveness while exhibiting a fondness for "Southern manners" that led him "to contemn the manly simplicity and firmness of the delegates from New England." As a Revolutionary War general, his steadfast cultivation of "new means of dissipation" rendered him totally incapable of leading by example. And as governor, he appointed numerous public officials whose only qualification for office was their friendship with him, and who through "their ignorance and folly, injured the reputation of government, perverted the laws, and proved a curse to society," thereby paving the way for Shays' Rebellion.[12]

On a related matter, old-schoolers worried about the constancy of wealthy associates when political principle clashed with economic interest. This concern first surfaced at mid-decade during the struggle over Jay's Treaty. Though not entirely satisfied with the treaty themselves, Federalist leaders believed any agreement that promised peaceful relations with England and undermined the position of France's American friends deserved their support. They were not happy when regional merchants, dissatisfied with the pact's provisions on the West India trade, initially joined anti-treaty demonstrations. Even though most of these merchants subsequently backed the agreement, the fact that they could be so easily misled disturbed old-schoolers. Speaking for many of his colleagues, Fisher Ames wrote: "I could neither repress my indignation, nor disguise my contempt for the blindness and gullibility of the rich men who so readily lend their strength to the party which is thirsting for the contents of their iron chests." Later in the decade, during the Quasi-War with France, George Cabot expressed serious doubts as to whether merchants engaged in the West India trade could resist the temptation to take advantage of rising prices in the French islands. Recognizing that one could not ignore the "commercial spirit" that dictated merchant conduct, Cabot urged Secretary of Treasury Oliver Wolcott to "authorize indiscriminate reprisals on French property," in the hope that "Avarice would fight our battles."[13]

Old-schoolers further regretted that merchants failed to do their part in financing the military buildup of the late 1790s. The reluctance of wealthy traders to subscribe generously to government loans forced the administration to pay higher interest rates than was politically wise, given popular resentment of the increased taxes levied to fund the war program. But as Stephen Higginson explained in a letter to Wolcott, this could not be helped. With current trade prospects "too flattering to be resisted," active merchants had most of their funds tied up in various commercial ventures. Nor could "money-holders who have retired from trade" be expected to relieve pressure on the government: "A moment like the present," Higginson noted, "is to such men, the time for harvest; their private interest is opposed to the object in view; and we must expect them to combine to reduce, rather than raise the price of stocks, that they may purchase with more advantage." In concluding, Higginson advised that government should attempt to bolster confidence through the systematic adoption of wise policies.[14]

That Higginson could do no better than this was of particular significance. A principled man who strongly believed that people of privilege had a special duty to behave responsibly, he had never been an apologist for elite foibles. In addition to his flaying of John Hancock, he had been a sharp critic of Robert Morris's financial machinations in the Second Continental Congress. And when Alexander Hamilton put together his financial program, Higginson recommended that public securities obtained at depreciated prices be redeemed at reduced interest rates, so as to remove the impression that the funding plan constituted nothing more than a contrivance for "stripping the poor to increase the wealth & influence of the rich." His lame counsel on the war loan reflected a major shortcoming of Federalist thought: an inability to resolve the contradiction between marketplace dictates and desired elite conduct. It was a dilemma that, for obvious reasons, old-schoolers never fully confronted. To have done so would have required the promotion of government initiatives that restricted their own economic activities. Rather than consider this unwelcome prospect, they found it much easier to propose policies that would make avarice an ally of good principles.[15]

The Quasi-War with France marked a major turning point in Federalist fortunes. Begun with high hopes and broad public support, it ended in disaster. One problem was the Federalist war program, which reawakened fears of a standing army and necessitated the imposition of a burdensome land tax that caused widespread alarm among small farmers. Just as troublesome were disagreements among leading Federalists over how to deal with France. When John Adams opted for peace, party ideologues, led by Alexander Hamilton, openly broke with the president. This created a dilemma for Massachusetts old-schoolers, who shared Hamilton's views but recognized that a clear majority of other Bay Staters strongly endorsed Adams and his policies. Thus immobilized, they sat out the ensuing presidential contest, privately lamenting the personal idiosyncrasies and muddled political thinking that had prompted Adams to pursue so misguided a course. Long before these intraparty squabbles could be resolved— if indeed they ever were—Thomas Jefferson had moved into the White House.[16]

Despite Jefferson's victory, Federalism remained a powerful force in Massachusetts politics. But most old-schoolers, believing that history had passed them by, derived limited satisfaction from continued state successes. The ever-pessimistic George Cabot had sensed that the end was near as early as 1797. "Whenever I go out of my house, or have guests within it, I am led to distrust my reasoning and conclusions," he observed in a letter to Oliver Wolcott. "I find myself in the errors of the French revolutionists, who maintain that the people understand their true interests, and will always vindicate them." Though Cabot never accepted such beliefs, he felt that little could be done to combat their spread. "After all," he added, "we must take the world as it is, and by expecting less, expose ourselves to less chagrin." With Jefferson's triumph, Cabot and other old-schoolers who had remained politically active largely withdrew from involvement in political affairs.[17]

The next several years were a transitional period in the evolution of Bay State Federalism. For a time, a group of younger men who championed old-school beliefs, but recognized the need to court popular opinion, attempted to devise a means of broadening Federalism's appeal without sacrificing party principles. The most notable of them was Fisher Ames, a Dedham lawyer whose slight frame and correct manners masked a fiery temperament. Driven as much by impulse as reflection, Ames was by his own admission "habitually a zealot in politics": "I burn and freeze, am lethargic, raving, sanguine and despondent, as often as the wind shifts." In what might have served as a comment on much of his writing, he said of one letter, "I have written thus far as fast as I could make my pen go— too fast, perhaps, for my discretion to follow." On another occasion he remarked, "With a warm heart, and an hot head, I often dupe my friends and myself."[18]

Although economic circumstances had forced Ames to retire from Congress in 1797 and "truck off reputation for cash" by resuming the full-time practice of law, he maintained a keen interest in party affairs. Convinced that Jefferson's election posed a dire threat to all that Federalists held dear, Ames sharply criticized the old-schoolers' withdrawal, which he attributed to a debilitating preoccupation with wealth and leisure. When they largely ignored his urgent warnings, he lashed out in disgust, condemning their sacrifice of principle for "money-getting" and pleasure: "He that robs me of my good name, takes trash. What is it but a little foul breath, tainted from every sot's lungs? But he who takes my purse, robs me of that which enriches him, instead of me, and therefore I will have vengeance." A long-time critic of such attitudes, Ames believed that people content to wait for the actual day of expropriation were already doomed. And despite failing health, he resolved to employ what energies he still possessed to combat Jeffersonian heresies. "If Jacobinism makes haste," he wrote to Timothy Pickering, "I may yet live to be hanged."[19]

Turning his attention to party problems, Ames believed that Federalism most needed an effective and appropriate means of shaping public opinion. However much he despised the Republican press, Ames appreciated its contributions to party successes and felt that Federalists had yet to make full use of this powerful electoral weapon. Accordingly, he urged the creation of a first-rate newspaper—one that would provide a forum for the thoughtful analyses of "able men" rather than the scribblings of "uneducated printers, shop-boys, and raw schoolmasters" that all too frequently littered the columns of existing party publications. Unlike these wretched sheets, the journal Ames envisioned would "be fastidiously polite and well-bred. It should whip Jacobins as a gentleman would a chimney-sweeper, and keeping aloof from his soot."[20]

With the establishment in 1801 of the *Palladium*, Ames got his newspaper. But he got little else. Younger party regulars welcomed Ames's enthusiasm and energy; they had much less use for his ideas about political journalism. By mid-decade, the *Palladium* was indistinguishable from other party papers, and Ames had for all intents and purposes joined his more aged old-school associates in political retirement. He recorded his disillusionment in an unpublished 1805 essay, "The Dangers of American Liberty," whose unrelievedly grim analysis of political developments made the gloomy speculations of George Cabot seem cheerful by comparison. Ames now saw that the press offered no solution; "by rendering men indocile and presumptuous," it was more often than not part of the problem. Nor could he see any way of reversing America's downward course, there being "no society without jacobins; no free society without a formidable host of them; and no democracy whose powers they will not usurp, nor whose liberties, if it be not absurd to suppose a democracy can have any, they will not destroy."[21]

By 1805 Ames had come to realize—as Cabot had nearly a decade earlier—that old-school principles could not be reconciled with the demands of popular politics. Recognizing the nation's irrevocable commitment to a democratic future, he belatedly accepted the fact that people like himself had little place in public life, as democracy was "of all governments that very one in which the wise and good are completely reduced to impotence." He and other old-schoolers remained Federalists only because they had no choice, the alternatives being so much worse. "The people will not knowingly employ nor voluntarily support a government whose acts contravene their favorite purpose, which are those of their worse passions," Cabot remarked. As a result, he added, "Some of our best men in high stations are kept in office because they forbear to exert any influence, and not because they possess right principles."[22]

The younger men who replaced the departing old-schoolers shared many of their misgivings. But as Fisher Ames learned when he sought to make the *Palladium* a journal of polite opinion, the young Federalists were mainly concerned about winning elections and would do whatever was necessary to keep the party in power. Their most important contributions were in the area of party organization. Apart from a legislative caucus formed in 1800,

Massachusetts Federalism during the early nineteenth century remained a loosely structured band of like-minded individuals that relied primarily on the self-induced prompting of traditional party loyalties for electoral success; little was done to get voters to the polls or to recruit new members. All this changed in 1804, when Republican advances underscored the need for more effective organization. That year witnessed the creation of a state Central Committee to manage party affairs during those long periods when the legislature was not in session; the establishment of country and town committees that looked to the "Headquarters of good principles" for guidance soon followed. With these developments, the party possessed a tightly knit pyramidal structure capable of mobilizing rank-and-filers throughout the state for mass rallies as well as getting out the vote on election day.[23]

The new emphasis on organization also strengthened the position of a group whose contributions to party development have been largely overlooked: the printer-editors whom Ames so cavalierly dismissed when making plans for the *Palladium*. During this period, the most prominent was Benjamin Russell, longtime publisher of Boston's *Columbian Centinel*. The son of a stonemason, Russell learned his craft under the tutelage of Worcester's Isaiah Thomas, who was for many years the dean of Bay State printer-editors. Although Russell's formal schooling ended at an early age, he was by no means "uneducated." A gifted writer and polemicist with a keen instinct for the jugular, Russell himself produced many of the provocative editorials and entertaining poems that appeared in the *Centinel*'s columns. His influence as a political journalist extended well beyond Boston. Rural printers of this era relied on metropolitan papers for editorial opinion and news to fill their own sheets, and in Massachusetts no Federalist journal supplied more than the *Columbian Centinel*.[24]

Russell was in most respects a profoundly conservative man. In addition to being a staunch defender of law and order, he had a reverence for honorary titles that reflected a deep regard for hierarchical social arrangements. At the same time, however, he had risen from humble beginnings. As Joseph T. Buckingham, who would later replace Russell as Boston's leading exponent of popular conservatism, observed of the *Centinel* editor: "he never forgot that he was a mechanic, and would, at almost any time, withdraw from a political committee, or conference, to attend a meeting of mechanics." Throughout his long life, Russell rarely missed an opportunity to demonstrate the respectability of the craftsman's calling. One of a group of artisans who assembled at Boston's Green Dragon Tavern in 1789 to draft a memorial supporting ratification of the Constitution, he was later a founding member and president of the Massachusetts Charitable Mechanic Association, an organization of manufacturers and master workmen

committed to protecting and advancing mechanic interests "by promoting mutual good offices and fellowship;—by assisting the necessitous;—
encouraging the ingenious;—and rewarding the faithful."[25]

Russell's efforts to defend mechanic interests sometimes brought him
into conflict with the Federalist elite. The most notable instance occurred
in 1803 over an application for a bank charter. The project was initiated
by twenty or so prominent Bostonians who, Harrison Gray Otis informed
John Quincy Adams, represented "all the great and respectable interests of
the town." The problem was that they planned to restrict stock ownership
to other men of "respectable character," word of which soon leaked out.
When it did, Russell opened the *Centinel*'s columns to protesting members
of the middling interest. Taking the lead, "Justice" asked: "Are the rich, because they are rich and powerful, to receive the exclusive privilege of being
incorporated into a Banking Company? Are a few individuals, who have
already made fortunes by Banks, and other incorporated money interests,
to be made still richer and more powerful, by the patronage of government,
to the exclusion of men of less property, who are equally entitled to such patronage?" "Justice" certainly hoped not, and he proposed that subscriptions
for bank stock be opened to the general public.[26]

These concerns, which centered on the vitally important question of access to capital, excited considerable interest among members of the middling classes. As Naomi Lamoreaux has written, most New England banks
of the period functioned as "investment clubs" designed to meet the credit
requirements of stockholders. Anyone in need of a loan who did not have
a financial stake in one institution or another could expect little assistance
from banks. "Justice" knew this; so did the bank's projectors, though they
were hardly ready to admit as much. And when "Steady" responded to "Justice's" attack, he shamelessly contended that the bank's promoters sought to
break the monopolistic stranglehold of existing financial institutions. Un-
surprisingly, "Justice" was not persuaded, and in a rejoinder said of "Steady":
"I presume he is a gentleman, and largely interested in the contemplated
bank, and I presume his interests and his wishes" prevented him from
speaking more forthrightly about the project.[27]

The controversy then abated for several months, resuming in April when
reports circulated that bank promoters were holding organizational meetings. Taking up where "Justice" left off, "Public Good" condemned the
handful of "rich purse-proud men" who thought they had a "prescriptive
right" to dominate all financial institutions and announced: "It is time that
numerous and respectable body of citizens, which constitute the middling
interest, and which are emphatically the people, should not only feel their
own importance, but make others sensible of it." To provide people of

modest means easier access to capital, "Public Good" recommended that a plan be adopted that would enable borrowers to use real estate as collateral for loans. This proposal was later included in a petition for a "Town and Country Bank" submitted to the legislature by a politically bipartisan group comprised of men of substantial wealth as well as representatives of the middling interest, one of whom was Benjamin Russell.[28]

Although the "Town and Country Bank" never received a charter, the debate surrounding it was nevertheless significant, and not only for what it revealed about the social tensions within Bay State Federalism. No less important was the role Russell played in the controversy, which was as much political as economic. Though plainly pursuing his class interests, he also acted in the interests of the Federalist Party. By allowing both sides to state their case in the *Centinel* and later joining a bipartisan effort to form the "Town and Country Bank," Russell helped depoliticize a question that Boston Republicans wanted to turn into a party issue. In so doing, he doubtless prevented further defections among those members of the middling interest who still voted the Federalist ticket. And however much elite Federalists may have resented Russell, they desperately needed people like him if the party was to remain a viable force in Massachusetts politics.

As it was, things were not going well at all. The organizational innovations accompanying the formation of the state Central Committee slowed but did not halt Republican advances. By 1807, Federalists had lost both the governorship and lower house of the General Court. One problem was Jefferson's enormous popularity, which extended well beyond traditional Republican strongholds to once hostile New England. Viewed against the backdrop of peace, prosperity, and national expansion that marked the Virginian's first administration, Federalist predictions of impending doom appeared futile, if not ridiculous.

A related problem was the inability of Massachusetts Federalists to identify an issue that would enable them to broaden the party's appeal. Some old-schoolers had hoped the Louisiana Purchase might be just such an issue. Asserting that the acquisition formed part of a deliberate plot by "Virginia Lordlings" to undermine the wealth and power of New England, they urged Bay Staters to stand up for their rights. Almost nobody listened. One young Federalist, more in tune with popular opinion, conceded that the purchase was "a master stroke" on Jefferson's part; and the *Centinel* publication of correspondence that both condemned and applauded the measure showed that even some party members thought the president had acted wisely.[29]

At the time, the anti-Louisiana campaign seemed yet another indication of the extent to which old-schoolers were out of touch with popular sentiment. Some of the wiser heads among them realized as much. In an 1804 letter to Timothy Pickering, George Cabot observed: "If we should be made to feel a very great calamity from the abuse of power by the national administration, we might do almost anything; but it would be idle to talk to the deaf,—to warn the people of distant evils." It turned out that the evils to which Cabot alluded were not as distant as he imagined. And as the people of Massachusetts came to experience them, the sectional appeal that had found so few listeners in 1803 proved much more compelling. It is to these later developments that we now turn.[30]

A MAJOR REASON for Napoleon's willingness to sell Louisiana to the United States was that by 1803 any visions he might have entertained of creating an American empire had yielded to more pressing concerns at home. With the termination of the short-lived Peace of Amiens, France and England resumed an already decade-old struggle that would convulse Europe for another dozen years. New England Federalists had little trouble choosing sides in this conflict. Having long viewed France as the embodiment of all evil and a threat to everything they cherished, they unreservedly believed that, as Congressman Samuel Taggart put it, "England at this time is fighting the battles of the civilized world."[31]

This did not mean that Federalists approved all facets of British war policy. Measures that jeopardized their commercial interests elicited immediate protest. Such was the case in 1805 when an English admiralty court handed down the *Essex* decision, which imposed tighter restrictions on the reexport trade between the West Indies and Europe, while sanctioning renewed seizures of American vessels by the Royal Navy. To Boston merchants, Britain's actions were, Christopher Gore declared, "not only unjust, but perfidious"; in response, Boston merchants drafted a memorial to the president and Congress demanding policies to "disembarrass our commerce, assert our rights, and support the dignity of the United States."[32]

Such bold words should not be taken at face value. Nearly all Federalist merchants opposed any actions on the government's part that would further restrict commerce, and no one wanted a war with Great Britain. Nor did they wish to see the European conflict brought to a quick close. As Gore later observed in an August 1806 letter to Rufus King, "Our Merchants are now trembling at the Expectation of a general Peace, which would greatly derange their Plans and Enterprises, as these are founded on the basis of a continued War in Europe for several years." What they really wanted was the dispatch of a negotiating mission that would resolve existing tensions and allow them to carry on their business without interference. Ideally, the agreement they envisioned would—as Jay's Treaty had a decade earlier—not only restore Anglo-American relations, but give a British tilt to U.S. policy, thereby placing the nation behind efforts to crush Napoleon.[33]

For a brief time, it appeared that Federalist wishes might be granted. The Monroe-Pinkney Treaty of 1806 gave Britain all that it wanted; had the treaty been accepted, the agreement would unquestionably have tilted U.S. policy toward Britain. Unfortunately for New England's Federalist merchants, the pact was so favorable to England that Jefferson flatly rejected it. Whatever hopes Federalists afterward retained for an Anglo-American rapprochement disappeared in a cloud of cannon fire on the morning of June 22, 1807, when H.M.S. *Leopard* shelled the U.S. frigate *Chesapeake* and impressed four members of its crew. Meanwhile, a series of British orders in council and France's Berlin and Milan decrees placed ever-tighter restrictions on neutral trade. These developments created a serious dilemma for Jefferson. Wishing to avoid war, yet believing that some response was imperative, the president opted for what he felt was a reasonable middle ground and asked Congress to enact an embargo. Passed on December 22, 1807, the Embargo Act prohibited the clearance of all American vessels for foreign ports; it would remain in effect until March 1809.[34]

Jefferson believed the embargo would expose British and French dependence on American trade, thus forcing the two warring nations to abandon their attacks on neutral commerce. New England Federalists disagreed. In their view, nothing short of war would compel a nation to sacrifice hard-won advantages—and since Lord Nelson's victory two years earlier in the Battle of Trafalgar, Britain undeniably ruled the waves. As a consequence, George Cabot noted, "they who exclusively possess the empire of the sea must be consulted" by anyone seeking to do business in their domain. To believe otherwise was foolhardy. "The ideas which some people entertain that there ought to be a perfect Freedom of Commerce through out the world," Salem's Benjamin Goodhue observed of an earlier embargo proposal, were utterly "visionary," for "every Nation will look out for their own interest without regard to any other."[35]

Worse, Jefferson's policy was not only quixotic but promised to be destructive as well. Writing from Congress on the very day the embargo was enacted, Franklin County's Samuel Taggart described the initiative as "a mode of warfare" that he could not approve: "A man humps upon my toe and hurts a corn; to be revenged I knock my own brains out, our boasted revenue destroyed at one blow; the produce of the farmer and planter rotting on his hand, public and private credit ruined, people out of employ; our seamen either turned out to starve, or driven to seek their bread in foreign countries; failures and bankruptcies will be some of the evils attending the measure." Taggart's salvo was the opening shot in what turned out to be a sustained fifteen-month assault on the administration. Reflecting on the period years later, Jefferson would remark, "I felt the foundation of the government shaken under my feet by the New England townships."[36]

From the outset, regional criticism of the embargo followed Taggart's lead and focused on economic distress and dislocation. In remarks made shortly after the measure's passage, George Cabot expected to see thousands of Bostonians "without subsistence in a few days because there is no employment for them." If the Federalist press is to be believed, he saw this and more. In the ensuing weeks and months, there were frequent stories of starving laborers and impoverished seamen. Some observers maintained that even war would be preferable to existing conditions, as "the poor would have *some employ*." Although most such accounts came from port towns, people from inland areas of the commonwealth were also troubled by these developments. In 1807, Massachusetts was the nation's leading shipper, with total tonnage per capita twice that of any other state. Citizens of central and western Massachusetts knew that they could not long escape the crippling impact that administration policy was having on so large a segment of the economy. As a March memorial from the Connecticut River Valley town of Northampton stated, many of the destitute from coastal areas were being "thrown back upon the interior in a state of wretchedness," thereby extending the embargo's "disastrous consequences to the door of almost every citizen."[37]

No less alarming was the embargo's effect on state morality. For many New Englanders, it required little imagination to see how economic distress could quickly lead to moral decay. Speaking on behalf of old-school Federalists, George Cabot warned that "all our commercial cities will experience that degree of suffering which must destroy order and subordination." How this might occur was explained in a March memorial from the Merchants and Others of the Town of Boston, which expressed concern about those "who are strong in bodily powers & have heretofore gained an honest livelihood by daily labor & by cruising the ocean, and who have willingness to work [but] are now deprived of the means of subsistence & the very bread taken from the mouths of their families." Reduced to a state of beggary, these individuals found themselves committing illicit acts "at which in other times they would have shuddered." The citizens of Lynn voiced similar fears. Were something not done soon to provide gainful employment to those whom the embargo had idled, they informed Jefferson in a September petition, "depravity of morals, ignorance, sloth, & barbarism will be the offspring of this monastic *retirement within ourselves.*"[38]

The most significant political consequence of the embargo was the opportunity it gave Federalists to pose as defenders of the middling interest. This theme appeared early and remained a staple of party rhetoric through the War of 1812. A particularly strong appeal was directed at farmers, who suffered from a variety of embargo-induced problems. One was falling crop prices caused by the closure of customary markets. In an open letter to Governor Sullivan published in Worcester's *Massachusetts Spy,* "Timothy" observed that reduced returns were having an especially deleterious effect on "young men of industrious habits, who calculating upon the sale of . . . [their] produce, to pay for their farms, have been nearly ruined." A related problem was debt. According to "Curtius," during the first quarter of 1808 creditors entered eight hundred suits on the docket of Worcester's Court of Common Pleas; if prevailing conditions continued much longer, he told readers, sheriffs and lawyers "will be the only men among you who will not start with horror, at the sight of a prison!" To people who still remembered Shays' Rebellion two decades earlier, such developments were not taken lightly—as "Curtius" doubtless knew when he added that the current spate of debt prosecutions was "almost double the number which have been known since the rebellion in Massachusetts."[39]

The embargo also enabled Federalist merchants to restore popular regard for their occupation. It was a commonly held tenet in eighteenth-century economic thought that civilization depended on commerce. Although such beliefs had not disappeared, Federalist merchants—particularly those in the carrying trade—had squandered much of this precious legacy through their often-insufferable elitism. But when Jeffersonian trade policy crippled regional commerce, their reputation as social benefactors revived. "Trained up in the belief that *Agriculture* and *Commerce* are reciprocal in their supports, and inseparable in their interest," a Lancaster petition asserted, "we cannot silently endure the long continuance of the Embargo." A Northborough petition echoed these sentiments, declaring that "commerce and agriculture are so inseparably connected that a suspension of the former removes almost all encouragement to the latter." Nor were farmers the only ones to express their appreciation. To Lynn's shoe manufacturers, commerce contributed to all that was good in American society: "it multiplies the means of subsistence, equalizes the distribution of wealth, levels the lofty pretensions of agrarian aristocracy, cherishes the sciences and useful arts, and promotes all the designs and objects for the accomplishment of which civil government is instituted." The shoe producers did not explain how trade did all this. But that really didn't matter, at least not so far as Federalist merchants were concerned. They had never been more popular, and if they owed their new status to the misguided measures of their political adversaries, then so be it.[40]

As embargo-induced misery spread, Bay State Federalists reinforced their defense of commerce and the middling interest with an appeal to regional loyalties. In its more benign form, the sectional critique attributed administration policy to southern and western ignorance of New England society. Various commentators expressed dismay that a band of planters and backwoodsmen, "who perhaps never saw the ocean but on a map, nor conceived the taste of it except from a *salt-lick*," would enact legislation on commercial matters. These were subjects better left to merchants who knew something about foreign trade. After all, a *Centinel* editorialist quipped, "we do not apply to a cobbler to regulate and repair a *watch*."[41]

Other Federalists viewed the embargo as part of a broader design to transform New England society. Pointing to Jefferson's observations in his *Notes on Virginia* as evidence, they contended that the president had long been hostile to commerce. Thus, it followed that a major aim of administration policy was, as Congressman William Ely informed his Hampshire County constituents, "to prostrate the navigating interests of the United States" and "change this whole country, and especially the Commercialists at the Northward, into Agriculturists and Manufacturers." In a variation on this theme, some Federalists claimed that southerners envied New England's commercial prowess and saw the embargo as a way of establishing interregional parity. "Jealous of our prosperity," "Curtius" remarked of such people, "they have been resolved to cripple our economy, as the most effectual means of reducing us to the same degraded level as themselves."[42]

Over time, such regional consciousness gradually assumed an even harder edge. When Jefferson paid little attention to New England petitions seeking repeal of the embargo, regional Federalists began to view administration aims in a much more sinister light. By the summer of 1808, letters and editorials in party newspapers spoke increasingly of "Virginia Tyranny" and the malicious intentions of "our Virginia Masters." With this shift in emphasis, critics depicted the embargo as a threat to the liberties as well as the livelihood of New Englanders. Meanwhile, there were growing calls for resistance, often accompanied by references to the sacrifices of the Revolutionary War generation. After reminding *Centinel* readers of how their fathers had responded to assaults on their rights and interests, "Spirit of the Times" asked, "How much more then will you deserve the curses of *posterity* if, without a struggle you abandon that freedom they have so dearly won?" "Gracchus" established a similar context for his assertion that "there is a point beyond which submission is cowardice, and patience a disgrace."[43]

These were powerful appeals, particularly when coupled with party dec-larations on behalf of the middling interest. To counter them, Bay State Republicans had to defend both administration policy and their party's southern leadership. In so doing, they largely ignored the embargo's dele-terious effect on the regional economy, focusing instead on the pro-British orientation of New England Federalism. According to "Unity," Federalist hatred of the "respectable democratic state of Virginia" stemmed from the party's desire to refashion American government along British lines. There was no reason, Republicans claimed, for Bay Staters to distrust Virginians. After all, said a Boston editor, farmers of the two states had everything in common. "They cannot be enemies, by the instigation of a few Boston Lawyers in connection with a desperate Faction whose fathers were in league with England" during the American Revolution. As Federalist use of the sectional theme intensified, Republicans further contended that the party was "unequivocally" committed to a separation of the states.[44]

In private, Bay State Republicans expressed greater concern about the sectional issue than these remarks suggest. The problem was that many southern politicians exhibited a wary approach to commercial matters that could easily be misinterpreted. Though not hostile to commerce per se, Joseph Story explained, "they have a system of reasoning on the subject which is abstract and peculiar; and their opposition to it results less from dislike, than from a fear that all other objects will be sacrificed to it." Story was making a rather fine distinction here, and some of his Republican col-leagues in Congress continued to wonder whether party leaders were duly mindful of New England interests. Orchard Cook of the Maine district felt sufficiently troubled about administration "partiality" that he sought reassurance from James Madison; after receiving it, Cook tried to arrange the selection of a New Englander for vice-president or secretary of state in order to "still the clamours of our State against southern influence."[45]

Despite some lingering doubts of their own, Republicans dealt reason-ably well with the sectional issue at this juncture. The same cannot be said of their efforts to blunt Federalist appeals to the middling interest. Apart from charging that "old Toryism" was responsible for the problems of the "[r]eal farmer, tradesman and merchant" whom they claimed to represent, Republicans had little to say about the embargo's economic consequences or what might be done to mitigate the mounting material woes of New Englanders. On those few occasions when they attempted to confront the matter directly, the result was embarrassing. A good example was an *Inde-pendent Chronicle* editorial commenting on the Federalists' capture of the Massachusetts legislature in the 1808 spring elections. Whatever difficul-ties administration policy may have caused, the editorial stated, the newly elected Federalist representatives had a duty to resolve them: "If the embargo is a bad thing, we shall look to them to propose a better substitute. If our seamen and tradesmen are out of employ, we shall call on them to fulfill their promises by setting them to work. If our merchants are complaining of captures, we shall demand protection—if the produce of the farmer lies on hand, we shall call on them for good markets." What the editor failed to note—and what most citizens knew—was that regional Federalists did have a solution for all these problems: repeal the embargo and let trade resume its natural course. But this was a matter for the president and Congress; the Massachusetts legislature could do nothing about it, as a moment's reflection would have told the *Chronicle* editor. To suggest otherwise only underscored the intellectual bankruptcy of Bay State Republicans.[46]

A party reduced to this sort of fatuous reasoning was in real trouble, and election returns bore this out. Although Republican managed to re-elect James Sullivan as governor in 1808, Federalists regained control of the legislature; the following year they captured the governorship as well. But the Federalist resurgence proved remarkably short-lived. By 1810, the Republicans were again riding high, with every indication that they would soon eliminate Federalism as a serious force in Bay State politics. There were several reasons for this turnabout, and we need to examine them before looking at the Federalist revival during the War of 1812.

One factor that contributed to the loss of Federalist power was the manner in which Federalist public statements seemed to confirm Republican charges that the party had a pro-British orientation. This was something that shrewder party members understood. "My own opinion concerning the fault of conduct in the federalists," said Josiah Quincy, "has been the zeal with which they have advocated every point between this country and Great Britain, in favour of the latter." Quincy's observation was right on the mark, as was his further comment that Republicans consistently took advantage of this unfortunate tendency. But he could do little to silence the party's looser cannons.[47]

The most egregious offender was Timothy Pickering, an old-school senator and congressman from Salem who had served in the cabinets of both Washington and Adams. Six feet tall, "with a frame nobly set and a nose with the true Julian hook in it," Pickering did possess certain positive qualities. Probably the least pretentious of the old-schoolers, he never tried to present himself as anything other than what he was. When his son offered to refurbish his residence, Pickering refused, stating that "for me to change the arrangement of my house, without any *necessity*, is utterly incompatible with my poverty." And as a person of modest means, Pickering had more than a passing acquaintance with hard physical labor; he was doubtless the only ex-secretary of state to win a plowing contest at age seventy-five.[48]

Unfortunately for New England Federalism, a host of less flattering characteristics more than balanced Pickering's few admirable qualities. A bitter partisan, who as secretary of state in the Adams administration had been chief enforcement officer of the repressive Alien and Sedition Acts, his political adversaries viewed him in the darkest possible light. To his fellow Salemite Rev. William Bentley, Pickering was "that pest of Society, the Ex-Secretary, the enemy of Washington, the enemy of Adams, & the enemy of talents, & all men, who would not submit to the tyranny of his false ambition." Pickering's personality, Bentley added, did nothing to compensate for these defects: "An obstinate temper, and irresistible pride of dominion, an oppressive envy, & haughty demeanor with little judgment & incessant enmities have given this man his character, & a determination to go to all lengths has made him an acceptable tool of an enraged faction." However unchristian, Bentley's characterization was not entirely unjust. Pickering was a notoriously vindictive person who forgot little and forgave less. At the foundation of his politics lay a set of personal grudges upon which he had built an elaborate polemical superstructure. Perhaps the best example was his virulent Francophobia, which stemmed less from any actions on the part of France than from resentment at the personal abuse he had received from French minister Pierre Adet and various Jeffersonians during the struggle over Jay's Treaty.[49]

As a party spokesman, Pickering was unsurpassed at preaching to the choir or getting under the skin of Republican leaders. Jefferson said of one particularly "malevolent & incendiary" attack on administration policy: "The author would merit exemplary punishment for so flagit[i]ous a libel, were not the torment of his own abominable temper punishment sufficient for even as base a crime as this." The problem was that Pickering's most widely publicized writings read like briefs for the British Foreign Office. This seriously hampered Federalist efforts to reach the unconverted. Any disillusioned Republicans perusing one of Pickering's tracts would immediately be reminded of why they had joined the party of Jefferson in the first place. And any uncommitted voter doing the same would likely come away with grave questions about the national loyalties of Federalist leaders—a matter of no small consequence during a period when large numbers of Bay Staters were becoming politically active for the first time.[50]

Another reason for the party's declining fortunes after 1809 was the choice of Christopher Gore to head the state ticket in 1810 and 1811. If Federalists really wanted to present themselves as the party of the middling interest, they could not have selected a more inappropriate standard-bearer.

Party activists seemed to realize as much and tried to repair the damage by asserting that Gore was "the Son of a Mechanic, the brother of Mechanics, and friend of the Mechanic, the Merchant, the Farmer, and the Fisherman." But such appeals fell flat. No one who knew him could ever envision Christopher Gore in a leather apron. One of the era's leading exemplars of conspicuous consumption, Gore manifestly lacked the common touch. As the *Chronicle* quipped during one campaign, "Whose carriage is that, that rolls so majestically thro the street, decked in scarlet and gold? . . . One might as well elect the Duke of York." It was a good line, made all the more effective by its aptness. That Gore won the 1809 gubernatorial contest demonstrates just how badly the embargo hurt Republicans; that he lost in 1810 and 1811 was not the least bit surprising.[51]

Federalist blunders were not the only reasons for the Republicans' post-1809 resurgence. Bay State Jeffersonians also benefited from James Sullivan's conduct as governor, which helped reduce political damage resulting from the embargo. A kindly man of moderate political bent, Sullivan cared deeply about the people of Massachusetts, particularly those of small fortune. Comparing Sullivan with his brother John, a Revolutionary War general and political archreactionary, Stephen Higginson had earlier observed: "James may plume himself upon being the official, constitutional guardian of the weak, against the ambition and pride of the mighty; and [John] is not less vain of being viewed, as the great protector of the natural right of the great fishes to eat up the little Ones whenever they can catch them." Sullivan's response to a group of seamen, who several weeks after the embargo's enactment marched on the governor's residence seeking relief, was characteristic of how he interacted with those less fortunate than himself. After informing the unemployed sailors that he lacked the power to grant their wishes, he told them where they might petition for aid and pledged to donate as much as he was able should a subscription be raised on their behalf.[52]

What truly distinguished Sullivan's service during this period were his actions to mitigate the economic destructiveness of administration policy. The worst violations of the embargo involved craft engaged in the coasting trade. To control this commerce, the administration required such vessels to post heavy bonds; it also sought to regulate the amount of provisions shipped to any given state by establishing a licensing system, which was to be administered by state governors. Governors, policymakers reasoned, best knew their state's needs and would license only that trade needed to fulfill them. It soon became apparent, however, that the system was not working as planned in Massachusetts. Rather than carefully monitoring state requirements and issuing the appropriate number of certificates, Sullivan was

passing out licenses with both hands to all applicants. The resulting surpluses were being sent to Canada, then on to Britain's West Indian islands.[53]

By July Jefferson had seen enough and demanded that Sullivan discon-
tinue issuing licenses. The governor's response could not have made the
president happy. "You may depend upon it," Sullivan wrote, "that three
weeks after these certificates shall be refused an artificial and actual scarcity
will involve this state in mob riots and convulsions pretendedly on account
of the Embargo." And before Jefferson had time to digest this unwelcome
news, Sullivan dispatched a longer and even less reassuring missive. In it,
he informed the president that because administration policy was having
no discernible effect on Britain or France, the embargo had lost support
even among Republican stalwarts, many of whom feared it would soon
reduce the people of Massachusetts "to suffering and poverty." Accordingly, Sullivan strongly advised against any measure that would prohibit
the coastal trade. Such a step, he noted, would be taken "as proof positive
that the President has no confidence in the northern part of the nation;
but relies on Virginia." Were this not enough, the letter also included this
extraordinary statement: "The habits of this State, contracted under the
royal Government and yet continued, lead to smuggling and the contra-
vention of embargo laws; and other laws restricting commerce. I believe the
present embargo laws have been as much respected, as laws of this nature
have heretofore been; nor do I believe, that until lately, there have been any
evasion of them, worthy of notice."[54]

One can only guess what Jefferson made of all this. It certainly did little
to restore his flagging confidence in the Massachusetts governor. But that
was the least of Sullivan's concerns. As he saw it, his first priority was to
take care of fellow Bay Staters—and that he did, as Secretary of Treasury
Albert Gallatin's ongoing complaints about Sullivan's openhanded issuance
of licenses attest. By placing state interests before administration demands,
Sullivan also performed a major service for Massachusetts Republicans.
Electoral backlash would almost certainly have been much greater had he
been more zealously committed to enforcing the embargo.[55]

A final reason Federalist gains did not prove more enduring was that
New England Republicans banded together to repeal the embargo before
regional opposition turned into insurrection. By December 1808, the measure had been in place for a year, and Bay Staters were growing increasingly
restive. This was especially the case on the North Shore. On the embargo's
first anniversary, bells tolled, flags on local vessels were hoisted to half-mast,
and sailors "wearing crepe on the left arm, and marshalled by an officer,
marched with muffled drums through the principal streets" of these hard-
pressed ports. Oppositional rhetoric assumed ever more menacing tones.

"Will the people of New England remain mute and quiet," "Coaster" asked, "while the chains are forging for them, and their Southern Masters standing ready to clap them on, as they would on their factious negroes . . . [?]" Federalist leaders, fearing matters might soon get out of hand, believed they would not. "Our Citizens are suffering under great poverty," Christopher Gore observed, "& will, I am satisfied, break into open violence against the existing laws unless they can violate them with Impunity." Nor could much help be expected from the legislature, Harrison Gray Otis added. "Our general Court will soon meet," he told Josiah Quincy, "and I doubt not the majority will require the bridle rather than the spur."[56]

The Jefferson administration willfully disregarded these stirrings. Rather than taking steps to moderate existing commercial restrictions, it passed an Enforcement Act that made the embargo all the more onerous. The response was immediate. Towns throughout the commonwealth, including heretofore staunchly Republican areas of the Maine district, passed resolutions condemning the action. A number of locales also gave notice that those who assisted federal officials could expect rough handling. Thus Gloucester, in an effort to discourage "pimping spies and nightwalkers, who fatten on the spoils of their suffering fellow citizens," appointed a Committee of Public Safety "to suppress all disturbers of the peace, and notice every abuse offered by any individuals, or combination of men, patrolling our streets and wharves, . . . and have them apprehended and punished at the expense of the town." In neighboring Salem, "Columbian" warned that anyone complying with the act "will receive the 'mark of the Beast in their foreheads and in their hands.'"[57]

These developments were the last straw for Republican congressmen from the region, many of whom had begun to waver even before passage of the Enforcement Act. John Quincy Adams had been supplying leading members with reports on the rebellious temper of New Englanders since at least November; by the following month, they were receiving increasing pressure from Republican merchants, who had doubtless learned of rising commodity prices in Europe and the West Indies. Initially disorganized and uncertain about what to do, many of the congressmen reluctantly supported the Enforcement Act. But this was the last such vote the administration would get from them. As Orchard Cook informed Adams a week before the measure's enactment, a consensus was forming "that we have already more Embargo Law than can be enforc'd, among a people totally averse from such measures—& that if it is to be enforced *Physical strength* & not paper Law is alone necessary to be added." When subsequent events confirmed the wisdom of this judgment, regional Republicans demanded that the embargo be lifted as soon as practicable. Despite administration counterarguments, they held their ground, forcing a March repeal of the hated restrictions.[58]

Some Federalists had seen early that the embargo alone could not transform national politics. Though gladdened by party successes in the 1808 elections, Salem's Leverett Saltonstall feared that "they were no more than a temporary mound" to the inexorable advance of democracy. George Cabot agreed, observing that "the *natural downward* course is for the moment obstructed or changed by accidental causes." But this reversal was only temporary. Both men believed that something more than a momentary lapse of judgment on the part of Republican leaders was needed to save New England Federalism, and the elections of 1810 and 1811 showed that they were right. It was surely too much to hope that Jefferson's successor would learn nothing from his folly. At the time, no one foresaw "Mr. Madison's War."[59]

ALTHOUGH REPEAL of the embargo allowed New England merchants to resume their activities without government interference, the administration had no intention of completely abandoning its policy of economic coercion. So long as Britain's orders in council and Napoleon's decrees continued to inhibit the free flow of commerce, Republican leaders believed that national honor demanded some response. To replace the embargo, Congress passed the Non-Intercourse Act, which prohibited British and French imports and barred U.S. trade with the two warring nations. It was soon apparent, however, that the measure contained serious flaws. Once an American vessel cleared port, authorities had no means of controlling where it went. And since Britain dominated the seas, most ships could be expected to follow trade routes that favored England to the detriment of France.[60]

This was hardly the administration's intent, and when the Non-Intercourse Act expired in May 1810, no one pressed for its renewal. Congress instead enacted Macon's Bill Number Two, which reopened trade with all countries; it also stipulated that if either Britain or France lifted its commercial restrictions, the United States would ban trade with the nation refusing to do so. Napoleon was the first to act. In August his foreign minister, the Duke of Cadore, handed U.S. Minister to France John Armstrong an ambiguously phrased letter stating that the Berlin and Milan decrees would be revoked by November. Madison knew as well as anyone that the French emperor could not be trusted, but he could see no other way to exert leverage on Britain. Putting his doubts aside, he accepted Napoleon's assurances—such as they were—and in February 1811, Congress passed a bill ratifying Madison's renewal of nonintercourse with Britain.[61]

During the next year, administration officials focused their wrath on British unwillingness to suspend the orders, while ignoring evidence that Napoleon continued to seize American ships. They also revived the long dormant but always explosive impressment issue. Meanwhile, there were growing indications that England might be ready for compromise. This was the first time that imposition of U.S. commercial restrictions had coincided with a serious downturn in the British economy, and English manufacturing interests, worried about losing the American market, mounted a campaign to repeal the orders. None of this made any impression on Madison, who had come to believe that war was the only language Britain understood. And on June 1, 1812, he asked Congress for a formal declaration of hostilities. Three weeks later, Britain revoked the orders in council. But it was too late; the administration was irrevocably committed to a conflict that large segments of the populace did not want.[62]

This was nowhere more so than in Massachusetts. Even after the embargo's repeal, Federalists had continued to warn of anticommercial southern plots designed to strip New Englanders of their independence and reduce the middling interest to "hewers of wood and drawers of water." There had also been incessant complaints about the pro-French tilt of Madison's foreign policy. As the nation drifted toward war, and administration officials acted in ways that gave credence to charges that they were collaborating with the "monster of Europe," these and related attacks appeared ever more plausible. The political consequences were not hard to predict. In the spring elections of 1812, Bay State Federalists recaptured both the legislature and the governorship.[63]

They were no doubt helped by their choice for party leader. A widely admired revolutionary patriot, Caleb Strong exemplified the moral virtues rather than the material excesses of old-school Federalism. To certain easterners, the unassuming Hampshire County politician possessed none of the qualities they so admired. Fisher Ames once described him as "a man who lives a hundred miles from salt water, whose wife wears blue stockings, and who, with his household, calls hasty pudding luxury." But this was just what the party needed, given how badly it had done with Christopher Gore heading the state ticket during the previous two elections. Indeed, the differences between the plainspoken Northampton lawyer and Waltham epicure could not have been greater. Where Gore exuded aristocratic opulence, Strong "had nothing of the polish of cities in his demeanor." William Sullivan may well have had just such a comparison in mind when he later said of Strong, "Perhaps no man in the United States could have been so unlike a monarchist."[64]

War opponents expected much of the governor. Having lost all faith in the federal government, they looked to the state to protect them from the ravages of an unwanted and unnecessary conflict. Thus Strong, not Madison, was their commander in chief; they would, a Newburyport address declared, "march under no other." The governor did not disappoint them. In his first act following the declaration of hostilities, he proclaimed a day of public fasting, humiliation, and prayer, in the hope that God "would humble the pride and subdue the lust and passions of men, from whence Wars proceed, and that Peace may speedily be restored to us, upon safe and Equitable terms." Afterward, Strong steadfastly resisted all efforts to employ Massachusetts militia outside the state.[65]

Meanwhile, the Federalists' legislative caucus was at work organizing grassroots protest of the war. At the resulting series of town meetings and county conventions, citizens throughout the commonwealth expressed their opposition to administration policy. Though the addresses issued by these assemblies strongly resembled those produced at earlier anti-embargo gatherings, they exhibited a number of subtle but noteworthy differences. One was their greater emphasis on the administration's servility to French interests, which was hardly surprising given the ambiguities surrounding Madison's most widely publicized foreign policy initiatives.

Even more significant, certain addresses began to employ warnings of impending enslavement as a rhetorical link connecting broad features of the antiwar critique. The envisioned threat was twofold. On one hand, French aggression, abetted by treacherous administration officials, imperiled American liberties. "Whatever *domestick* sufferings the people of New England are prepared to encounter," the Worcester County convention declared, "they will not submit to become the slaves of a *foreign* despotism, to be fastened upon them under the specious pretense of aiding in the vindication of their rights." At the same time, war-related economic dislocations such as the destruction of commerce threatened Bay Staters with another, no less oppressive form of bondage. As the Gloucester town meeting explained: "wealth is the sinew of a nation—poverty is the badge of Slavery, and to this degrading situation we find ourselves fast approximating." Other commentators then connected the dots by resurrecting condemnations of the "inordinate ambition" of a "Virginia cabal" that was using its domination of the federal government to destroy regional commercial interests.[66]

Despite the growing ferocity of Federalist attacks, regional war opposition remained largely rhetorical during the first eighteen months of the conflict. This was, for the most part, a period of watchful waiting—a time of sullen passivity brightened only by the grim satisfaction derived from reports of the manifest incompetence with which federal authorities prosecuted the conflict. All this changed in December 1813 when, at Madison's request, Congress enacted a second embargo. To make matters worse, reimposition of trade restrictions coincided with collection of land taxes levied earlier in the year to fund the financially strapped war effort. Although the embargo did not last long, the damage had been done. Repeal softened but by no means eliminated the rage that passage of the measure aroused in Bay Staters; in its wake, antisouthern animosity flared with heretofore unseen intensity.[67]

To understand why resumption of the embargo proved so explosive, we need to keep in mind that complaints about administration attacks on regional well-being did not begin in June 1812. Rather, they formed part of a broader series of grievances that stretched back to the first embargo's enactment in December 1807. The second embargo was thus seen as the "last blood-thirsty act" in what had already been six years of "unprincipled war upon our commercial rights." For those who shared this perspective—and they appear to have been numerous—assaults on the anti-New England animus of southern-born political leaders had moved from rhetorical posturing to a description of reality.[68]

Though this shift in outlook happened at different times to different people, in some instances we can see it taking place. A good example was Josiah Quincy. In a December 1808 letter to John Adams, Quincy observed that even though administration policy "was ruining the last hopes of New England," he could not determine Jefferson's actual intentions. After Madison's acceptance of the Cadore letter, suspension of trade with Great Britain, and warnings about impending war, all doubts disappeared. Writing to Harrison Gray Otis in November 1811, Quincy said he was now totally convinced that Republican leaders were trying to ruin New England and that regional Federalists had an obligation to show their constituents the administration's "real design": "to embarrass commerce and annihilate its influence as part of a system" in an effort to produce "the permanent elevation of the planting states over the commercial."[69]

At almost exactly the same time—and for much the same reasons—Samuel Taggart reached a similar conclusion. The Franklin County congressman had long been a partisan critic of Republican foibles. But Madison's bellicose congressional message of November 1811 prompted a degree of genuine anger that had been absent from Taggart's earlier, more cynical commentaries. The administration, he wrote, planned to use the current crisis in foreign relations to "destroy commerce which when done will seal our insignificance in the political scale." The economic and social consequences would be even more devastating, Taggart added: "Our merchants and men of capital must either abandon the country and become landholders and slave-holders in the western or southern country, or they must vest their capital in manufactories; our sailors must be converted into cotton spinners; our laborers in various mechanic arts and our enterprising young men, but without fortunes to begin with must become literally heavers of wood and drawers of water to the wealthy. One part of the community, viz., a very few may arrive at the enviable situation of the rude magnificence of the feudal barons, and the great body of the people degraded to a situation but little different from that of slaves and vassals of feudal times; or but little above that of a West India or South Carolina negro."[70]

This is a remarkable statement that merits more than passing attention. In it, Taggart expressed some of the most deeply held concerns of New Englanders. As inhabitants of a region with few natural endowments, they had long worried about how to provide for their children's livelihood. Since the early eighteenth century, a growing population and scarcity of fertile land in eastern Massachusetts had forced increasing numbers of parents to make special provisions for their offspring, if the latter were to secure the middling status to which all respectable New Englanders aspired. While some moved west, others looked eastward to the various maritime industries that had been developing since the mid-seventeenth century. What the land could not furnish the ocean would, and it was here that many Bay Staters saw a way of creating the wealth needed to escape the poverty that the Gloucester town meeting considered a "badge of Slavery." As trade flourished, producers of timber, cattle, and other commodities benefited as well. Appreciation of what all this meant extended well beyond Essex County and other seaboard areas. "Your memorialists, residing in the interior of the country, are none of [us] personally engaged in navigation or Commerce," a Northampton antiwar petition declared, "but the interests of the Merchant are so closely blended with those of the Mechanic and Husbandman, that any measures, hostile to the rights and happiness of either, maintain the same character in relation to all."[71]

An even more noteworthy feature of Taggart's statement was its striking parallels with Revolutionary-era conceptions of exploitation and oppression. According to Richard L. Bushman, many Bay Colonists feared that the plundering exactions of a corrupt patronage system threatened to destroy the "middling Sort" and create a two-class society of "those who worked and the great network of indolent task-masters who lived off the workers' toil." To New Englanders of the period, Bushman adds, such a prospect represented the "very essence of slavery"; there was no other name for a society in which members of the producing classes could not enjoy the fruits of their labor. In Taggart's reworking of this traditional construct, tyrannical slaveholding politicians replaced avaricious British placemen. But the result was the same: where an autonomous, broad-based middling interest of household producers had once held sway, a small group of "feudal barons" now dominated a vast, groaning mass of "slaves and vassals."[72]

Popular images of southern planters added to the plausibility of such a conspiracy. To many New Englanders, slaveholders exhibited the same dissolute characteristics that had made British colonial officials so dangerous. Speaking of his southern colleagues in the Continental Congress, Nathan Dane remarked that Philadelphia's many social diversions were "not very favourable to the industry of men not naturally inclined to it." With the subsequent rise of Jeffersonianism, Federalist newspapers were even less charitable. "The planters," a writer in the Newburyport *Herald* declared, "are generally extremely ignorant, excessively idle, and addicted to all the low vices of drinking, gambling, etc." That they had no regard for the labor of others made them all the more reprehensible. "What real satisfaction can that man feel," the Worcester congressman Abijah Bigelow wrote in a letter to his wife, "who lives in idleness and luxury, who rolls about in his carriage, when he reflects that he is enabled so to do, merely from the sweat of slaves, whom he keeps in ignorance, that they may not desert him, or rise upon him and assert their rights, and whom he half starves and half clothes to pamper his own Epicurean appetite, and gratify his vain ambition for shew and splendor."[73]

The moral vacuity of southern planters appeared even more glaring and insidious when set beside popular images New Englanders had of themselves. "The God of Nature, in his infinite wisdom, has made the people of New England to excel every other people that ever existed in the world," "Warren" asserted in a *Centinel* article attacking Madison's embargo. "What people," this writer asked, "ever carried industry and enterprize to the extent you have done? What people in their infancy ever filled every nook and corner of the earth with their name, as you have done?" It was little wonder that southerners so envied New England's commercial successes, or that one could now hear "slave representatives of the South exclaim on the floor of Congress, with an air of triumph; We have chained Every Vessel To The Wharf." If Bay Staters submitted to this "fatal encroachment" on their rights, "Warren" declared, "Massachusetts is little better than the slave of Virginia."[74]

"Warren" was by no means the only person who felt this way. Other war opponents repeated his warnings while invoking the Revolutionary generation's example to incite regional resistance to federal impositions. "Our patriotic forefathers in 1776, preferred death to slavery," said a Salem editorialist. "Shall it be said that the sons of such sires are willing to return to the mean condition of servitude?" The citizens of neighboring Newbury certainly hoped not. "We remember the resistance of our fathers to oppressions, which dwindle into insignificance when compared with those we are now called on to endure," they stated in a memorial protesting the wartime embargo. This state of affairs could no longer be tolerated, and it was now time for action: "We call on our State Legislature to protect us in the enjoyment of those privileges, to assert which our fathers died; and to defend which, we profess ourselves *ready to resist unto blood.*"[75]

Thus it was that Madison's embargo created a potentially more disruptive crisis than that produced by the Enforcement Act of 1809. Leading Federalists reacted to these developments in much the same way they had then. On the one hand, they were grateful for the growing magnitude of party electoral successes. On the other, they feared that matters might soon get out of control if they did not take steps to direct the mounting discontent into constructive channels. As Harrison Gray Otis had said of the earlier ferment, popular outrage "must not be extinguished for want of sympathy, nor permitted to break forth into impudent excess." To ensure that it did not, party leaders assumed control of the movement for a regionwide assembly to defend New England's economic and political interests. They may have acted just in time, Otis later remarked. In a letter written shortly before the Hartford Convention met in December 1814, he observed that many believed "a reliance upon some *effectual suggestions* from that body, alone prevents a violent sentiment and open opposition in many places."[76]

Despite some disagreement, proponents of moderation had their way at the convention. Their influence can be seen in the final report, which avoided all mention of the disunionist schemes then being advanced by certain extremists yet contained a number of those "effectual suggestions" that Otis deemed so necessary. The most important appeared in a series of proposed constitutional amendments that, if ratified, would have restored New England's place in national affairs. To reduce southern congressional power, the delegates called for elimination of the Three-fifths Clause, which counted every five slaves as three people for purposes of representation; to regulate the political consequences of westward expansion, they demanded that a two-thirds vote of both houses of Congress be required for admission of new states; and to check Virginia domination of the executive branch, they proposed that presidents be limited to a single term, and that persons from the same state be barred from election to successive terms. Although there was little likelihood that any of these amendments would receive serious attention, the delegates had acted shrewdly. Their demands represented a controlled expression of regional dissent that, without exacerbating current tensions, addressed the sense of sectional grievance that had fueled the Federalist electoral resurgence in Massachusetts.[77]

The war ended shortly afterward. With the onset of what *Centinel* editor Benjamin Russell dubbed the "Era of Good Feelings," both party and sectional conflict abated as many Bay Staters were happy to let bygones be bygones. The transition was so abrupt that the long-term significance of what had happened during the previous seven years is often overlooked. In most historical accounts, the year 1815 marks the end of an era; what followed is presented as a new beginning, shaped largely by new forces and new issues. It is unlikely that this was truly the case anywhere, and it was certainly not so in Massachusetts. In at least two respects, subsequent developments would be profoundly influenced by events surrounding the embargo and the War of 1812.

The first was a marked rise in regional awareness of the ways in which slavery set the South apart from New England. This is not to contend that a fully developed antislavery creed emerged during these years. It did not. For one thing, most antisouthern attacks focused on Virginia rather than the South as a whole. At the same time, many Bay Staters feared the West just as much as they did the South. This was especially so among members of the elite, many of whom had served in Congress with southern Federalists, continued to correspond with them, and had no deep misgivings about slavery. On at least one earlier occasion, Harrison Gray Otis had assisted the South Carolina politician and jurist John Rutledge in his efforts to apprehend a runaway slave. When party leaders periodically took steps to temper regional dissent, they were doubtless motivated as much by these associations as by general fears of social disorder.[78]

Yet, Otis did not represent the entire elite. There were always a certain number of mavericks such as Josiah Quincy who charted their own course on this and other issues. And outside elite circles, the antisouthern critique took particularly strong hold among members of the middling interest. Although few stated the threat as clearly and as elaborately as that crusty Presbyterian minister from Franklin County, Samuel Taggart, did, countless other Bay Staters now viewed slavery in a new light. Rather than a regional idiosyncrasy, the peculiar institution had become something much more ominous. The resulting substitution of southern slaveholders for British placemen in an updated structure of exploitation and oppression represented a conceptual transference of enormous significance. While it did not give birth to a full-blown slave power conspiracy thesis, it did establish an ideological framework for interpreting later acts of southern aggression.

That this framework had its roots in the American Revolution would make such analyses appear all the more compelling.[79]

More significant for the immediate future was the effect the embargo and war-related events had on the distribution of political power in Massachusetts. In 1807, Bay State Federalism had seemed fated for an early and unmourned death. Eight years later, the commercial elite who controlled party affairs possessed unprecedented authority and prestige. This resurgence is in part explained by their successful adaptation to the era of popular politics ushered in by the rise of Jeffersonianism. In addition to such organizational innovations as the formation of an integrated network of state, county, and town committees, important shifts in party rhetoric also occurred. One of the more noteworthy was the infrequency with which Federalists now referred to Republicans as "Jacobins." By 1815 this once ubiquitous term of opprobrium, though still heard occasionally, had become an anachronism. The party doubtless benefited from its passing, for no term better illustrated the sneering elitism that was old-school Federalism's least attractive feature. By speaking instead of Napoleonic despotism and Virginia tyranny, party polemicists were able to develop rhetorical themes that had wide appeal.

These changes were undeniably important. Without them, the party may well have disappeared during those dark years preceding the embargo. But other Federalists in other states made similar adaptations with notably less success. The real key to Federalism's revival in Massachusetts was the ability of party leaders to identify themselves—both as merchants and as Federalists—with the hopes and fears of New England's middling interest. Where old-school Federalists stood before the people as exemplars of traditional virtues, the embargo and the War of 1812 gave their younger, more innovative successors an opportunity to pose as defenders of regional economic interests. A vote for Federalism thus became a vote for both moral order and material progress. State election returns testify to the popularity of this appeal. Yet the wealthy merchants who benefited most from these developments could not stand still—not if they wished to maintain their newly won prominence as champions of New England civilization. By 1815 the economic foundation of their political power was gradually shifting from commerce to manufacturing, a change that presented new challenges as well as new opportunities. How they responded is the subject of the next chapter.

CHAPTER TWO

From Federalism to Whiggery

THOUGH POSTWAR BOSTON was a much more democratic place than it had been during the heyday of old-school Federalism, traditional patterns of deference did not disappear overnight. A good example was a largely unnoticed exchange that took place on an early spring day in 1831, when a group of the city's master artisans called on Harrison Gray Otis. They were there to present Otis with a tortoise-shell walking cane, "as a symbol of the *support* which the substantial classes are ever ready to yield to well tried worth and distinct greatness." Otis had emerged as a major tariff proponent during the previous decade, and the mechanics wanted to express their appreciation while reaffirming "the mutual interest and good feeling, which should ever exist between the people and their public servants." Gratified by the tribute, Otis assumed his part in this social ritual with characteristic grace, telling the group that having grown up among the artisans of Old Boston, he had learned in life "to judge *that body of men by their own standard*. And to look to it as containing all the valuable qualities" that made for an industrious and prosperous community.[1]

Even more significant than the exchange itself was the mechanics' reason for honoring Otis. By the early 1830s, tariff protection had become the hottest national issue in Massachusetts politics. The dramatic expansion of textile production during the previous decade had linked the economic fortunes of increasing numbers of Bay Staters to industrial development, and recent efforts by South Carolina nullifiers to abolish protective duties had set the stage for a congressional showdown that promised to enhance the Boston elite's image as a defender of regional interests. The mechanics certainly saw Otis in this light, and their testimonial suggests that Brahmin leaders made the transition from commerce to manufacturing without any serious challenge to their political hegemony.

Viewed from one perspective, they did just that. During the 1820s, the Boston elite encountered nothing comparable to the harsh assaults they would later endure. Yet the period was by no means trouble-free. As political and sectional tensions abated during the Era of Good Feelings, rank-and-file Federalists from the middling classes turned inward and took a closer look at the party's leadership and organizational practices. What they found was the same elitism and arrogance that had doomed old-school Federalism. Their ensuing protests had barely been contained when the party all but disappeared at mid-decade.

Meanwhile, economic divisions surfaced within elite ranks. Despite the hefty profits of Francis Cabot Lowell's Boston Manufacturing Company, many Brahmins were slow to invest in manufacturing. Reluctant to commit their capital to what they considered a risky experiment, these skeptics not only opposed higher tariff duties but derided manufacturing in general, raising questions about its moral and social consequences. Though nearly all of them ultimately embraced the new economic order, their initial resistance undermined elite unity during a period of political uncertainty.

It took time, but by the early 1830s everything had come together. As the region's burgeoning textile industry provided an investment outlet for ever greater amounts of Brahmin capital, the Boston elite became more socially cohesive and economically secure than ever before. And as southern opposition to industrial protectionism mounted, manufacturers were able to reconstruct the popular conservatism of the war years on a new foundation. Our examination of these developments begins in 1817, with James Monroe's presidential tour of New England.

"WE TALK HERE as you do in Congress of the perfect Extinction of the Party Spirit," said Christopher Gore in a January 1817 letter to Rufus King, "and there are not a few of our first rate Patriots, perfectly willing to avail themselves of this general Sentiment to take sides with any man in any party, and approve & promote any Measures, however contrary to former Condition & former Professions, provided they can by such measures, slide into Office & attain Distinction." Though plainly unhappy with this turn of events, Gore knew that there was little he could do about it. Conciliatory policies had an irresistible appeal to Federalist politicians who, not having joined Gore in retirement, faced a lifetime of exclusion from federal office. Even more important, postwar prosperity diverted public attention from partisan squabbles at a time when the surge of nationalism unleashed by American successes in the war's closing weeks had enveloped New England as well as those regions where the conflict had been popular.[2]

Just six months later, in June 1817, President Monroe embarked on a goodwill tour of the region. Undertaken at the urging of Harrison Gray Otis and other Federalist leaders, Monroe's visit was intended to further the process of reconciliation. By all accounts, it was a spectacular success. Thundering cannons, ringing bells, and cheering crowds greeted Monroe everywhere he stopped. Harvard awarded him an honorary Doctor of Law degree, and even Timothy Pickering appeared at a public dinner that prominent Bostonians arranged on the president's behalf. Several days after Monroe's departure, when *Centinel* editor Benjamin Russell announced the commencement of an "Era of Good Feelings," nearly everyone applauded his felicity. Polemical assaults on "Virginia tyranny" had no place in this climate of opinion.[3]

However understandable, the Federalist response to postwar political developments gave rise to problems that few party leaders perceived. The popular conservatism of the war period had been forged in the white heat of partisan and sectional strife, combining appeals to both class and regional interests. Rather than hardening into a compelling political ideology, it lost whatever firmness it possessed when exposed to the cool air of postwar reconciliation. All of this points to a contradiction between the national and local requisites of Federalist policy. To be taken seriously in Washington, party leaders needed to erase memories of earlier intersectional tensions; to consolidate and extend their hold on Bay State opinion, they had to avail themselves of every opportunity to pose as champions of New England civilization. There were, to be sure, few such occasions in the immediate postwar period, particularly in the wake of Monroe's goodwill tour. But as time passed, opportunities to refurbish the party's regional image did arise. And when they did, Federalist leaders proved unable to take full advantage. Perhaps the best example was their response to the Missouri question.

The controversy began in February 1819, when Republican congressman from New York James Tallmadge, Jr., introduced two amendments to a Missouri statehood measure. One barred the future movement of slaves into Missouri; the other would free at age twenty-five all slaves born after Missouri's admission to the Union. Tallmadge's amendments had broad bipartisan support among northern legislators but faced equally broad opposition from enraged southerners. Although both initiatives passed the House on a largely sectional vote, they were defeated in the Senate. Congress adjourned before differences could be resolved, and when debate resumed early the following year, Senator Jesse Thomas of Illinois sought to break the deadlock by proposing a two-part compromise. His first measure, admitting Maine as a free state to balance Missouri's admission as a slave state, was designed to maintain sectional parity in Congress; the second restricted the further geographical expansion of human bondage by banning slavery north of the 36°30' line in the Louisiana Purchase territory.[4]

Thomas's proposals received little support in Massachusetts. In preceding months, bipartisan city and county meetings throughout the state had passed resolutions condemning slavery as a "great moral and political evil" whose extension would "pave the way for the general depression and submission of our Republican form of government." Individual contributors to Federalist newspapers were even more adamant in their opposition. "Freeman" felt that adding another slave state to the Union was a "[l]ife or death" matter; to "D," the question was whether America would become "a nation of Freemen" or "a nation of Slaves"; "Neptune" thought it better to "let the nation be dissolved rather than extend slavery"; and a writer in the *Boston Advertiser*, who believed the controversy had truly frightening implications, declared: "The agitation of this question has brought to our startled vision, the full view of the horrible reptile whose colossal size was hid in the swamps and wilds of the South.—We see the glare of his baneful eyes and hear his envenomed hissing; if Missouri is placed within his reach he will spring at once to involve the union in his hideous folds."[5]

Even Bay State Republicans found the Missouri question troubling. Although the *Independent Chronicle* and other leading newspapers eventually adopted an equivocal stance—deploring slave expansionism while endorsing compromise efforts—prominent figures within the party put principle before partisanship. Congressman Timothy Fuller of Cambridge was among the first speakers to second Tallmadge's amendments on the House floor. His colleague, Edward Dowse of Scituate, felt that the compromise disgraced America "in the eyes of the civilized nations of the earth." And Dedham's Nathaniel Ames, the crusty, irascible brother of Federalist firebrand Fisher Ames, exploded when informed that a Missouri politician had declared slavery compatible with Republican principles: "Such ignorant apes ought to be chained, blacked and taught. No wonder western emigrants are ranked below savages."[6]

Even more interesting was Joseph Story's response. A one-time Republican congressman from Marblehead now serving on the U.S. Supreme Court, Story had earlier played a pivotal part in rallying northern Republican opposition to continuance of the embargo. Then, he believed Jefferson oblivious to the embargo's effect on New Englanders and resisted administration pressure to toe the line. Over time, however, his suspicions about southern intentions had grown. When the Missouri controversy erupted, Story abandoned his lifelong practice of avoiding public comment on political questions while serving on the bench. At a December 1819 Missouri meeting in Salem, he affirmed Congress's authority to ban slavery in the territories. His private comments on the issue had a much sharper edge. In a letter to Edward Everett several months later, he lashed out at the claim that anticompromise initiatives were part of a Federalist ploy to regain power, likening such partisan contentions to the "cry of 'mad dog.'" What particularly alarmed Story was that Virginia continued to dominate the North politically through a "divide and conquer" strategy. "We have foolishly suffered ourselves to be wheedled by Southern politicians," he told Everett, "until we have almost forgotten that the honors and the Constitution of the Union are as much our birthright and our protection, as of the rest of the United States." He saw no reason for this. New England had at least as much "talent, enterprise, and industry" as any section of the country, and former political divisions within the region had all but disappeared. Accordingly, Story pledged to do whatever he could "to restore harmony and solid confidence among the federalists and republicans of Massachusetts."[7]

Federalist leaders appreciated what Story was saying. As Harrison Gray Otis observed of Bay State politics, "we are occupied in an eternal struggle for the ascendancy of party without reference to local interests, while in the South party and local interests are combined in one" as a result of a common commitment to slavery. Otis and other party bosses also recognized the political potency of appeals to regional interest. But that was the problem. They had learned during the war years that popular resistance to southern aggression could not be turned on and off at will; once ignited, it could all too easily get out of hand, leaving New England politically isolated and stripping it of any chance to resume its place in national affairs. Yet, Federalist chieftains knew they had to do something. Apart from their own opposition to slave expansionism, they realized that popular opinion demanded some action from party leaders.[8]

How they attempted to resolve the dilemma can best be seen in the tortuous course pursued by Harrison Gray Otis, serving at the time in the U.S. Senate. An ardent supporter of James Monroe's reconciliation policy, Otis hoped to soften war-inspired animosity toward Massachusetts and in 1819 voted against both of the Tallmadge amendments. Afterward, Otis claimed that he did not initially understand the full implications of the Missouri question and had voted without thinking. This may well have been so, for he appears to have experienced a genuine awakening, later remarking that if slavery were not restricted southern "feet will be upon our necks forever." Whatever the case, Otis attempted to make amends the following January by speaking out, in a lengthy Senate address, against Missouri's admission as a slave state. The speech was a cautious, legalistic effort that focused on constitutional matters. In it, Otis made clear his opposition to slave expansionism but did so in a manner calculated to make the issue a matter of elite rather than popular discourse; its intent was to keep the controversy alive without further inflaming restive rank-and-filers and without exposing Massachusetts Federalists to renewed charges of disunionism.[9]

Otis viewed the January speech as the first step in a two-part scheme. The second was to orchestrate press discussion of the issue. Otis believed that Republican journals should be encouraged to take a strong antislavery stance. "Let the Democracy *lead*," he instructed William Sullivan, "and urge them into the foreground, and take care to *support* them." At the same time, he added, "Don't permit violent expressions, or reflections, or recrimination to appear in the *Federal* papers; but let them show a firm solemn determination." As it turned out, Otis was too clever by half. Although his plan had only one flaw, it proved fatal. He had failed to anticipate the pro-compromise stance subsequently adopted by leading Republican newspapers; when that stance came to light, Otis had no fallback position. Nor did Boston's Federalist press, whose restrained commentary on the question elicited derision from disappointed party members.[10]

Some of the more caustic observations came from Christopher Gore, who accused Otis and his associates of a willful desertion of principle. These charges were unfair. Federalist leaders bitterly resented southern actions during the Missouri controversy and believed their strategy would prevent the territory's admission as a slave state. That said, Gore came uncomfortably close to the truth when he added: "Everything must give way to the Production of a right Understanding relative to the Hartford Convention, and to the Establishment of the fair Fame of its members, which would be interfered with, if this Disposition against Slavery was expressed too loudly." And the ex-governor was right on the mark when he stated that the people of Massachusetts were "a great way in advance of their leaders" on the Missouri question. This brings us to the main point of the foregoing: Even as they came to realize that southern views of national reconciliation differed sharply from their own, Federalist leaders could not overcome an abiding distrust of the masses. Throughout the Missouri crisis, concerns about slave expansionism competed with fears about losing control of an impassioned populace. As a result, they not only squandered a golden opportunity to reinforce the party's reputation as a defender of regional interests, but lost face in the process.[11]

The actions of Boston congressman Jonathan Mason proved particularly embarrassing. A one-time Federalist who had been Otis's partner in various real estate ventures, Mason secured the Suffolk seat in 1817 with support from a bipartisan coalition. Massachusetts then sought federal payment of wartime militia claims, and Mason's Federalist backers believed such a candidate would be well placed to obtain reimbursement. The congress-man's subsequent performance was doubly disappointing. Not only did the claims remain unpaid, but in 1820 he was one of two Massachusetts repre-sentatives who voted for the Missouri Compromise. Although he was no longer a Federalist, his vote put party leaders on the spot, as everyone knew that nobody went to Congress from Boston without elite approval. They apparently decided that the best way to deal with the problem was to ignore it. Of Boston's leading Federalist newspapers, only the *Advertiser* criticized Mason, and its relatively restrained commentary was in keeping with the genteel sensibilities of editor Nathan Hale. Pressure further abated when Mason afterward resigned his seat.[12]

It was nevertheless a close call. In private, some Federalists expressed sharp disapproval of Mason's conduct, William Tudor angrily remarking that the militia payments "had better be at the bottom of the ocean than held up to induce the most ruinous sacrifice of great political considera-tions." Other observers combined criticism of Mason with a broader at-tack on the reconciliationist policies of party leaders. In a *Salem Gazette* article titled "Slavery or Death," "'75'" noted that the congressman had been elected during the Era of Good Feelings, a time "when every man was stigmatized as an *uncandid* partisan who did not hold *good principles* and *bad principles* in equal favor." No one should therefore be surprised that Mason acted as he did, for "it would be directly at war with the era of good feelings to refuse to vote for Slavery, when our southern friends" are so devoted to the institution. Even more biting were the comments of Joseph T. Buckingham, editor of the *New England Galaxy and Masonic Magazine*, who cautioned readers about relying on "our era-of-good-feelings men" to do the right thing: "An invitation to dinner or to a ball, will turn their good feelings into any direction, their host desires; and the same mouth, which yesterday breathed pity for the slave, will to-day blow approbation for the driver."[13]

Had their equivocal stance on the Missouri question been the only prob-lem facing Federalist leaders, such criticism could have been easily ab-sorbed. They were not so lucky. Coming at a time of mounting discontent among Boston's middling interest, the Missouri controversy added to rank-and-file disgruntlement with the party's elitist mode of operation. It also coincided with the Panic of 1819. Although Federalist leaders could not be blamed for the depression, neither could they blame anyone else, given their reconciliationist stance on national issues. The result was a further diminu-tion of elite prestige. As economic distress spread, claims that the material well-being of all Bay Staters depended on merchant prosperity sounded considerably less compelling than they had when Federalist leaders were combating Republican restrictions on regional commerce. Indeed, the first direct challenge to elite political rule in Boston revolved around a question that suggested just the opposite.

The issue was auction sales. Initiated by British manufacturers in the late 1810s, the sales bypassed local merchants and exposed them to cut-rate competition. The merchants' claims that the system threatened to disrupt the entire local economy made little impression on Boston consumers, who benefited from the purchase of imported goods at reduced prices and who viewed the practice as an ideal way of determining the true value of such products. The General Court proved more responsive to elite concerns. At the merchants' urging, legislators imposed prohibitive taxes on auction sales, and Boston's Federalist selectmen ensured strict enforcement of the measure. Angered by this open use of government to protect merchant interests, proponents of the sales responded by organizing a bipartisan "Union List" of candidates for selectmen, which swept the field in the 1820 elections.[14]

Subsequent events showed that the 1820 revolt was not an isolated phenomenon confined strictly to economic matters. Over the next several years, dissenting forces gathered momentum and cohesion as they expanded their critique of elite rule. In 1821, they mounted a retrenchment campaign to reduce the cost of government and demanded a more equitable system of local taxation. The following year, they formed the Middling Interest Association, a broad-based organization composed mainly of mechanics and small tradesmen with some support from wealthy Bostonians who either opposed the current drift of Federalist policy or had not gained full admittance to elite circles.[15]

The association's 1822 campaign focused on two issues, one of which was ward voting. When Boston became a city that year, the state legislature ignored a recent referendum in which a clear majority supported ward voting and issued a charter continuing the traditional system of having all ballots cast at Faneuil Hall. The General Court doubtless acted at the behest of local Federalist leaders, many of whom feared that the innovation would strip them of their ability to exact electoral deference from middling-class party members. Proponents of the measure backed ward voting for exactly that reason. Without such a change, "A Mechanic" said, local artisans and shopkeepers would never be able to register their "full weight" in public affairs. After Boston voters again, in a second election, endorsed the ward system by a substantial margin, Federalist leaders realized that they would have to give way.[16]

The second issue involved local building practices. Here the middling interest sought repeal of an 1803 law prohibiting construction of wooden buildings over ten feet in height. To community leaders, the ban was a necessary safety precaution that no prudent citizen could find objectionable in an era when fire posed a major threat to urban life and property. Members of the middling interest viewed things differently. To them, removing the prohibition would enable artisans and tradesmen to increase the stock of local housing, thereby providing themselves with more comfortable dwellings and reducing rents for the poorer classes. As Joseph Buckingham put it, the wooden-buildings question was a simple matter of "self-interest, in which the purse-proud landlord is arrayed against the mechanic." Again, Federalist leaders gave way when they saw that the controversy might erupt into an even broader assault on their diminishing control of local affairs.[17]

The middling-interest insurgency stemmed primarily from two interrelated developments. We have already said much about one of them: the disinclination of Federalist leaders to consult rank-and-filers when formulating party policy. According to Buckingham, most members of the Middling Interest Association were Federalists who, having been excluded from participation in the decision-making process, "thought fit to withdraw from a party which has never used them but as humble instruments to effect purposes in which the mechanics and middling classes of people had no concern." When Harrison Gray Otis claimed that these people had no reason to withdraw, Buckingham promptly asked if anyone could honestly deny middling-class marginality. Nobody, he said, would dare to do so "who is not an overgrown purse-proud nabob, a bank director, stock-and-exchange broker to their serene majesties of the nobility, or the mere pimps and scullions which these several classes keep in their employ."[18]

The second development was Boston's dramatic growth during preceding decades. Between 1780 and 1820, local population increased fourfold—from 10,000 to 43,398 people. As time passed, many of these newcomers found that they were not receiving the social recognition they believed their gradually accumulating wealth and attainments merited. Joseph T. Buckingham represented perhaps the best example of this phenomenon. After a grim childhood immersed in rural poverty, he apprenticed as a printer and moved to Boston in 1800, where he hoped to make his mark in the world. During the next two decades, the aspiring editor engaged in a variety of journalistic ventures with varying degrees of success. By the early 1820s, his *New England Galaxy* had a circulation of more than one thousand, and he was sufficiently prosperous that he could withdraw from manual labor, leaving the supervision of mechanical operations to a hired manager.[19]

Buckingham had done well and expected some acknowledgment of his ascent. But this had not happened. Despite his accomplishments, he remained an outsider, largely ignored by Boston's elite and with limited influence in political affairs. The middling-interest insurgency thus reflected Buckingham's own thwarted hopes and propelled him to join other discontented members of the middling classes in giving vent to these frustrations. As a leading dissident and spokesman, Buckingham combined principle and ambition in his assertions. He genuinely detested the undemocratic practices of Federalist leaders and believed their reconciliationist posture betrayed an alarming dearth of integrity that threatened Federalism's very existence. But he also saw the revolt as a means of realizing some of his own aspirations.

All this was most evident in the way Buckingham singled out *Centinel* editor Benjamin Russell for abuse. Over the course of his long career, Russell had risen from obscurity to become one of Boston's leading citizens. As a member of the Federalist State Central Committee, his influence on party policy far exceeded that of relative newcomers such as Buckingham; as longtime president of the Massachusetts Charitable Mechanic Association, Russell enjoyed an equally enviable reputation as the foremost representative of local artisans. During the insurgency, Buckingham criticized Russell's conduct in both roles. One line of attack centered on the *Centinel*'s reconciliationist editorial position. In 1817, Russell had coined the phrase "Era of Good Feelings." Since then, Buckingham later declared, the paper had "persevered in a course of the most disgusting and odious servility to the federal administration,—indicating a littleness of mind and a prostration of all that could be considered as honest in principle, or honourable in feeling." At the same time, Buckingham condemned the Mechanic Association's undemocratic procedures for electing officers, lampooned its attachment to outmoded ceremonies, and suggested that the real purpose of an apprentices' library established at the *Centinel* office was to bolster Russell's prestige rather than to assist fledgling artisans.[20]

Yet for all his polemical vehemence, Buckingham had no wish to topple the Boston elite. Throughout the insurgency, he expressed greater concern about middling-class opportunities than about the structure of local power relations. What he found most objectionable was the unwillingness of Federalist leaders "to keep their ranks recruited with young men." Given the way things now stood, he later remarked with characteristic overstatement: "There is no more possibility of a young man's gaining political distinction among the federalists, than there is of a West India negro becoming a member of the Holy Alliance." These observations help explain why he focused his wrath on Benjamin Russell. As the leading representative of Boston's mechanic interest, Russell had an obligation to promote policies that advanced the well-being of this important social group; his role was to serve as a mediator between the elite and middling classes. Buckingham did not want to abolish the position, but rather wanted to see it filled by some ambitious, enterprising individual better equipped to do the job—someone exactly like himself.[21]

In March 1824, Buckingham took a giant step toward displacing Russell when he established the *Courier,* a Boston daily that would later function as the state's foremost middling-class exponent of a revived popular conservatism. And just as his thwarted ambitions reveal much about the insurgency's origins, his growing prominence sheds light on its decline. Several months after the *Courier*'s founding, "Middling Interest" complained about a construction project that threatened to deprive local residents of the refreshing view of the countryside adjacent to the common's western boundary. Whereas wealthy Bostonians could regularly escape the city's "sultry atmosphere" by traveling to Europe and other vacation spots, the "poor man must stay, and it is therefore for his interest to oppose every proposition which may lessen his happiness and comforts." This was just the kind of issue that a few years earlier would have called forth Buckingham's choicest invective. But that was then. Rather than attacking the avaricious behavior of interested real estate developers, he now chided "Middling Interest" and other critics for displaying "more temper than the occasion can justify." These people did not seem to realize that if the project were approved, nearly three hundred acres of land currently "lying in a state worse than useless, may be brought into the market, and converted into abodes for industry and wealth."[22]

Buckingham's editorial comments provide a fitting epitaph to the middling-interest revolt. But they do so only to the extent that the movement was confined to Boston, and only to the degree that it represented a temporary outburst of middling-class frustration. These caveats are important, for as Ronald P. Formisano has observed, "the Middling Interest mentality was widespread." Outside Boston, it could be seen in protests against imprisonment for debt and disputes over internal improvement projects. Of even greater significance, the depression-induced economic insecurity that had helped ignite the insurgency did not disappear with the return of better times. For large elements of the middling class, such insecurity remained an unnerving fact of life throughout the antebellum period. In their efforts to create a more stable material environment, many would be drawn to Antimasonry, the workingmen's party, and other dissident movements.[23]

It would be some years yet before all this was apparent. In the meantime, Bay State Federalism had entered its final days. The political turmoil unleashed by Boston's middling-interest insurgency was one sign of approaching doom. If Federalists could not maintain order at "the Headquarters of good principles," they could hardly expect to control the state. In the 1823 elections, Republicans reclaimed the chief executive's chair for the first time in more than a decade. When they triumphed again the following year, political editors began writing of Federalism's imminent demise. Formal obituaries soon followed, as the 1824 contest was the last election of the Republican-Federalist era in Massachusetts.[24]

Apart from the heartfelt laments of a few die-hard partisans, Federalism's passing went largely unmourned. To some old-schoolers, the party had for years been a hollow shell, without principle or purpose. Christopher Gore expressed this viewpoint when he bitterly observed, "What used to be the Federal Party died long since by Suicide." Others, though sorry to see it go, believed the party could no longer effectively perform what many elite Bostonians saw as its most important function: maintaining social order. This at least was the opinion of Isaac Parker, chief justice of the Massachusetts Supreme Judicial Court. After noting that it had been a while since Federalists had disagreed with a major legislative initiative of state Republicans, he told Daniel Webster, "I cannot but think that the ark is more secure with them, for the reason only that they are nearer allied to the people, . . . and their doings will be more cheerfully approved."[25]

However gloomy things looked, the demise of Federalism did not signal the end of Brahmin political control. Even as Parker spoke, Boston's elite was forging the economic bases for a new party that would dominate Massachusetts's politics into the 1850s. During the mid-1820s, massive amounts of capital poured into the state's emergent textile industry. As it did so, textile investors rallied around a revamped political program that promised to revive middling-interest support of elite rule while protecting their stock portfolios. In the chapter's final two sections, we will look at how the rise of manufacturing enabled the elite to resolve economic differences among themselves and to sell that program to Bay State voters.

"THE MANUFACTURING INTEREST has become a *strong distinct political party.* This you may rely upon." So wrote Daniel Webster in an 1816 letter commenting on the manner in which the tariff issue had divided both Federalists and Republicans. Read as a prediction of future developments, Webster's remarks were well taken. But they hardly described what was happening at the time in Massachusetts. During the immediate postwar period, most Bay State textile mills were small, undercapitalized concerns, struggling for survival amid an inundation of British imports unleashed by the Treaty of Ghent. The one exception, Francis Cabot Lowell's Boston Manufacturing Company (BMC), had yet to fulfill its promise. As late as August 1817, total sales amounted to less than $35,000. And with only twelve shareholders, four of whom controlled a majority of the stock, the

BMC provided little basis for the formation of a "strong distinct political party." Moreover, Boston's wealthiest merchants and shipowners staunchly opposed protective tariffs and would continue to do so for another decade, during which time their main spokesman would be none other than Daniel Webster.[26]

Though somewhat misleading, Webster's remarks are useful in at least one respect. By linking the rise of a "manufacturing interest" to tariff politics, he furnished us with an excellent means of determining how such an interest took shape. When antebellum Americans debated protectionism, they rarely confined their comments to mind-numbing arguments about how much a certain duty should be raised or lowered. Rather, these disputes invariably turned to broader issues of political economy—to such matters as the nature and pace of industrial development, governmental promotion of class interests, and the intersectional balance of power. By following their lead, much can be learned about the relationship between the formation of a manufacturing elite and the emergence of the second party system in Massachusetts.

Few New Englanders flatly opposed industrialization. Nearly everyone assumed that factory production would play an increasingly prominent role in the region's future. Disagreement centered on the question of timing. Despite the wartime expansion of textile operations, many Bay Staters doubted that American manufactures could long withstand British competition without extensive governmental assistance. According to one popular belief, land-population ratios did not yet favor industrial development, which made efforts to shift resources away from customary forms of economic endeavor as unwise as they were unnecessary. Even in New England, where compared with other regions "population is vastly greater in proportion to the quantity of land," a "Massachusetts Yeoman" stated that "we can more profitably employ our citizens in cultivating the land, in preparing timber for market, in making pot and pearl-ashes, than in weaving cloth, or in making locks and hinges. We have neither the hands nor the capital requisite to the establishment of such existing manufactories as would enable us to supply ourselves cheaper than we could purchase from *Great-Britain*."[27]

This was not altogether true. The capital needed to establish successful industrial operations did exist. The problem was that most Boston and North Shore merchants still had serious doubts about manufacturing. Their misgivings stemmed in part from entrepreneurial inertia. As an 1820 Salem memorial protesting increased duties stated, "men are slow to engage their capital in new pursuits. They have a natural timidity in embarking in enterprises, to which they are not accustomed." The failure of earlier industrial initiatives added to their skepticism. During the late eighteenth century, a combination of inadequate machinery, expensive cotton, and British imports had doomed George Cabot's short-lived Beverly Cotton Manufactory. When Francis Cabot Lowell later sought his support, Cabot not only refused, but predicted that his nephew's venture would end just as disastrously as his had. Lowell's cousin and business associate, Henry Lee, said much the same thing. Even Nathan Appleton, who was troubled by the growing insecurity of commerce and would soon emerge as the manufacturing interest's leading public spokesman, got cold feet at the last minute. Asked by Lowell to purchase $10,000 of BMC stock, Appleton hesitated, subscribing only half the requested sum.[28]

Unlike Appleton, who was then considering alternatives to commerce, most merchants had little intention of abandoning the carrying trade. This further dampened their enthusiasm for manufacturing. Sensing that the rise of domestic industry threatened their mercantile operations, they opposed governmental initiatives to promote manufactures. In 1816, when Francis Cabot Lowell sought tariff revisions that would hamper the importation of coarse India cottons, even his BMC co-investor Israel Thorndike joined Essex County merchants in protesting the measure. But where Thorndike would accept a compromise that delayed implementation of the act until his vessels had returned from Asian waters, other shippers had deeper objections. Their views were perhaps best expressed by George Cabot, who told congressman Timothy Pickering that Bay State merchants could not be expected to "long acquiesce in any system which should take money from their pockets to sustain a particular class," unless doing so plainly served some broader interest. Manufactures requiring permanent aid, Cabot added, "are not connected with good economy—they retard the progress of wealth & diminish the proportion of comfort to the labourer;—to sell dear & buy cheap, is obviously for our interest—the widest market & freest competition secure these in the best manner."[29]

Merchant protest notwithstanding, the 1816 tariff bill contained provisions that seriously undermined the East Indies cotton trade. Believing that this was only the beginning of a wide-ranging assault on its interests, the Boston—North Shore mercantile community was well prepared when the tariff issue resurfaced four years later. Whereas opposition had been confined largely to private lobbying efforts in 1816, now Boston and Salem merchants took their case public—organizing meetings, circulating memorials, and enlisting the support of regional editors. In so doing, they expanded their critique to embrace broader community interests. Providing special assistance to manufactures, they contended, not only violated the laws of economic development by encouraging speculative activity in enterprises unable to stand on their own; it also threatened the rights and well-being of ordinary citizens by facilitating the creation of monopolistic corporations, controlled by a new class of privileged investors.

At the heart of the merchant critique was a vigorous restatement of the interdependence of merchants, farmers, and mechanics. "For the promotion of agriculture and the ordinary mechanic arts," the congressman Ezekiel Whitman declared, "there is nothing to be compared to commerce." Among those agreeing was a master shipbuilder from Boston who feared that encouraging manufactures would unleash forces capable of turning artisans into spinners and weavers, and who accordingly urged his fellow mechanics to "bestow their suffrage on those only, who are known friends of Agriculture, Commerce, and the Mechanic Arts." Authors of Salem tariff memorials expressed similar sentiments, contending that trade "has contributed largely to the employment of the capital, the industry, and the enterprise of our citizens." They further argued that the proposed tariff was part of a broader scheme on the part of manufacturers to "absorb the whole moneyed capital of the nation." The main effects of its enactment would be "to throw the great business and trade of the nation into the hands of a few capitalists, to the exclusion of the industrious and enterprising of other classes; to introduce general distress among commercial artisans and agriculturists; . . . and, in fine, to destroy many of the great objects for which the Constitution of the United States was originally framed and adopted." Boston memorialists repeated many of these assertions, adding that such developments could not help but "corrupt the morals of the people."[30]

Although most of these critics claimed that they bore no animus against manufacturers, their declarations plainly suggested otherwise. Yet, BMC investors issued no immediate response. One reason for their restraint was that they, too, opposed the 1820 tariff. Because the BMC had prospered under the existing bill, company owners believed it unwise to back a measure that might discredit the very concept of protection. As Israel Thorndike had earlier observed, should increased duties push cloth prices high enough to prompt consumer complaints, legislators "*may* be induced to listen to the popular voice & take off the whole or so high a portion of the duty on cottons as will blunt the future prospects of the manufacturers, & leave them to perish." That something of this sort might happen did not seem farfetched at the time, given the intensity of regional opposition to the 1820 tariff.[31]

Some charged that BMC owners had a more sinister motive for their opposition. Compared with Lowell's Waltham enterprise, which was heavily capitalized and equipped with the best machinery in the industry, most regional textile concerns operated much closer to the margin. The resumption of British imports after the War of 1812 had sent many textile operations under, and the Panic of 1819 deepened the devastation. Where the BMC could amass substantial profits without further protection, these firms could not; more than a few teetered on the verge of bankruptcy. People such as Pittsfield's Thomas R. Gold, who held stock in a small struggling Berkshire County mill, were at first puzzled by the BMC's approach to tariff matters. When Francis Cabot Lowell said that "little if any protection was wanted as to cottons" in the 1816 tariff, Gold asked his son-in-law, Nathan Appleton, "Can this be so?" It was indeed, and when BMC investors later opposed the 1820 bill, other regional manufacturers believed they knew why: the Bostonians hoped to clear the way for an expansion of their operations by driving hard-pressed competitors out of business. Appleton stoutly denied these accusations, noting that the BMC had no need to increase its already comfortable returns by raising prices. He was probably telling the truth. Although BMC investors were hardly troubled by the woes of other companies, there is no evidence that they viewed tariff opposition as a means of eliminating competition.[32]

This still does not explain why BMC owners made no effort to refute antitariff activists' attacks on manufacturers; nor does it tell us why at least one activist, Israel Thorndike, Jr., endorsed the Boston resolutions. A more satisfactory explanation of their behavior must begin by noting that they were industrial latecomers in their region. Whereas Rhode Island textile mills had been operating continuously since 1790, the Bostonians showed little interest in manufacturing before the 1810s. With the exception of those individuals directly engaged in the production process, most BMC investors were slow to develop an industrial consciousness. Having spent much of their lives in commerce, many remained active merchants long after they had purchased their first shares of manufacturing stock. It took time for them to shed older mercantile biases and begin thinking of themselves as manufacturers; some of them never would.[33]

Another important point is that at the time of the 1820 tariff debates, few if any BMC owners knew what the future held in store for them. In light of company successes, there was certainly talk about expansion; however, no firm decision had yet been made. All this changed the following year, when BMC owners began purchasing land in Chelmsford and laying plans to construct what would soon become the industrial center of Lowell. With so much more now at stake, it dawned on project promoters that the popular image of mill owners might cause problems. If they were to secure needed supplies of capital and labor, perceptions of manufacturers as grasping monopolists intent on destroying the rights and well-being of

New England's middling classes could not be allowed to go unchallenged. Someone had to stand up and make a case for industrial development.

That person turned out to be Nathan Appleton. An original BMC investor whose initial skepticism about the venture was soon replaced by a strong commitment to industrialization, Appleton had emerged as one of the strongest proponents of expansion. Although he lacked the innovative genius of Francis Cabot Lowell, Appleton possessed superb organizational skills and a clear, logical mind. A vigilant defender of the honor and interests of Boston's merchant-manufacturers, he was the type of individual who felt compelled to justify what he was doing, and once having convinced himself, to convince others. When a local minister stated that the mercantile code could not be reconciled with the principles of Christianity, Appleton immediately set the man straight, informing him that no merchant who acted unethically in his business dealings could maintain a reputation for respectability. Industrial promoters seeking someone to put their actions in the best possible light could not have found a better spokesman.[34]

Appleton's defense appeared during the summer of 1821 in a series of articles published in Nathan Hale's *Boston Advertiser*. Although the series was titled "The New Tariff," Appleton evinced little concern about protectionism. After acknowledging that commerce functioned best when least restricted, he quickly set about refuting the assertions of antitariff activists. "There was no necessity," he declared, "for going out of the way, to stigmatize the occupation of a manufacturer as calculated to debase the moral order, or to attempt to make it appear that more labor is employed in freighting a bale of cotton to Europe, than in converting it into cloth at home." Charges of worker immorality, he believed, were based entirely on the English experience. New England operatives constituted an entirely different class of wage earners. The "universal diffusion of school education" made them more virtuous and intelligent than their British counterparts, and access to a broader range of opportunities outside the mills sharply limited the degree to which they could be exploited inside the mills; industrial labor "cannot be depressed below the level of other labour, until our population shall have filled up the immense regions which are open to us in the west." Turning to a related matter, Appleton also dismissed contentions that manufacturing made the "rich richer, and the poor poorer," stating that "capital in this business can do nothing" unless it forms "a copartnership with skill." Industrial workers certainly did as well as mercantile wage earners. After all, he asked, "Do the operatives of a merchant, consigning his ships to a foreign merchant, require him to divide a larger portion of his profits, with [those] employed in carrying them into effect, than the operatives of a manufacturer?" It was a good question. The early nineteenth century was hardly a golden age for dockworkers and seamen, and as Appleton doubtless anticipated, no merchant stepped forward to answer his query.[35]

The main thrust of Appleton's case concerned the role of industrialization in New England's future development. Young people had been moving westward within Massachusetts and neighboring states for more than a century. With the opening of the Old Northwest following the American Revolution, they were deserting the region altogether. The problem, Appleton explained, was that New England's existing resources provided insufficient opportunities for these ambitious and industrious youths. "Let her commerce and her agriculture put forth all their energies," he declared, "they cannot give employment to her swelling population. Manufactures alone can stop the tide of emigration in search of milder skies and richer soils." Industrialization, he claimed, would benefit all classes; no one need fear the consequences: "As respects New England, it is not her farmers or her merchants who are to leave their occupations and become manufacturers;—it is a new class added to her population, increasing the consumption of the products of agriculture, and opening new branches of trade to the merchant." Appleton's aim here was to redefine accepted notions of economic interdependence in order to show that commerce, agriculture, and the mechanic arts depended not only on each other, but on manufacturing as well. As he later put it, "we have no other resource to increase our population. And without population, how are we to have commerce?" At the time, Appleton convinced few Boston merchants. When tariff advocates proposed a new bill in 1824, they again attacked the measure in a remonstrance that repeated many of the same arguments they had made four years earlier. But the broader economic context for their opposition had changed significantly since 1820. With the rise of Lowell, where the first of the new mills began production in September 1823, opportunities for industrial investment expanded. And given the BMC's spectacular performance in recent years, more than a few merchants were interested. As increasing amounts of their capital flowed into textiles, a foundation was being laid for reassessment of what Appleton called "the occupation of a manufacturer."[36]

Congressional approval of the 1824 tariff marked a major turning point. Even though Lowell promoters made no effort to influence the measure, it substantially increased protection of cottons. Investors reacted immediately. As Appleton later observed, capital had already been "rushing into that branch of business more rapidly than at any former period, when the additional stimulus was applied, which could have no other effect than to urge on the wild spirit." By 1825, demand for shares in cotton mills had become "a perfect mania." Some investors, led by Abbott Lawrence, plunged into woolens as well. And the movement that resulted in the 1828 tariff, which sought to do for woolens what the 1824 bill had done for cottons, began at a meeting in Boston's Exchange Coffee House. It was quite a turnabout. Within the space of a few years, a majority of the city's wealthiest citizens had abandoned free trade to become outspoken proponents of protectionism.[37]

Noting the rapidity of this shift, some critics afterward leveled charges of ideological inconsistency against the Boston elite and its leading congressional spokesman, Daniel Webster. Such criticism was based on a misconception of elite views of how the world worked. Although wealthy Bostonians sometimes spoke in ideological terms, they were by no means ideologues. In their minds, the purpose of political economy was to justify—not dictate—economic behavior. In an 1827 letter to an English correspondent, Boston merchant Henry Lee complained that "the manufacturing policy is upheld entirely upon a principle of pecuniary & sectional benefit & the most intelligent supporters of it do not pretend to have any better reasons to offer in its favor." This may have been so, but as Lee himself doubtless understood, members of Boston's emerging manufacturing interest did not feel they needed any better reasons. To them, free traders such as Lee who based their arguments on the writings of British political economists were "theorists" or "visionaries"—people who had trouble dealing with reality. And the 1824 tariff was one of those realities. Once the tariff was enacted, investors responded accordingly, and the government had a responsibility to face the consequences of its actions. In the words of Bay State congressman John Reed, "We cannot by acts of legislation, induce our citizens to make large investments, in ships, factories, machinery, or any other valuable property, and then destroy them, by repealing the laws which gave them being, and upon which they depend for life and support." It was a wonderful argument. The rise of Lowell had fortuitously coincided with the tariff's passage, and Boston mill promoters intended to take full polemical advantage of that happy coincidence. That the actual movement of capital into manufactures had begun somewhat earlier was quickly forgotten. All that mattered now was that the shift had taken place, and it was time for other New Englanders to fall in and follow their economic and political lead.[38]

The tariff would play a major part in elite efforts to secure that support. In an 1824 commentary on the death of the first party system in Massachusetts, Joseph Buckingham had observed: "Some other questions, some other principles, than those, which have heretofore been the distin-

guishing characteristics of federalists and democrats, will next agitate our
political world, and produce a division, which will take place without regard
to former partialities or animosities." Protectionism was the first and most
potent of those questions, and Boston's manufacturing interest used it to
create a new political party.[39]

AS THEY SET ABOUT fashioning a popular post-Federalist political appeal, Boston manufacturers received unwitting assistance from a small band
of antiprotectionists who refused to accept the new economic order. Led by
Henry Lee, these diehard free traders opposed all increases in tariff duties.
They found Abbott Lawrence's campaign to boost woolen rates particularly
disturbing, and in 1827 they issued a lengthy *Report on Importations* that
challenged manufacturer claims. The report itself presented no problem.
Few people outside elite circles noticed its publication, and even fewer took
the time to wade through it. As one local wag said of the document, "it is
unquestionably fortunate for the reputation of its authors, that the *size of the
book* and the *tedious manner* in which it is composed are effectual antidotes
to any danger of its being extensively read." Ordinarily, a treatise of this
sort would have disappeared quickly without arousing any interest. What
made the report different was what Lee and his cohorts did with it: they
sent it to Senator Robert Y. Hayne of South Carolina for presentation in
Congress as an antitariff memorial.[40]

   If the Boston merchants were seeking public reaction to their work, they
got it—good and hard. The push for higher woolen duties had prompted
a growing number of slave-state politicians to attack protectionism in ways
calculated to inflame the ever-latent antisouthernism of New Englanders.
It was bad enough that a group of wealthy Bostonians would abet such
a movement; that they had turned to someone from South Carolina for
support was especially upsetting. No southern state had a greater reputation for militant sectionalism. According to "Valens," Hayne represented
a people for whom "'*the very name of Massachusetts* is hateful'—a people
who talk as flippantly and as loftily of separating from us, as they would
of discarding a useless or obnoxious servant." When dealing with southern
sectionalists, the only appropriate response was to close ranks and resist
their arrogant impositions. But this had not happened, nor would it happen
so long as the North was home to treacherous "dough-faces" such as the
Boston memorialists. "That it has ever been so," "Valens" lamented. "While
the people of the slave holding states have stood shoulder to shoulder, in
their opposition to northern men, and northern manners, the people of
the north have allowed petty jealousies, and local circumstances, to divide
themselves upon great national questions."[41]

Attacks on the Boston memorialists were not confined to charges of regional disloyalty. Critics also condemned them for being backward-looking theorists who had no understanding of contemporary economic developments. To *Courier* editor Joseph Buckingham, whose paper led the assault, they comprised a group of men "who, having been long engaged in a certain routine of mercantile operations, are amazed to find that enterprize and perseverance have discovered other modes of investing capital, and that wealth may be obtained in other channels, if government would but grant the same protection and the same facilities which were originally granted to the mercantile adventurer." Other commentators were even less charitable. "Clarendon" believed that the free-trade principles advocated by the memorialists had "been rendered worse than obsolete, not only by an alteration in *our own* circumstances, but also by a most decided change in the circumstances of the *whole civilized world.*" To base economic policy on their "idle vagaries," "Aurelius" asserted, would "reduce our country to the situation in which Portugal stands or rather *lies* to Old England, viz: a situation of complete *commercial dependence* and *virtual subjugation!!*" Though willing to concede that free trade reduced prices, these critics contended that such arguments missed the point. It was not consumption that mattered, but rather the production and the employment it created. As "K.I.K." observed, "it is insulting to talk to any men or nation, of the *cheapness* or *abundance,* of an article in a foreign land, when you know they *have not the means* to buy."[42]

In short, Massachusetts needed manufactures. Adopting an Appletonian interpretation of economic interdependence, the memorialists' critics linked the well-being of farmers, merchants, and mechanics to industrial growth. "To increase our agriculture without at the same time increasing the number of manufacturers and mechanics," "Thurlow" declared, "would only be throwing a dead stock of raw products upon the country." The same held true for commerce. After acknowledging that Boston remained a commercial city, Buckingham asked, "how is her navigation to be maintained and carried on without the reciprocal aid of the mechanic and the manufacturer?" As a regional entrepôt, Boston could be no stronger than its hinterland. By checking the "tide of emigration," Buckingham explained, the spread of factory production had given a "new impetus" to commerce: "men of enterprize and intelligence have permanently settled in the city and state, who would otherwise have been raising corn in Illinois, for which they could find no market, or perhaps distilling it into whiskey, to furnish subjects for prisons, almshouses, and penitentiaries."[43]

However chastened they may have been by this onslaught, the Boston memorialists were not yet ready to concede defeat. They recognized that the day had passed when advocates of protectionism stood alone, the object of merchant taunts, and that they themselves now occupied this unenviable position. But they believed free trade still defensible. In 1830 they made their final stand, when Henry Lee announced his candidacy for Boston's congressional seat. The 1828 impost, the so-called "tariff of abominations," had excited considerable controversy, particularly in the slave states; South Carolinians threatened to nullify the measure if protective duties were not reduced to revenue levels. With a major showdown on protectionism looming, Boston free traders hoped to influence the debate by placing one of their own in Congress. The city's manufacturing interest also realized what was at stake. Its candidate was Nathan Appleton, the region's most articulate and knowledgeable proponent of industrial development.[44]

As it turned out, Lee never had a chance. Although his supporters claimed that he opposed total repeal of the tariff because such "a large amount of property is vested in manufacturing establishments," concessions of this sort did not go nearly far enough to satisfy local advocates of industrial expansion. Buckingham's *Courier* again led the editorial charge, casting Lee and his followers in the role of monopolistic exploiters earlier reserved for manufacturers. The free-trade regime they hoped to establish, Buckingham wrote, "might perhaps enable two or three—perhaps half a dozen—ship-owners to amass mountains of wealth, and become 'greedy monopolists' or an 'aristocracy' of importers; but it would soon leave the farmers of the country *free* to mortgage their farms to those lords of free trade, and the mechanics *free* to beg their way from the seaports, cities and villages of Massachusetts to that delightful Paradise at the mouth of the Oregon." As the foremost spokesman of Boston's middling interest, Buckingham made a special effort to reach local artisans, reprinting their 1788 and 1819 tariff petitions and composing editorial statements that appealed to their most cherished aims. "Is it possible," he asked, "that the mechanics of this city, a bold enterprizing, industrious race, who have made themselves independent by the labor of their hands under the protection of the government, will consent to give up the privilege of sustaining that independence and transmitting it to their children?" Buckingham could not believe they would, not if they were the thoughtful and sagacious citizens he had long known them to be.[45]

Placed on the defensive throughout, Lee's supporters had little opportunity to present a compelling appeal of their own. When they were not refuting accusations that Lee had embraced Jacksonianism, they had to contend with renewed charges of regional disloyalty. According to "Elector," the main issue facing voters was whether Bostonians wanted to be identified with South Carolina's nullifiers, whom he characterized as "the most desperate and infuriate junto, to judge from their speeches, that ever belched out hostility to Yankees over their cups." Was there anyone, he asked, "who has so little public spirit—so little national feeling—so little New-England feeling—as to wish to put us into this awkward and mortifying Predicament?" Now more than ever, Appleton's backers declared, New Englanders needed to stand together and resist southern assaults on their interests. That at least was the opinion of "An Old Merchant," who drew a parallel between the current situation and earlier instances of southern economic aggression. Just as internal differences had opened New England to the commercial depredations of the embargo and war period, the *Courier* correspondent stated, people of the region could expect "a new series of equally disastrous measures, if, after having invested an immense amount of property in manufactures, we shall again suffer ourselves to be divided, and our influence lost by a mistaken view of our true interest."[46]

The most serious blow to Lee's candidacy came from a totally unexpected source. His followers knew where Buckingham stood and could hardly have been surprised by the *Courier*'s stance. What they did not anticipate was that Nathan Hale's *Advertiser* would also come out for Appleton. During the previous decade, Hale's paper had been the city's leading forum of merchant opinion, and Hale himself had been a staunch proponent of free-trade principles; his press had published the 1827 *Report on Importations*. Although Hale still considered himself a free trader, he could not ignore what was happening around him. Unlike Buckingham, who thrived on political strife, the *Advertiser* editor favored a more genteel approach to public affairs. He certainly did not like being denounced as a tool of "the Virginian Vatican," as he had during the memorialists' controversy. By endorsing Appleton, he doubtless hoped to reduce the level of invective unleashed by the free trade-protectionist debate. More important, Boston was a place where money talked, and Hale knew as well as anyone where the real money now was. As he later told Lee, his own views on political economy had been eclipsed by broader economic developments, and he did not see how the protective system could "be abandoned without the most serious consequences."[47]

Election day finally arrived, and as expected Appleton defeated Lee by a comfortable 3,343 to 2,475 votes; the only surprise was that he did not win by more. In addition to demonstrating the growing political power of Boston's manufacturing interest, Appleton's triumph marked an important step in the formation of the second party system in Massachusetts. As Buckingham observed, "The election cannot fail to terminate in fixing upon every man his name, and the name of the church to which he belongs." Though it would be another three years or so before advocates of industrial expansion began referring to themselves as Whigs, their message was already in place. With Buckingham's able assistance, they had made great strides toward fashioning a political appeal that reached well beyond their own narrow interests by redefining traditional notions of economic interdependence to include manufacturing, and by identifying southern antitariff activities as a threat to regional development. It was a compelling mix that bore a striking resemblance to the popular conservatism of the embargo and war period. All that remained was to extend the appeal to other areas of the state; the Twenty-second Congress would provide ample opportunity to do just that.[48]

All indications were that if Congress did nothing else in the forthcoming session, it would deal with the tariff. And the debate was certain to have strong sectional overtones. The 1828 tariff had aroused considerable antagonism throughout the South, and nowhere more so than in South Carolina. Between 1818 and 1829, prices for the short-staple cotton grown by the state's upcountry planters had plummeted 72 percent. The resulting depression was exacerbated by the deteriorating fertility of upcountry lands and growing competition from producers in the soil-rich areas of the expanding Southwest. Although most South Carolina planters understood the broader causes of their plight, they had come to view protectionism as the main source of their troubles. John C. Calhoun made the connection in his 1828 *Exposition*, which declared protective tariffs unconstitutional and asserted that states possessed the authority to nullify such legislation. However inflammatory his beliefs may have seemed to outsiders, Calhoun saw himself as a moderate, trying to check the excesses of hotheaded colleagues by stating South Carolina's case in a rational, legalistic manner.[49]

Chief among those assuming a more militant stance was Congressman George McDuffie, a gloomy, excitable former nationalist turned state's rights zealot whose platform style one observer likened to that of "a mad man in Bedlam." His main contribution to the tariff debate was the forty-bale theory. Carolinians had long claimed that protective duties threatened planter interests by raising the specter of retaliatory foreign tariffs. McDuffie went a step further, contending that the tariff took money out of planter pockets regardless of what importing nations did. According to the forty-bale theory, Britain paid for cotton imports with manufactures rather than cash, and the money returned to exporting planters came from the sale of these goods in America. With no tariff in effect, southern producers would be paid the full value of whatever they exported; with a 40 percent tariff, they would be required to leave a comparable proportion of the finished goods they received in payment for their cotton with customs authorities. Although the theory made no sense economically, it was wildly popular among all classes of Carolinians. Where Calhoun might be willing to negotiate with northern protectionists, McDuffie and his followers were utterly uncompromising. They demanded abolition of all protective duties.[50]

Boston manufacturers had no intention of submitting. Most were delighted with the 1828 tariff. Once amendments had been added to protect woolens, Abbott Lawrence felt the measure would "keep the South and West in debt to New England the next hundred years." He further believed that southerners could not "be appeased by any concessions" and urged Nathan Appleton to reject all compromises. His normally conciliatory brother Amos offered much the same advice. Resentful of the way Carolinians issued ultimatums "with their fists in our faces," he had nothing but "contempt" for their threats and considered resistance to nullification a matter of regional pride. "I think it against good taste, to say the least," he wrote to Appleton, "for these gentlemen to be *eternally* sounding in our ears, their *gallantry,* their chivalry, their generosity and such like compliments; as tho' these traits belonged to them only." He was willing to "go as far in their praise as they wish, but certainly will never admit that my own section of the union is a whit behind them, in any one valuable quality, and whenever I hear these boasts (which seem to imply superiority) my feelings suffer a shock, and *deny the demand.*" The conservative jurist Peter Oxenbridge Thacher was equally unsympathetic, noting that southern planters were "unwilling to labour" and relied on their slaves for everything. "If this is founded in truth," he told Appleton, "it is an incurable evil"— certainly not something that could be remedied through an adjustment of tariff rates.[51]

Such counsel notwithstanding, Appleton was willing to compromise. He had never considered high tariffs necessary or even desirable, as they tended to promote overproduction. He also knew that many well-intentioned people felt existing duties were excessive and needed to be reduced. At the same time, though, he adamantly rejected any suggestion that "the principle of protection" be abandoned. Like Thacher, Appleton believed the Carolinians' problems were largely of their own making, a view reinforced by the observations of a South Carolina correspondent who attributed planter woes to overproduction, "*imprudent* and *extravagant* purchases of *Lands* and *Negroes,*" and the greater productivity of southwestern soils. Were this indeed the case, eliminating protective duties could provide at best marginal relief.[52]

Of much greater importance was the role protectionism played in the manufacturing interest's industrial development strategy. Appleton viewed product diversification as the key to successful expansion. To prevent overproduction of a narrow range of goods, new firms needed to develop fabrics that did not compete directly with existing product lines. At Lowell, he constantly urged manufacturers to vary their output through the introduction of finer goods. Companies that did so need not fear competition from more established British producers, for it was here that protectionism entered the picture. As Appleton observed, the greatest profits were to be made from those quality fabrics "farthest removed from home competition and nearest to that of foreigners and the protection of the tariff." Knowledgeable investors shared Appleton's views. When it later appeared that cotton duties would be substantially reduced, Harrison Gray Otis noted that existing mills would do well enough, as coarse goods could still be manufactured profitably; however, new companies seeking to produce finer fabrics had little hope of survival.[53]

According to some economic historians, there was no real basis for these fears: Antebellum textile producers could have successfully upgraded product lines without tariff protection. They may be right, but Appleton would have disagreed—and with good reason during the early 1830s. Before 1840, mill promoters had limited access to long-term industrial loans. Individual investors were still the main source of capital, and tariff politics strongly influenced what these people did with their money. Otis was a good example. Without protection, he wanted nothing to do with textiles. In the letter noted above, where he described the effect that abolishing protective duties would have on industrial expansion, Otis confided: "I shall, between us, avail myself of the first opportunity to diminish very considerably my manufacturing stock."[54]

That someone of Otis's stature within the tightly knit Boston investment community would make such a decision was of more than passing significance. As the textile industry expanded, it attracted growing numbers of passive investors who knew little about manufacturing and were making no effort to learn more. Instead, they relied on word of mouth and the example of people such as Otis. Industrial promoters knew this better than anyone. As part of his campaign to raise capital for the Boston and Worcester Railroad, George Morey urged the former Federalist leader to purchase a few shares. Those expressing interest in the enterprise, he explained, often "wish to look over the list of stockholders, & I have several times heard the remark that our stockholders seem to be amongst our *active* & *enterprising* citizens, but that there are very few of our *shrewd capitalists*." In this latter regard, Morey added, many people had asked specifically about Otis. If the removal of protection prompted textile investors to begin asking similar questions, it could have disastrous consequences. At the very least, plans for further development would have to be shelved. And Appleton did not want to see this happen, believing as he did that such expansion-related activities as land and machinery sales, waterpower provision, and mill construction generated significantly greater returns than cloth production ever would.[55]

As the Bay State delegation's point man on protectionism, Appleton arrived in Washington ready to do battle with southern free traders. Expecting the debate to be "violent & angry," he knew that he would have to confront George McDuffie, whose forty-bale theory he determined beforehand to treat with "contempt," while "preserving all due respect" for its author. Making such fine distinctions is never easy, and Appleton was not altogether successful. In the course of demolishing McDuffie's formulation, he characterized it as a "tissue of sophistries," the product of a hallucinatory mind imbued with "downright fanaticism," adding that he used such language "in the conviction of its truth, and in the spirit of charity." McDuffie can certainly be pardoned if he failed to see the good will in these remarks; and Appleton should not have been surprised when the South Carolina congressman displayed "a good deal of spiteful ill nature in a subsequent speech."[56]

Appleton's refutation of McDuffie's forty-bale theory formed only a small part of his lengthy address. Aware that many New Englanders still harbored doubts about industrialization, Appleton was more concerned about northern skeptics than southern rebels, and the bulk of his speech reflected that concern. Of particular interest was his fascinating commentary on intersectional class relations. Regarding the South, Appleton found it remarkable "that we never hear from that region the voice of the working man: it is only capital that we hear speak." He also thought it noteworthy that tariff opposition was most intense in those states where slaves comprised a large proportion of the total population. These ruminations led him to question the effect of slave labor on "the industry of the whites." By contrast, conditions in the North could not be more different, and the protective system had done much to make them so. "All industry," Appleton explained, "is set in motion by capital, and this system seeks to induce capital to devote itself to the employment of domestic industry; because, by adding to the means of comfort and happiness in the laboring classes, their character and standing in society is elevated, and they are better fitted to discharge the duties of citizens."[57]

In a later speech, the Worcester lawyer John Davis elaborated on Appleton's observations. Drawing a distinction between free and slave labor, he noted that slaves could not really be considered labor because they did not work for themselves; their exertions were "but the operation of capital, the same as we see it in horses or cattle." "How widely different," he exclaimed, "the objects of a freeman! He labors for himself. . . . He aims at something higher than food, raiment, and lodging." That he did so had broader political implications. In a free society, Davis said, "Every voter is identified with, and constitutes a portion of, this Government; and nothing is more certain than that it will fall when the voters become too poor to educate their families—too poor to be enlightened themselves—too poor and debased to care whether they are freemen or slaves."[58]

These statements were part of an important shift in regional social ideology. More than simply a response to the growing militancy of southern antitariff activists, they represented a further redefinition of accepted notions of economic interdependence. The proportion of dependent wage earners in the New England economy had been increasing steadily since the late eighteenth century, and the spread of factory production had accelerated the process. It was no longer sufficient to speak only of the ways in which merchants, manufacturers, farmers, and mechanics depended on each other; with the recent emergence of workingmen's organizations in Massachusetts, something also needed to be said about this "new class" that was being added to the population. The confrontation with southern free traders not only prompted elite spokesmen to look more closely at their own society; it also provided an opportune context for the reconceptualization of regional social relations. So long as comparisons with slave society obscured memories of New England's relatively egalitarian preindustrial past, one could speak with real certitude about the interdependence of capital and labor.[59]

This formulation did not supplant older views of social relations. Rather, the two were fused to form a new synthesis. Protective duties, tariff advocates contended, aided workers as well as manufacturers, and what benefited these two groups helped everyone else. Abbott Lawrence certainly saw things that way. In a January 1833 letter to Appleton criticizing Henry Clay's compromise tariff, he asked whether Congress would "bring down the laborers wages in this country to the standards of the pauper labor of Europe. Will the government destroy the middle classes in this great Republic— the bone & sinew of the country, and place the property of the many in the hands of the few[?]"[60] These were also the central themes of a series of county gatherings held during the same month that Appleton and Davis addressed Congress. Typical were two resolutions contained in a petition drafted by a meeting of Hampshire County farmers, mechanics, and other citizens that clarified Lawrence's remarks in the letter quoted above:

Resolved, That we do not wish to impair the comforts of the laboring class of our fellow citizens, by forcing them into an unnatural competition with the half-fed and half-clothed paupers of Great Britain.

Resolved, That the interest of the agricultural community is indissolubly
connected with the success of manufactures, since the price of labor is
sustained and enhanced by them, and the domestic market essentially
improved, to the direct and manifest benefit of the farmer.[61]

These were powerful sentiments, and as the county meetings broadcast
them throughout the commonwealth, increasing numbers of Bay Staters
received the message. An 1832 congressional petition from the working
people of Essex County that linked protection to high wages perhaps best
stated what it meant to them. Echoing Appleton and Davis, the memorialists declared "any measure that shall tend to reduce the price of labor below
a sum sufficient to enable a laborer to furnish a comfortable subsistence
to his family, and to give his children an education that will qualify them to
discharge the duties of citizens with intelligence, must have a tendency to
degrade, if not entirely break down that character for intelligence and independence, which should ever distinguish the citizen of a free republic."[62]

Meanwhile, developments in South Carolina made the protectionists'
appeal even more compelling. Although the 1832 tariff reduced duties on
a broad range of items, southern militants felt that the measure did not
go far enough. No bill "that does not give up the principle of protection,"
Appleton's Charleston correspondent had predicted, would ever satisfy proponents of nullification. He was right. That October, a special session of
the South Carolina legislature called a convention to determine the state's
response. The assembly convened the following month and issued an or-
dinance declaring the 1828 and 1832 tariffs unconstitutional; after February
1, 1833, federal revenue laws would be considered null and void in South
Carolina.[63]

In Massachusetts, nullification was seen as a direct attack on state interests. Although a few conciliatory voices could be heard, most people
believed that the time for compromise had passed. The South had a "settled determination" to destroy the protective system, said Supreme Court
Justice Joseph Story. "We may as well see the truth at once, and meet it like
men." Story's one-time political adversary, William Sullivan, felt the same
way. "So far as the public sentiment is known to me," he wrote to Appleton,
"it is, that the protective system must be preserved; and that this matter is
now understood by the classes of persons, who know whence their daily
bread come." Sullivan could not "submit to the tyranny of the South, and
the prostration of all means of honest living in this quarter." Neither could
John Lowell, another former Federalist leader whose spirited opposition
to the embargo and War of 1812 had earned him such nicknames as "The
Boston Rebel" and "Crazy Jack." "I would let the manufacturers go to ruin,"

he told Appleton, "if it would secure our peace, dignity, & freedom but the principles set up by the South leave us no hope of future security under any system of finance or legislation whatever." Without protection, Lowell added, "our labour would be necessarily reduced to that of the slave labour of the South or of the White Slaves of England, France & Germany."[64]

Outside elite circles, Joseph Buckingham enlarged on these themes in his efforts to rally the middling interest. "They gravely misapprehend the public sentiment of the North, who believe the present crisis is only a controversy between a few manufacturing monopolists, and the advocates of unrestricted commerce," the *Courier* editor declared. "Though every great manufacturer should consent to surrender the system, a voice of strong and earnest protest would be sent forth from every work-shop, every farm-house, every valley and hill-top of New England." Abolishing protective duties threatened to impoverish New Englanders, forcing them to abandon such cherished institutions as schools and colleges by reducing regional "labor and its profits to the standards of the labor and production of slaves." Nor would tariff reduction help the South, for its problems were rooted in its social system. Slave societies, Buckingham said, "cannot be prosperous, under any system of policy, unless in a combination of physical advantages, which few countries possess." It is time, he believed, to let southerners know "that slavery is their only grievance,—the wasting disease that is consuming them by inches. . . . It is time to proclaim that best established maxim of political economy, that prosperity and slavery cannot co-exist."[65]

Among those who heeded Buckingham's call, none did so more force-fully than John Quincy Adams. Two years after his 1828 defeat for reelection to the presidency, he had taken a seat in Congress where his Committee on Manufactures drafted the 1832 tariff. Adams was by all accounts a difficult man. As a young adult he had remarked, "Human Nature, how inexplicable art thou! Oh, may I learn before I advance upon the political stage (if I ever do) not to put my trust in thee!" He rarely did. Austere, self-righteous, and morosely introspective, Adams viewed the world through a dark prism. Perhaps the most learned American of his generation, he did not suffer fools gladly. His few devoted friends and admirers were far outnumbered by a legion of detractors. The latter included most members of the Boston elite, who resented Adams's tendency to chart his own course without first consulting them. "I have been fearful of this man," said Peter Chardon Brooks, an Adams in-law, because "he is so apt to act independently,—which must often embarrass his friends—and is set about everything which he once assumes." As recently as 1829, Adams had engaged Harrison Gray Otis and other former Federalists in a heated public dispute concerning the secessionist inclinations of Hartford Convention delegates.[66]

Boston mill investors thus worried about the kind of tariff Adams's committee would present to Congress. Apart from personal animosities, they knew that Adams had long placed national concerns before regional interests, and that he had never been a notably staunch advocate of protective duties. Their fears turned out to be groundless. Although Adams thought some concessions in order, he was just as committed as Nathan Appleton to maintaining the principle of protectionism. He felt that the tariff reported by his committee represented a reasonable compromise, which addressed southern objections to the 1828 bill without harming the manufacturing interest. When South Carolina announced its intention to nullify the act, Adams put aside all thoughts of conciliation. The "real question," he believed, was slavery, and if southerners refused to discuss protectionism in those terms, he would. At the very least, they needed to be shown the extent to which their peculiar institution depended on federal support.[67]

Adams did not have to wait long for a suitable opportunity to make his case. During the course of an antitariff tirade, Congressman Augustus Smith Clayton of Georgia declared, "*Our slaves are our machinery,* and we have as good a right to profit by them as do Northern men by the machinery they employ." Referring to the speech in a subsequent address of his own, Adams informed southerners that their "machinery" already had ample protection. It included the Fugitive Slave Law and the Three-fifths Clause, which added more than twenty representatives to the region's congressional delegation and thereby gave slaveholders a type of protection denied northern owners of industrial machinery. Even more noteworthy was the constitutional protection against domestic violence. It was no secret, Adams explained, that the danger of rebellion posed a constant threat to those living in areas reliant on the South's peculiar form of machinery, "because that machinery sometimes exerted a self-moving power." If southern legislators insisted on removing "protection from the free white labor of the North, then it ought to be withdrawn from the machinery of the South." After all, Adams observed, his Bay State "constituents possessed as much right to say to the people of the South—we will not submit to the protection of your interests; as the people of the South had to address such language to them."[68]

Although the speech enraged southern congressman, who accused Adams of hurling "a firebrand into the Hall," it delighted New Englanders. According to Joseph Buckingham, a longtime Adams critic who had never forgiven him for deserting Federalism a quarter-century earlier, the former president's speech was just what "the crisis demanded, telling honest, unvarnished truth, directly and plainly." Across the state in Hampshire County, the *Northampton Courier* agreed. "There was no cringing or mincing the matter," its editor wrote. "Small arms had been used so long without effect, that all were impatient or in despair. Mr. Adams, at last, threw in his potent bomb, which immediately scattered the sophistry and small talk of the House." Adding to the applause, the Antimasonic leader Benjamin F. Hallett spoke for countless Bay Staters when he told Adams that he could "not but believe that such sentiments if expressed with manliness by representatives of the North, would have a salutary effect upon the South."[69]

Unaccustomed to such praise, Adams expressed surprise at the reaction, remarking that he had no idea this "*chiffon* of a speech upon the Southern Machinery would have been the most popular thing I ever said or did." That it was so can be attributed to the manufacturers' success in developing a broad appeal linking their interests to those of New England's middling and laboring classes. To be sure, it was not Adams's purpose to assist them. As a longtime foe of elite Boston, he did not speak for the city's mill promoters; as an Antimason, his political aims differed markedly from theirs. But what he had to say was in perfect accord with their own message. Commenting on his speech in a letter to Benjamin Hallett, Adams wrote: "I opened the field, upon which in my opinion, the free labour of the country is to be defended against the operation of *Southern Machinery*. That field had not before been assumed in Congress; but it is the Flanders upon which the parties to the conflict between free and slave labour must as Mr. Webster says come to a better understanding with each other." This was not entirely true. Nathan Appleton and John Davis had "opened the field" a year earlier; Adams's more confrontational speech underscored and clarified their contentions. As he told Hallett, "The Free System and Slave System are there in full contrast, and I am anxious that they should be seen and considered throughout New England."[70]

The tariff would never again play so prominent a role in Massachusetts politics. Henry Clay's compromise bill—which called for a series of biennial reductions, the most substantial of which were scheduled for 1842—not only resolved the nullification crisis but effectively depoliticized the tariff question for a decade. Later clashes over protectionism were relatively tame affairs when compared with the 1832–1833 conflict. Yet the earlier debates left their mark, and perceptive Bay State Democrats knew this better than anyone. Writing to John C. Calhoun in 1829, Marcus Morton told the Carolinian that two issues worked against him in Massachusetts: slavery and the tariff. Morton might have added that the same two issues hampered Democrats generally in state elections. Although Morton himself detested slavery and avoided confrontation on the tariff, he belonged to a party whose most influential northern spokesman, Martin Van Buren, sought to forge an alliance "between the planters of the South and the plain Republicans of the North." Morton would never be able to urge Bay State voters—as John Davis did during the 1840 elections—to "cast aside the demagoging politicians who hang on the skirts of the slave holders to obtain some paltry office, and speak in a tone that shall startle these usurpers." Nor could he advise a congressman, as Abbott Lawrence did Leverett Saltonstall: "You have no fear so long as you manifest a sincere desire to promote the great interests of the country—and those are best served by looking to the importance and magnitude of New England and giving to them a hearty support." Amos Lawrence explained why that was so in an 1831 letter urging his son to "use all the talents and powers you may possess in the advancement of the moral political influence of New England. New England, I say; for here is to be the stronghold of liberty, and the seat of influence to the vast multitude of millions who are to people this republic."[71]

Thus it was that BMC-Lowell mill promoters reestablished the Boston elite's reputation as a defender of regional interests. That they did so during the late 1820s and early 1830s was especially significant. This was a period of political transition, when older party loyalties had faded and new attachments were being formed. Voters who came to identify with what would soon be called the Whig Party during this formative juncture remained staunch supporters long afterward. Over the next two decades, the Whigs would dominate state politics in much the same way—and for many of the same reasons—that the Federalists had before them.[72]

These years were also a time of economic transition, when no one yet knew what the social consequences of industrialization would be. This too helped Boston's proto-Whig manufacturing interest. Most people looked to the future with mixed feelings of hope and trepidation. The Whig appeal, with its optimistic talk about moral and material progress, gave them reason to believe that all would turn out well. Yet not everyone was persuaded. The dissenting views of certain Bay State working people could already be heard. Over the next several decades, their numbers would increase and their voices would grow louder. What they had to say and how the elite responded is the subject of the next chapter.

CHAPTER THREE

Labor and Challenges to Elite Rule

IN APRIL 1825, SIX HUNDRED Boston house carpenters deserted local building sites in one of the largest strikes in the northeastern United States up to that time. They demanded increased wages and a ten-hour day, and because they had acted at a particularly opportune moment—during the spring when construction had just begun and there was a strong demand for building craftsmen—merchant contractors and master carpenters were quick to respond. At an April 15 meeting, the latter issued a set of resolutions that appealed to the carpenters' popular image as worthy "Sons of New England" and residents of a city, "the early rising and industry of whose inhabitants are universally proverbial": "we consider such a combination as unworthy of that useful and industrious class of the community who are engaged in it; that it is fraught with numerous and pernicious evils, not only as respects their employers, but the public at large, and especially themselves; for all Journeymen of good character and of skill, may very soon expect to become masters, and like us the employers of others; and by the measure which they are now inclined to adopt, they will entail upon themselves the inconvenience to which they seem desirous that we should now be exposed!" The statement revealed much about the world in which many of the masters had grown up. In traditional artisanal society, nearly all craftsmen saw themselves as incipient entrepreneurs. It was a place where, after achieving proficiency in their trade, artisans rose from apprentice to journeyman and gradually accumulated the resources needed to become masters in their own right.[1]

By the 1820s, that world either had ended or was passing for many craftsmen. Assumptions that few artisans would remain permanent wage earners no longer held true, nor had they for some years. Whereas during the Revolutionary era a clear majority of Boston mechanics could describe themselves as "Master Workmen," there were three to six times as many journeymen as masters by 1800. And the merchant contractors' resolutions notwithstanding, no one seriously believed that the ratio would improve in the future. Meanwhile, as competition among employers intensified, the casual work-pace of an earlier era disappeared. The workday had once been punctuated by regular bouts of conviviality, during which masters often joined journeymen in a few bowls of rum; now, a growing proportion of employers embraced a new industrial morality that stressed hard work, temperance, and self-discipline. Worse still, in many occupations the craft skills that set artisans apart from common laborers were being eroded by an increased division of labor and the replacement of hand tools by machinery.[2]

These changes did not occur overnight. The degradation of craft life was a gradual, uneven process that affected different groups of artisans at different times. As late as 1850 in most northern cities, more than half the members of certain crafts continued to work in small shops that employed no more than five wage earners. Nevertheless, the trend was clear for mounting numbers of journeymen. No longer able to assume that anyone with ordinary skill and enterprise would as a matter of course become a master, they had to get what they could now. As such convictions spread and deepened, disputes over wages, hours, and working conditions multiplied.

To prevent further erosion of their position, journeymen began organizing. The first major initiative in Boston occurred during the summer of 1830, when local wage earners created a workingmen's party that viewed "all attempts to degrade the working classes as so many blows aimed at the destruction of popular virtue—without which no human government can long subsist." Although the party fared poorly in municipal elections and disappeared the following year, workers continued to seek tangible ways of expressing their solidarity. In 1832 they organized the New England Association of Farmers, Mechanics, and Other Workingmen to unify the "laboring classes" behind efforts to regulate the number of hours they worked, expand their educational opportunities, and "maintain their rights, as American Freemen." At the same time, individual trades such as masons, bakers, and house carpenters created a host of craft-based associations that joined forces in early 1834 to form the Boston Trades' Union.[3]

The labor movement of the 1830s faded after mid-decade and did not survive the depression of 1837. By the early 1840s, however, there were signs of renewed agitation. In Massachusetts, the decade's most significant organizational development originated in Fall River, where a ten-hour campaign launch by local mechanics spread to northern mill centers and resulted in the formation of two important groups: the New England Workingmen's Association (NEWA) and the Lowell Female Labor Reform Association (LFLRA). Before the movement's demise in the late

1840s, activists associated with these and related organizations championed such initiatives as land reform, communitarianism, and the creation of consumer cooperatives, in addition to coordinating efforts to shorten the workday.[4]

It is easy to dismiss the Bay State labor movement of the 1830s and 1840s. In terms of concrete achievement, these groups had little to show for their efforts. They nevertheless made a difference. At a time when both major parties accepted most features of the new economic order, labor activists boldly contested the bland assurances of Boston's manufacturing interest. Focusing on the costs rather than the benefits of industrialization, they argued that the disproportionate share of those costs borne by working people threatened to destroy the social and moral fabric of New England society. To an elite whose political authority was based on its reputation as a defender of regional civilization, this was a serious challenge indeed. Our assessment of that challenge begins with an examination of labor's critique.

ANTEBELLUM LABOR ACTIVISTS demanded a broad range of reforms. In addition to shorter hours, which remained their primary aim throughout the period, at various times they sought to simplify the legal code, abolish imprisonment for debt and compulsory militia duty, enact mechanics' lien laws, and promote land reform and communitarianism. Overshadowing all these objectives was an abiding preoccupation with education. To the mechanics who formed the Boston workingmen's party in 1830, the creation of "a liberal system of education, attainable by all, should be among the first efforts of every lawgiver who desires the continuance of national independence." Leaders of the New England Association of Farmers, Mechanics, and Other Working Men seconded these sentiments, making the "all important subject of General Education" their foremost concern. So did the NEWA convention participants, who in 1846 resolved that "the cause of popular, adult education, ought to find its strongest support among the friends of radical reform; no obstacles in the way of such reform being greater, than the low state of moral and intellectual culture."[5]

As the foregoing resolution indicates, labor activists did not view education as something for youths alone; nor did the term refer only to schooling. Their much broader definition of education embraced anything that contributed to the moral and intellectual development of working people of all ages. What one learned from lectures and labor newspapers was often more important than information received through formal instruction. And reading rooms, libraries, debating clubs, mechanics' institutes, and self-improvement circles had as prominent a place in the worker's educational world as the schoolhouse.

Even more noteworthy were the different purposes of worker education. Two of them—self-improvement and cultural maintenance—embodied values and beliefs shared by nearly all Bay Staters. But for labor activists, education had a third purpose, what might be called a counterhegemonic function. Through the exercise of this function, they expressed their dissatisfaction with the existing order and sought alternatives to it. Antebellum labor leaders, Bruce Laurie has written, subscribed to "a loose and variable body of thought" that is "best and broadly described as radicalism." What made them radicals was their unwillingness to accept elite assertions about how society worked and their determination to fashion a world view that gave voice to labor's needs and interests. These concerns also set them apart from other working people—as well as many members of the middling classes—with whom they otherwise had much in common. All of this makes education an ideal vantage point for the examination of class relations in antebellum Massachusetts. While elite Bostonians were well versed in the language of self-improvement and cultural maintenance, they were unprepared to engage—much less accommodate—the counterhegemonic claims of labor radicals.[6]

In Massachusetts, concerns about self-improvement were as old as New England itself. The region's Puritan settlers embraced a Calvinist work ethnic that made "improving the time" a religious duty. Though later drained of its spiritual content, this behavioral code continued to influence popular attitudes through the widespread inculcation of such moral-pecuniary values as industry, temperance, punctuality, and thrift. As children, New Englanders learned from both teacher and primer that "The Idle *Fool* is whipt as School." Youths attending private academies received a similar message. When George Bancroft, cofounder of Northampton's Round Hill School, told his sister that the main object of education was to teach young people "that they are born to work, and not to while away life in pastime," he spoke for generations of regional schoolmasters.[7]

There were several forms of worker self-improvement in antebellum Massachusetts. One arose in response to changes in the master-apprentice relationship. Traditionally, apprentices had lived with their master's family, where they received moral instruction as well as craft training. By the early decades of the nineteenth century, such arrangements had become increasingly rare. To deal with resulting problems of labor control, master artisans established organizations in many urban locales that were intended to serve as surrogates for the disappearing family-based mode of apprenticeship. One such organization was Springfield's Hampden Mechanics' Association, which opened its library to local apprentices and sponsored a school that provided instruction in bookkeeping, simple arithmetic, writing, and other skills that fledgling mechanics needed to obtain a competence in a marketplace society. The association also monitored apprentice behavior, awarding temperance medals to those who had "abstained from the use of ardent spirits" and conducted themselves "in an honest, obedient, and orderly manner." In an editorial commending the association's work, the *Springfield Republican* observed that if any local working people did not feel they received the respect due them, "they must attribute it in a great measure to the neglect of advantages now within their power and to a want of respect to themselves."[8]

Other self-improvement institutions focused on the needs of journeymen, combining prudential counsel with scientific instruction in an effort to foster "the intellectual improvement of the Mechanics, and the advancement of the Mechanic Arts." Perhaps the best example of this type of organization was the Boston Mechanics' Lyceum. Founded in 1831 by Timothy Claxton, an English-born instrument maker who later became president of the Boston auxiliary of the New England Association of Farmers, Mechanics and Other Working Men, the lyceum arranged lectures, organized debates, and published the *Young Mechanic*. In its pages, and those of successor journals such as the *Mechanics' Magazine, The Mechanic,* and *Boston Mechanic,* journeymen learned about various technical innovations and scientific theories while being advised to work hard, practice economy, select prudent wives, avoid indebtedness, and exercise "virtuous ambition."[9]

Urban mechanics were not the only antebellum workers who evinced an interest in self-improvement. The young women who tended the looms and spindles in regional textile centers established an enviable record of their own. Most of them hailed from farm villages, where hard physical labor had long been part of their daily routine and where opportunities for personal development were limited. Lowell and other mill towns not only offered paid employment, but provided what Lucy Larcom called "an opening into freer life." As soon as they had adapted to their new surroundings, these women enrolled in evening schools, attended lectures, and formed self-improvement circles. They also produced a substantial body of literary work, which appeared in *The Lowell Offering* and other operative-edited journals.[10]

Radicals shared this commitment to intellectual and moral development. But they did so in their own way. In line with the counterhegemonic impulse that shaped radical thought, they insisted that self-improvement initiatives be managed by and for labor alone, independent of the influence of other social groups. "The fault is all our own that we are considered the lower class," said "An Old Worker" in an 1833 letter to the *New England Artisan* that recommended the formation of reading rooms: "We have been governed in our own ideas and opinions by the ideas and opinions of others. It is now time that we began to form opinions of our own." Making the point even more forcefully, another *Artisan* contributor expressed concern about the "overwhelming influence of wealth, and talents, which are profusely lavished to perpetuate error and to secure, by a mock show of learning, a confident people, who now thirst after knowledge." To help blunt the malign effect that the unchecked dissemination of elite views had on popular consciousness, this correspondent urged Boston mechanics not to attend public lectures "until they can devise the means of having Lectures of their own."[11]

On occasion, conflicting approaches to self-improvement exploded into open confrontation. One such dispute occurred in Lowell during the mid-1840s and pitted LFLRA president Sarah Bagley against Harriet Farley, editor of the corporation-sponsored *Lowell Offering*. The two women knew each other well and had much in common. As the author of such essays as the "Pleasures of Factory Life," Bagley had been a frequent contributor to the *Offering* and remained a staunch proponent of self-improvement, describing it as a duty that working women owed to themselves and society. But they had other duties as well, one of which was to protest their deteriorating position in Lowell mills. When the *Offering* refused to print articles she had written criticizing local labor conditions, Bagley denounced the journal at an 1845 Independence Day rally. The main points of her critique, which she developed at some length in an ensuing exchange with Farley, are easily summarized: The *Offering* presented a distorted picture of factory life, and it did so because it was not an independent labor periodical, but a tool of ownership. "This is *undeniable*," Bagley claimed, "and we wish to have the Offering stand on its own bottom, instead of going out as the united voice of the Lowell Operatives, while it wears the Corporation lock and their apologizers hold the keys."[12]

At issue here and throughout the foregoing discussion was an important distinction among labor spokespersons. Whereas people such as Harriet Farley and Timothy Claxton believed in the sufficiency of self-improvement, radicals did not. This can be seen in the different ways each employed the expression "knowledge is power." Although Claxton recognized that "men do become the dupes of those better informed," the lyceum leader more often stressed the rewards of individual effort when speaking about the power of learning. "To my young friends I would say," he wrote in his memoirs, "knowledge is power, wealth, and distinction; that industry and prudence will in general, lead to independence and respect; while idleness and dissipation, will end in slavery and disgrace." A writer in Claxton's journal, *The Mechanic*, spoke from a similar perspective when recommending that people "be ranked according to the sum total of their real, personal, and *mental* property."[13]

Radicals did not disagree with these sentiments, but their emphasis was much different. They were more concerned about the ways in which elite spokespersons used an unequal distribution of knowledge to create and justify broader social inequities. In the *New England Artisan*'s premier issue, an article titled "Knowledge and Understanding" explained how this occurred. With "proper opportunities, and a due proportion of zeal," its author observed, all people were "capable of acquiring a competent knowledge, and a good understanding of those objects toward which they direct their pursuit." Too often, however, working people let others do their thinking for them. "It is in this way," the writer said, "that knowledge gives power—It is for this reason, more than any other, that the labors of the many are made subservient to the interest and the pleasure of the few—It is for this reason, in fact, that any distinction of rank exists at all, in this free country, except such as is formed on the legitimate moral basis, the merits of virtue, and the demerits of vice."[14]

Radicals further emphasized the need to link learning with action. Understanding how society functioned would produce few changes if working people failed to act on the knowledge they had obtained. In a presidential address before the New England Association of Farmers, Mechanics, and Other Working Men, *Artisan* editor Charles Douglas thus urged his listeners to make their motto: "knowledge, whose consequence is power[;] union, that results in efficient strength; and perseverance, which ensures victory." Writing more than a decade later, the editor of Lynn's *Awl* echoed Douglas's counsel when he told local shoemakers that despite their superior numbers, they had permitted "themselves to be ruled and governed at the pleasure of the few, who *think* instead of working"; by combining thought and action, working people could claim their rightful place in society.[15]

But what was labor's place in society? And why did radicals consider the existing state of social relations so unjust? To answer these questions, we need to take a closer look at the second purpose of worker education: cultural maintenance, which in antebellum New England referred to the preservation of social and moral order in a republican society. Like the popular commitment to self-improvement, concerns about cultural maintenance had deep roots in regional history. Seventeenth-century Puritans had departed their homeland to escape both the religious oppression of Anglican authorities and what they saw as the appallingly low moral standards of Stuart England. Once in Massachusetts, they made discipline and obedience distinguishing characteristics of early New England society. This did not mean that they were rigid authoritarians. The Puritans believed in liberty, but it was a special kind of liberty—what the historian David Hackett Fischer has called ordered liberty. According to this conception, liberty was not the prerogative of individuals, acting in their own self-interest; most New Englanders expected and accepted restraints on personal behavior. For them, liberty was collective, something that belonged to the whole community. It was, as they described it, "publick liberty": the freedom of citizens, acting together, to create social rules that all members of the community had a responsibility to obey.[16]

As with the Calvinist work ethic, this concept lost much of its religious content over time. By the early nineteenth century, no Bay Stater seriously hoped to establish a "Bible Commonwealth" that would inspire people everywhere to take up God's work. There had also been a considerable relaxation of colonial laws governing personal conduct. But notions of ordered liberty persisted, and education became a central means of maintaining it in the republican society created by the Revolution. "Shortlived, indeed, would be the fame of our ancestors," said a writer in Horace Mann's *Common School Journal*, "if they had established such a frame of government without providing some extensive guaranty that it should escape the misrule of ignorance and licentiousness." These were not simply the views of middle-class reformers. Seth Luther, the era's most articulate and assertive labor activist, believed a widespread diffusion of knowledge the "only sure foundation of freedom and public safety" in a democratic society, for those who lacked "learning and moral virtue" were doomed to lives of "idleness, dissipation and crime." Leaders of the LFLRA adopted a similar perspective when speaking of their cause. "Its great and leading object," wrote Sarah Bagley in an 1845 report, "is to give the laborer more time to attend to his or her mental, moral and physical wants—cultivate and bring out the hidden treasures of the inner being—to subdue the low, the animal nature, and elevate, ennoble and perfect the good, the true and the Godlike which dwells in all the children of the common Parent." Creating such conditions, Bagley stressed, would benefit the "entire community," not just working people.[17]

The concept of ordered liberty embodied rights as well as duties. And it was here that antebellum radicals parted company with most middle-class exponents of cultural maintenance, for they believed those rights were in grave peril. These fears were not new. They had been voiced earlier by William Manning, a Billerica farmer and Revolutionary War veteran, whose 1799 essay, "The Key to Liberty," contained the first known proposal for a national organization of workers and their political allies. Driven by the same counterhegemonic impulse that inspired labor radicals, Manning approached the problem in much the same way they later did. "Learning and education," he wrote, are "essential to the preservation of liberty; and unless we have more of it among us, we cannot support our liberties long." This was so, Manning explained, because the "foundation on which the Few build all their schemes to destroy free government is the ignorance and superstition of, or the want of knowledge among, the Many." According to leaders of the New England Association of Farmers, Mechanics, and Other Working Men, little had changed three decades later. In an 1832 memorial to Congress, they charged that the growth of "extensive monopolies" obstructed "the spread of knowledge and the 'march of intellect,'" while "subject[ing] the great mass of the people to the arbitrary sway of a monied aristocracy."[18]

How radicals approached cultural maintenance issues can be seen in their response to child labor, another problem addressed by the 1832 memorial as well as an earlier association report on education. Although New England youths had always worked, they had traditionally done so within familial settings where parents or employers made some provision for their moral and intellectual development. This was not happening in regional factories, the association reported: young people who labored thirteen to fourteen hours a day had no time for self-improvement, and family dependence on child earnings made it unlikely that many of these youths would ever see the inside of a schoolhouse after they began work. In directing attention to these developments, association leaders worried not only about the stunted lives to which such children were too often condemned. Equally troubling were the social and political consequences of an uneducated populace. These youths would soon be adults, and to fulfill their responsibilities as citizens, they needed "an education suitable to the character of American freemen." Without it, they would be ill-prepared to preserve their independence in the face of elite manipulation and cajolery—a situation that would almost certainly end in "the final prostration of their liberties at the shrine of a powerful aristocracy."[19]

Radicals also linked concerns about cultural maintenance to their demand for shorter hours, stressing the need for what two historians of the workday have aptly described as "citizenship time." In their influential "Ten Hours Circular" of 1835, Boston trade unionists questioned the patriotism of employers who refused to recognize that workers "have duties to perform as American Citizens and members of society, which forbid [them] to dispose of more than Ten Hours for a day's work." Adopting a similar tack, *Artisan* editor Charles Douglas asked regional manufacturers, "Gentlemen, do you love your country?" If so, he urged, consider the consequences of requiring wage earners to work excessive hours: "By the system you now pursue, you are doing all in your power to foster ignorance," thereby creating a generation of working people who lack any sense of responsibility and who "will at some future day, become fit instruments to establish domestic slavery, or, reduce your country to the lowest state of degradation, tamely to surrender it to a foreign despot."[20]

Although they could not vote, women radicals joined male artisans in making the demand for "citizenship time" part of their campaign for shorter hours. They did so by drawing on popular beliefs about maternal duties that could be traced back to the early years of the republic. Today's mill women, they noted, would be the wives and mothers of tomorrow, charged with the responsibility of preparing their children for the duties of citizenship. To carry out this vital task, women needed to be at least as knowledgeable as men, because "the mother educates the man." But acquiring such knowledge was all but impossible for working women, Sarah Bagley said, so long as manufacturers "inclosed them within the brick walls of a cotton mill from twelve and a half to thirteen and a half hours per day." To enlist male support for ten-hour legislation, the LFLRA leader reminded men that they, too, had duties. In a shrewdly calculated appeal to the "Fathers of our own happy, free New England" that deftly combined patriarchal and republican themes, she asked: "Do you sanction this long hours system? Are you willing that your sons, aye, your daughters, too, shall thus go out into the world? Are you the sons of those who fought so nobly for freedom? Are you the sons of the fathers of '76?"[21]

Throughout the antebellum period and beyond, no issue more frequently mobilized Bay State wage earners than the demand for a reduced workday. That it did so is not surprising. In addition to creating bonds between male mechanics and women mill operatives, the shorter-hours question addressed concerns about self-improvement as well as cultural maintenance. Without greater leisure, working people could not realize their full potential. As Charles Douglas observed of a report praising Connecticut's high literacy rate, it mattered little that workers could read when they did not have time to reflect on what they were reading and apply the knowledge thus obtained to some useful aim. This was particularly significant to radicals, who stressed the importance of linking thought to action, and who saw self-improvement as an integral part of their broader counterhegemonic enterprise. What shorter hours meant to them was perhaps best captured in an 1847 letter from the Lowell Union of Associationists, a local Fourierist organization whose membership included Sarah Bagley and other LFLRA activists. "We are all dependent upon our own labor for support," its author wrote, "with but little money, and a still greater lack of that which our own kind Father bestowed alike on all,—Time,— which is here monopolized by the few,—time to cultivate those tastes and talents which we humbly believe were bestowed upon us, as upon our more favored sisters."[22]

The statement reveals much about the widespread appeal that shorter hours had for antebellum workers. Stripped of its reference to the monopolistic practices of Lowell mill owners, it could just as easily have been voiced by Harriet Farley, who despite her conflict with LFLRA leaders valued time just as much as they did. As it was, Lucy Larcom, a *Lowell Offering* contributor who shared Farley's belief in the sufficiency of self-improvement, expressed in her autobiography sentiments similar to those quoted above. Describing her move from a well-paying but demanding job to a position that promised greater leisure, Larcom recalled the paymaster asking if she had arranged the transfer to make more money: " 'No,' I answered, 'I am going to where I can have more time.' 'Ah, yes!' he said sententiously, 'time is money.' But that was not my thought about it. 'Time is education,' I thought to myself; for that is what I meant it should be to me."[23]

Radicals would have been more gratified than surprised to hear such remarks uttered by someone who distanced herself from their activities, for they viewed efforts to promote education as a way of reaching out to other groups in the community. New Englanders had long held learning in high esteem, and radicals felt that demonstrating their commitment to "educating the uneducated" would convince all but the hopelessly avaricious of their good intentions. "When intelligent men see that those who are demanding from others an amelioration of their condition, are also trying to improve themselves," said an *Artisan* contributor who proposed the establishment of circuit schools for mill children and evening schools for adults, "they cannot withhold their own vote of approbation." At the same time, wage earners who profited from this increased diffusion of knowledge would soon be doing their part to further labor's cause. There were many working people, a Fall River editor believed, "who, if they had an opportunity to improve their intellectual faculties, could and would, exert a beneficial influence over, at least, a portion of the community."[24]

Several factors influenced these efforts to secure middling-class support. One was the economic insecurity felt by many master mechanics, shopkeepers, and farmers caught up in the market revolution that was transforming antebellum society. Radicals sensed the organizational opportunities such fears and uncertainties engendered, and they did what they could to exploit them. "A Boston Mechanic" demonstrated how they did so in an 1834 letter defending the local practice of allowing master artisans to join trade unions. After noting that "hard luck" often forced boss mechanics back into the ranks of wage labor, this writer proceeded to describe the material bases for worker-middling class cooperation. "Mechanics, farmers, artisans, and all who labor, whether as boss or journeyman" he declared, "have a common interest in sustaining each other—the rich men, the professional men, and all who now live, or who intend hereafter to live without useful labor, depending on the sweat of their neighbor's brow for support, have also a common interest. And their interest is promoted by working us hard, and working us cheap."[25]

Popular attachment to traditional notions of social harmony also influenced radical outreach initiatives. Elite proponents of industrialization acted shrewdly when they appropriated the rhetoric of social interdependence to justify their activities. These beliefs were deeply rooted in regional culture, and radicals could not ignore them without adding to their own marginalization. The resolutions issued by workers' conventions contained ample evidence of their sensitivity on this point. Labor organizers rarely met without condemning social unrest or denouncing class conflict, though in doing so they did not allow such disavowals to dilute the counterhegemonic thrust of their broader critique. A good example can be found in Seth Luther's famous *Address to the Workingmen of New England*. Labor activists held no "views hostile to any body or profession, of men, as *such*," the radical carpenter assured listeners, "for we believe the interests of all classes are involved in the *intelligence* and *welfare* of those who labour—those who produce *all* the wealth and enjoy so *small* a portion of it themselves."[26]

Luther's remarks, which could be heard wherever radicals gathered, cut to the heart of the matter. Whatever the case may have been in earlier periods, labor could no longer assume that other classes would be mindful of its interests. Whereas manufacturers claimed that their business activities reinforced traditional forms of social interdependence, radicals charged that recent developments destroyed any basis for interclass cooperation. By exposing capital's assault on the producing classes, they sought to repair rather than exacerbate existing social divisions—in the words of the labor lecturer S. C. Hewitt, "to fill up the awful chasm which is already existing between the laborer and the capitalist—to heal the breach which their present antagonism is continually making more alarming." And they hoped they could do so without pitting employers against workers in bitter personal confrontations. "Let it be understood," said *Voice* editor William F. Young, "that the workingmen's warfare is not with *individuals* but *systems*—systems which make the rich tyrannical, powerful, haughty, aristocratic, hardened and neglectful of the duties they owe to their race and their fellow men around them; and the poor envious and contentious, or servile and obedient to the mandates of wealth, and those more favored."[27]

In sum, the radicals' critique combined opposition to current injustices with concerns about broader cultural trends. On one level, their protest centered on questions of basic equity. Here they sought to provide working people with the same time and resources for personal development enjoyed by members of other social groups, and to end a state of affairs where an operative could be defined as someone "who is employed in a Factory, and who generally earns three times as much as he or she receives." On another level, they questioned the new economic order's effects on traditional social values. Particularly worrisome was the growing power of "mere money" to distort popular perceptions of what mattered. The tension between material acquisitiveness and moral duty that had troubled earlier generations of New Englanders appeared to have been resolved in favor of unrestrained accumulation. People were now defined by what they owned, not by what they did or how they behaved. "Rich and poor have bowed down together before the God of Wealth," an *Awl* correspondent observed, "and mere external circumstances have dictated to men the station they should occupy in society." Labor could never prosper in such a world. "But let the opposite principle prevail," this writer added, "that every honest profession is alike honorable, and that men are to be esteemed according to their intelligence and virtue, and the foundation is established for a series of efforts that will tell with tremendous effect in favor of the working men of our country."[28]

These inspiring words tell us much about radical aims. They further reveal the extent to which radicals remained very much a part of the society they hoped to transform. This was both a strength and a weakness: posing as champions of traditional moral concerns widened the audience for their appeal, while blunting the force of their critique. Members of Boston's manufacturing interest also believed that people should "be esteemed according to their intelligence and virtue." Indeed, they claimed to be creating just such a world. It is now time to see how they justified their creation.[29]

THE BOSTON ELITE's response to the rise of organized labor was by no means uniform. To those who had imbibed the buoyant optimism of antebellum Whiggery, labor's growing assertiveness did little to shake their belief in moral and material progress. Confident that all would benefit in the new economic order, they viewed the radical critique with uncomprehending dismay, to the degree that they noticed it at all. By contrast, those whose social and political convictions had been forged in an earlier era felt they were living in a world turned upside down. To these Federalist leaders, increased labor unrest signaled a breakdown in social order that would only get worse over time. "The spirit of insubordination is fearful and universal in the country," said Harrison Gray Otis after reading a handbill urging New York workers to protest a judicial decision against that city's journeymen tailors. His longtime friend and political colleague, William Sullivan, expressed even greater alarm. If something were not done to strengthen the militia, he warned in an 1832 letter to Nathan Appleton, "we shall presently be disarmed, and in a few years a band of desperate operatives may burn the whole town of Lowell, without resistance."[30]

Although such hysteria was hardly typical, it is worth pausing to examine its sources, as the fears and biases of these aging Federalists provide a useful counterpoint to significant features of Whig social and political thought. One reason people such as Otis and Sullivan found growing worker activism so troubling was their tendency to see social protest as a reflection of broader political developments. In their minds, labor radicals took their cue from Jacksonian demagogues bent on aggrandizing their power at the expense of everything decent in society. And it could all be traced back to the election of 1800. Like certain late twentieth-century conservatives who view the student radicalism and counterculture of the 1960s as the fount of all evil, these men held Thomas Jefferson responsible for everything wrong with society. The Virginian "drew the line between rich and poor," Sullivan declared. "The perils, sufferings, and dread of the present hour, are all from his impulse." Salem attorney Benjamin Merrill also believed the country was "still reaping the fruits of the seeds sowed by Jefferson," who as party leader had instilled in the masses "hatred and jealousy of the rich and of corporations and capitalists"; "the virus yet infects the people, and till it is worked out, they will never be sane and in health."[31]

Otis probed even deeper in his efforts to explain what had gone wrong. The problem, he concluded, lay in the class dynamics of democracy. As a younger man, Otis had done as much as anyone to make Federalism appealing to the state's middling interest. But whatever faith he might have had in that social group had long since faded. Drawing on language that could have been copied from George Cabot's correspondence, he told Benjamin Pickman that "jealousy of a monied interest always prevails in popular governments. It is the foible of the middling classes and with the lower it is a ruling passion, which the ambitious and unprincipled leaders of the democracy always rouse into dangerous activity and direct against any men they wish to put down." Members of these two classes, he added in another letter, were often political allies and together constituted a powerful force that could be used by unscrupulous politicians to establish "the despotism of the poor many over the rich few, which has been found in every popular government."[32]

In their gloomier moments, these men also voiced disapproval of contemporary elite conduct. Here too things had changed, and mostly for the worse. "To one who looks back on what the social world was," Sullivan remarked, "it seems as though money-making, and selfishness, had frozen the currents of the heart. That frank, friendly, social, hospitable intercourse, which was once the delight of this land, is gone (it is feared) for ever; and the cold, calculating spirit of accumulation, or the worthless emulation of show and splendor, has succeeded." Sullivan doubtless overstated the extent to which social life had retrogressed. In a community populated with such masters of highbrow chatter as George Ticknor and Edward Everett, whose lives revolved around their dining arrangements, there was no dearth of elegant discourse at antebellum social gatherings. Nor did all upper-class social functions of the earlier period display the genteel refinement of which Sullivan spoke. As Henry Adams wrote of the state dinners then so popular among urban elites, they were not the light repasts that "France introduced into an amusement-loving world, but the serious dinner of Sir Robert Walpole and Lord North, where gout and plethora waited behind the chairs; an effort of animal endurance."[33]

Though one might also question whether Whigs were appreciably more acquisitive than Federalists, the two groups did differ in one important respect. Where Whigs equated material prosperity with social progress, Federalists had serious doubts about the ameliorative powers of money-making and economic development. This skepticism stemmed in part from their bleak assessment of human nature. Despite their embrace of religious liberalism, Federalist elites had a decidedly Calvinist view of popular behavior, and they could not see how the release of acquisitiveness made people more virtuous. A second reason for their skepticism was the fragile foundation on which much of Federalist wealth had rested during their formative years. When contemporary observers referred to Napoleonic era commercial ventures as "speculations," they were not passing judgment on merchant behavior but stating an unsettling fact of mercantile life. In the hectic, unpredictable world of the transatlantic carrying trade, a few bad decisions or unforeseen disasters could wipe out the heftiest fortune.

The expanding enterprises of the Boston Associates had a much more stable base. Just how stable was perhaps best stated by Amos A. Lawrence, the son of Amos and nephew of Abbott Lawrence, who as a Harvard senior felt he could confidently look forward to a prosperous and trouble-free future. "My advantages for becoming rich are great," he observed. "[I]f I have mere mercantile tact enough to carry on the immense though safe machine which my father and uncle have put in operation, it will turn out gold to me as fast as I could wish." That "machine" was already in place by the 1830s, and at midcentury its dimensions were truly impressive. With the erection of additional factory towns at Chicopee, Lawrence, and Holyoke in Massachusetts, and at various sites in Maine and New Hampshire, the Associates owned 20 percent of the nation's textile spindlage; they also controlled 40 percent of Boston banking capital, 39 percent of Massachusetts insurance capital, and 30 percent of the state's railroad mileage. Given the breadth of their holdings and the seeming ease with which they had increased them, it was little wonder why they placed such faith in economic progress, why they believed few problems existed that a booming economy could not resolve, or why they occasionally appeared somewhat vulgar to former Federalist leaders such as William Sullivan.[34]

Confident that they had vanquished economic uncertainty and with few doubts about their own rectitude, the Associates believed they knew how to deal with labor's growing restiveness. In their minds, there was no reason for radical attacks on elite society. "We are literally all working-men," said Amos Lawrence, "and the attempt to get up a 'Working-men's party' is a libel upon the whole population, as it implies that there are among us large numbers who are not working-men." The noted Brahmin orator, educator, and politician Edward Everett elaborated on Lawrence's comments in an 1830 "Lecture on the Workingmen's Party" that made no reference to labor politics. His main point—expressed with mind-numbing prolixity—was that all but the immoral and the indolent were workers. Outside elite circles, important organs of middling-class opinion reacted in similar fashion. "We cannot of course answer for the character of industry of many places where this party is agitated," the Springfield Republican editorialized, "but we believe the great body of our own community, embracing every class and profession, may justly be called workingmen; nor do we believe enough can be found who are not such, to make even a decent party of drones."[35]

Members of Boston's emergent Whig leadership found statements of this sort particularly gratifying. Although they did not share Otis's deep distrust of the middling classes, they knew their reputation for independence. So long as shopkeepers, master artisans, and other petty entrepreneurs accepted elite definitions of social interdependence, radical initiatives could be isolated and contained. Should these groups become receptive to radical appeals, however, the existing balance of social forces might be disrupted in ways that threatened elite control. It was therefore important to keep the middling classes in line, even if it required some coercion.

One such incident, involving Joseph Buckingham, occurred during the 1832 Boston shipwrights' strike. The Courier editor had come a long way in the past decade. In addition to displacing Benjamin Russell as the city's leading exponent of middling-class opinion, Buckingham had a growing statewide reputation. The Worcester lawyer-archivist C. C. Baldwin, who relied on the Courier "more than any other paper," believed that "[a]s a pithy editor there were few equal to him in the country." What Buckingham did not have was the respect of local elites, and their inattention plainly bothered him. "There is a clannish spirit in this city and vicinity," he wrote to Daniel Webster, "which is in nothing more manifest than the opinions respecting the Press." To the Lowells, Cabots, Appletons, and other elite families, Nathan Hale's *Advertiser* was the only Boston newspaper worth reading, and any article that did not first appear there was unlikely to elicit their notice. Buckingham thus felt that he had little inducement to elevate the tone of the local press. "It would cost me labor and money," he explained, "and I should be sneered at as a *mechanic* by the aristocracy, and laughed at by professional contemporaries as a *fool,* for entering with zeal into a political warfare where I have everything to lose and nothing to gain." His safest course was "to be as tame and as passive as one can be with decency to make friends of the *Mammon of unrighteousness.*"[36]

But "decency" is a very subjective term, and Buckingham was not by nature a passive man. Moreover, as spokesman for Boston's middling classes— those who stood between rich and poor, "holding them together as one body politic, like the cement of the solder which the mechanic uses to make different materials cohere and form one indivisible mass"—he saw himself as a social mediator, with a responsibility to remind the city's various social groups of the duties they owed each other. When waterfront employers proved unwilling to meet local shipwrights halfway in an 1832 shorter-hours dispute, he decided to intervene by publishing a letter from an "old friend" who felt that the striking workers had real cause for dissatisfaction. Appearing less than a month after Buckingham had confided to Webster, the letter did more than defend the hard-pressed journeymen; it also contained a withering critique of employer conduct. Responding to merchant assertions that they sought mainly to combat the unjustified demands of an "unlawful combination," this correspondent asked: "What was their own meeting? A convention, no doubt, of high-minded gentlemen: but for what? *To compel the caulkers to work hard and to work cheap.*" These merchants and shipowners apparently believed that their wealth and social position gave them the right to do anything they wished to the "men dependent upon them for employment." If that were indeed the case, the writer informed them, they had it all wrong: "they have mistaken the public opinion, and have miscalculated the effect which an array of names can produce."[37]

Buckingham did not have to wait long for the merchants' response. Their committee immediately issued a statement condemning the communication and expressing regret that the *Courier* had published it. Several days later, committee members confronted Buckingham at his office and demanded that he reveal the writer's identity. Although Buckingham refused to do so, he got the message: any more such interventions in the shipwrights' strike could have costly repercussions. Later that month, "A Non-Producer" had to submit a letter criticizing the merchants to the *New England Artisan* because the *Courier* refused to publish it. And the following January, after Judge Peter O. Thacher had condemned unlawful combinations in a charge to the Suffolk County grand jury, Buckingham applauded Thacher's defense of law and order. Buckingham thus restored his reputation as a faithful "watchman on the walls of our political Zion," as he later described himself in a loan request to Nathan Appleton.[38]

Although fear and self-interest certainly influenced Buckingham's conduct, he did not act from such motives alone. The *Courier* editor sincerely felt that all could prosper in the new economic order, and he genuinely detested social unrest. Apart from his steadfast support for protectionism, Buckingham's enthusiastic promotion of social interdependence constituted his greatest service to elite Boston. Not content simply to show how industrial development benefited agriculture, commerce, and the mechanic arts, he also championed the doctrine of stewardship, urging the rich to remember their social duties and assuring the less fortunate that a merciful God had "put it into the hearts of men to provide relief for the poor and him who hath no home."[39]

This was music to Brahmin ears. Duties of this sort accorded well with elite perceptions of themselves as virtuous and upstanding citizens. Assuming the responsibilities of stewardship also helped them to resolve any doubts they might have had about the deleterious consequences of their moneymaking pursuits. No one can now determine how extensive this self-questioning was, but it did happen. "It is mean and unaccountable that our desire for property or power is so great," said William Appleton, "when we reflect on the entire uselessness of it for the little time which we can remain with it." Peter Chardon Brooks, who made a fortune in marine insurance during the Napoleonic era and was reputedly Boston's wealthiest citizen, expressed similar concerns when he remarked that "there is more danger of having too much than too little," for "[m]oney rarely makes us better." And having acquired the bulk of his wealth in a relatively short time, he worried about the effect it would have on himself and his family, confiding to his diary: "Few can behave with propriety under a change so sudden and considerable." But this troubling thought apparently passed quickly, as his next words were: "God grant that I might be one of those few!"[40]

That Brooks could so easily cast aside such reservations by asking divine assistance owed much to the doctrine of stewardship. It was one feature of the region's Puritan heritage that Boston's Unitarian ministers continued to stress, and it was not surprising that their wealthy congregants responded to these appeals. As a people long accustomed to viewing both spiritual and temporal matters in contractual terms, elite Bostonians were strongly predisposed to embrace a doctrine that linked benevolence and salvation in an implicit agreement between oneself and one's God. "I would earnestly strive to keep in mind the fact that he *will* call," Amos Lawrence said of the final judgment, "and that when he calls, the question will be, How have you used these? Not How much have you hoarded?" To Lawrence, increased wealth added to one's social responsibilities, and believing that as agents of the Lord everyone "must at last render an account," he implored: "God grant that mine be found correct!" It doubtless was, as Lawrence—who gave more than a half million dollars to various charitable projects between 1841 and 1852 alone—took his duties as a social steward very seriously.[41]

Few of his social peers matched Lawrence's piety or generosity or typically assisted so broad a range of causes. Much of their philanthropic giving went to institutions such as Harvard University and the Boston Athenaeum that helped the elite define, differentiate, and sustain itself. At the same time, though, other concerns reinforced their commitment to the ethic of stewardship. Of these, none was more important than the preservation of social harmony. In an 1827 discussion of the responsibilities of wealth, the Harvard theologian James Walker observed that the day had passed "when the few could trample with indifference on the interests and feelings of the many, and make sport of their complaints with impunity." Elite Bostonians would do well to recognize that fact, the city's Central Board of the Benevolent Fraternity of Churches declared, if they wanted to maintain social order. Governmental stability and "the security of property," the board warned, are "very much in the hands of what in Europe are called the poorer classes. They hold the votes, they wield the power; and a fearful one it will prove, unless directed by moral and religious principle." Boston's elite took these warnings seriously, and the church board's Sunday schools and city missions received the funding needed to carry on their work.[42]

So did a host of other philanthropic societies. Between 1830 and 1850, the number of such institutions in Boston increased sixfold, from 26 to nearly 160 at midcentury. The Associates exhibited a particularly strong interest in educational initiatives. Some, such as the evening schools, libraries, and lecture programs they established in Lowell and other factory towns, responded to worker longings for self-improvement. Others linked individual achievement to economic development. During the 1820s, the New England Society for the Encouragement of the Manufacturing and Mechanic Arts—whose members included John Lowell, Amos Lawrence, Nathan Appleton, and Patrick Tracy Jackson—sought to promote domestic industry by providing financial inducements to artisan-inventors.

Similar concerns influenced Abbott Lawrence when he later gave the Massachusetts Charitable Mechanic Association twenty thousand dollars to help erect a school "in which the apprentices of Boston Mechanics may be instructed in those branches of education most appropriate to their wants," and when he laid out an even larger sum for the creation of a scientific school at Harvard "to diversify the occupations" of New Englanders.[43]

Like labor radicals, the Associates viewed cultural maintenance as a major function of education. Needless to say, they were not talking about the same things. Where radicals hoped to promote public virtue by restoring the more egalitarian conditions of New England's past, elite Bostonians were more concerned about inducing popular submission to their political and economic hegemony. This was one area where Whigs agreed fully with their Federalist predecessors. To Fisher Ames, who took pride in the fact "that the New England people are better taught than any other," those who thought "ignorance produce[d] loyalty" needed further instruction themselves. Shays' Rebellion demonstrated otherwise, he said, "and I believe it will ever be found that the best informed people are the most governable." Daniel Webster made much the same point when he later described public education "as a wise and liberal system of police, by which property, and life, and the peace of society are secured." So did the Brahmin educator George Ticknor when he explained to Maria Edgeworth: "The principle, that the property of the country is bound to educate *all* the children of the country, is as firmly settled in New England as any principle of the British Constitution is settled in your empire; and as it is alike for the interest of the majority, who have little of the property that is taxed to pay for the education, and for the interest of the rich, who protect their property by this moral police, it is likely to be long sustained."[44]

It is easy enough to show that wealthy Bostonians placed social control before social reform. But at this juncture, a more important question needs to be asked: Did it matter that the aims of elite stewardship were often so self-serving? At least one Brahmin felt that it did not. In an 1845 journal article on Boston charities, Samuel A. Eliot acknowledged that local philanthropists acted from a variety of motives—"benevolence, vanity, love of influence, ambition, or whatever else may be imagined." Eliot himself preferred to believe that elite charity stemmed primarily from feelings of benevolence. But, he added, if prompted by "any of the lesser motives, still it produces active sympathy,—a sympathy between those who act in concert, and sympathy with those to whose benefit their action is directed. Thus is society knit together by feelings and by interests intertwining in every direction, and scarcely can one bond be broken without its being widely felt and speedily repaired."[45]

However overstated, these observations represented more than wishful thinking on Eliot's part. Though radicals might condemn such reasoning, other working people had fewer questions about the objectives of elite stewardship. To Harriet Farley, Lucy Larcom, and the many mill operatives who believed in the sufficiency of self-improvement, it was enough that manufacturers made provisions for their educational needs. And to proponents of mechanics' lyceums such as Timothy Claxton, who appreciated the Associates' enthusiasm for technological innovation and economic development, these questions were of even less consequence. At the Massachusetts Charitable Mechanic Association's fiftieth anniversary dinner, members acknowledged Abbott Lawrence's generosity by toasting the health of this "prince among merchants"—sentiments no doubt shared by many of the apprentices who benefited from instructions offered in the free school that Lawrence's twenty-thousand-dollar gift helped establish. In short, while elite philanthropy did not change the minds of radicals, it did blunt their appeal to New England working people. And they knew this better than anyone, as their efforts to create autonomous labor institutions clearly testify.[46]

Another factor shielding the Associates from radical criticism during the 1830s was worker receptiveness to protectionist arguments. Although *Artisan* editor Charles Douglas tried to convince readers that higher tariffs benefited mill owners alone, it was a hard sell. Too many workers shared "A Mechanic's" fears about competition from British "pauper labor." The actions of South Carolina nullifiers made Douglas's task even more difficult. His assertion that the controversy could best be viewed as a "contest between rich and avaricious planters" and "rich and avaricious manufacturers" did not satisfy *Artisan* correspondents who attributed nullification to slavery and southern jealousy of northern prosperity. Even readers who worried that the conflict might "draw the people from their own cause" refused to concede protectionism's irrelevance. It was true that working people would never receive the full benefits of increased duties without additional economic and political reforms, said one such correspondent. But this did not justify the dismantling of the protective system. Doing so, this writer contended, would only "sink the power and resources of free labour, and diminish immensely the amount of its income." Though none of these letter writers said anything about the interdependence of capital and labor—as manufacturers invariably did when discussing protectionism—the fact that many radicals supported protective tariffs suggests that the issue had real appeal to wage earners in general.[47]

The Associates also escaped criticism on two of the more inflammatory issues of the 1830s. One was child labor. Whereas the family labor system found in the Slater-type factories of southern New England employed numerous children, the women who worked in Waltham-Lowell mills were for the most part young adults. And the 1832 education report issued by the New England Association of Farmers, Mechanics, and other Working Men noted the relative absence of child labor at Chicopee and Lowell firms controlled by Boston capital. The demand for shorter hours was a second issue that the Associates did not have to face during the 1830s— at least not in their main enterprises. Although mill conditions at Lowell were by no means idyllic, the work pace was sufficiently undemanding that operatives could read and talk with each other while on the job; being able to exchange tasks, share work, and leave the mill for short periods further broke the monotony of the twelve-hour workdays. When Lowell workers walked out in 1834 and again in 1836, their grievances centered on wage-related concerns.[48]

The Waltham-Lowell firms would not be so lucky during the 1840s. In the depression following the Panic of 1837, mounting competition in a contracting market caused a steady decline in cloth prices. As profits and dividends fell, owners placed pressure on mill agents to boost productivity. The resulting speedups and stretchouts increased machine speeds while adding to the number of looms and frames assigned to operatives. And as workloads grew, mill workers found the industry's long workdays increasingly oppressive. When Fall River workers launched a statewide movement for shorter hours, Lowell operatives showed themselves more than ready to do their part.[49]

Between 1842 and 1846, Massachusetts working people flooded the legislature with petitions requesting enactment of laws to limit the workday. Though Whig leaders had no intention of passing such legislation, neither did they want to alienate working-class voters. So they did what politicians customarily do at such moments: they tried to talk their way through the dilemma. Responding to an 1842 petition from Fall River workers, Governor John Davis said that he concurred fully with the principles expressed in the group's constitution: "that the rewards of those who are industrious in any necessary and useful employment, should be sufficient to enable them with prudence and economy to secure for themselves, and their families, opportunities for mental, moral, and religious improvement; to obtain the necessaries, conveniences, and comforts of life; and to accumulate enough to ensure a comfortable support in sickness and old age." Indeed, he added, when "the state of things is such as to forbid the attainment of these most reasonable and desireable ends, it furnished strong presumptive proof that there is a great fault in legislation somewhere, which needs correction." That said, Davis told the petitioners he could not support a bill that prevented wage earners who so desired from working longer than ten hours.[50]

This was plainly not good enough, and the petitions kept on coming. By mid-decade, Lowell operatives had assumed a leading role in the campaign; in 1845, when legislators appointed a committee to investigate the hours of labor in Massachusetts's workplaces, the chairman William Schouler requested their presence at the hearings. Replying on behalf of her fellow petitioners, Sarah Bagley informed Schouler that they were prepared to present their case whenever the committee would consent to hear them. In their subsequent testimony, the six women of the Lowell delegation furnished an able defense of the ten-hour workday, noting how the present system impaired workers' health without giving operatives time for "intellectual, moral and religious" development.[51]

Their account of working conditions at Lowell made little impression on the committee. Nor did it sway Schouler, who as editor of the *Lowell Daily Courier* had a vested interest in protecting the reputation of local mills, and who as a man of some ambition hoped that manufacturers would support his plans to establish a Boston daily. In the committee's report, which he authored, Schouler dismissed concerns about health, claimed that shorter hours would mean lower wages, and declared that "[l]abor is intelligent enough to make its own bargains, and look out for its own interests without any interference from us." Any needed reforms, he concluded with a characteristic Whig flourish, must be sought elsewhere—"in the progressive improvement in art and science, in a higher appreciation of man's destiny, in a less love of money, and a more ardent love for social happiness and intellectual superiority."[52]

Although Schouler's recommendations kept him in good standing with mill owners, they hardly satisfied discontented factory operatives. To *Voice* editor William Young, the report removed any doubt that Schouler was nothing more than a "tool sent by the Lowell Corporations to the Massachusetts legislature, to uphold and foster those rotten hearted and inhuman institutions." LFLRA activists agreed. Meeting shortly after the report's publication, they condemned "the cringing servility to corporate monopolies" exhibited by committee members and vowed to use their "best endeavors and influence to keep [Schouler] in the 'city of spindles,' where he belongs, and not trouble Boston folks with him." That November, when the *Courier* editor lost his bid for reelection, the LFLRA thanked local voters for "consigning" him "to the obscurity he so justly deserves."[53]

Care must be taken in assessing the significance of Schouler's defeat. For one thing, shorter-hours legislation was not the only question at issue. Lowell Whigs went into the contest divided over a railroad extension to

Andover, and Schouler apparently came out on the short end of the dispute. Local Democrats, who had no candidates in the race, lined up behind a "railroad ticket" of four Whigs that did not include the *Courier* editor. Nor did the election signal a shift to increased political activism on the part of labor radicals. "So long as the inducement exists for men to abuse power gained by political action," William Young declared, "there is danger in relying too much upon it to renovate society." Worried about the corrupting effect that involvement in electoral politics had on working people, Young urged them to concentrate on acquiring the knowledge and moral strength needed to withstand such temptations. Such advice could hardly have gladdened working people whose problems stemmed from their lack of power. Young's position nevertheless received support from other NEWA leaders who thought that a resort to political action had helped destroy the workingmen's movement of the 1830s. The organization thus limited its electoral activities to questioning candidates on labor-related issues.[54]

Yet LFLRA opposition did contribute to Schouler's defeat, and given the state's political demography, this spelled potential trouble for Massachusetts Whigs. As Daniel Webster had remarked several years earlier, party dominance of state affairs depended on electoral victories in Boston, Lowell, and other major population centers. There had been few problems to date, Webster added, "[b]ut this is a frail basis, to rest party hopes upon, for time to come." It was indeed, and shorter-hours agitation made that foundation all the more fragile. Though the LFLRA soon dissolved, other proponents of ten-hour legislation built on the women's example. By the early 1850s, mill-town elections turned increasingly on where candidates stood on the workday issue. This was bad news for Bay State Whigs.[55]

If the Associates noticed what was happening, they gave little indication. Although the stretchouts and speedups of the post-1837 period made a mockery of their claims to being good stewards, public statements about life in Lowell and other mill towns continued to be framed in terms of the paternalistic vision of the founders. And when they talked about labor's current needs, they invariably did so within the context of a broader discussion of protectionism. Good examples were Abbott Lawrence and Nathan Appleton, two of the best-known and most powerful industrialists of the period. Lawrence was an outgoing, even-tempered person of great charm and engaging sociability, whom even John Quincy Adams found "frank [and] open-hearted." His enormous wealth notwithstanding, he considered himself a man of the people, someone squarely in touch with popular sensibilities. On an 1828 lobbying trip to Washington, he found far too many lawyers in Congress, writing to his brother Amos: "More farmers and Mechanics and practical men of all sorts are wanted." He "cultivates the mob as well as the aristocracy," one British observer later said of Lawrence, probably the only member of Boston's elite who could, with a straight face, declare that he had long supported policies designed to give "the Many the greatest amount of prosperity and happiness, believing the Few can always take care of themselves." But the policies of which Lawrence spoke rarely went beyond a demand for higher duties. Should American industry be left unprotected from foreign imports, he contended, "the rich will become richer, and the poor and middling classes poorer." In 1850, as ambassador to Great Britain, he was still collecting data that would show how competition from "the half pauper labor of this country" threatened the well-being of American wage earners.[56]

While adopting a somewhat more elaborate tack when discussing labor, Appleton also emphasized the benefits that working people derived from protectionism. The best summary of his views appeared in an 1844 article written for *Hunt's Merchants' Magazine*. He began by asserting that "[h]uman labor is the only source of wealth" and then proceeded to compare conditions in Europe and the United States. Unlike Europe, where a hereditary ruling class viewed workers with contempt, Appleton observed, America was "a great novel experiment" with much different aims—"an attempt to amalgamate, equalize and improve the whole mass of population, by elevating the lower portions from their usual abject state, and depressing the higher, in dispensing with a privileged aristocracy." Thus far the experiment had been a wonderful success, he believed, and for two reasons. One was a liberal land policy that had turned the western region into a safety valve for eastern workers. The other was a system of protective tariffs that kept wages high by restricting the importation of goods produced by "the cheaper and more degraded labor of Europe." In repudiating the doctrine of free trade, Appleton argued, Americans rejected its assumption "that labor is everywhere in excess" and could be treated accordingly.[57]

The article was well received in elite circles. Although the Harvard theologian Andrews Norton felt that Appleton could have placed greater emphasis on the salutary role played by American institutions, he fully agreed with the article's main premise: "There are with us no permanent classes of rich and poor." More noteworthy was the response of James S. Amory, who wanted to have a thousand copies of the article printed. He believed Appleton's analysis "eminently calculated for general and extensive circulation, not as a political tract, but as a very clear exposition of the fundamental principles of our whole structure of society." It was a telling observation. At a time of growing concern about the social consequences of industrialization—when the center of labor protest had shifted from Boston and Fall River to Lowell and when increasing numbers of middling-class radicals were seeking communitarian alternatives to the new economic order—the Associates could not have been more satisfied with the world they had created.[58]

The uncertainty and discontent that they neither felt nor saw was perhaps best captured by John Allen, a one-time Universalist minister and Brook Farm communitarian who briefly interrupted his work as a Fourierist lecturer to edit the *Voice of Industry* during the summer and fall of 1846. In several open letters to Abbott Lawrence, he described a much darker future than that envisioned by the Associates. It was true, he conceded, that most factory operatives were well-educated and virtuous citizens, but only because their minds had been "nurtured in the Common School or the village Academy, before they left their homes to be shut up fourteen hours per day in the factory bastilles." Allen worried about what would happen when workers without this type of upbringing replaced them. Should the populations of regional mill towns "become permanent as they are in Europe, and as in a few years they surely will [be here], must not some ignorance prevail here as there?" he asked. To suggest that higher tariffs could prevent these developments added insult to injury. The protection such legislation provided for working people could be likened to "the protection the Vulture offers the Dove, or the Wolf gives the Lamb." If Lawrence really cared about the men and women who labored in his mills, he would "[r]educe the hours of daily labor." Only then might they have a chance to escape what otherwise promised to be a lifetime of unremitting toil and grinding poverty.[59]

As noted, the Whig appeal was forged during a period of economic transition when no one really knew what industrialization portended, and when people could still hope for the best. By the mid-1840s, many feared that the future might not be as bright as advertised. One did not have to accept the radical critique to see that the spread of factory production increased social dependence; nor did one have to work in a textile mill to realize that tending a machine twelve hours a day, six days a week, robbed people of the time and energy needed to better their condition. With each passing year, the Associates' continued insistence that economic prosperity would solve all such problems sounded less and less reassuring. Meanwhile, there were growing troubles on another front, where their inclination to look for easy answers to tough questions in the working of impersonal economic forces would place them in even worse repute.[60]

CHAPTER FOUR

Antislavery and Challenges
to Elite Rule

O N NEW YEAR'S DAY 1831, the first issue of what would become
America's most famous antislavery newspaper appeared on the streets
of Boston. Aptly titled the *Liberator,* its editor, William Lloyd Garrison,
introduced the new publication with a forthright assertiveness that left no
room for misunderstanding. If the Declaration of Independence meant
anything, he told readers, the "popular but pernicious doctrine of *gradual*
abolition" must be replaced by a commitment to immediate emancipation.
That was his message, and he would not rest until the nation acted on it.
"I *will* be as harsh as truth, and as uncompromising as justice," Garrison
declared. "I am in earnest—I will not equivocate—I will not excuse—I will
not retreat a single inch—And I will be Heard."[1]

These were brash words from a hitherto unknown journeyman printer,
whose rhetorical boldness contrasted starkly with his humble origins and
slim prospects for recognition. But Garrison was nothing if not persevering.
Despite persistent financial troubles, the *Liberator* survived. Even more
surprising, he was heard—and within a relatively short while. That August, in Southampton County, Virginia, a slave revolt led by a charismatic
preacher named Nat Turner sent shock waves throughout Dixie. In its
wake, alarmed southerners who believed that Turner had been influenced
by Garrison's writings flooded Boston mayor Harrison Gray Otis with letters demanding the *Liberator's* suppression. At the time, Otis knew nothing
about the paper, and after determining that Garrison had few subscribers
and operated out of an "obscure hole" in Merchants Hall, he assured his
southern correspondents that "the new fanaticism had not made, nor was
likely to make, proselytes among the respectable classes of our people."[2]

Although Otis underestimated Garrison's tenacity, he was certainly right
about Boston's "respectable classes." With a few notable exceptions, abolitionism had little appeal among the select group of merchants, manufactur-

ers, and professionals with whom he socialized. The state's middling classes proved more responsive. This was particularly so outside Boston, where mechanics, shopkeepers, and small-town professionals could ignore upper-class opposition to antislavery initiatives with much greater impunity than their metropolitan counterparts. Meanwhile, a series of events, beginning with the elite-sponsored Faneuil Hall anti-abolition meeting of 1835 and culminating in the petition campaign of later years, awakened antislavery sentiment throughout the commonwealth. By decade's end, few politically ambitious Bay Staters could adopt Otis's dismissive attitude, regardless of what the respectable classes thought.

These developments marked the high point of Garrisonian influence. During the late 1830s and early 1840s, disputes about tactics, the role of women, and other issues created deep divisions within abolitionist ranks. The increasing politicization of antislavery caused further problems for the Garrisonians, who resolutely opposed political action. Despite its hatred of Garrison, Boston's elite derived small comfort from this turn of events, as intersectional amity seemed more distant than ever. Mounting popular concern about slave expansionism was especially worrisome. And when the annexation of Texas raised antisouthern feeling in New England to fever-pitch, the Associates felt compelled to devise their own solutions to the growing sectional crisis. This chapter's final section examines how they attempted to meet that challenge.

AT FIRST GLANCE, William Lloyd Garrison seemed the most unlikely of radicals. As a young man, he ardently championed the old-school Fed-eralism of his native Essex County. It was the only political party that he ever truly loved, and his earliest heroes included such conservative stalwarts as Timothy Pickering, Rufus King, and Fisher Ames. To Garrison, Feder-alism's subsequent demise represented a rejection of "correct principles" by an ungrateful and unthinking electorate. From his thoroughly conventional perspective, the preservation of social order depended on the example set by virtuous leaders. And though never far from destitution during his youth, he identified much more readily with his social betters than with others of his own class. When he turned to moral reform several years later, he did so in good Federalist fashion, observing "that the readiest way to operate on the mass of society is to begin with the opulent."[3]

Garrison never entirely abandoned these views, which were particularly evident in his early days at the *Liberator*. In the paper's first issue, in an editorial statement that claimed everyone suffered from existing social evils, he condemned workingmen's associations for attempting to incite class warfare. Chided by a correspondent for making light of labor's grievances,

Garrison declared inequality inevitable in a republican society where opportunities for advancement were "open to all." And this could not be changed. "Those who attempt to level," he said, quoting Edmund Burke, "never equalize. In all societies consisting of various descriptions of citizens, some description must be uppermost." More to the point, Garrison added, critics of elite oppression had no basis for such charges. It could certainly not be "found in their manufacturing establishments, which multiply labor and cheapen the necessities of the poor." While Garrisonians such as Parker Pillsbury later made special efforts to enlist worker support, tensions remained—even though New England labor radicals also sought the destruction of slavery; indeed, they considered their own movement and abolitionism to be parts "of the one great question of *Labor.*" But they also felt that few antislavery leaders shared this perspective, and their occasional complaints about the *Liberator*'s "exclusive and aristocratic tendencies" revealed the social distance that separated the two groups.[4]

Whereas Garrison reached an uneasy truce with labor radicals, his relations with elite Boston started badly and never improved. Apart from the small group of Brahmins who became leading Garrisonians, elite Bostonians viewed abolitionism as a form of fanaticism that threatened social order. This did not mean that they approved of human bondage. To Nathan Appleton, slavery was a "social and political evil" that "degrade[d] labor, the very foundation of all civilization." There were, however, real limits to what they were willing to do about it. In his biography of Harrison Gray Otis, the distinguished Brahmin historian Samuel Eliot Morison observed: "He had the slight moral repugnance for [slavery] that was common to almost all Northerners, but his conscience was not greatly troubled by the existence of wrongs he did not feel or see." The same might be said of elite Boston in general. As a young man traveling in the South, Appleton witnessed a Charleston slave auction and was appalled by "the horrid sight of the sale of human flesh, a sight at which human nature unperverted by custom must ever revolt." But this sense of horror passed quickly. Four weeks later, as he prepared to return north, he did so "with considerable regret," grateful for the hospitality white Charlestonians had shown him.[5]

Appleton's experience sheds light on an important source of elite anti-abolitionism. Unlike the average New England yeoman or mechanic, most Brahmins had some personal acquaintance with slaveholding southerners. Many young planters studied at Harvard and other northern colleges, where they formed friendships with their Yankee counterparts. And many planter families vacationed at such popular pleasure spots as Saratoga, Niagara Falls, and Newport, where they too socialized with wealthy and powerful northerners. In other instances, intersectional contacts were based on those commercial links that prompted William Ellery Channing's complaint about "the all-devouring passion for gain, accumulation, which leaves little leisure for sympathy for any suffering which does not meet our eye, and which will listen to no invocation, by which the old channels of trade may be obstructed."[6]

It is unlikely that these relationships changed many northerners' negative views of slavery. They did, however, increase elite sensitivity to planter problems. One slaveholder who tried to take advantage of these ties was the Maryland politician Daniel Jenifer, who served with Nathan Appleton in the Twenty-second Congress. In 1834, he asked Appleton for financial assistance to transfer his slaves to a plantation in the Lower South. The movement, Jenifer explained, was necessary "to render valuable that description of property which with us in many instances, particularly in the present time, is an expense." He also hoped to make sufficient profits to free "those most deserving." Appleton doubtless found the request troubling, and there is no evidence in his papers that he agreed to the loan. But he certainly understood Jenifer's concerns. "As a question of property," he later said of slave emancipation, "it involves an amount of about a thousand millions of Dollars." The Salem congressman Leverett Saltonstall made the point even more clearly in an 1839 letter to his wife. Northerners must remember, he said, that abolition "affects *all* their property—at least in their opinion. What would their country be good for without slave labor—at present?"[7]

However much they sympathized with planter rage at the growing fury of abolitionist rhetoric, elite Bostonians recognized that they had to proceed cautiously against Garrison. When prominent southerners urged Harrison Gray Otis to suppress the *Liberator* after the Turner uprising, the Boston mayor informed them that such a heavy-handed response would only drive local moderates into antislavery ranks. Apart from Peter O. Thacher's attack on abolitionist dissemination of "incendiary publications" in his March 1832 charge to the Boston Municipal Court, city leaders took no action to curb Garrison before mid-decade. Another reason for restraint was the bad feeling engendered by the nullification crisis. While most Brahmins could readily commiserate with southern planters as a beleaguered elite, they had no intention of bowing to slaveholder dictation, particularly on matters that concerned their own economic interests. Even Otis, who was then trying to drum up support for a compensated emancipation scheme, could not contain his anger. "Your father," he wrote to Theodore Sedgwick, "belonged to a party who forty years ago, well understood that the negroholders when they ceased to govern us, would refuse to be governed by us." The current conflict showed that planters had lost little of their political power. "They govern us effectively thus far, and I believe will blast the prosperity of N. England this very Anno Domini."[8]

By 1835, tensions had cooled and elite Bostonians were much more willing to entertain planter grievances. That spring, when the American Anti-Slavery Society launched a broad-ranging campaign to flood the nation with abolitionist literature, southern leaders demanded that something be done to suppress the effort. As spring turned to summer and their cries became increasingly hysterical, prominent businesspeople from throughout the Northeast responded by organizing a series of well-publicized anti-abolition gatherings. The call for a Boston meeting appeared in Richard Haughton's Websterite *Atlas* in late July. According to *Advocate* editor Benjamin Hallett, Haughton issued the summons to help Webster win southern votes in the upcoming presidential contest. Whether he did so at Webster's urging is not clear. The Bay State senator did not attend the meeting; there is no evidence that he contacted Haughton beforehand; and the *Atlas* editor was quite capable of acting on his own. Moreover, had Haughton not taken the initiative, someone else doubtless would have.[9]

Webster was one of the few prominent figures in Boston society who failed to appear at the Faneuil Hall gathering that August. Leading participants included Harrison Gray Otis, industrialists Amos Lawrence and Patrick Tracy Jackson, merchant Henry Lee, attorney Peleg Sprague, congressman Richard Fletcher, and mayor Theodore Lyman, Jr. They were there, Otis said, because "it seemed proper to make an exertion to show to the South that the general sentiment in the North is correct upon the Slave question." The meeting, Abbott Lawrence told John Quincy Adams, would show southerners that "there was no diversity of opinion" in Boston about the need to suppress abolitionism. The ever-skeptical Adams had his doubts. "If the measures [proposed] are vaporing resolutions," he confided to his diary, "they will pass unanimously, and be inefficient. If the measures are efficient, there will be diversity of opinion."[10]

Adams's observations were right on the mark. The Faneuil Hall meeting exhibited great unanimity only because it passed "vaporing resolutions" that did little to pacify southern critics, who declared the measures "not thorough enough for their taste." Joseph Buckingham explained why it could not have been otherwise. Although the *Courier* editor served on the resolutions committee of a Cambridge anti-abolition meeting, he recognized that such gatherings could go only so far in condemning abolitionism. When South Carolina afterward demanded that laws be enacted to prevent the discussion of slavery in Massachusetts, he observed that southerners had much to learn about northern principles: "The mere suggestion by a Boston meeting that the legislature should put an end to discussions of slavery, *by the strong arm of the law,* would be the signal for revolution." Buckingham also worried that many anti-abolition meetings sent the wrong message when they passed resolutions that exhibited "a lamentable want of self-respect, and manifestations of an overflowing spirit of cowardly truckling to Southern arrogance and presumption."[11]

Buckingham's behavior was not as contradictory as it might seem. In several important respects, his was the real voice of Bay State Whiggery. As representatives of the party of property and social order, Whigs believed that they had an obligation to check the perceived excesses of potentially disruptive groups. It thus made perfect sense for a party activist such as Buckingham to participate in an anti-abolition meeting. At the same time, however, Whigs posed as defenders of New England civilization against the impositions of an overbearing planter class. To some party leaders—particularly those who wished to create a viable national organization with a strong southern wing—this role could be discarded whenever circumstances dictated. Buckingham saw things differently. He had been an outspoken critic of the reconciliationist policy adopted by Massachusetts Federalists after the War of 1812, and the lesson he drew from their subsequent demise was that a party without principles was a party without supporters. He now warned Whig leaders not to repeat Federalist mistakes.

Meanwhile, local abolitionists could not have been happier. Garrison's brother-in-law, Henry E. Benson, believed that the Faneuil Hall meeting helped rather than hurt the cause. "The excitement," he told Amos A. Phelps, "has created a ravenous appetite & our publications are perused with intense interest." Garrison, who thrived on controversy, felt much the same way. He used the occasion to administer a blistering public chastisement to Harrison Gray Otis and Peleg Sprague, two of the principal speakers at the gathering. That Garrison turned so savagely on Otis was particularly notable. The former Federalist leader had long been one of Garrison's idols, and Garrison may well have been thinking of the several instances on which he had written or spoken on Otis's behalf when he now asked: "Sir, do you wish to put it within the power of impartial truth, after your death, to place upon your tomb-stone this awful inscription?"

Here lies the body of

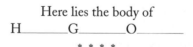

* * * *

Reader, weep at human inconsistency and frailty!
The last public act of his life,
A Life conspicuous for many honorable traits,
Was an earnest defence of

The Rights of Tyrants And Slave-Mongers
To hold in bondage, as their property,
The bodies and souls of millions of his own countrymen![12]

In addition to being a year of anti-abolition meetings, 1835 also witnessed a marked increase in anti-abolition violence. Exactly two months after the Faneuil Hall gathering, Boston became the scene of one of the era's more memorable attacks on antislavery activists. The mob's intended victim was George Thompson, an English abolitionist whom newspapers throughout the Northeast had depicted as the leading agent in a British conspiracy to disrupt American society. In the weeks preceding the Boston Female Anti-Slavery Society meeting at which Thompson was scheduled to speak, Haughton's *Atlas* accused Thompson of promoting racial amalgamation and encouraging slaves to slash their masters' throats. As it turned out, Thompson did not appear at the meeting. But Garrison did. Seized by the crowd, he was led through the streets of Boston with a rope around his body before being rescued and placed in the Leverett Street jail for protection.[13]

Most Boston newspapers blamed Garrison for the riot, but they were soon thrown on the defensive. The most adverse commentary centered on the "respectable" composition of the mob. To many editors outside the city, a mob was a mob regardless of how many gentlemen participated in it. Inside Boston, criticism assumed much sharper class overtones. Writing in the *Reformer,* "A Working Man" saw the riot as part of a broader elite assault on popular freedoms. "How long will the restless spirit of Aristocracy be content with an easy victory over the liberty of *one* defenceless man?" he asked. "How long will an insatiable thrust for power be stayed by *one* victim to its ferocity?" In a letter to the same journal, "A Democrat" adopted a similar perspective, exclaiming, "Now talk of a war of the poor against the rich! The war has begun already, but the order is reversed. The *rich* have trampled down the *poor* in the heart of Boston, and no man cries shame upon them." And lest anyone forget, working-class abolitionist William Comstock reminded *Liberator* readers that everything had started with the Faneuil Hall gathering: "The time-serving orators of that impious meeting, like the man within the brazen bull, had but to open their mouths to set the monster of popular fury in a roar."[14]

At this point, elite Bostonians would have been wise to cut their losses and let Garrison do as he wished. Rather than restraining local abolitionists, their actions thus far had tarnished their own reputations while enlarging the *Liberator's* subscription list. Such wisdom was apparently in short supply. During the summer of 1835, William Sullivan had written a pamphlet urging the enactment of laws barring the circulation of antislavery literature and making the holding of abolitionist meetings an indictable offense. In his message to the legislature that winter, Governor Edward Everett condemned abolition societies and asked the General Court to act on Sullivan's suggestions, thereby setting the stage for yet another fiasco. A major problem was George Lunt, the Essex senator who headed the committee appointed to consider Everett's request. A young attorney "of small practice" with more ambition than good sense, Lunt soon demonstrated that he was in over his head. Unwilling to let abolitionists who testified before the committee state their case, the senator showed himself to be rude, carping, and hypercritical. His behavior was so obnoxious that it aroused the ire of George Bond, a wealthy and well-respected Boston merchant who had participated in the Faneuil Hall meeting. The anti-abolition campaign of the previous seven months had lurched from one disaster to another, and Bond had seen enough. After informing Lunt that his conduct only added to the "excitement," he told the senator that he did not want "to see grounds given for the gentlemen and their friends to say they have been denied a hearing." As Bond concluded, a voice from the gallery called out, "I say Amen"; others quickly seconded the sentiment.[15]

Bond's intervention hardly signaled a sea change in the way elite Bostonians viewed abolitionism. In their eyes, Garrison remained a troublemaking fanatic who required close watching. It did show, however, that a few people were finally coming to their senses. Responding to a letter from George Lunt several weeks after Bond's appearance, *Advocate* editor Benjamin Hallett condemned the senator for having disgraced "Massachusetts by attempting to make her the first free State to crouch to the insolent demands of the South, for gag laws and censures of freedom of speech, upon the citizens of a Commonwealth, who boasts her origin from those bold advocates of free discussion, the Pilgrim Fathers." Hallett's comments could just as easily—indeed, more appropriately—have been directed at Boston's leading citizens. Had the Lunt Committee succeeded in carrying out Everett's mandate, their political candidates might well have met the same rejection that befell the Essex senator in his bid for reelection later that year. It was a close call. Hereafter, they would be more cautious.[16]

The Lunt Committee was not the only legislative body then seeking to restrain the free discussion of antislavery issues. In May 1836, Congress passed a "gag rule" that prohibited action on any petitions related to the subject of slavery. The ban prompted what proved to be one of the most popular campaigns ever undertaken by antislavery forces. Over the next two years, northern communities bombarded Congress with more than two hundred thousand petitions, a majority of which sought abolition of slavery and the slave trade in Washington, D.C.; others demanded repeal of the gag rule, protested the admission of new slave states, opposed the annexation of Texas, and called for abolition of the interstate slave trade. Many of the petitions ended up on the desk of John Quincy Adams, who spearheaded congressional opposition to the ban, and a large number of them came from Massachusetts.[17]

Not all Bay Staters approved of Adams's role in the struggle. According to one Adams correspondent, "some of *the most respectable souls* in Boston" believed that the former president had lost his mind. But theirs was a minority opinion. Elsewhere in the commonwealth, Adams had become "the new folk hero." Had his critics been able to read the numerous letters he received from petitioners, they would have been truly distressed. Some praised Adams as a defender of regional interests. New England's hopes were in Adams's hands, said Morton Eddy of Bridgewater—"all eyes are turned to you." Others felt Adams's actions marked the high point of his long and distinguished public career. "I am fully persuaded," wrote Springfield's Samuel Osgood, "that your personal noble stand in defence of human rights will be followed with a richer harvest of fame, than you have ever reaped."[18]

Even more alarming from an anti-abolitionist standpoint were two other features of these letters. One was the insistence with which petitioners proclaimed their respectability. Denying that they sought trouble, these individuals declared themselves intelligent concerned citizens, motivated by deep commitment to moral and religious principle. Also noteworthy was the number of writers who either opposed or disclaimed any attachment to abolitionism. Despite their aversion to Garrison and organized antislavery, they fully supported Adams's efforts to defend the right of petition. This was a particularly significant development. It meant that, as one petitioner observed, "the subject of Slavery and the Rights of the Free are rapidly coming to associate and identify themselves in the minds of the Citizens of this State." As they did, anti-abolition sentiment softened to the point that some believed it might disappear altogether. Should current trends continue, wrote another correspondent, "the time will soon come when denials of any affection for or sympathy with the abolitionists and their cause will not be *required* by the people of Massachusetts from their representatives in Congress or elsewhere."[19]

One reason the petition campaign proved so effective was tradition. Popular reverence for the right of petition had deep roots in regional political culture. Before the Revolution, petitioning furnished one of the few legitimate means of conveying grievances to the crown; to deny colonial New Englanders this cherished right invited rebellion. Some abolitionists also believed that the simple act of signing a petition deepened one's antislavery convictions. "So much force and definiteness do our principles gain by ex-pression," explained the Garrisonian attorney Ellis Gray Loring. "So much oral vigor does a man acquire by openly taking sides." Though one might question the degree to which this actually happened, Bay State politicians were not taking any chances. In the spring of 1837, legislators adopted res-olutions condemning the gag rule by the near unanimous margins of 32–1 in the Senate and 378–16 in the House. This was quite a turnabout. A legislative body that only a year earlier had considered ways to suppress antislavery activity now attacked Congress for doing exactly that.[20]

Outside the General Court, other politicians followed its lead. In August 1835, Boston representative Richard Fletcher had played a leading role in the Faneuil Hall meeting; two months later, Anne Weston observed him standing amid the Garrison mob, viewing the proceedings *"with a pleased expression of face."* The petition struggle turned Fletcher into a new man. In the Twenty-fifth Congress (1837–39), he not only opposed the gag rule but supported efforts to abolish slavery in the District of Columbia and outlaw the interstate slave trade. When an Illinois mob destroyed Elijah Lovejoy's Alton *Observer* and murdered the antislavery editor, Fletcher offered to help finance the establishment of another newspaper.[21]

Whereas Fletcher appears to have experienced a genuine change of heart, others acted from simple opportunism. Perhaps the best example was Governor Edward Everett, a former minister who had decided early in life that a small Unitarian parish provided inadequate scope for his ambitions. Through hard study and a keen instinct for saying the right things to the right people—he had all "the blandishments of a courtier," said one critic—he acquired a reputation as a scholar, orator, and man of the world; his marriage to Peter Chardon Brooks's daughter gave him a secure foothold in the upper reaches of Boston society. Vacillating by nature and with no moral compass, Everett had little objection to human bondage. As a Har-vard professor, he defended slavery before his students, later repeating the performance on the floor of Congress in an address that elicited derisive notice from Timothy Pickering and other old-school Federalists. In 1832, Brooks cut short Everett's plans to invest in a Louisiana plantation, telling him that he could think of nothing "more mortifying" than to learn that his son-in-law had become a slaveowner. Four years later, Everett gave the Lunt Committee its marching orders. That he could now declare slavery "a *social, political,* and *moral evil* of the *first* magnitude" demonstrated that the times were indeed changing.[22]

For those who still had doubts, a careful reading of Haughton's *Atlas* was certain to remove them. No one had played a more conspicuous role in the mid-decade anti-abolition campaign than the Websterite editor, nor had anyone greeted the gag rule with greater enthusiasm. But that was then. As public opinion shifted, so did Haughton. By the spring of 1837, he had emerged as one of the city's most outspoken defenders of the right of petition, declaring in a March editorial: "If the northern slaves in the House are willing to surrender the most obvious and valuable rights of their constituents, . . . [t]here will be at least one voice raised in remonstrance, and this is the voice of Massachusetts." At this point, the only major Whig holdout in Boston was Nathan Hale's *Advertiser;* "as usual," Haughton quipped, it was "about two years behind the times." The same could no doubt be said for many of Hale's elite patrons. Yet even they were not altogether insensitive to what was taking place around them. If nothing else, they had at least learned to keep a low profile.[23]

Bay State Whigs were the main political beneficiaries of these developments. Despite Hale's intransigence and the blatant opportunism of Everett, Haughton, and others, the party's position on slavery compared well with that of its Democratic adversaries. In Congress, northern Democrats furnished the votes needed to pass the gag rule, and as president, Martin Van Buren sought to reassure southerners by promising to protect slavery in the District of Columbia. The national party's stance had little effect on David Henshaw's Boston machine, which followed John C. Calhoun's lead on these matters. But it did limit what Marcus Morton's more progressive Van Burenite faction could do. Morton associate George Bancroft is a case in point. Asked to give substance to his frequent pronouncements on the glories of American liberty by signing a petition to abolish slavery in the nation's capital, the historian refused because "he did not think it right to throw such an apple of discord into Congress." Edward Everett could not have put it better.[24]

In an 1842 letter to John Quincy Adams, Edmund Quincy wrote that "it is no insignificant sign of the times that Faneuil Hall should be granted by the civic authorities of Boston for a public meeting in favor of the immediate abolition of slavery." The Brahmin abolitionist found it remarkable "that in a little more than six years from the great sympathizing meeting, at which Messrs. Otis, Sprague, Fletcher and others performed the *kotow* before their imperial (or rather imperious) masters, and licked up the slave-holding spittle (tobacco juice & all) without so much as a wry face, the very principles they had thought they had killed should fill the same hall to overflowing." Quincy had good reason to feel exuberant. Although a distinct minority of Bay Staters considered themselves abolitionists, the climate of opinion had certainly changed. Antislavery activists had acquired a degree of respectability that was unimaginable during the mid-1830s. More often than not, their adversaries now found themselves on the defensive.[25]

In at least one respect, Quincy appeared much too optimistic. By 1842, abolitionism as an organized movement was coming apart at the seams. Two years earlier, Garrison's attempt to take over the American Anti-Slavery Society had split the organization in two. Unwilling to accept the New Englander's commitment to no-government principles or his advanced position on women's rights, Lewis Tappan, his brother Arthur, and others broke ranks to form the competing American and Foreign Anti-Slavery Society. Meanwhile, social and religious differences prompted an exodus of middling-class women from the elite-dominated Boston Female Anti-Slavery Society. And Garrison's adoption of disunionism further reduced his appeal among antislavery northerners, large numbers of whom rejected his description of the Constitution as "a covenant with death and an agreement with hell."[26]

Formation of the Liberty Party in 1840 added to the confusion. Believing politics to be inherently corrupting, Garrison condemned the party and everyone associated with it. Not all of his followers agreed. Ellis Gray Loring, who considered abolition the only question "on which the whole North can be brought to unite," had long defended political action. In 1841, he refused to attend a convention organized to attack the Libertyites, observing that it would be best to "[l]et them work in their own way without obstruction." By censuring people simply because they did not adhere to pure Garrisonian doctrine, Loring exclaimed, "we are interfering with the freedom & breaking down the influence of men who hold as firmly as we, the Abolition faith, but who differ with us on measures!" No one of importance in the movement listened. Despite reports from western lecturers of growing enthusiasm for antislavery politics, leading Garrisonians continued to disparage the Liberty Party, likening it to the accommodationist American Colonization Society.[27]

Describing his fellow Garrisonians in an 1845 letter to the Irish abolitionist Richard Webb, Edmund Quincy observed: "They are a remarkable body of men and women,—the choice of the elect,—who have been winnowed over & over again, till nothing but the good seed is left." That was one way of looking at it. Others adopted a less charitable view. Whereas Quincy saw virtuous dedication in the Garrisonian refusal to condone alternative approaches to abolitionism, the Quaker poet John Greenleaf Whittier saw "vanity and pride," an inclination "to forget that flesh and blood and immortal souls were involved—and to talk about the subject as if *we* were alone interested in the success of the cause." As these tendencies hardened after 1840, Garrison's influence contracted.[28]

This said, it must be added that too much can be made of the fact that so few people became or remained Garrisonians. For all his shortcomings—

and they were many—Garrison always had one thing going for him: he was incontestably right on the greatest moral issue of his time, and he never let anyone forget it. Hypocrites, timeservers, and the like could always deride or dismiss his attacks on slavery; principled people could not. And those who attempted to engage the Garrisonian critique were inevitably drawn left. Because many such people in turn influenced others, it is worth observing how this occurred. We will do so by examining the evolving antislavery convictions of William Ellery Channing. As Boston's most distinguished Unitarian minister, Channing spoke with an authority that could not easily be ignored. What he had to say sheds further light on the challenge antislavery posed to elite rule.

BORN IN 1780, William Ellery Channing was a native of Newport, Rhode Island, who after graduating from Harvard served for nearly four decades as pastor of Boston's prestigious Federal Street Church. Although he first achieved prominence during the Unitarian controversy of the 1810s, Channing spent much of his life in search of consensus. By nature shy and retiring, he instinctively equated passion with disorder. "Your enthusiasm sometimes lacks sobriety," he once told a good friend. No one ever had occasion to offer Channing similar counsel. His lofty objectives, delicate feelings, and refined sentiments, said his nephew and biographer, "guarded him from all familiar contact with rude radicalism." When contemplating social questions, he was painstakingly deliberate and reached conclusions slowly. Believing that all sides of an issue merited equal consideration, he could be maddeningly equivocal. Lydia Maria Child observed that in conversation, he invariably prefaced statements about controversial matters with "I am doubtful" or "I am afraid"; in print, some qualifying phrase often followed his boldest comments. As Channing himself conceded, "I am made of but poor material for a reformer."[29]

Many abolitionists certainly thought so. To Maria Weston Chapman, Channing was nothing more than a religious front-man for Boston's elite—someone who "had been selected by a set of money-making men for piety, as Edward Everett was their representative gentleman and scholar, Judge Story their jurist and companion in social life, and Daniel Webster their representative statesman and advocate looking after their interests in Congress." Child felt much the same way for a time. Though she later came to appreciate Channing's contributions to the antislavery cause, her early impressions had been far from favorable. "A smile of contempt passed over my face at the value he placed on the attentions of *rich* abolitionists," she said after one conversation. "My soul has suffered many a shivering ague-fit in attempting to melt, or batter away, the glaciers of his prejudice, false refinement, and beautiful *theories,* into which the breath of life was never infused by being brought into *action.*"[30]

Voiced in 1836, Child's observations were not entirely unfair. Channing had only recently stepped forward as an antislavery spokesman and was still feeling his way. He had yet to move beyond the cautious conservatism expressed in an 1828 letter to Daniel Webster. At that time, Channing had proposed using revenue from the sale of public lands to finance a program of compensated emancipation. Well aware of southern sensitivity on the subject, he hoped the plan could be sold to planters without arousing sectional hostility; whatever happened, he felt the Union must be preserved at all costs. It was thus important that antislavery agitation be confined to safe channels. "Appeals will probably be made soon to the people here," he told Webster, "and I wish that wise men would save us from the rashness of enthusiasts, and from the perils to which our very virtues expose us."[31]

As Channing anticipated, antislavery protest increased markedly in the coming years. But he took little notice of these developments before the 1833 publication of Child's *Appeal in Favor of That Class of Americans Called Africans.* Impressed by the young Garrisonian's account, he immediately contacted Child. During the three-hour conversation that followed, he told her the book had convinced him that he could no longer remain silent. Afterward, discussions with his abolitionist colleague Samuel J. May and growing anti-abolition repression further stiffened Channing's resolve to take a public stand on the issue. Two decades earlier, orthodox efforts to curb discussion of liberal religious doctrines had spurred him to assume an active part in the Unitarian controversy. He believed in freedom of expression just as strongly now as he had then. If nothing else, regional tradition demanded a steadfast defense of civil liberties. "Could such encroachments be borne," he later asked in his first major statement on slavery, "would not the soil of New England, so long trodden by freemen, quake under the steps of her degenerate sons?"[32]

The public apathy he saw all around him also disturbed Channing. One could not read most newspapers, he stated in an October 1834 address, "without seeing the profound unconcern, which pervades the country on the subject of slavery." Worse, this criticism could be extended to most religious bodies, including his own. Edmund Quincy said of Boston Unitarians that they "are the rich; well educated as a general thing. They hire men to preach to them who can write essays that will not shock their taste & with the tacit understanding that they will never preach anything that would make them uncomfortable." Antislavery was one such topic. According to an 1837 survey conducted by Amos A. Phelps, only one of eight Unitarian ministers in eastern Massachusetts had strong objections to slavery. Channing would have been disappointed but not surprised by Phelps's findings. "At the present day," he believed, "there is little need of cautioning ministers against rashness in reproving evil. The danger is all on the other side. As a class, they are most slow to give offense."[33]

By early 1835, Channing had substantially completed *Slavery,* his first important work on the subject. But the arguments of local elites persuaded him to withhold the manuscript. They were then considering ways to restrain Garrison, and the publication of an antislavery treatise by the city's most eminent minister hardly fit into their plans. As it turned out, the events of that summer and fall removed any reservations Channing had about going public. Despite his own objections to certain Garrisonian practices, he expected nothing good from the August anti-abolition meeting at Faneuil Hall. "That *Boston* should in any way lend itself to the cause of oppression," he wrote to John Warren several days before the gathering, "would be a dark omen indeed." When Garrison was mobbed two months later, Channing's patience ran out and *Slavery* went to press soon afterward. "I have perceived a faint-heartedness in the cause of human rights," he said of his decision to publish. "The condemnation, which has been passed on Abolitionists, has seemed to be settling into acquiescence in slavery."[34]

Slavery was an uneven combination of moral exhortation and cautious commentary. On one hand, Channing roundly condemned human bondage as an irremediable evil that had no place in a civilized society. At the same time, he urged readers to be mindful of slaveowner sensibilities, rejected immediate emancipation, and recommended that a system of guardianship be instituted to oversee the transition from slavery to freedom. Channing also criticized abolitionists for causing undue excitement, a problem that could have been avoided had they adopted more selective recruitment procedures. If there was an actual need for antislavery societies, he said, "[m]en of strong moral principle, judiciousness, sobriety, should have been carefully sought as members."[35]

Had *Slavery* appeared a decade later, its tame counsel and carefully phrased admonitions would have excited little notice. Similarly, had the book been written by anyone other than Channing, it is unlikely that it would have had much impact then. But the mid-1830s was a time when many northerners had just begun to sort out their feelings about slavery, and the Federal Street pastor was one of the nation's best-known clergymen. The mere fact that Channing authored such a work made it significant. "Being, as he is, one of the most distinguished and popular of American writers," said one Garrisonian, "his book has introduced the cause of the slaves to thousands, who would turn contemptuously from our pages, without a perusal." And despite the pains Channing had taken to pacify southerners, *Slavery* did contain many forceful passages. To John Quincy Adams—who noted the equivocating, "Jesuitical" nature of the Boston Unitarian's main arguments—the book was "an inflammatory, if not an incendiary, publication." Even more interesting was Garrison's response. In public, the *Liberator* editor attacked the work in a scathing twenty-five-point rebuttal. In private, he seemed much less upset, writing to Samuel J. May that if Channing "does not soon have a hornet's nest about his ears, then it will be because hornets have respect unto the persons of men!"[36]

Garrison knew something about hornets—more at least than Channing did. Shortly after *Slavery*'s publication, its author told Noah Worcester that many of those who tried to dissuade him from writing on the subject found nothing objectionable in the work. Channing spoke too soon. According to Richard Haughton, other Bostonians considered the book "ill-timed and dangerous." One of them was James T. Austin, the commonwealth's thuggish attorney general, who blasted *Slavery* in an anonymous pamphlet that showed little respect for Channing's esteemed position in local society. Like most of Boston's elite, Austin believed the most appropriate northern response to slavery was to do nothing. That a clergyman would step outside his "*proper sphere*" to criticize the institution particularly disturbed him. Should ministers persist in such conduct, he warned, "any man may be prophet enough to foretell that their holy office will soon come to an end." The attorney general was not speaking for himself alone. However "ill humoured" Austin's pamphlet may have been, Harrison Gary Otis remarked, Channing had "most indiscreetly 'shot from his sphere' & deserved a scoring." Some ministers, he lamented, could not be happy without interfering in secular matters that did not concern them: "We have great trouble in store from this quarter."[37]

Bay State ministers would not prove quite as troublesome as Otis feared. But as the aging Federalist doubtless sensed, Channing would be heard from again. However much he might have preferred retiring to the safe confines of his study, Channing could not ignore the call of duty. As the antislavery struggle intensified, he continued to make his presence felt. At the Lunt Committee hearings, he walked across the room to shake hands with Garrison. It was a significant gesture that may well have influenced George Bond, the Boston merchant who criticized Lunt's conduct during the proceedings. As an active Unitarian layman, Bond held Channing in high regard and was disgusted by Austin's intemperate assault on the clergyman. The hearings not only offended his sense of fair play, but provided an opportunity to show his support for the Federal Street pastor.[38]

Channing also played a central role in the controversy surrounding a meeting to eulogize Elijah Lovejoy. In November 1837, after an Alton, Illinois, mob murdered the antislavery editor, Boston abolitionists made plans to honor their fallen colleague. Because Channing's "name would have greater weight than that of any other person in the city," they asked permission to place it at the head of a petition seeking the use of Faneuil Hall. Channing "cheerfully" assented, though he hoped that he would not be required to speak at the gathering. The mayor and board of alderman were not impressed. In rejecting the request, they asserted that the resolutions likely to be passed by the petition's signers "ought not be regarded as the public voice of this city." Angered by their response, Channing immediately began preparing an open letter to the citizens of Boston, which urged readers to remember who they were. "Has Boston fallen so low? May not its citizens be trusted to come together to express the great principles of liberty, for which their fathers died?" he asked. "If such be our degradation, we ought to know the awful truth; and those among us who retain a portion of the spirit of our ancestors, should set themselves to work to recover their degenerate posterity."[39]

Any fears Channing might have had soon disappeared. The "spirit" about which he spoke was still alive and well. Although the *Atlas* and the *Advertiser* lent their support, the aldermen were nearly alone. Outside Boston, numerous newspapers joined the *Fitchburg Courier* in refusing "to cringe before the audacious encroachments upon our liberties, which have been countenanced by the self-styled 'gentlemen of property and standing,' who have taken upon themselves the guardianship of the press, among '*the white slaves of the North.*'" Charles Francis Adams expressed similar sentiments when he wrote, "The craven spirit has got about as far in Boston as it can go." Informed that others shared his opinion, the ex-president's son remarked, "We are not all broken into the cotton interest then." Among those who did so was George Bond, who chaired a public meeting that passed resolutions criticizing the board's decision and appointed ward committees to collect signatures for another petition. "On its presentation to the Board of Aldermen," one abolitionist observed, the "request was granted quite obsequiously!"[40]

The meeting took place on December 7 at Faneuil Hall, and its heterogeneous audience included large numbers of elite Bostonians as well as antislavery activists from all walks of life. James T. Austin also made an appearance. In a viciously uncompromising address, the attorney general likened blacks to wild beasts, declared that "Lovejoy died as a fool dieth," and compared the Alton mob to the Boston Tea Party. He was followed by Wendell Phillips, whose often-quoted reply announced his coming-out as a Garrisonian stalwart. Though rarely mentioned, one other speaker addressed the crowd that evening. George Bond had not intended to say anything; however, after listening to Austin, he changed his mind. Over the previous two years, Bond stated, there had been repeated efforts to suppress free discussion in Boston—efforts that had been "regarded by a large portion of the community with silent acquiescence, if not with decided approbation." If they would not speak out, he would. And in words dripping with contempt, Bond let the audience know how detestable he found the attorney general and all that he had said.[41]

Had Bond represented a majority of elite Bostonians, Channing would have been a happy man. Given his Federalist background and long, intimate association with city leaders, he was perfectly comfortable living in a society where a small, wealthy, educated elite guided the social conduct of everyone else. "To communicate the intelligence and blessings of the higher classes to the lower," he said in an 1831 letter to an English correspondent, "should be the end and sure result of all social institutions, and they are essentially defective where such is not their operation." Unfortunately for Channing's peace of mind, Bond did not speak for others of his class. As Charles Francis Adams noted, "a large and powerful party of respectable men" had applauded nearly every sentence of Austin's speech at the Lovejoy meeting. Moreover, many of these same people belonged to Channing's Federal Street Church, where recent attempts to read abolition notices from the pulpit and open the building to antislavery gatherings had provoked a hostile response from enraged parishioners. On at least one occasion, several members of the congregation, "doubling up their fists in his face," confronted Channing and demanded the names of those providing him with the notices. Even more upsetting was the Federal Street Standing Committee's later refusal to allow him to hold a memorial service at the church for his close friend Charles Follen, the abolitionist minister.[42]

These and similar incidents forced Channing to reconsider his elitist conceptions of how society functioned. He was learning that, as Lydia Maria Child put it, "you cannot raise a solid anti Slavery structure upon an aristocratic ground-work. There is no moral cement by which the two things can be held together." At the antislavery gatherings he attended, Channing could not help but notice "the absence of what is called the influential part of the community." He soon realized that little support could be expected from such people. "The prosperous and distinguished of this world, given as they are to epicurean self-indulgence and to vain show," he wrote shortly after the Lovejoy meeting, "are among the last to comprehend the worth of a human being, to penetrate the evils of society, or to impart to it a fresh impulse."[43]

In attempting to explain elite indifference to slavery, Channing some-times focused on specific economic interests. "The slaves' toil is the North-ern merchant's wealth," he observed in an 1839 letter that foreshadowed the Conscience Whig critique of the mid-1840s, "for it produces the great staple on which all the commercial dealings of the country turn. As our merchants and manufacturers cast their eyes southward, what do they see? Cotton, Cotton, nothing but Cotton." More often, however, Channing attributed elite behavior to the materialistic spirit of the age. An all-consuming preoc-cupation with gain had blunted the moral senses of the rich and powerful. He could see it in the eyes of his own parishioners. "I have often been struck with the entire composure with which a congregation will hear their worldliness rebuked," he told an English acquaintance, "when they would wince if any acknowledged vice were charged on them. They really see no guilt in an entire absorption in outward interests."[44]

Despite his frequent criticism of acquisitive behavior, Channing was not an inveterate foe of economic development. Commercial expansion, he believed, had destroyed feudalism, checked the spread of militarism, reduced conflict among nations, and obliterated irrational prejudices. He even conceded that material progress might be a precondition for moral and intellectual advance. And Channing was nothing if not an optimist. Of all the problems facing society, he told one correspondent, "[t]he want of faith in improvement which you deplore, is the darkest symptom." But such attitudes could be found largely among "what are called 'the better classes.' These are always timid, and never originate improvements worthy of the name." The reform impulse lay elsewhere, in the middling classes that were slowly acquiring the power "to balance the aristocracy" and defend "liberal principles."[45]

It was to this group that Channing looked for progress in the struggle against slavery. Without pressure from below, "the better classes" would never respond to the cries of suffering humanity; that pressure had to come from the "middle and laboring ranks" of the community. Leading aboli-tionists shared these views. Edmund Quincy, who believed "the prejudices of property are almost invariably arrayed on the side of the slaveholder," felt that human bondage would be abolished "not by the highest or the lowest classes of society, but by the middle classes, who are removed equally from the temptations of the rich and the poor." The antislavery movement, he noted, drew its greatest support from "farmers, merchants, teachers & persons of small capitals scattered over the country towns." Among working people, Quincy added, the movement received further aid from "the native laboring classes who are much above the generality of the Irish emigrants in intelligence."[46]

Although Channing avoided such nativist slurs, he too distinguished among different groups of working people. On one hand, there were the aimless and dissolute, those whose troubles stemmed less "from physical causes" than "from moral want." For the sake of "order and good principles," workers of this sort required some supervision, as "[a] moral care over the tempted and ignorant portion of the state is a primary duty of society." But there were also respectable workers, people who were trying diligently to better themselves. As one of the era's most ardent proponents of self-improvement, Channing believed that their efforts deserved all the assistance society could reasonably furnish. Moving beyond the stewardship doctrine of elite philanthropists such as Abbot Lawrence, he even endorsed the demand for shorter hours. Opposition to the reform most often came from individuals "who think more of property than of any other human interest"; if their claim that shorter hours meant reduced output proved true, then so be it. Adding to the world's stock of material goods was not the be all and end all of human existence. Though production might decline, he said, "the character and the spirit of the people would effect a much more equal distribution of what would be produced; and the happiness of a community depends vastly more on the distribution than on the amount of its wealth."[47]

Channing's incipient radicalism on labor questions mirrored changes in his approach to emancipation. In *Slavery*, published in 1835, he had strongly opposed Garrisonian immediatism. "The slave," he observed in one particularly striking passage, "should not, in the first instance, be allowed to wander at his will beyond the plantation on which he toils; and if he cannot be induced to work by rational and natural motives, he should be obliged to labor; on the same principles on which the vagrant in other communities is confined and compelled to earn his bread." By decade's end, Channing had disavowed these views. He did so in part because he thought the success of emancipation in the West Indies had shown immediate freedom to be "safer than a gradual loosening of the chain." His changing perceptions of labor also influenced him. Where earlier he had worried about the willingness of freed slaves to engage in productive activities without planter supervision, he now stated that they might well choose to work less. But this did not matter. "Has man nothing to do but work?" he asked. "Are not too many here overworked?" A final factor was Channing's new understanding of how society functioned. Although he had long feared disruption from below, he now believed that the most potent sources of social disorder lay elsewhere. "It ought to be understood that the great enemies to society are not found in its poorer ranks," he declared in an 1841 address. "The mass may, indeed, be used as a mob; but the stirring and guiding powers of insurrection are found above. Communities fall by the vices of the prosperous ranks."[48]

At the time of his death in 1842, Channing was not the same person he had been a decade earlier. As his antislavery convictions deepened, he began to look at the world in different ways. His changing views did not go unnoticed. Heretofore, John Quincy Adams remarked, elite Bostonians "had almost worshipped him as a saint; they now call him a Jacobin." They had good reason for doing so. Although Channing never became an abolitionist, much less a labor radical, his withering commentary on elite behavior raised disturbing questions about the ability and willingness of Boston's "better classes" to shoulder the moral responsibilities of leadership. More such questions would be asked in the decade to come, and a number of those asking them would remember the Federal Street pastor. When Charles Sumner later condemned Congressman Robert C. Winthrop's conduct during the Mexican War—an action that signaled his own break with elite Boston—he did so because he believed that the Boston representative had a duty "to see that the influence of the city of Channing was not thrown on the side of injustice."[49]

Channing's death coincided with the end of what might be called the first phase of antislavery agitation in Massachusetts. During this period, attention centered on questions of free speech and the right of petition. Despite their clumsy response to abolitionist initiatives, elite Bostonians managed to maintain their position in state politics without serious loss of authority. However grudgingly, most ultimately followed the lead of enlightened conservatives such as George Bond, thereby minimizing the damage caused by earlier acts of repression. After 1842, however, attention shifted to the much more explosive issue of slave expansionism. In one of his last speeches, Channing declared that annexing Texas constituted sufficient cause for dissolving the Union. When John Tyler afterward took steps to do exactly that, the resulting uproar was unprecedented in its scope and intensity. Containing it without loss of reputation would require greater skill than simply knowing when to control one's more authoritarian instincts.[50]

LIKE THEIR FEDERALIST FOREBEARS, Massachusetts Whigs opposed territorial expansion in general. As they saw it, the acquisition of new lands reduced regional political influence and undermined national unity. They particularly objected to any initiative that would add new slave states to the Union. In addition to moral considerations, there were good economic reasons for restricting the spread of slavery. No one had forgotten the nullification controversy of the early 1830s, and the South remained an overwhelmingly agricultural region whose material interests differed markedly from those of New England mill owners. When a Whig activist told *Lowell Daily Courier* editor William Schouler that he had heard southern politicians "say they would go the annexation of Texas to put down the *damned northern manufacturers*," Bay State party leaders had little trouble believing that most planters viewed the issue in exactly those terms.[51]

During the spring of 1844, as word leaked out that the Tyler administration was attempting to obtain Texas, Abbott Lawrence began organizing an opposition movement. Seven years earlier, when Andrew Jackson officially recognized the fledgling republic, Lawrence had urged Bay Staters to resist any further acquisitions of slave territory—and his views had not changed. His brother Amos felt the same way. "The damning sin of adding [Texas] to this nation to extend slavery," he wrote to one acquaintance, "will be as certain to destroy us as death is to overtake us." At the same time, however, the Lawrences and other elite Bostonians did not want to alienate southern Whigs. By taking the initiative, they hoped to confine protest within "official" channels. It appeared for a while that they might be successful. In June, Tyler sent the Texas treaty to the Senate, where southern Whigs joined their northern counterparts in voting against annexation.[52]

But this was just the first round. Recognizing that he would never secure the two-thirds vote needed to pass a treaty in the Senate, Tyler made plans to achieve his ends through a joint resolution of both houses, which required only majority approval. That November, when James K. Polk was elected president on an expansionist platform, Democratic publicists hailed his victory as a mandate for annexation. And as the movement to acquire Texas gathered force, any hopes Abbott Lawrence might have had of controlling the expression of anti-annexation sentiment vanished. Anger at Tyler's actions was so great that even party conservatives such as Leverett Saltonstall were making uncharacteristically radical noises. A longtime advocate of restraint on slavery-related issues, the Salem congressman had "never before felt so deeply on any public question" and recommended "*dissolution* rather than *annexation*."[53]

In January 1845, Bay State Whigs, joined by regional abolitionists, organized a massive protest meeting at Faneuil Hall. Among the more conspicuous absentees were Lawrence and fellow manufacturer Nathan Appleton. Unable to impose their moderate counsel on the anti-Texas resistance, they decided against participating at all. After Congress passed Tyler's annexation resolution in early March, they considered the matter closed and refused to support the ongoing activities of antislavery Whigs opposed to Texas statehood. "Massachusetts has done her duty," Appleton declared that fall when asked to sign a petition being circulated by the Texas State

Committee, gratuitously adding that he wanted no part of an organization whose membership included abolitionists. Appleton believed that abolitionist excesses had "postponed emancipation in the more northern slave states," and it was to these states that he and Lawrence now directed their attention. Having lost the struggle against annexation, they hoped to rally sufficient southern support to preserve the tariff of 1842, whose protective provisions had been targeted for elimination by the Polk administration.[54]

How they sought to do so can best be seen in a series of public letters that Lawrence addressed to the prominent Virginia Whig, William C. Rives. The Old Dominion, Lawrence observed, had lost much of its former prosperity in recent decades; its future appeared even more bleak, given the state's inability to compete with western grain-producing regions. To reverse its declining fortunes, Virginia had to create a more diversified economy in which "mental culture" played at least as great a role as "active physical power." In addition to establishing manufactures and constructing modern transportation facilities, the state needed to develop an effective public school system, which Lawrence described as "the lever to all permanent improvement." Without an educated and efficient labor force, Virginia would never reclaim its rightful place in the Union. "Let the lawmakers . . . so act as to give an impetus to labor; let it be considered respectable for every man to have a vocation, and to follow it," he declared. Once embarked on this line of development, Virginians would soon recognize the benefits to be derived from protectionism. "If you propose now to enter upon those pursuits that are certain in their operation to give employment, and that of a profitable kind, to your people, and to create a market at home for your agricultural products, what object can there be in transferring our workshops to Great Britain?"[55]

Lawrence spoke like a man who had seen the future and believed that it looked exactly like New England. Were this just another declaration of regional chauvinism, there would be little to add. New Englanders had been issuing such statements since the early colonial era. But this was not what Lawrence intended, nor was he concerned only about maintaining protective duties at current levels. Although the Rives letters made no mention of slavery, they need to be seen as an expression of what might be called the market-forces theory of emancipation. According to the leading exponent of this notion, the Philadelphia economist Henry C. Carey, slavery marked a transitional stage in southern development. As the region's economy matured, Carey argued, free labor would gradually displace slave labor. And because this was a natural process that could not be hastened by government action, northerners should leave the South alone and let economic forces do their work. "There is but one way to free the negroes," he wrote to Charles Sumner, "and that is to produce competition for the purchase of his labour." When industrialization created such competition, slavery would disappear.[56]

Given their aversion to intersectional conflict, elite Bostonians found the market-forces argument extremely appealing. "Slave labor can never, in the long run, come into successful competition with free labor," said George Ticknor, "and in time slaves, therefore, will everywhere cease to be valuable as property." Meanwhile, northerners could best advance their own interests by doing nothing. "The Southern States are not only losing their *relative* consequence in the Union, but, from the inherent and manifold mischiefs of slavery, they are positively growing poorer." This was especially so in the Upper South, where worn-out lands and competition from soil-rich western areas made plantation agriculture an increasingly precarious enterprise. Nathan Appleton, who considered the problem of human bondage "beyond the power of man to solve," had "little doubt that slavery will gradually be abolished in the most northern of the slave states. It may," he added, "be abolished in all of them when slave labor ceases to be profitable." Abbott Lawrence agreed. The South's peculiar institution was already on the verge of extinction in at least six states, he told Edward Everett—and "for the best reason in the world": *they cannot afford it.*[57]

Stated in 1850, Lawrence's observation would not have been out of place in the Rives letters. His description of Virginia's productive shortcomings, his call for economic diversification, and his comments on worker education all pointed toward the creation of a free labor economy. That he did not say as much attracted critical notice from various Massachusetts commentators. Still bitter about the recent annexation of Texas, many Bay Staters felt that this was no time for regional political leaders to be pulling their punches when addressing southerners on slavery-related matters. Even William Schouler's *Lowell Courier* believed Lawrence should have informed Virginians that manufactures and free schools could never thrive in a state where "slavery is suffered to remain."[58]

Lawrence's harshest critic turned out to be Charles Francis Adams. The ex-president's son was a leading member of a group of antislavery Whigs who had spearheaded opposition to Texas annexation and statehood. In the course of doing so, these Conscience Whigs developed serious doubts about the moral integrity of the manufacturers who dominated party affairs. They were particularly incensed at Lawrence and Appleton for opposing the January 1845 anti-annexation meeting at Faneuil Hall and for refusing to support resistance to Texas statehood. They also discovered that, with the exception of Buckingham's *Courier*, they had no Boston outlet for expressing their dissatisfaction. And Buckingham would go only so far, because his paper was financed in part by Cotton Whigs. As he later told Charles Sumner, "I am not in *independent circumstances,* and must submit to influences, from which I should be most heartily glad to be free." To escape restraints imposed by those same influences, Adams and other Conscience Whigs decided that they needed a newspaper of their own. In June 1846, they secured control of the *Boston Daily Whig,* a nearly moribund local party sheet whose owner could no longer make ends meet with a mere 212 subscribers.[59]

As editor, Adams wasted little time letting readers know what he thought of Lawrence's views. In mid-June, he began reviewing the Rives letters in a long series of articles addressed "To the Hon. Abbott Lawrence." Writing under the pen name "Sagitta," Adams started where the *Lowell Courier* had left off: by asking Lawrence why he had said nothing about slavery in the letters. He was, after all, urging Virginians to change their entire way of life, and he must surely have known that they could "never become a manufacturing people so long as the laboring class are in chains." Rives doubtless appreciated his reticence. "But this politeness is not without its cost," Adams said. "People who are under no obligation to be quiet, will ask impertinent questions about your motives for taking so singular a course." As one of those people, Adams offered his own explanation: "You . . . thought it expedient to make your principles bend to your interest, and to promote the Tariff at the expense of a full statement of truth." Concerned only about the new factory center being constructed north of Lowell on the banks of the Merrimack—a city that would bear his name as well as add to his fortune—Lawrence failed to see that while he was trying "to make Virginians think well of sheep and cotton, they were winding around man the cords intended to fasten him forever helpless to earth."[60]

Adams further noted that Lawrence received nothing in return for his sacrifice of principle. Congress had recently repealed the tariff of 1842, replacing it with a revenue measure that left northern manufacturers unprotected against foreign competition. Adams believed that the textile magnate should have seen this coming. That he did not reflected a basic misunderstanding of southern aims. Planter opposition to protectionism, Adams explained, "is political and radical in its character. They are jealous of power, and insofar as money is power, they are jealous of money." Slaveholders could not be placated with alluring promises of industrial prosperity; slavery itself had to be confronted. He hoped that anyone who thereafter wrote about southern society would feel shame at not doing so.[61]

What Lawrence had yet to learn, Adams concluded, was that protectionism, banking, and other economic questions no longer occupied a central place in American politics. He himself could not support a platform devoted to these questions alone, and neither would half the party. Adams observed, "There is a deep and growing conviction . . . that Slavery creates the power which now rules the country to its great injury." Though still important, protectionism had become a secondary concern. "I am ready to work for the Tariff because it is in my opinion useful to our people and to the country," said one *Whig* correspondent, "but I cannot make it out as equal to any principle mentioned in the Declaration of Independence." Adams and other Conscience Whigs believed party leaders could ill afford to ignore such sentiments. As Charles Sumner put it, "They must recognize the dominion of right, or there will be none left who will recognize the dominion of party."[62]

This was the kind of language Lawrence usually understood. More so than most of the Boston Associates, he had taken an active part in party affairs, doing whatever he could to advance Whig fortunes. It is therefore worth asking why he proved so resistant to Conscience Whig concerns about the slave power. If questioned on the matter, Lawrence doubtless would have said, as he did on a later occasion: "*I am a Union man,* and have never been any thing else." But this was not entirely true. Had he reviewed his correspondence, he would have found that during the nullification controversy he had declared himself ready to tell whoever cared to listen "that the evil of separation to the Free States would be far less than the abandonment of protecting their industry." Expressed in the heat of the moment, the statement cannot be taken at face value. Yet it did reflect the intense regional consciousness Lawrence then felt—a consciousness that Bay State Whigs made one of the primary bases of their political appeal.[63]

Another question thus arises: What had changed? Several things had. One was the New England textile industry, which had matured considerably since the early 1830s and no longer seemed so vulnerable to the political assaults of free traders. Although Lawrence continued to believe protective duties essential for the industry's further development, he could feel reasonably assured that the legislative machinations of southern sectionalists did not critically threaten his core economic interests. The general political situation was also much different. As memories of the Hartford Convention faded and the proto-Whiggery of the nullification period gave way to a truly national party, elite Bostonians escaped the political isolation that had been their lot throughout much of the 1820s. That many southern Whigs shared or were at least receptive to their views on industrialization, protectionism, and related matters made them all the more ready to adopt a conciliatory stance on questions that threatened intersectional harmony.[64]

A letter Lawrence wrote several years later to John Davis sheds further light on his new outlook. In it, he listed his vast holdings: his cotton, iron, wool, machinery, and railroad investments; the seven ships in which he had an interest; his fire and marine insurance stock; and the property he owned in Boston and various other locales. "I have been somewhat particular," he told Davis, "that you may understand that my interests are those of the whole country, and cannot be separated." This did not mean that Lawrence's unionism was simply a by-product of his expanding portfolio. He was genuinely proud of American achievements. "I am every day more satisfied with the mighty power [that] our country and its institutions are exercising not only here, but in every part of Europe," he later observed while serving as ambassador to Great Britain. "The eyes of all Christendom appear to be turned toward the United States." And he feared that intersectional conflict would destroy that influence, "for when we begin to break up the Federal Union no one can tell where the divisions will end." Thus, Lawrence now saw himself as part of a national rather than a regional elite. The fears and hopes of New Englanders still mattered, but not nearly as much as they had a decade or so earlier. As he came to operate on a broader economic and political stage, Lawrence developed new priorities that set him at odds with dissident Whigs, who continued to view the party as a champion of regional interests and values.[65]

In Lawrence's case, these tensions were exacerbated by a thoroughly materialistic view of historical processes that rendered him tone deaf to appeals based on moral principle. His embrace of the market-forces theory of emancipation was not simply a matter of self-interest, but a logical application of his understanding of how the world worked. In a letter to Henry Clay, written shortly after the Kentuckian had resolved the nullification crisis, Lawrence contended that economic growth provided the surest means of reconciling intersectional differences. "If the system of internal improvements could go on for a few years, with vigor," he declared, "there is not a doubt upon my mind, that this Union would be bound by ties stronger than all the constitutions that human wisdom could devise. A railroad from New England to Georgia, would do more to harmonize the feelings of the whole country, than any amendments that can be offered or adopted to the Constitution." As the Rives letters made clear, Lawrence still believed that material forces dictated public policy. This left him and those who shared his perspective woefully ill-equipped to deal with the Conscience Whig critique. In the opening paragraph of *Slavery*, William Ellery Channing had written: "The first question to be proposed by a rational being is, not what is profitable, but what is Right. . . . This is the fundamental truth, the supreme law of reason; and the mind which does not start from this, in its inquiries into human affairs, is doomed to great, perhaps fatal error." Channing penned these observations at a time when most Bay Staters had just begun to respond to abolitionist attacks on slavery, and when elite Bostonians could still dismiss such admonitions as visionary claptrap. With the rise of Conscience Whiggery, it was no longer quite so easy.[66]

CHAPTER FIVE

The Revolt of the Subelites

IN SEPTEMBER 1846, just as Charles Francis Adams was concluding his "Sagitta" letters, Bay State Whigs gathered at Faneuil Hall in
Boston for the their annual convention. In recent months, intraparty relations had grown increasingly acrimonious. In addition to Adams's thrusts
at Lawrence, Conscience Whigs had leveled their sights on Robert C.
Winthrop, a Boston congressman then being groomed to replace the aging
Daniel Webster as the elite's main political spokesman. After a May border
skirmish between Mexican and U.S. troops had given the Polk administration a pretext for declaring war, Winthrop was the only Massachusetts representative to support a military appropriations bill whose preamble blamed
Mexico for initiating hostilities. That Winthrop's vote provided cover for
administration recklessness and duplicity was bad enough in the eyes of
Conscience Whigs; that he had broken ranks with his colleagues because
he "could not bear that the whole Delegation should be mixed up with a
little knot of ultraists" added insult to injury. The ensuing assault focused
on Winthrop's character and integrity, leaving him deeply embittered and
expecting little good from the September convention. "If the Boston Whig
is to be our organ, & Adams & Sumner our fuglemen," he told a party
associate, "I, for one, see nothing worth fighting for."[1]

Conscience Whigs approached the convention with equal trepidation.
Despite assurances that they would not be muzzled, they expected the worst
from their more conservative adversaries. In the end, both groups expressed
dissatisfaction with the proceedings. On one hand, efforts by Conscience
Whigs to push through a strong set of antislavery resolutions compelled
party leaders to take a more forceful stand on the issue than they would have
liked. "It is plain," Winthrop said afterward, "that the Factionalists must be
cut adrift, or they will swamp us." On the other hand, Conscience Whigs
felt that they had been consistently overpowered and outmaneuvered by

their wealthier foes. In a post-convention analysis that exposed the critical role played by individuals with close links to the manufacturing interest, a *Whig* correspondent declared: "It is the party of cotton against the party of conscience." These Cotton Whigs cared only about protecting their investments, and citizens of the commonwealth would soon have to decide whether "liberty and humanity, the Declaration of Independence as it is, and the Constitution as it was" should "be dearer in their eyes, than huge Woollen Mills and great Cotton Corporations."[2]

For all their discontent, Conscience Whigs were not yet ready to chart an independent course. They wanted to reform—not destroy—Whiggery. The party had long functioned as a suitable vehicle for the principled expression of regional values, and they felt it could do so again. Creating a third party, many believed, would be "suicidal." Despite Winthrop's gloomy forebodings, most Cotton Whigs also hoped to keep the organization intact. They still dominated party affairs and saw little reason why that should change anytime soon; with a presidential election looming, maintaining a united front was all the more important. The uneasy truce that resulted began to unravel at the 1847 state convention. When Conscience Whigs announced their unwillingness to support any presidential candidate who refused to oppose slavery, party leaders defeated a resolution embodying the demand. Afterward, Cotton Whigs cut off all contact with disaffected party members and threw their support behind the presidential candidacy of Zachary Taylor, a Louisiana slaveholder and Mexican War hero. Taylor's nomination the following June signaled a final parting of the ways. As party regulars fired cannons on Boston Common to celebrate Taylor's selection, Conscience Whigs issued a call for separate action.[3]

The time for compromise had passed, and in late June they assembled at Worcester to condemn the "aggressive slavocracy" and urge an end to northern submission to planter dominion. Charles Sumner best expressed their anger when he declared that "the usurpations of the Slave Power" had rendered the tariff, banking, and other such issues "obsolete." Those Bay State party leaders who refused to recognize this development were largely responsible for Taylor's nomination. With no concerns other than making money, Sumner charged, they had become eager participants in an unholy alliance "between the cotton planters and flesh-mongers of Louisiana and Mississippi, and the cotton spinners and trafficers of New England— between the lords of the lash and the lords of the loom."[4]

Sumner's remarks, which were harsh even by Conscience Whig standards, did not go uncontested. Among those taking notice was Nathan Appleton, who resented the claim that New England manufacturers had joined southern planters in a proslavery conspiracy. Writing to Sumner shortly after the convention, Appleton demanded to know if he truly believed that the two groups were acting together. He did indeed, Sumner responded, adding that the industrialist had no right to question him. This was not what Appleton wanted to hear. That the *Boston Whig* had characterized him as "the living embodiment of the cotton manufacturing feeling," he informed Sumner, gave him all the right he needed to make such inquiries. At this, Sumner recounted a series of incidents during the previous four years in which "certain prominent gentlemen 'interested in the cotton manufacture' and exercising much influence as 'politicians' over our Commonwealth, have generally discountenanced those measures whose objective was to oppose the extension of Slavery & the aggressions of the Slave Power."[5]

Though still not satisfied, Appleton realized that nothing could be gained by continuing the correspondence. Their differences were simply too great. In a final letter, he told Sumner that he felt no personal animosity toward him. "I have regretted your course during the last two years. But more in sorrow than in anger. I have regretted to see talents so brilliant as yours, and from which I had hoped much for our country, take a course in which I consider them more than thrown away." The sentiments were sincere. Related to Sumner by marriage, Appleton had taken a genuine interest in his accomplishments. So had other elite Bostonians. A protégé of Harvard law professor and Supreme Court justice Joseph Story, Sumner was widely viewed as one of the best and brightest of the coming generation. During a European tour earlier in the decade, he had dazzled Britain's aristocracy with his social skills and intellectual attainments, in the process making no small impression on status-conscious Brahmins who prized the scholar-gentleman ideal every bit as much as their English counterparts. In 1845, city fathers chose Sumner to deliver Boston's annual Fourth of July oration, an honor generally reserved for young men from whom much was expected. That he seemed intent on throwing all this away caused dismay as well as anger in elite circles.[6]

It also caused some worry. Appleton, Lawrence, and the other merchant-manufacturers who had created the Waltham-Lowell system and controlled state politics for the past two decades were not getting any younger. Death and diminished capacity would soon force their withdrawal from public affairs, and someone had to be there to replace them. If they could not count on their most talented young people, the future promised to be much different than the past. And that was the problem. Sumner belonged to what Adams described as "a young generation" untrained "in the schools of expediency that were favorites in the preceding generation. These men feel and reason for themselves—money cannot buy nor the hope of office

seduce them—they will demand consistent action as well as fine words."
They formed what might be called a subelite: individuals who had not
attained full elite status, but who could expect to do so as their elders passed
on the torch of leadership.[7]

Three of these people are the subject of this chapter: Charles Francis Adams, who engineered the initial challenge to elite political rule;
Theodore Parker, Boston's most popular and most learned minister of the
period; and Horace Mann, who better than anyone embodied the stewardship ethic that furnished a rationale for elite hegemony. Apart from their
dissatisfaction with the existing social order, the three had little in common.
As the son and grandson of presidents, Adams had a much more distinguished lineage than either Parker or Mann, both of whom hailed from
yeoman backgrounds; Adams's marriage to a daughter of Peter Chardon
Brooks further enhanced his status in Brahmin eyes. Their personalities
also differed. Whereas Adams and Mann often appeared reluctant rebels,
the unrestrained fury of Parker's attacks alarmed even his friends. "You
must slay more gently," said Samuel Gridley Howe, "you must *put to death*,
not *kill*, the moral vermin it is your mission to remove." More significant,
each of these men traveled different paths to rebellion. While Adams believed that Whig political compromises on slavery-related issues dishon-
ored the commonwealth, Parker's discontent arose from what he saw as
the theological rigidity and moral lethargy of Unitarianism, and Mann
developed serious doubts about the elite's commitment to educating the
uneducated.[8]

That the three men acted from such different motives highlights an important feature of the challenge posed by the subelites. Though their critique ultimately centered on the slavery question, the sources of their unease
were much broader. Examining how these diverse strands of dissent came
to intersect provides a revealing look at heretofore unexamined dimensions
of the crisis of authority facing Boston's elite at midcentury.

THE FIRST—and most important—thing one needs to know about
Charles Francis Adams is that he was an Adams. The achievements of
his father and grandfather loomed large in Charles Francis's mind. "The
world tries the sons of distinguished men by the standard of the qualities of their fathers," he told Theodore Parker. Should the bearer of an
honorable name fall beneath that standard, he wrote on another occasion,
"then comes a comforting tale about the degeneracy of families. If he does
himself credit enough to escape that, there follows no disposition to award
him any particular praise." Always on guard, Charles Francis approached
others with a certain wariness, revealing little and never letting himself

go. "Our highest duty as a people," he told Bostonians in a Fourth of July address, "is self-restraint." The burden of family reputation made it particularly imperative that he exercise such control. As his father often reminded him, the Adamses had their share of enemies, people only too eager to see them humiliated. "Your father and grandfather have fought their way through the world against hosts of adversaries open and close, disguised and masked," with few true friends to aid them, John Quincy warned. "The world is and will continue to be prolific of such characters. Live in peace with them. Never upbraid. Never trust them."[9]

No one had a greater influence on Charles Francis than his father. To the younger Adams, John Quincy was an awesome figure whose intellectual powers seemed even more impressive than his political accomplishments. "It astonishes more and more to perceive the extent and reach of the acquisitions of my father," he confided to his diary. "There is no subject on which he does not know a great deal and explain it with the greatest beauty of language." John Quincy's example provided a model for his own daily regimen. Trained in the law, a profession he found thoroughly uninteresting, Charles Francis channeled his energies and ambitions into a disciplined self-improvement program of reading and writing, each evening noting the day's progress in his diary. If he could not match his father's attainments, it would not be for a lack of trying. And should any opportunity for public renown ever come, he would certainly be ready.[10]

As much as Charles Francis revered his father, the two men did not always see eye to eye. Although the younger Adams hoped some day to make his mark in the public sphere, he long resisted John Quincy's urgings to enter politics. Worse, he did not seem to be doing much of anything for a time. It was not until the 1830s, when he assumed responsibility for overseeing the family's finances, that Charles Francis began to prove his worth. John Quincy knew little about business, and the family fortune was fast disappearing under his careless stewardship. By contrast, Charles Francis possessed the attention to detail and hardheaded pragmatism of a banker. He observed that unlike his father, whose visionary bent left John Quincy ill-equipped to deal with such mundane matters as money management: "My mind does not know the theoretical any farther than as it *clearly* guides to a practical end." If John Quincy did not always appreciate this side of Charles Francis's personality, his father-in-law, Peter Chardon Brooks, did. As the two got to know each other better, the retired insurance magnate came to think so highly of Adams's abilities that he proposed giving him full control of his wife's inheritance, an offer Charles Francis declined because he feared that accepting would reflect badly on the husbands of Brooks's other daughters. In the case of Edward Everett, whom Brooks on at least one occasion admonished for his lax approach to financial obligations, Charles Francis was doubtless right.[11]

Though proud of his competence as a financial manager, Charles Francis kept such matters in perspective. He certainly hoped to retain what wealth he had. After all, he observed, "It is idle to say that poverty is not an evil when so much care is taken to avoid it." But he worried about the inordinate influence money had on society. Sermons criticizing acquisitiveness invariably prompted an approving diary entry. "In this community, this subject needs often pressing," he wrote after listening to one such exhortation. "The great vice of this New England people is their adoration of Mammon. And rooted as it is in the character, the tree has now attained immense luxuriance and bids fair to overshadow us all." Of an acquaintance who left a position in an insurance office to study for the ministry, he noted with some bitterness: "Poor fellow, I pity him. He forgets the fact that Wealth gives Power, learning only indigence and contempt." Clergymen truly had a hard row to hoe, he afterward observed with equal asperity: "A man who should tell us that Charity, Piety, Faith, Benevolence, Meekness, and the rest of the virtues are good things to practise, would be laughed at for his pains. Yet these are the great topics of our Religion, and the cultivation of them the great purposes of preaching."[12]

These and similar observations did not stem from any deep discontent on Adams's part. Generally satisfied with the existing social structure and his own place within it, he had little use for the workingmen's party or other radical movements. When Alexander Everett asked him to subscribe to a newspaper committed to reconciling differences between labor reformers and Jacksonians, Charles Francis dismissed the request with elite disdain. "To take up a radical paper with my feelings and principles, would be either self degradation or desperation," he remarked. "I must either be expected to bend to a tone which would please the reformers, a tone which I despise, or to raise them up to me which is a vain and absurd hope." Nor did he have much respect for working people in general. When a local minister equated artisans with statesmen in a sermon on the mechanic arts, Adams objected, observing that "it would have been fair to draw a line between the inventors and the mere executors." Those mechanics who introduced technological innovations merited "a high place in intellectual rank, but the others rank but one degree over animals—at least when considered only in reference to results."[13]

Despite these views, which were common in elite circles, Adams did not fit comfortably into Brahmin society. "I am an aristocrat," he said while still a youth, "but not one of Boston." Though appreciative of the city's philanthropic spirit, he despised its "purse proud ostentation." Unlike most Harvard students of the era, who during their years in Cambridge established a network of relationships that remained intact throughout their lives, Charles Francis made no close friends in college. "Among all the men I met there," he later said, "not one did I find with a character at all congenial to mine." He bore them no "illwill," but neither did he take any "pleasure in their society."[14]

Little digging is necessary to uncover the reasons for this frostiness. As a young boy visiting his grandfather at the family homestead in Quincy, Charles Francis doubtless heard numerous tales of elite treachery from that loquacious and indiscreet worthy. His father's ongoing conflicts with local Federalists and the shabby treatment John Quincy received at the hands of state Whig leaders deepened his conviction that "family prejudices" made Boston a place "eminently unfavorable" to someone of his background. Even his marriage to Abigail Brooks had its unpleasant side. That many Brahmins believed he had married "up" was an insult no Adams could easily abide. When Charles Francis joined his father in embracing Antimasonry, he acted not only from filial loyalty, but from a desire to undercut elite power by "break[ing] down the Whig party, that thing of shreds and patches which is more tyrannical where it has exclusive sway than any party that ever existed in this Government." For a time, his opposition to Whiggery grew so intense that he backed Martin Van Buren in the 1836 presidential contest.[15]

It was during these years that Adams began paying serious attention to the slavery question. Apart from a few disparaging comments on abolitionist tactics, he largely ignored antislavery agitation before the mid-1830s. His awakening owed much to the repressive activities of elite Bostonians. He found the August 1835 anti-abolition meeting at Faneuil Hall, together with the mobbing of Garrison several months later, particularly upsetting. These were the kinds of actions one might expect from people who had forgotten "the history of the founders of our own Commonwealth." Those responsible, he wrote, seemed to believe that "men who felt themselves under a solemn *duty* to go forward and preach equality of rights to the slaveholder, were of the same class as those who stand in bodies upon occasions of ordinary political contention—who bow to the nod of the file leader and march in squads to the place commanded." When city authorities later denied Channing's request to use Faneuil Hall for a meeting to protest Elijah Lovejoy's murder, he angrily denounced their "craven spirit."[16]

The South's growing aggressiveness made such behavior particularly disturbing. "The cause of Freedom is becoming secondary to the cause of Slavery," Adams observed in an 1836 essay. His father's struggle on behalf of the right of petition provided all the evidence he needed of this alarming turn in national affairs. Northerners, Charles Francis feared, were ill-prepared to resist the onslaught. Their tendency to subordinate public affairs to private interests placed them at a marked disadvantage in any political competition with the slaveholding South, where every adult white was "a politician by trade." Though he did not say as much, the message was clear: if northern citizens hoped to preserve their rights, they needed to rearrange their priorities.[17]

As Adams's antislavery convictions deepened, his brief flirtation with Jacksonianism came swiftly to an end. Despite his "innate aversion to the dirty dictates of the Whigs of this place," Charles Francis soon realized that he had little choice as to party affiliation. The willingness of Van Buren's administration to pacify southern planters ruled out any alliance with the Democrats. When the New Yorker lost his bid for reelection in 1840, Adams hoped it would be a lesson to "the Northern man with Southern principles" who sacrificed regional interests "for the sake of truckling to slaveholders." Meanwhile, Charles Francis had decided to take an active part in state politics. However strenuously he had resisted his father's urgings that he enter public life, he knew more was expected of him. On his thirtieth birthday, he noted in his diary: "Half of the ordinary period of a man's life is gone, and I am as yet somewhat of a drone upon the earth's surface." In 1840, he finally relented and accepted the Whig nomination to a seat in the Massachusetts House of Representatives.[18]

Although Adams was a conscientious legislator who distinguished himself on several slavery-related issues during his years in the General Court, he soon grew bored with public service. By 1844, the novelty of being a legislator had worn off, and he feared that he was becoming "a mere hack, working in party traces." Though proud of his accomplishments on the antislavery front, he doubted that much more could be achieved. And while still a Whig, he believed Whiggery destined for an ignominious end: "A party tied together by no principles and led on by political gamblers can have no other fate." What most troubled the country, he observed in the spring of 1844, was "the selfishness of the few and the indolence of the many." Yet even as he wrote, the ground was being prepared for a conflict that would cut through popular apathy and propel him into the forefront of a popular movement based on conscience. In the course of this struggle, he would have much to say about elite selfishness.[19]

Adams had been introduced to the Texas issue well before most Bay Staters. In 1836, his father claimed that leading Jacksonians had instigated the Texas rebellion as part of an insidious plot to reimpose slavery on a region where Mexican law barred the institution. Afterward, the elder Adams came to see Texas annexation as the central component of a great slave-power conspiracy designed to expand southern political authority and make government the compliant tool of a planter aristocracy. Charles Francis could not avoid being influenced by John Quincy's views; if Charles Francis never embraced the slave-power thesis with quite the same fervor that his father did, he certainly appreciated the threat Texas annexation posed to northern interests. At both the 1843 and 1844 sessions of the Massachusetts legislature, he presented resolutions condemning efforts to acquire the territory. Outside the General Court, he supported initiatives to mobilize public opinion on the issue.[20]

From the outset, Adams had doubts about the extent to which opponents of annexation could rely on elite backing. Although Boston industrialists claimed to feel just as strongly about the question as he did, their actions did not inspire confidence. At a March 1844 meeting, held at Abbott Lawrence's home and attended by some of the most distinguished figures in Brahmin society, Adams found Lawrence most concerned about devising ways to contain abolitionist excesses. To be sure, everyone recognized that annexing Texas presented real dangers, "but few had the right spirit." He could not help but conclude "that the wealthy classes have become inactive. They care but little for an abstract principle, and not much for any agitation whatsoever." Adams's skepticism about elite intentions deepened when, during that year's presidential campaign, he heard Whig leaders insist that Bay State voters cared only about the tariff. In a December article for Buckingham's *Courier,* he wrote that certain members of the "slaveholding party" were offering to endorse protectionism in exchange for support on annexation. Planters seemed "to imagine that Yankees would abandon any principle, however sacred, for money," as though New England's long history of "self-sacrifice" on behalf of noble causes meant nothing. It is hard to believe that much conviction lay behind these comments, at least so far as they applied to Boston's elite. His faith in Brahmin readiness to do the right thing—never great to begin with—was fast disappearing.[21]

The events of 1845 confirmed Adams's reservations about elite integrity. Appleton and Lawrence's early withdrawal from the anti-annexation movement, followed by their refusal to oppose Texas statehood, told him all he needed to know about the Associates' priorities. There could no longer be any doubt, as he later put it, that "[t]he rights of cotton sounded more loudly in their ears than the rights of men." Yet knowing where the problem lay and deciding what do to about it were two entirely different matters. After observing that any movement led by Lawrence and Appleton would "chain us to the cart of slavery, forever," a Vermont associate asked, "Shall we be bound?" That was indeed the question. More so than ever, Adams felt constrained by party ties and longed to cast them aside.[22]

In light of the foregoing, it was not surprising that Adams agreed to edit the *Whig*. He had long considered newspapers "the great engines" for shaping popular opinion in America, and he knew that Conscience Whigs could not rely on Boston's leading party journals to broadcast their views. Editing a paper was a natural extension of his own ideas about political insurgency. As he later observed, the process by which people came to challenge an established order passed through three stages: "First, they begin to *think* for themselves. Next, they go on to speak the result of their thoughts. And last of all they determine to act." The main problem was moving people from stage one to stage two, for it was here that the "old combinations" offered the greatest resistance; it was here, also, that an independent newspaper could do the most good.[23]

It was even less surprising that Adams began his editorship with a broad-ranging assault on Abbott Lawrence and the manufacturing interest. Given the elite's ability to dominate public discourse, little could be accomplished without first checking its power and demystifying its stance on slavery-related issues. "The changes of trade and the growth of manufactures," he wrote, "have created strong sympathies with the institution of slavery, which it will take a long while for an abstract principle to struggle with to succeed." By exposing these links, he hoped to spur the kind of questioning that constituted the first stage of political insurgency. In the process, he aroused the ire of party bosses who resented intimations that material self-interest dictated their tepid response to slave expansionism. That could not be helped, Adams told them. As much as he regretted having to employ such tactics, recent events had convinced him that manufacturers exerted a malign influence on public policy, and citizens had a right to know why their leaders acted as they did.[24]

These expressions of regret were by no means disingenuous. For one thing, Adams did not enjoy personal confrontation. He would have much preferred using "peaceful measures" to accomplish his aims. Nor did he object to mixing politics and economics. As a longtime proponent of protective duties, Adams believed that New England politicians had a responsibility to safeguard regional interests. Declaring himself a "friend of the Tariff of 1842," he told Lawrence that he shared his alarm at its repeal by a "slaveholding alliance." But this made it all the more imperative that the manufacturer abandon his conciliatory course, which could only "alienate men at home, who might have been friends, without gaining others abroad who will always be enemies." Adams also felt considerable ambivalence toward Brahmin society. On one hand, he knew most of these people personally and even liked some of them. "I am glad it is the last," he said of the final "Sagitta" letter, "for there is something amiable about Mr. Lawrence that had made me reluctant" to continue the series. At the same time, though, he believed they had lost their moral mandate as political leaders. If it could be restored without destroying the existing structure of authority, Charles Francis would not be altogether displeased, given his own elitist sensibilities; if it could not, he was prepared to bear the consequences.[25]

Whenever the opportunity arose, Adams eagerly embraced potential elite allies. One was David Sears, a wealthy land developer whose family fortune rested on his father's successes in the carrying trade. "Brought up amid the traditions of New England Federalism," a biographer wrote, Sears felt perfectly content with the existing power structure. Although ready to support policies providing for " 'the greatest good of the greatest number,' " he never hid "his belief that the credulity and the ignorance and the prejudices of the 'greatest number' often unfit them for any intelligent distinction between good and evil." Like Adams, however, he had been disappointed by the lackluster performance of Whig leaders during the Texas annexation struggle and feared that slavery might be extended indefinitely; repeal of the tariff of 1842 further angered him. Unless something were done to stop them, he said, "indolent and ignorant" slaveowners, "without education or industry," would soon "guide the destinies of this mighty empire." In late 1846, he revived an emancipation scheme that he had first submitted to John Quincy Adams three years earlier. According to the plan, all slave children born after July 4, 1850, would be freed and their owners compensated by the federal government. Sears thought the proposal would be particularly popular in the border states, where slave labor was no longer productive and where residents could see that their northern neighbors were "rapidly advancing upon them in wealth and strength." If the Lower South chose to go its own way, then so be it. "I do not fear a dissolution of the Union," he told John Quincy. Within five years, any states that seceded would be begging for readmission: "They cannot exist without us,—yet being with us, and of little comparative value in the statistics of power, and the elements of greatness,—they govern us at their own caprice."[26]

Although Charles Francis did not believe that planters possessed "a right of property in slaves," he had no objection to their being compensated, and he welcomed Sears's contribution. This was the kind of talk Adams liked—bold, forthright, brimming over with regional chauvinism. He was especially gratified to hear it from one of the more prominent members of Boston's elite. Sears's proposal, he told *Whig* readers, showed that not all of Nathan Appleton's friends were afraid to tackle the slavery question. He soon realized, however, that Sears spoke largely for himself and had few elite supporters. With the exception of Henry Lee, who published a thirteen-part series in Buckingham's *Courier* elaborating on the plan, no other Brahmin stepped forward to back Sears's initiative. Moreover, as Lee later observed, no Whig editor in Boston apart from Buckingham and Adams would print his articles.[27]

By late 1847, Adams felt it only a matter of time before Conscience Whigs struck out on their own. The shabby treatment they had received at the recent state convention, coupled with growing indications that the cotton faction supported Zachary Taylor's presidential bid, had all but severed their already slender ties to Whiggery. "I am now convinced that we have got to break," he wrote to John Gorham Palfrey that December. The only question was where to go. The Democrats, he noted, had no more to offer than the Whigs: "Principle is a secondary consideration with both." The Liberty Party, on the other hand, now looked much better. As late as August, Adams had informed antislavery editor Gamaliel Bailey that he did not believe he could ever work together with leading political abolitionists. But with nowhere else to turn, earlier misunderstandings no longer seemed so significant, and prospects for an antislavery coalition appeared extremely promising.[28]

Meanwhile, state Whig leaders had decided that they could do without the conscience faction. "I cannot but hope that we may soon drive them from the Whig party," Lawrence wrote in a February 1848 letter to Winthrop. "We gain nothing by allowing any portion of those people to attend our primary or other public political meetings." He did not have to wait long to see his wish realized. Taylor's nomination that June ended any hope of reconciliation. To Adams, the selection represented an unexampled "piece of highhanded villainy," made all the more "mortifying" by the part Lawrence and other elite Bostonians played in it. He could not believe he was the only Bay Stater who felt that way. "The introduction of the Manufacturing influence has materially affected the principles of the State," he told the Ohio congressman Joshua Giddings, "but there is yet a profound attachment to truth and right, a love of morality as well in politics as in all other departments of human action which will resist if only the means be presented by which to do it." Nor did he have any doubt as to where his duty lay at this critical moment. "It has been the fate of three generations of our race to stand as the guardians of Liberty in this commonwealth against the corrupting principles of a moneyed combination," he confided to his diary that fall. And so long as he drew breath, the state could count on yet another Adams to "denounce every bargain that shall trade away the honor of his country."[29]

By the time Charles Francis penned these lines, Conscience Whigs had joined Libertyites and dissident Democrats to form the Free Soil Party. Willing to forget past differences, Adams put aside his reservations about

Democratic integrity and urged others to do so as well. At the party convention in August, delegates acknowledged his contributions and paid tribute to his recently deceased father by nominating Charles Francis for vice-president. Although the Free Soilers failed to carry Massachusetts in November, they did place second and there was every reason to hope they would do better in the future. Adams certainly had no intention of turning back. Whatever obstacles lay ahead, he told Palfrey, "our duty remains unchanged. The only pure moral influences which regulate the passions of man in the United States come from the land of the Puritans." That some prominent Bay Staters "have yielded to the seductions of the harlot, must be only an additional incentive" to carry on the struggle. Adams himself needed no added incentive. During the course of 1848, he had become a new man. "Altogether the most important year of my life," he wrote in his diary that December. "In it my relations have changed to every thing around me. The world looks like a wholly different thing." With his father's death, he became "[t]he sole representative of a family which in the preceding two generations has gathered to itself extraordinary honor," and he had shown he could uphold that tradition in the face of attacks from some of the state's most powerful men.[30]

In doing so, he set an important example for others. No one prior to Whiggery's demise, the Free Soil editor William S. Robinson later wrote of Adams, proved "more fearless or able than he on the antislavery side"; nobody "had less regard for the social and political environments of Boston and Massachusetts Whiggism." These observations were not entirely accurate. As his diary makes clear, Adams felt considerable trepidation throughout. He knew that "[a] party which commands so much money and which has so much fancied interest at stake was not going to abandon every thing without a struggle." But he never let his fears and doubts show. And because he represented an alternative elite tradition established by his father and grandfather, each of whom had his differences with Brahmin society, he found it easier than most to feign disregard for what Robinson called the "political environment of Boston."[31]

What made all this so significant was the deferential nature of social relations within elite society. Members of the subelite who hoped to advance socially or economically were well advised to comply with the wishes of their betters. In one particularly telling incident, Nathan Appleton informed Channing's Federal Street assistant, Ezra S. Gannett, that he could not agree with the sentiments expressed in a recent sermon questioning mercantile ethics. Nothing more needed to be said. Gannett not only acknowledged his error the following Sunday, but five years later wrote to Appleton thanking him for the chastisement. "Your letter & other sources of information," he said, "convinced me that my language was too strong & general, and might be liable to the comments you made upon it." Although Gannett's indiscretion occurred in 1828, elite expectations of subelite deference did not diminish over the years, nor did they alter the imperious tone in which they communicated their displeasure to those who stepped out of line.[32]

But the response they received did change. Years later, when Appleton wrote to John Gorham Palfrey about a critical article in the *Whig*, the former Harvard theology professor was anything but contrite. Complaining of the industrialist's "overbearing language," he told Appleton: "It is best that we should understand one another. I am not to be overborne. Doubtless, in station and influence you have greatly the advantage of me. But I, as much as yourself, am a freeman of Massachusetts, in the enjoyment as yet of political privileges, inherited from ancestors who did their full part in winning them, and which, please God, I will do my best to secure for their posterity and mine." For someone of Palfrey's precarious social standing to issue such a reply took real courage, and Adams's example helped infuse that courage in those around him. It was no small contribution to the Conscience Whig–Free Soil insurgency of the 1840s.[33]

"IT IS AMUSING to see what antics these gentlemen of the cloth exhibit when they assume the political costume." Thus did Harrison Gray Otis assure Appleton that Palfrey need not be taken seriously. The aging Federalist had fixed ideas about the clergy's role in society. He fully agreed with Rufus Choate's observation that the minister should focus solely on religious matters: "for that exactly we prize, and for that exactly we pay him." Clergymen who stepped outside their assigned "sphere" invited public ridicule and should be treated accordingly. Otis never lived to observe Theodore Parker in full flight. Had he done so, he would not have been amused. Once aroused, Parker flayed the elite with an uncompromising savagery. In numerous addresses and sermons throughout the 1850s, he distinguished between the churches of Christianity and the churches of commerce, noting how the latter's "lower law" ministers sacrificed principle to prestige in service to "our first men"—a ruling class that placed financial gain before everything and dominated society through the manipulation of public law and public opinion. To such people, "[m]oney supplies defects of character, defects of culture. It is deemed better than education, talent, genius, and character, all put together." How one acquired it mattered little. "You may be a senator from Massachusetts," he said in obvious reference to Daniel Webster, "and you may take the 'trust fund,' offered you by the manufacturers of cotton, and be bound as their 'retained attorney,' by your 'retaining fee,' and you are still the 'Honourable Senator from Massachusetts,' not hurt one jot in the eyes of the controlling classes." And so he continued, barely pausing for breath, never missing a beat, smashing one elite icon after another.[34]

The two muskets mounted above his fireplace said much about the man. One had belonged to his grandfather, Captain John Parker, who commanded patriot militia at the Battle of Lexington; the other was the first weapon taken from British forces in the Revolution. His grandfather's exploits on April 19, 1775, and the Revolution generally were never far from Parker's thoughts. As he sat down to write, he often looked at the two muskets, drawing inspiration from what they represented. Though he hated war, it was not in Parker's nature to turn the other cheek, for he did not share the pacifist convictions of his many Garrisonian friends. His maxim was that of the Puritan fathers: "Trust in God, but keep your *powder* dry." Springfield editor Samuel Bowles exaggerated when he said that Parker resembled Luther and Calvin—"had he lived earlier he would have burned his enemies . . . and gloated over it." But such overstatements can be pardoned. Parker gloried in the fact that, like himself, most Bay Staters could trace their lineage to the Covenanters of the English Revolution. That their forebears had resisted the impositions of a series of British monarchs in their struggle for political and religious liberty should be, he believed, a matter of pride to all New Englanders.[35]

Reviewing these aspects of Parker's character, it is easy to forget that he was first and foremost a man of God. But this is where any serious examination of his life must begin, for Parker loved being a minister; he could conceive of no higher calling. Spiritual concerns shaped his highest aims and provided his greatest disappointments. On one hand, he never stopped hoping that of the four great social forces—market, state, church, and press—religion might someday reclaim its place as the first among them. At the same time, he recognized that most contemporary clergymen followed rather than formed public opinion. Ministers, he observed in an 1843 sermon, faced two dangers. One was an overweening confidence that resulted in the teaching of "mere whimsies." The other was a readiness to accept the world as it is, to affirm without comment or reflection the beliefs of one's congregation. Such a minister typically viewed sectarian doctrine and local prejudice as truth and most often became "a Prophet of lies, a blind leader of blind men, fit only to dangle about the tables of rich men."[36]

There was never any likelihood that Parker's ministry would end on this sorry note. From the very beginning, he questioned popular beliefs, forcing parishioners and ministerial colleagues alike to reconsider what religion meant to them. The most significant such challenge occurred in May

1841, when he preached his "Discourse of the Transient and Permanent in Christianity" at the ordination ceremony of Charles C. Shackford. Parker's main argument in this controversial address rested on what he described as the distinction between religion and theology. The primary elements of religion, he contended, were piety and goodness, the love of God and the love of humankind. This had been so since the beginnings of Christianity and would remain so until the end of time. Theology, on the other hand, had a much more evanescent character. It was not religion per se, but the mere "form religion takes." That being the case, he explained, it "can never be the same in any two centuries or two men; for since the sum of religious doctrines is both the result and the measure of a man's total growth in wisdom, virtue, and piety, and since men will always differ in these respects, so religious *doctrines* and *forms* will always differ, will always be transient, as Christianity goes forth and scatters the seed she bears in her hand."[37]

The discourse contained the seeds of Parker's own theology. As his religious thought matured, three interrelated doctrines emerged as core elements. One was the infinite perfection of God. Parker had no time for ministers who spoke about the "cruel character of God, rejoicing in his hell and its legion of devils"; such professions were the "fundamental vice" of popular theology. The notion that God was a "perfect Creator" formed the "cornerstone" of his religious teaching, and he believed "the relative perfection of all that He creates" was an unavoidable corollary. It followed that, as the highest of those creations, humanity possessed the powers necessary to accomplish all the ends God had intended. "In the primal instincts and automatic desires of man," Parker observed, "I have found a prophecy that what he wants is possible, and shall one day be actual." The final element in Parker's theology was his concept of natural religion: the development and use of one's emotional, intellectual, and practical powers to achieve one's natural aims. No belief system that ignored the progressive evolution of these faculties could be a true faith. That all the great religions to date did so was their main shortcoming. They claimed "to have come miraculously from God, not normally from man; and, spite of the excellence which they contain, and the vast service the humblest of them has done, yet each must ere long prove a hindrance to human welfare, for it claims to be a finality, and makes the whole of human nature wait upon an accident of human history—and that accident the whim of some single man."[38]

In light of the foregoing, it is easy to see why Parker's relations with ministerial colleagues deteriorated so rapidly during the 1840s. Although his followers found these doctrines liberating, there was a certain boundlessness to Parker's thought that could be truly terrifying to people of more conservative outlook and limited vision. This group included most of Boston's

Unitarian clergy. Worse, at least from the perspective of those with whom he disagreed, Parker could be a very intimidating presence. As a child, he could memorize poems of up to a thousand lines after a single reading; as a young schoolteacher, he often spent ten to twelve hours studying after classes—an exhausting regimen that he continued throughout much of his life. He thus brought formidable intellectual powers to bear on any question. And everyone—his adversaries particularly—recognized Parker's genius. In a typical comment, Robert Winthrop remarked that he "is as mischievous as he is brilliant."[39]

To this it should be added that Parker did not believe in false modesty. His aim as a minister, he told a friend, was "to lay the foundation of my religious teachings so deep that nothing could move or shake it." And he never doubted the correctness of his course. As he stated in a letter to Ezra S. Gannett, "when the grass grows over my level grave, when my name has perished from amongst men, the hearts of men shall flame with the truths that I have tried to teach." If Boston Unitarians did not care to go along, so much the worse for them. He did not really need them anyway. "There are few of the clergy I respect or esteem," he observed in an 1846 letter to Charles Sumner. "Few of them are intellectually competent to their task, fewer still morally capable of doing any good thing for mankind. Among the more respectable portion of society, religion—using that word in its widest and best sense—is not the leading influence."[40]

By the time he wrote these words, Parker had few clerical friends left in Boston. Many of his colleagues had begun avoiding him five years earlier, shortly after he delivered his "Discourse of the Transient and Permanent in Christianity." Some passed him by on the street in silence; others got up and took another seat when he sat down next to them at public gatherings. On several occasions, Parker sought reconciliation, urging clerical leaders to remember the difference between religion and theology—"that while there is only one religion, there may be a great many and quite diverse theologies, each imperfect, yet each helping towards the truth, and that a man may have the Christian religion in his heart and live it, too, who has neither your theology nor mine." It was to no avail. Though other members of the Boston Unitarian Association also believed theological debate served a useful purpose, the denomination's "controlling men" felt otherwise and had apparently decided: "This young man must be silenced!" When Parker refused to submit, they severed all contact and did what they could to obstruct his work. The Lexington dissident was doubtless thinking of his own relations with the Boston clergy when he later wrote to Samuel J. May: "If there is not an eternal Hell it will not be for lack of ministers to pray that you might be put in it."[41]

Efforts to restrict Parker's influence proceeded on two tracks. By mid-decade, he found that he could no longer publish in religious journals; most newspapers were also closed to him. For someone who had always expected "to do more through the *Press* than *Pulpit*," this was a major setback. Parker also discovered that few of his colleagues would exchange pulpits with him; although he still had friends in the ministry, the climate of opinion in leading Unitarian circles was such that he hesitated to call on them for assistance. "If you had proposed an exchange," he wrote to one correspondent, "I should have declined it, on the ground that it would only bring you into trouble or suspicion, possibly with your parish; certainly with your professional acquaintances." This ostracism not only limited the audience for Parker's teachings, but forced him to devote most of his energies to preparing original weekly sermons for his own congregation, thus leaving little time for theological study.[42]

As much as Parker loved and respected his West Roxbury parishioners, he required a larger stage on which to perform. He had not labored to become New England's most learned minister to see his influence confined to a small country parish. In early 1845, a number of friends in Boston's reform community came to his rescue. They believed that the city needed to hear what Parker had to say, and at their invitation he began preaching at the Melodeon that February; the following January he was installed there as pastor of the Twenty-eighth Congregational Society, a free church whose heterogeneous membership included independent-minded men and women from all walks of life, who were not afraid to court elite disapproval by supporting the well-known dissident. With as many as seven thousand people on its rolls, about five hundred of whom attended services regularly, the Twenty-eighth Congregational Society was the city's largest congregation. In 1848, Parker added to his audience by hitting the lecture circuit. Over the next decade or so, he spoke to between sixty thousand and a hundred thousand people annually on a wide range of topics.[43]

Such impressive numbers only begin to describe Parker's influence. From both platform and pulpit, his performances made a lasting impression on those who heard him. Decades after Parker's death, Thomas Wentworth Higginson could still vividly recall listening to him preach—"the great, free, eager congregation; the strong, serious, commanding presence of the preacher; his reverent and earnest prayer; his comprehensive hour-long sermon full of sense, knowledge, feeling, courage, he being not afraid even of his own learning, absolutely holding his audience in the hollow of his hand." Even those who found his views offensive could not help but be impressed. In what is one of the better extant descriptions we have of Parker in action, an otherwise critical reporter from the *Boston Daily Bee* marveled at the "power he seems to exert over the minds and feelings of those who listen to him notwithstanding the prejudices with which they may have entered his doors." What made Parker so compelling a speaker, this observer noted, was his ability to present everyday truths "in their most striking and simplest lights"; "he gives a very uncommon cast to thoughts and ideas really the most common among men."[44]

These were shrewd and insightful observations. As much a sociologist as a theologian, Parker had a real talent for exposing the underside of contemporary social relations. Once he had finished such a probe, his audience could begin to see patterns of influence and power that they had never before noticed. A good example can be seen in his essay on the mercantile classes, a broad social grouping in which he included manufacturers as well as merchants. In modern U.S. society, he observed, merchants occupied much the same place that warriors and later the nobility had in earlier historical epochs, and still did in most parts of Europe. Where these civilizations tended to prize martial prowess above all else, Americans placed a similar valuation on material accumulation. And just as military chieftains and landed aristocrats ruled these nations, merchants dominated the state in America: "Our politics are chiefly mercantile, politics in which money is preferred, and man postponed. When the two come into collision, the man goes to the wall and the street is left clear for the dollars." This hegemony, he added, extended to church and press. Ministers "are unconsciously bought up, their speech paid for, or their silence. As a class," he asked, "did they ever denounce a public sin?" It was a provocative commentary intended as much to arouse as to inform. Listening to it, one can certainly understand why Nathan Appleton's wife told a houseguest who inquired about attending services at the Melodeon: "Mr. Hilliard, we cannot accompany you; we do not go to hear Mr. Theodore Parker in Boston."[45]

Yet like Channing before him, Parker was no foe of economic development. As someone who claimed familiarity with the value of money, he felt perfectly comfortable advising a young relative in training for a mercantile career to learn bookkeeping, make a careful study of market conditions, and "[b]e fair and honest while you are fore casting and shrewd." More important were the social consequences of commercial and industrial expansion. Inclined to view all facets of human activity in developmental terms, Parker believed that moral and material progress advanced hand in hand. Whereas the technological backwardness of the South and various European states prompted scornful comment from Parker, he had nothing but praise for New England's industrial growth and felt that the Boston Associates had earned their millions. Despite certain excesses, he wrote, regional prosperity was "laying the foundation for a spiritual civilization in some future age, more grand, I think, than mankind has hitherto rejoiced in." Ever the optimist, Parker further believed that the moral character of trade was constantly improving. This was the case even in Boston, he remarked, offering as evidence the observation that one no longer heard it said that "if a Yankee was to sell salt water at high tide, he would yet cheat in the bargain."[46]

As much as he appreciated the benefits of economic development, Parker recognized that some had been left behind. One of his major aims upon moving to Boston in the mid-1840s was to assist the struggling members of what he called "the perishing class." Despite his intentions, Parker never gave labor-related social problems the time he would have liked. A major reason was his increased involvement in antislavery activities after 1845. There was never any question as to where Parker stood on slavery. When Boston city officials initially barred the use of Faneuil Hall for the 1837 Lovejoy meeting, he lashed out at the servility of "those vile Boobies." But with the exception of his 1841 "A Sermon of Slavery" in which he seemed most concerned about people who had become bond servants of avarice and intemperance, Parker had little to say about human bondage before Texas annexation and the Mexican War focused attention on the issue at mid-decade. Swept up in the ensuing furor, he began thinking much more seriously about slavery. As he did so, he observed how others reacted to these events, writing to Samuel J. May that he was "amazed at the way men and Politicians look at the matter—amazed at their silence." In 1845, when the American Unitarian Association issued an antislavery protest, nearly every prominent minister of the denomination refused to sign. This Parker also noticed, and it made him all the more conscious of his own silence.[47]

During the next decade and a half, Parker fully atoned for his earlier in-activity. By the time of his death in 1860, he was widely recognized as one of the nation's most outspoken critics of the South's peculiar institution. From the outset, he made elite treachery a major theme of the many antislavery sermons and addresses he delivered during the period. To the rhetorical question as to why northerners didn't stop Texas annexation, he answered: "They knew they could make money by it." As regional manufacturers looked south, they could see only cotton and could "speak audibly but two words—Tariff, Tariff, Dividends, Dividends. The talent of the North is blinded, deafened, gagged with its own cotton." Elite support for Zachary Taylor's presidential bid could be similarly explained. The general, Parker wrote to Horace Mann, "must have promised (in private) his aid in restoring the tariff of '42. I know of nothing else that could have so excited their enthusiasm." Their social standing rested upon money, and as members of a party that considered property more important than people, they did not care how they obtained it. By the 1850s, Parker was telling audiences that America was ruled by "two very different classes of men;—by mercantile men, who covet money, actual or expectant capitalists; and by political men, who want power, actual or expectant office-holders." Each looked out for the interests of the other, ever willing to make whatever sacrifice of principle necessary to achieve its aims.[48]

"The great men of Boston," William Robinson later wrote, "find nobody to look up to them, and plenty of leisure for introspection and self-worship. All this is Parker's work more than any other man's." However arguable, the observation contains a good deal of truth. Parker did as much as anyone to shatter the moral authority of Boston's ruling elite. After listening to him, no one ever viewed Brahmin pretensions in quite the same way again. Not surprisingly, radicals of all sorts recognized a kindred spirit in the Lexington dissident. Despite doctrinal differences, the editor of Boston's free-thought newspaper warmly welcomed him to the city because "we have sympathy for the *Man,* knowing as we do that he is persecuted by a set of bigots who posses not a tithe part of his ability or moral worth." And where Brook Farm Associationists praised Parker's analyses of social problems, labor radicals applauded his humanity. "The pulpit from which you learn what the Gospel teaches," said a *Voice of Industry* correspondent in an open letter to Abbott Lawrence, "is closed to Theodore Parker, because he happens to believe that the Gospel teaches that the only love to God, is that which shows itself in a love for man whether black or white; and a stern love of truth and justice which will lead us to love our neighbor as ourselves." It was an accurate summation of Parker's beliefs that explains much about his appeal to working people in general. "God speed you Brother," wrote one "poor obscure mechanic," who appreciated Parker's "liberalizing" work. Another told Parker that elite condemnation only added to his honor, while providing assurance that "[t]he poor love you as they love no other man." And this write believed he had as much authority as anyone to make such a statement: "I am poor and I love you."[49]

Thus it happened that someone qualified to become one of elite society's brightest ornaments chose instead to become its harshest critic. But Parker was not alone. Others, less brilliant and considerably more conservative, followed a similar course during the period. One of them was Horace Mann, the first secretary of the Massachusetts State Board of Education.

ON A SUMMER DAY in 1847, the secretary of the Massachusetts State Board of Education entered the law office of Richard Henry Dana, Jr. Earlier in the decade, Dana had published *Two Years before the Mast,* a graphic account of his experiences on a voyage around Cape Horn to California that Mann believed might be a suitable addition to a series of volumes being planned by the board. He felt, however, that the work needed revision, and he was there to discuss the matter with its author. As Mann explained, "merit & value in a book consisted in its moral teachings, & the information it conveyed as to matters of fact." On both scores, he told Dana, *Two Years* fell short of his standards. At first, Dana tried to humor the unwelcome intruder by suggesting that unity and coherence were also considerations when assessing a written work. It was to no avail. Totally oblivious to Dana's growing irritation, Mann pressed on, unwittingly piling one insult upon another. "If some enemy had employed him to come & try my patience to the utmost," the attorney later confided to his journal, "he could not have executed his task better." Adopting another tack, Dana expressed some particularly "barbarous sentiments on the subject of education" in an effort to unnerve this "school master gone crasy." This approach had equally little effect. The book, Mann persisted, needed more facts and additional moral lessons.[50]

It was an illuminating exchange that revealed as much about Mann as the two muskets resting above his fireplace said of Parker. The obtuse didacticism that so infuriated Dana was a product of the moral intensity Mann brought to his work. Always quick to distinguish between right and wrong, the educational reformer combined an uncompromising sense of duty with a black-and-white view of human affairs that allowed for little intermediate shading. When as president of Antioch College he proposed denying degrees to students of "immoral character," Samuel Gridley Howe had to remind him that there was no easy way of determining whether "John is a sheep and Harry a goat, though one may be decidedly sheepish, the other decidedly goatish." This unrelenting earnestness stamped nearly all of Mann's activities. In his daily life, he had little time for small talk and none whatsoever for recreational reading, believing as he did that "*light reading makes light minds.*" And while capable of humor, he had limited appreciation of life's more comical moments, particularly when some moral issue was at stake. That he could find nothing amusing about a William Makepeace Thackeray lecture in which the British satirist "spoke of the intemperate habits of the wits of Queen Anne's time as if he would have like to have drunk with them" was wholly in character.[51]

To his moralism, Mann added a bleak view of human nature that fit uncomfortably with his belief in social progress. According to Theodore Parker, this side of Mann's thought resulted from early exposure to an especially harsh brand of religious orthodoxy. "Bred in the worst form of Calvinism," the Unitarian maverick observed, "he never quite wiped off the dreadful smooch it makes on the character—nay, he did not extract the dark colors it *bites in* to the spiritual nature of the unlucky child. Hence his low estimate of men, hence his unforgiving disposition." Although Parker's own hatred of orthodoxy made him a less than objective commentator on such matters, there is something to be said for his explanation. Despite Mann's rejection of Calvinism and lifelong doubts about religion in general, his sermonic mode of expression unmistakably marked him as a son of Puritan New England.[52]

Although Mann's youthful experiences influenced his later development, it was by no means fated that he would become the person he did. As a child growing up on a small farm in Franklin, Massachusetts, he decided early on that he wanted more from life. "I believe in the rugged nursing of Toil," Mann once said of these years, "but she nursed me too much." A degree from Brown University, followed by further study at Judge Tapping Reeve's famous law school in Litchfield, Connecticut, provided a way out. By 1827, he had a growing legal practice in Dedham and, with his brother Stanley, owned a controlling interest in two small textile companies. That same year he secured a seat in the Massachusetts House of Representatives, where he soon emerged as a leading proponent of railroad construction and other programs designed to promote industrialization. However preoccupied he may have been with material gain and political advancement, Mann also made time for various reform activities. As Jonathan Messerli has written, "his system of values would not let him divorce self-interest from social responsibility." During this period, he fulfilled that duty by lecturing temperance audiences on the evils of drink and by championing improved treatment for the insane.[53]

By the early 1830s, Mann was one of the rising stars of Massachusetts politics. Capable, prosperous, strongly committed to economic development, and with his reform impulses lodged in thoroughly respectable channels, the Dedham legislator seemed destined for a leadership role in the state's emergent Whig Party. Two events altered his course. The first—and most traumatic—was the loss of his wife Charlotte, who died in August 1832, less than two years after they had been married. Mann never fully recovered from the blow. Though he later married again, memories of Charlotte weighed heavily on him for the remainder of his life. His immediate reaction to her death was to withdraw from politics and cut off contact with nearly all friends and acquaintances. At the same time, he began to reorder his priorities. His quest for success and distinction, he later confided to his journal, had been entirely for her sake. As his ambitions revived, concerns about human betterment increasingly overshadowed his earlier focus on more commonplace forms of achievement.[54]

These years also witnessed the moral and financial demise of his brother Stanley. When a textile slump in the early 1830s reduced returns from their two mills, the brothers found themselves with a bulging packet of unpaid loans. Unwilling to face the consequences, Stanley deserted his family and relocated in Louisville, Kentucky, where his efforts to start anew proved even more disastrous. Destitute and unable to secure assistance from his brother, who refused to help him, Stanley died not long afterward, leaving Horace solely responsible for the repayment of their joint debts. Mann worried less about the money than what Stanley's conduct said about the age in which he lived. That someone from a background so identical to his own could behave so wretchedly added to his concerns about the moral shortcomings of antebellum society and sharpened his disillusionment with conventional definitions of success.[55]

As Mann tried to sort out his life amid these personal calamities, it appeared for a while that he might resume his former course. At the urging of Elizabeth Peabody, whose sister he later married, Mann reentered politics, in 1834 winning election to the state senate. His selection as senate president for the 1836 and 1837 sessions showed that Whig leaders continued to hold him in high regard. Still a young man, he could reasonably expect even greater honors in the future. But appearances were deceiving. Despite his promising political prospects, Mann was not happy. Where he had changed, those around him had not. His enthusiasm for economic development no longer matched that of party colleagues, who could think of little else, and his preoccupation with social betterment left him increasingly isolated, wondering what would become of a civilization whose leaders seemed incapable of recognizing their duties to society. Asked to accept the secretaryship of the newly formed Massachusetts State Board of Education, Mann weighed the offer carefully. He knew that taking the position would mean loss of power and prestige, not to mention giving up a lucrative law practice. Yet, he reasoned, "The interests of a client are small, compared with the interests of the next generation." And he could not resist this chance to "labor for something more enduring than myself."[56]

If he did not know it already, Mann quickly learned that not everyone shared his appreciation of the secretaryship's potential. What he considered a unique opportunity for personal fulfillment, his professional acquaintances viewed as an incomprehensible rejection of fame and fortune. "All men but one, so far as I know," he later told Theodore Parker, "thought me a fool, and most of them said so." They could not understand why anyone would take a substantial salary cut to accept an obscure position that led nowhere. Mann could not have been entirely surprised by this response. Over the past several years, he had seen all too much of the self-aggrandizing behavior that prompted such comments. These were hardly the kind of people from whom he sought approval, and their derision only strengthened his conviction that he had made the right decision. "If the Lord will prosper me for ten years," he vowed, "I will show them what way the balance of honor lies."[57]

Carrying out that pledge would take some doing. As Mann began his formal duties as secretary, he found many country elites as indifferent to public education as their metropolitan counterparts. Although everyone said they wanted better schools, few gave much thought to the issue; even fewer were willing to expend the time and money needed to improve existing facilities. On his annual circuits of the commonwealth, Mann encountered one disappointment after another in his efforts to promote interest in the cause. "To make an impression on Berkshire in regard to the schools," he said of one trip to northwestern Massachusetts, "is like attempting to batter down Gibraltar with one's fist." Things were no better out on Martha's Vineyard, where "[a]fter a miserable day, spent miserably at a miserable tavern, in the miserable town of Edgartown, & a miserable failure in attempting to get up a convention," he departed "in miserable humor, for this."[58]

Although Mann criticized people of all classes for their apathy, his wrath most often centered on the wealthy. With their riches, they had the most to give; they also had the most to lose if social order broke down under the weight of an uneducated citizenry. Of all people, he declared, they should understand "that whatever ills they feel or fear, are but the just retributions of a righteous heaven for neglected childhood." Mann believed that the main reason so many elites neglected their educational duties as social stewards was their reliance on private schools. In sending their offspring to such institutions, he contended, these parents diverted funds from public education and deprived common schools of students capable of establishing "an abstract standard of excellence" that children of the "lower classes" lacked. Worse, he added, private schools perverted "the social feelings of children,—to envy on the one side, to an assumption of superiority on the other." Though strongly argued, Mann's case was in the end unpersuasive. Most elite parents wanted their children educated with others of their class and refused to consider what Mann called "the American side of this question."[59]

One should not conclude from the foregoing that Mann's relations with elite Bay Staters were unreservedly hostile. That was hardly the case. Some of his staunchest supporters possessed solid Brahmin credentials, and he knew that whatever success he achieved would owe much to their continued backing. Even here, though, tensions sometimes emerged. A good example was Edmund Dwight, who had worked with Mann in the legislature to promote railroad development and as a member of the Board of Education gave generously of his time and money. Mann considered Dwight an outstanding individual, "free from the frivolity and emptiness" that constituted "the odious badge of so many of his class." But his friend and patron did have one defect: "A disposition to ridicule persons less educated, or less acquainted with the ways of the world," which to Mann was a "sure sign of *low breeding*." That he found such behavior offensive sheds light on Mann's conflicted notions of class. For all his own elitism, the Franklin native never entirely forgot his yeoman background. During an 1837 visit to Northampton, he met a representative of the local upper class who lamented "that the good old days of the aristocracy have gone by, when no upstart could ever obtain ingress into their ranks," and who thought "that one portion of mankind is to be refined and cultivated, the other to suffer, toil, and live and die in vulgarity." Despite this grandee's assurance that he intended no disrespect, Mann knew better, for "he insulted me and all my relatives twice most outrageously. That is their way." Mann doubtless had this conversation in mind when two weeks later he confided to his journal: "Many of our educated men need educating more than the ignorant. When shall we bring them up to the level of humanity?"[60]

For our purposes, the most noteworthy feature of Mann's later years as secretary was his effort to redefine the meaning of stewardship by substituting state paternalism for elite benevolence. Several factors influenced Mann's evolving views on the subject. One was a long-standing disposition that he shared with other antebellum Whigs to use government as an instrument of moral oversight. Every youth required schooling, he noted in his journal shortly after assuming the secretaryship: "If not educated by its own father, the state should appoint a father to it." Mann felt just as strongly a decade later, when in his *Eleventh Report* he stated that parents who neglected their children's education gave up their "parental rights." A second factor was Mann's declining faith in elite willingness to act as responsible stewards. However much he appreciated the support received from Edmund Dwight and other Brahmins, Mann felt that the wealthy classes could be doing much more. If nothing else, their preference for private schools would always be a source of resentment.[61]

A final factor influencing Mann was his changing perceptions of the perils facing the republic. By the mid-1840s, a wary skepticism had combined with recent experiences to raise disturbing questions in Mann's mind about the nation's future. A critical turning point was his 1843 European trip, during which he witnessed the abuse and exploitation of working people, the vast disparities among social classes, and what he considered a criminal misapplication of wealth. Although Mann's observations were hardly unique, the conclusions he drew differed from those of the typical tourist. While most visitors viewed Europe's social ills as evidence of American exceptionalism—a belief that national virtue made the United States immune to Old World problems—Mann saw a grim harbinger of what could yet happen on this side of the ocean.[62]

The information Mann collected in Europe provided the basis for his *Seventh Report*, which is best remembered for the pedagogical innovations he recommended and the hard feelings those proposals engendered among Boston schoolmasters. But reforming teaching practices in Bay State schools was only one of his aims in the document. As he later told James Stone, he also sought to caution working people about falling into a "degradation" similar to that of their European counterparts and to urge the wealthy classes to meet their social duties. Like exponents of American exceptionalism, Mann too believed that the societies created by the Pilgrim fathers and other founding groups represented an incalculable advance for humankind. He noted, however, that the nation had developed under uniquely propitious circumstances, and he worried that Americans might be squandering their inheritance. Have they, he asked, done all they could to abolish vice and poverty by ensuring that children of all classes received the training needed to make them virtuous and productive citizens? "Have the more fortunate classes amongst us,—the men of greater wealth, of superior knowledge, of more commanding influence,—have they periodically arrested their own upward march of improvement, and sounded the trumpet, and sent back guides and succors *to bring up the rear of society*?"[63]

Mann feared they had not and found it hard to believe they ever would. In an effort to deal with the troubling implications of these concerns, he attempted to devise an intellectual rationale for state paternalism. The results of his reflections were best stated in his *Tenth Report*, where he examined "the false notions which men entertain *respecting the nature of their rights to property*." In most cases, he argued, what people considered property "was prepared at the creation, and was laid up of old in the storehouses of nature." Because these vast natural riches did not exist for the benefit of any single individual or generation, but for all subsequent generations, there were limits to the "absolutism of ownership, which is so often claimed by the possessors of wealth." Property holders were in effect "trustees," with an obligation to serve as guardians to those who would follow them. As citizens, they collectively formed "one great Commonwealth" that was "*parental* in her government" and whose property was "pledged for the education of all its youth, up to such a point as will save them from poverty and vice, and prepare them for the adequate performance of their social and civil duties."[64]

According to the *Tenth Report*, Massachusetts already had such a government. To a degree, this was true. Compared with other states, the commonwealth had fewer reservations about using its powers and resources for purposes of social reform. Yet, as Mann knew from the private subsidies needed to advance his own work, much still depended on elite benevolence. And he continued to harbor doubts about the public spiritedness of the wealthy classes. "With all their pretended love for education, & their regard for me," he said of them in an 1848 letter to his wife, "there are not a half dozen men in Massachusetts, who would willingly and heartily give me a hundred dollars to keep me from the almshouse." But that did not mean one should give up the struggle, he added, "for this very fact shows how much need there is of vigorously prosecuting the only work which can make men better." In his final report, which he prepared that same year, Mann forcefully reminded Bay Staters of what was at stake. Drawing on his European experience, he warned that the commonwealth was "verging towards those extremes of opulence and penury, each of which unhumanizes the human mind." With every passing year, certain fortunes expanded as new pockets of destitution appeared elsewhere. "If this be so," he asked, "are we not in danger of naturalizing and domesticating among ourselves those hideous evils which are always engendered between Capital and Labor, when all the capital is in the hands of one class, and all the labor is thrown upon another?" Mann certainly thought the threat real. He further believed that these trends could only be reversed through education, "the great equalizer of the conditions of men—the balance-wheel of the social machinery."[65]

This is not the place to examine the limitations of Mann's social vision. It is enough to note that education alone could never fulfill all the expectations he had of it. The main object of the foregoing was to show that by 1848, when he replaced the recently deceased John Quincy Adams in Congress, Mann had serious reservations about the conduct of Bay State elites. Those reservations would soon deepen. Though not yet a Free Soiler, Mann stood apart from those elite Bostonians who dominated Bay State Whiggery, and the more observant knew it. "I have no feeling but kindness toward the nominee," Robert Winthrop said of his new colleague, "but all this rampant & transcendental philanthropy is anything but congenial to me." Winthrop had good reason to feel uneasy. Mann's strong suit was morality, not politics. Should the party adopt positions that conflicted with his principles, he could be expected to go his own way. And as the Thirty-first Congress confronted those slavery-related issues that formed the Compromise of

1850, it was not long before Mann was declaring his aversion to "men who make money their god" in letters and addresses relating how "the Slave Power of the South & the Money Power of the North have struck hands."[66]

Mann's brief congressional career ended in 1852, and his subsequent acceptance of the presidency of Antioch College concluded his active involvement in state politics. Although they did not leave the commonwealth, most subelites followed a similar course. By the early 1850s, they had completed their most significant work. With a few exceptions—Charles Sumner being the most notable—they either withdrew or were pushed to the margins of public life. As a group, they never wielded the kind of power so long exercised by their elite adversaries. But this is not altogether surprising, for they never constituted a coherent social class. What gave dissident subelites some semblance of cohesiveness was a shared conviction that the Boston Associates no longer possessed the moral authority that regional tradition demanded of a ruling class. More important, they had the courage and talent needed to articulate those convictions in ways their fellow Bay Staters found compelling. In so doing, they dynamited a fundamental prop of elite hegemony, thereby preparing the way for the establishment of a new political order in Massachusetts. How that order came into being is the subject of the final two chapters.

CHAPTER SIX

Whig Factionalism and the Coalition

O N SEPTEMBER 17, 1850, President Millard Fillmore signed a bill abolishing the slave trade in the District of Columbia. In the preceding ten days, he had approved other measures that admitted California as a free state, adjusted a border dispute between New Mexico and Texas, organized New Mexico and Utah as territories with no restrictions on slavery, and strengthened the fugitive slave law. Together, these bills formed the Compromise of 1850. To Fillmore, the legislation represented "a final settlement" to a sectional crisis that began four years earlier when the Pennsylvania congressman David Wilmot sought to amend an appropriation bill by adding a proviso barring human bondage in any territory acquired from Mexico. Henceforth, the president and other supporters of the Compromise believed, citizens from all regions could put aside differences over slavery and once again work together for shared national goals. Elite Bostonians certainly thought this to be the case. As news of Fillmore's actions spread north, the one hundred guns fired on Boston Common thundered their satisfaction with the Compromise.[1]

This and other celebrations proved premature. As the historian David Potter observed, the settlement did not really constitute a compromise but rather an armistice or truce between warring parties. Analysis of critical roll calls on the six compromise measures shows that sectional interest determined how most congressmen voted. On only one occasion in one house did a northern majority join a southern majority in endorsing a given bill. Just as significant, the Compromise failed to provide a long-term answer to the explosive question of slavery in the territories. No reasonably perceptive observer doubted that the issue would arise again, and when it did, it was likely to generate at least as much acrimony as it had during the late 1840s. Lastly, the Fugitive Slave Act contained provisions plainly at odds with northern conceptions of justice. Antislavery Whigs such as

Horace Mann believed the bill would "make abolitionists by battalions & regiments," and party conservatives feared it would do exactly that. "I admit the theoretical right of the South to an efficient extradition law," said Edward Everett, "but it is a right *that cannot be enforced.*"[2]

While the Compromise ultimately disappointed nearly everyone, Boston's Whig elite had even less reason than most to celebrate. Months before Fillmore put his signature to the settlement's final bill, disagreement over compromise measures had widened intraparty divisions that had been building since the Texas annexation dispute. On one side, a pro-compromise group, centered in Boston and led by Daniel Webster, was willing to make any concessions to reduce intersectional tensions. Pitted against them was a group of discontented party regulars, whose most prominent members included the State Central Committee chairman George Morey, the *Boston Atlas* editor William Schouler, and Senator John Davis. More strongly committed than the Websterites to those regional appeals that Davis had been among the first to enunciate during the nullification debates of the early 1830s, they recognized that the party's successes in Massachusetts rested on its reputation as a champion of New England civilization and worried about the consequences of sacrificing Bay State Whiggery's most precious asset. In their eyes, Webster's course endangered everything they had worked to achieve in the political sphere.

The Websterites had several reasons for acting as they did. Though primarily concerned about preventing the social and economic disorder that was certain to follow a breakup of the Union, they further believed that offering concessions on slavery-related matters would enable them to replace the free-trade tariff of 1846 with a more protectionist revenue bill. An overproduction crisis, beginning in the late 1840s, had hobbled textile operations, making the need for tariff revision more urgent than ever. Directing attention to the question might also furnish a solution to their mounting political woes. Two decades earlier, Boston's manufacturing interest had made protectionism central to a popular conservatism that celebrated class interdependence and promised prosperity to all. Some hoped that the issue could do again what it had then.

Those who did so had forgotten why Bay Staters found protectionist appeals so compelling in the first place. During the tariff struggle of the 1830s, manufacturers had linked declarations of economic interdependence to a bold defense of regional interests. Since then, however, they had adopted a much more conciliatory approach to intersectional questions. The change attracted increasing notice following passage of the Compromise and its Fugitive Slave Act, which Bay Staters found particularly repulsive. Elaborating on themes stated earlier by Charles Francis Adams in his "Sagitta" letters, Free Soilers charged elite Bostonians with participation in a conspiracy to barter freedom for personal gain. In so doing, they transformed the tariff—an issue that had long bolstered Whig hegemony—into a symbol of treachery and betrayal.

Meanwhile, a Free Soil-Democratic coalition directly challenged elite claims that the middling and laboring classes could best advance their interests by promoting those of the Boston Associates. Not content simply to condemn Whig pandering to southern planters, coalition leaders fashioned an anticorporate message that focused on the threat Boston's elite posed to cherished notions of interclass harmony. Its popularity could best be seen in Lowell, where a broad-based movement combined ten-hour agitation with demands for a secret ballot to break the Whigs' longtime stranglehold on local politics. Although the coalition's assault did not immediately kill Bay State Whiggery, it inflicted wounds from which the party never recovered.

DANIEL WEBSTER WAS, said George Frisbie Hoar, "the idol of the people." Though only five feet, nine inches tall, Webster always looked much bigger to those who noticed him. And nearly everybody did. As he walked through the streets of Boston, people turned and stared, pointing him out to acquaintances. Everything about Webster interested Bay Staters. "His beautiful black eyes shone out through the caverns of his deep brows like lustrous jewels," Hoar wrote. "His teeth were white and regular, and his smile when he was in a gracious mood, especially when talking to women, had an irresistible charm." The expansive brow held particular fascination for New Englanders awed by his legendary intellectual powers. "Under that hat is the greatest phrenological head in the civilised world," observed Richard Henry Dana, Jr., and "a larger & heavier brain than any of his race & a physical frame suited to its utmost needs."[3]

By 1850, Webster had been a public figure for nearly forty of his sixty-eight years, having first achieved notice as a New Hampshire representative during the War of 1812. Although he spent much of the period in Congress, Webster had never been a notably diligent legislator and his name was associated with no major enactments. What he did best—indeed better than any of his long-winded colleagues in that golden age of oratory—was talk. And he spoke most eloquently about the wisdom embodied in the U.S. Constitution and the glorious past and future of the government it had created. As the sectional crisis deepened at midcentury, increasing numbers of Capitol watchers expected some statement from the senior senator from Massachusetts. Webster could not let such an opportunity pass. Over the years, he had spoken so often and so ably about a perpetual Union that he had developed a proprietary interest in the concept. If nothing else, the demands of his massive ego required that he make his views known at this critical juncture.[4]

Shortly after the Senate convened at noon on March 7, 1850, Webster rose to deliver what would be the last major address of his life—an oration that became known as the Seventh of March speech. It differed from earlier such efforts in one important respect. In his most memorable orations—at the 1820 bicentennial anniversary of the Pilgrim's landing, at the Bunker Hill Monument dedication of 1825, and in the 1830 replies to South Carolina's Robert Y. Hayne—Webster had deftly combined appeals to regional pride with rousing tributes to national progress. In his address to the Senate in 1850, however, he seemed almost willfully disdainful of the concerns and values of New Englanders. In addition to dismissing antislavery activists as intolerant zealots who "deal with morals as with mathematics," he endorsed policy positions that went well beyond what most Bay Staters deemed acceptable. Addressing southern fears about the loss of sectional political parity, he contended that the government had a contractual obligation to create four new slave states out of Texas, should its citizens so desire. He also derided supporters of the Wilmot Proviso, declaring that geographical laws prevented slavery from taking root in the Southwest and announcing that he would vote against any resolution requiring California or New Mexico to insert provisions in their constitutions prohibiting the institution. Lastly, Webster asserted that southerners had good reason to complain about the disinclination of northerners "to perform fully their constitutional duties in regard to the return of persons bound to service who have escaped into the free States." The Senate Judiciary Committee was then considering a fugitive slave bill to deal with the matter, and he planned to give the measure his full backing.[5]

Webster did not have to wait long to learn what New Englanders thought of the address. The reaction was swift and in most cases vehement. To regional Free Soilers, the speech represented the worst form of betrayal. Webster's opening declaration that "he did not speak as a Massachusetts man," said the *Boston Republican,* hardly needed stating: "No man who reads this effort would suppose that its author ever breathed the air of Massachusetts, or ever imbibed any of her sentiments or principles." Other antislavery critics looked to the past for comparable instances of treachery. Theodore Parker knew of "no deed in American history, done by a son of New England," to which he might liken Webster's violation of trust "but the act of Benedict Arnold!" Ranging more broadly, Charles Francis Adams believed that Webster could best be compared to Judas Iscariot, the only difference between the two being that Judas had a conscience and hung himself afterward. No one expected any expression of regret from Webster, nor did many Free Soilers care by that point. Rumors of his ethical vacuity had circulated for years, and most now agreed with the journalist who told William Schouler: "*Morally* he is not worth the powder and ball it would take to end him."[6]

However much Webster enraged Free Soilers, they could at least use the address as a recruiting device. Antislavery Whigs who still retained some hope for the party had no such consolation. Few if any had anticipated what Webster would say, and the speech forced them to reassess their political commitments. Horace Mann spoke for many of them when he declared that the address "must be discarded thro' out Massachusetts, or Massachusetts Whiggery not only will go down, but it ought to go down." Mann himself quickly made it known where he stood. During his long tenure as secretary of the Board of Education, he had often concealed his true convictions on many issues as part of an effort to build support for educational reform. With those inhibitions lifted, years of pent-up frustration came pouring out in a series of pamphlets and speeches that, in Adams's words, "seize[d] Mr. Webster by the throat in the most summary way."[7]

Had criticism of the address been confined to Free Soilers and antislavery Whigs, Webster could have passed it off as the vindictive rantings of deluded moralists who "think what is right may be distinguished from what is wrong with the precision of an algebraic equation," and whose soft hearts and even softer heads rendered them incapable of making the hard choices that public life demanded of political leaders. But they were not alone. Numerous others, many of whom prided themselves on their toughmindedness, also believed Webster had gone too far. "I make no profession of a sensitive *conscience*," said the *Boston Atlas*'s Washington correspondent, Thomas Brewer, "but I should for ever be ashamed to look myself in the face if I attempted in any way to sustain, endorse, or approve the closing half of Mr. Webster's speech." *Atlas* editor William Schouler felt the same way. "His sentiments are not our sentiments," Schouler wrote of the address, nor were they "the sentiments of the Whigs of New England."[8]

Despite pressure to retreat and often at personal sacrifice, Schouler maintained this position in the months ahead. He did so for reasons that combined political calculation with a principled opposition to slave expansionism. During the mid-1840s, as editor of the *Lowell Daily Courier*, Schouler had taken a firm stand against Texas annexation, opening his columns to various Garrisonians and allowing his assistant William Robinson to give vent to his Conscience Whig convictions. On one occasion, Robinson recalled, Schouler even endorsed "a 'slashing' and 'crushing'" leading article directed at his patron and financial confidant, Abbott Lawrence. Robinson was probably referring to one of several pieces that chided Lawrence for not being more forthright in his correspondence with William C. Rives. Though hardly comparable to Adams's "Sagitta" letters, the *Courier* editorials did make it clear that none of Lawrence's aims could "be attained while slavery is suffered to remain."[9]

Schouler also recognized that Webster's address created serious problems for Bay State Whiggery. According to an *Atlas* survey, only six of seventy-six New England newspapers approved of the speech. No responsible party leader could ignore evidence of this sort, given the growing strength of state Free Soilers. They already controlled Worcester and Plymouth counties, and if Massachusetts Whigs suspected that their party had abandoned its defense of regional interests to pacify slaveholding planters, the future could be much darker. Moreover, Schouler believed, there was no compelling need to compromise. Zachary Taylor proposed admitting California and New Mexico to the Union as soon as they formed their own constitutions. Because no one doubted that they would seek admission as free states, the North could ask for no more than that. If southerners objected, let them take the matter up with their fellow slaveholder in the White House. That Webster was one of only two northern Whig senators who failed to see the wisdom of this course made his position all the more indefensible.[10]

Schouler nevertheless had a delicate line to walk. In trying to prevent further Free Soil defections, he knew he could only go so far without incurring the wrath of local elites. The dilemma this presented can best be seen in his handling of Horace Mann. On one hand, the *Atlas* editor published Mann's attacks on Webster, applauding the way in which the "repeated blows of his electric logic" hammered away at the senator's positions until they dropped "lifeless to the ground." At the same time, he and party chairman George Morey urged the famous educator to exercise greater restraint, particularly when referring to merchants. A majority of them, Schouler tried to convince Mann, "think as you and I do." Had this truly been the case, Schouler would have found it much easier to bridge the widening gap in party ranks. But as he probably knew, he had already gone farther than most elite Whigs cared to travel. Edward Everett was doubtless only one of many who could not understand why, "considering how very little short Mr. Mann stops of the most unmitigated free soilism," the *Atlas* would print and endorse his remarks.[11]

This does not mean that Schouler was on a fool's errand. He had simply miscalculated. For a time, in fact, it appeared that he might successfully rally broad elements of the party around Taylor's plan. According to Boston whale-oil manufacturer Samuel Downer, many local elites were themselves seeking some middle ground. Businesspeople who had initially greeted the Seventh of March speech with "unmixed satisfaction," Downer noted, soon learned from their more politically astute associates that Webster's course pointed toward the "certain death" of Bay State Whiggery. As this realization sunk in, support for Webster softened. Although a public letter endorsing the great man's position gathered more than seven hundred signatures from all major elements of the community, many of those who signed did so without enthusiasm. At a dinner party attended by Webster not long afterward, Everett observed that some of the senator's "fastest friends" turned on him as soon as he departed. No less significant, Everett added, anyone who cared could easily have compiled just as imposing a list of those who refused or neglected to append their names to the letter.[12]

What made Schouler's efforts so problematic was that opinion varied widely among those elites declining to sign. At one extreme stood David Sears, the wealthy real estate developer who was still attempting to push his compensated emancipation proposal through Congress. When early in the crisis a South Carolina congressman declared "that the Lords of the Loom, and the Lords of the Lash are so united by a common interest that they cannot live separate," an enraged Sears angrily denied the assertion. He continued to believe that southerners needed the Union much more than New Englanders did, and if they wanted to secede, he was perfectly happy to "let them *go in peace.*" That October, he refused to subscribe to a fund being raised on Webster's behalf. Once an ardent Websterite who on several earlier occasions had taken the lead in such promotions, Sears could no longer back a man whose supporters seemed intent on destroying Massachusetts Whiggery through their zealous adherence to "the new theories of the last winter."[13]

Unfortunately for Schouler, Sears did not speak for a majority of Boston's elite. More typical was Nathan Appleton's stance. Like Sears, Appleton deplored planter belligerence and felt that southerners had little to complain about. He could not, however, accept Sears's casual approach to disunionism. To Appleton, the destruction of intersectional bonds would be the signal for a catastrophic descent into anarchy. Whatever happened, he told one southern correspondent, his motto remained: "The union must be preserved." As threats of secession grew increasingly louder during the late spring and early summer of 1850, he abandoned any thought he might have had of standing up for regional interests. Whereas Sears and several of his friends declared that they would "see their factory stock annihilated & ruined before they would yield to the south one inch," Appleton was ready to support any compromise that promised to reduce sectional tensions.[14]

What finally doomed Schouler's initiative was Zachary Taylor's inordinate fondness for raw fruit and vegetables. After overindulging at a Fourth of July celebration, the president grew violently ill and died five days later.

At the time, said one Whig leader who believed that Taylor's plan would "poll the strongest vote throughout the State," he was probably the most popular national figure in Massachusetts. And as one of Old Rough and Ready's most outspoken supporters, Schouler had drawn strength from that popularity. The new administration, as Webster quickly noted, would not be nearly so hospitable to "half abolition Gentlemen." Not only did Millard Fillmore strongly support the Compromise, but by making Webster his secretary of state, he undermined Schouler's position at home. This promotion, Mann observed, "from the senate where he was already toppling to his fall, to the cabinet where he has much of the patronage of the government at his command," altered the balance of forces in Massachusetts Whig politics and rescued Webster from political oblivion. Party members who were either undecided or did not feel strongly about the compromise now had some incentive for backing him; those who continued to oppose him would have to calculate the added costs.[15]

Abbott Lawrence provides perhaps the best example of the effect Webster's elevation had on Bay State Whiggery. Relations between the two men had been strained for some time. Following Webster's dismal showing in the 1836 presidential contest, Lawrence had concluded that the senator could never be elected chief executive. That being the case, he began looking for more "available" candidates. After all, he had not achieved such phenomenal success in business by throwing good money after bad, and as a person of some ambition, he sought the power and prestige that came with backing a winner. In 1848, Lawrence had been one of Taylor's earliest and most enthusiastic supporters. With the general's election, Lawrence brushed past Webster to become the state's most influential Whig leader. Rewarded with the prestigious British ambassadorship, he was then in London awaiting Senate confirmation of his appointment.[16]

Schouler and his associates felt certain that they could count on the industrialist's backing. The *Atlas* editor had consistently sided with him over the years and knew that he was not, as Lawrence said of himself during an earlier dispute with Webster, a person "to be *muzzled* by the sophistry of great men, or alarmed at the sound of great names." What Schouler did not know was that Lawrence had begun distancing himself from the *Atlas* even before Taylor's death. While in Washington that June, Lowell mill agent Linus Child learned that southern senators were blocking confirmation of Lawrence's appointment because they thought Schouler spoke for him. Hearing this, several of the ambassador-designate's close friends rushed to assure Webster that this was not so in an effort to enlist his aid in breaking the deadlock; Webster's subsequent selection as secretary of state made securing his good favor all the more important. Lawrence certainly understood as much. Writing to Everett and others close to the secretary, he praised Webster's qualifications for the office, no doubt anticipating that they would show him the letters—which Everett at least did. The upshot was a tacit agreement between the two longtime political adversaries: Webster would push through Lawrence's appointment, while Lawrence would do nothing to assist anti-Websterite forces in Massachusetts. When Congress afterward passed the various compromise measures, Lawrence urged that they be accepted and enforced.[17]

Apart from Lawrence, most elite Bostonians had little interest in patronage matters. With their vast wealth, they were far more likely to create jobs for unemployed party operatives than to seek such positions themselves. Yet despite doubts about the Compromise's wisdom, they followed Lawrence's counsel and supported the pact. They did so for several reasons. In addition to worries about disunion, they feared that resistance would cripple their ability to influence federal legislation. Indeed, they often combined the two concerns when discussing party policy. As the *Advertiser* put it, adopting a stronger antislavery stand would place Bay State Whigs "in a hopeless minority in regard to National questions, if not in the still less enviable position of being the cause of dissension and attempts at secession in other portions of the Union." Of these national questions, none had greater significance than tariff revision. Why it meant so much to them at that particular moment is a matter that deserves more extensive examination.[18]

THE MID-1840S WERE boom years for Boston manufacturers and mill investors. As the long depression that began in 1837 finally lifted, a generally prosperous national economy combined with low cotton prices to produce record dividends and soaring stock values. Believing the time ripe for expansion, mill builders were quick to take advantage of this happy turnabout. In addition to major developments initiated by the Associates at Holyoke and Lawrence, new plants went up throughout the commonwealth. Between 1845 and 1850, spindlage in Bay State mills rose 57 percent, from 817,483 to 1,288,091 spindles. Other regions also registered significant advances in capacity.[19]

It was, as is so often the case at such moments, all too good to last. By decade's end, the storm clouds of overproduction had darkened New England's industrial landscape, dimming the spirits of even the most congenitally optimistic. With mills producing more fabric than could be sold, textile manufacturers found themselves caught in a cost-price squeeze: cloth prices declined or remained static while the cost of cotton and other inputs rose. As profits and stock values plummeted, investor interest in new concerns faded and development at Lawrence and Holyoke stalled.

Although other sources of capital existed, there was a limit to the amount of risk that promoters and financial institutions wished to assume; the more than one million dollars Abbott Lawrence poured into the project bearing his name left him far more exposed than he had planned. Building new mills also exacerbated several structural problems that already impeded adjustment to the mounting crisis. Because existing plants needed to operate at close to full capacity to achieve maximum efficiency, there was no easy or painless way to reduce output. And because commission agents dependent on revenue from cloth sales held major blocks of stock in most mills, any concerted effort to cut back production could expect stiff opposition.[20]

An era was coming to an end. Although the Associates controlled a diverse array of enterprises, mill building occupied a special place in their structure of accumulation. To many, it provided the motivating power for that gold-producing "machine" Amos A. Lawrence said his father and uncle had created. As Nathan Appleton observed, factory construction generated far greater returns than the productive operations of textile mills, and for the past quarter-century, leading Associates had demonstrated the wisdom of this counsel in numerous promotional endeavors. However extensive their other holdings may have become, the superprofits promised by such developmental activities possessed an allure that few could resist. Lawrence's uncle Abbott is perhaps the best example. Despite his seven ships, insurance stock, railroad interests, and other investments listed in his letter to John Davis, Abbott Lawrence leaped at the chance to participate in one more promotional scheme. He soon discovered, however, that the old formula no longer worked. Holyoke and Lawrence would be the last of the Associates' great mill-building campaigns. Each proved to be a major disappointment, particularly the Holyoke project, where investors would lose nearly everything during the Panic of 1857.[21]

With these developments, attention focused increasingly on the tariff. To regional mill owners, it was no coincidence that their current woes began shortly after enactment of the 1846 measure, which had sharply reduced rates on a broad range of goods. "The present condition of the cotton manufacture, and for the last two years, is that of extreme depression," Nathan Appleton informed the treasury secretary William Meredith in an 1849 letter, and it was so primarily because of "the change in the tariff." Abbott Lawrence—who had earlier said he would "recommend stopping one half of the machinery in Lowell, and every where else," if President Tyler vetoed the 1842 tariff—agreed with this analysis. "We must," he wrote from London in a letter to Appleton, "have a new Revenue Law before the Country can be in a rich position." Mill investors of all stripes felt the same way. Those who believed themselves overcommitted and wanted to "unload" depreciating stocks were especially "anxious" that something be done, said Lawrence's nephew Amos. Desperate to prevent further losses, these investors would support anything they could "call a new Tariff: they do not much care what it is."[22]

During these years, the younger Lawrence stood out as one of the Associates' more perceptive commentators on tariff legislation. Even though he, too, planned to shift some of his assets from manufacturing to real estate, he was not among those who would accept any change in revenue laws simply to boost flagging stock values. His family was in too deep for him to consider deserting textiles entirely, and a solution that provided only a short-term rise in stock prices had little appeal. And Lawrence saw more clearly than most where the industry's problems lay. He knew that the tariff alone was not responsible for the troubles facing cotton manufacturers. As he explained to Robert Winthrop, "We are producing too much at home; we have more than supplied our own markets," and there was not enough foreign demand to absorb existing surpluses. This especially applied "to the heavy cotton goods wh. are our great production, & wh. require no protection." The finer fabrics, he noted, were not doing too badly. From this, Lawrence concluded that New England producers did indeed need a new tariff, but they required a particular kind of tariff: one that would facilitate the production of greater amounts of fine goods.[23]

On a matter of equal interest to elite Bostonians, such a tariff furnished a means of preventing the industrial road to sectional reconciliation from being washed away by the textile industry's burgeoning output. Like his uncle and other leading Associates, Lawrence believed in the market-forces theory of emancipation and had supported the industrialization efforts on which that theory rested. As things stood in the later 1840s, however, increased southern capacity only added to market surpluses, creating havoc for producers in all regions. When the Rhode Island textile engineer Charles T. James issued a glowing prospectus for southern manufacturing in an 1849 piece in *Hunt's Merchants' Magazine,* Lawrence attempted to dampen the enthusiasm awakened by James's optimistic projections in two subsequent articles reviewing the dismal recent performance of New England mills. Yet, there was a way out. At almost exactly the same time he was preparing his response to James, Lawrence's father wrote to a South Carolina correspondent that he hoped the Palmetto State would soon spin all of its cotton, "for we of Massachusetts will gladly surrender to you the manufacture of coarse fabrics, and turn our industry to making fine articles." To bring about this mutually advantageous division of labor, he added, "nothing will help us all so much as specific duties."[24]

As the letter to Winthrop quoted earlier indicates, the younger Lawrence saw quickly what his father was saying. Who, he later asked William Appleton, would dare "embark in new projects under the present system of ad valorem duties?" The manipulation of ad valorem rates by importers not only reduced the level of protection a given duty was intended to furnish but made it nearly impossible for American producers to determine "what the foreign goods are to cost with which wh. we must compete." Without the certainty provided by specific duties, no one could be expected to invest in plant and machinery designed to produce fine goods that would compete directly with British fabrics. Yet if regional mills did not move into this line of production, the current crisis could drag on interminably. At the very least, plans for further development at Lawrence and Holyoke would have to be shelved. "Our great water powers are much less valuable if they must remain unimproved until there shall be a demand for coarse cotton goods beyond our present ability to produce them," Amos wrote to his uncle Abbott. "We must have something new in New England, or we must stand still." In the political sphere, this meant convincing southerners that they, too, would benefit from a tariff that facilitated fine goods production, "since they cannot make a profit by manufacturing when we cannot."[25]

Among those agreeing with Lawrence was William Gregg. Considered by many to be the South's leading industrialist, the South Carolina cotton manufacturer accepted the fact that it would be some years before regional mills moved beyond the production of coarse goods. Any proposal that promised to reduce northern output for those crowded markets had his approval. The main obstacle was the current political situation. "A reasonable tariff of protection would set every thing right at this time," he told Lawrence, "but unfortunately for the country, just when the south was ready to receive reasonable propositions on this head, you people of the North, East, & West, raise up a bone of contention which has spoiled all." Southerners viewed agitation on the Compromise of 1850 and related matters a malicious assault on everything they held dear. "With us," Gregg said, "slaves are property, and it amounts to Many Millions, the protection and free use of which is guaranteed to us by the Constitution." Without such protection, he added, southerners had little interest in the Union, much less tariff revision.[26]

Written in early September 1850, Gregg's missive confirmed what Lawrence and other prominent Bostonians had been hearing for months from Daniel Webster. Webster's message, repeated in numerous letters to local correspondents, is easily summarized: southern Whigs "will not give a single vote for the Tariff until this slavery business is settled." The Associates heard the same thing from Linus Child, the Lowell mill agent whom they had sent to Washington that spring on a lobbying mission, and who afterward could be seen scurrying about Boston, informing investors that no compromise meant no tariff. According to George Morey, this argument found a ready audience among elite Bostonians, many of whom believed that if they backed "Mr. W., we should have a tariff without any difficulty." Webster's strongest supporters, said one of Horace Mann's correspondents, were local selling agents for large corporations "who would consent to have Slavery spread all over the world, if by so doing it would improve their business."[27]

Mann did not doubt the truth of such reports. No one had to tell him about people "who, if they were to hear for the first time of the River of Life flowing past the throne of God, would instinctively ask whether there were any good mill sites on it." He had seen the "swarms" of lobbyists, many of them from Massachusetts, who converged on Washington whenever Congress was in session "to reinforce the interests of the manufacturers." He had also monitored the activities of Webster and Child. His observations convinced him that the two men had become the willing pawns of southern power brokers. Webster, Mann wrote to his wife, had for months been telling all who cared to listen "that if we would surrender Liberty, the South would withhold their opposition to a tariff. This has been the idea that has worked such a wonderful change in Boston & in those parts of the state connected by business with it, & almost all parts of the State are so connected." Appalled and angered by Websterite maneuvering, he nevertheless remained hopeful that some good might yet come of it. "[W]ill the people of Massachusetts bear to have the liberties of men bartered for the profits of trade?" he asked Charles Sumner. Mann did not believe so. He felt that if the motives behind elite support for the Compromise could be exposed, "their author would be crucified."[28]

Although Mann's suggestion was well taken, Free Soilers had to proceed cautiously on tariff matters. Despite the growing prominence of slavery-related questions in state politics, protectionist appeals could still mobilize voters when linked to a defense of free labor during a period of economic stagnation in textiles. As Samuel Downer remarked, a favorable adjustment of duties might well be used "to whitewash" the Compromise. "It is really of great consequence to legitimate and honest trade," he wrote to Mann, "to have a tariff of specific duties." And while Free Soilers claimed that "the people are sick of this annual cry—*this wail of Corporations and Capitalists*," they knew better than to press the point too far. In one of the few antiprotectionist statements to be found in Free Soil journals, the *Boston Republican* asserted: "Those Corporate managers [who continually raise the issue] should be taught that there is a limit to popular credulity, if there is no limit to their own stupidity. The tendency all over the globe is to free and unrestricted commerce among nations." A week later, however, after William Schouler had accused the *Republican* of opposing tariff reform, its editor recanted, declaring the charge "greatly unjust and false." Such retractions were rarely necessary elsewhere. This was especially so in industrial centers such as Lowell, where William S. Robinson consistently defended the principle of protectionism.[29]

Mann, too, championed protectionism. Like most former Whigs who became Free Soilers, he felt that government had an obligation "to encourage industry by securing the rewards of labor to the laborer." This and related beliefs had attracted him to Whiggery as a young man, and nothing had happened since then to change his mind. Yet when Websterite efforts to enact tariff legislation in the Thirty-first Congress failed, he expressed little disappointment. One reason was the grim satisfaction he derived from seeing an adversary foiled. "I regret as much as anyone the suffering of our laboring classes," he told his wife, "but there is a retribution in all this, which gratifies one's moral sense." He also saw that the defeat of tariff reform provided an ideal opportunity for exploiting the issue politically. In his "Sagitta" letters, Charles Francis Adams had observed that slaveholder opposition to protectionism was "political and radical in its character. They are jealous of power, and insofar as money is power, they are jealous of money." If Boston mill investors did not understand what Adams was saying, Mann did. The South, he wrote to the dissident Whig railroad magnate John Murray Forbes, had no intention of ever giving way on the tariff. It "proposes to control us thro' our love of office, and hopes of making money. They know, if they were to yield to us what we desire, they would at once surrender all their power over us, as a women who gives up her virtue loses a husband." The elite's apparent inability to recognize this basic fact of political life gave Mann a compelling framework for his exposure of the Websterite compromise behind the Compromise.[30]

In an October 1851 letter concerning a speech Mann intended to deliver in Lowell, the Free Soil activist Chauncey L. Knapp advised: "Show up the beauties of the Compromise—how it was done—how it, like its predecessor is *all on one side*—what was the consideration promised, but *not* given?" Such counsel was hardly necessary. For the past year, Mann had been doing exactly that in various public letters and addresses asking Bay Staters what they had received in exchange for submitting to southern dictation. For the benefit of those few who missed the rather obvious point he was trying to make, he had a second, more specific query: "Have we got the tariff?" Everyone knew the answer to that question. What many did not appreciate, Mann added, was that northern surrender on the slavery issue had bolstered planter power. "By our yielding to the south," he observed, "their party discipline has been immensely strengthened, and it is now more difficult than ever to obtain their votes for any measure conducive to northern interests." New Englanders had placed their trust in the hands of Whig leaders who had shown themselves to be as politically inept as they were morally bankrupt. "What have those now to say for themselves," he exclaimed, "who beguiled a portion of our people into the delusion, that they might safely barter human rights for pecuniary advantages, and have left to their dupes both the loss of the advantages, and the disgrace of abandoning their principles!"[31]

"A few years ago," a November 1851 editorial in a Boston Free Soil journal remarked, "protectionism was the most prominent of the cardinal articles of the Whig creed. Now, the leading Whig papers declare—you need expect no tariff—you can have none unless you sanction the compromise measures." Through their devastating critique of Websterite policy, Free Soilers ensured that few responded to such appeals. Commenting on a speech by Mann, one constituent told him that all "intelligent" citizens applauded his refusal to sacrifice "liberty, justice, manliness, self-respect, the sacred rights and interests of humanity, to pander to the vice of slaveholding & money-getting." Hyperbole aside, this correspondent had good reason to feel as he did. By this point, public discussion of protectionism more often than not added to Whig embarrassment. We can understand why by taking a closer look at how Bay Staters greeted efforts to enforce the Compromise of 1850.[32]

AMONG THE VARIOUS BILLS constituting the Compromise, none proved more inflammatory than the Fugitive Slave Act. In the spring of 1850, when Webster chided Bay Staters for opposing the measure and told them to "conquer their prejudices," an *Atlas* editorial flayed him for his inability to distinguish prejudice from the "strong moral and religious conviction" that had made Massachusetts "noble in the past, and beloved in the present." In September, newspapers throughout the commonwealth joined Schouler in condemning the enactment of a law "so utterly in defiance of public opinion that even its advocates can hardly expect that it should be enforced." Of all the columns penned by opponents of the measure, perhaps the most ominous for the friends of law and order was a little-noticed appeal that appeared in Henry Gere's *Northampton Courier*. Signed by ten fugitive slaves and addressed to local residents, it requested their attendance at a meeting to be held at the town hall to "adopt such resolutions as they may deem proper to prevent Massachusetts from being made slave hunting ground." Although it would be some months yet before Boston's black community provided a practical demonstration of what the appeal meant, its message was clear to anyone who cared to listen: the Fugitive Slave Act would be resisted in Massachusetts.[33]

In the meantime, confusion and despair reigned in Whig ranks. Robert Winthrop, who had voted against the fugitive slave bill, believed that its passage guaranteed Free Soil gains in the coming election. He was "by no means sure Massachusetts Whiggery w[ould] survive the shock, which this, & other things have given it." Boston attorney Franklin Dexter, who feared that Websterite disregard of "local interests" might well result in "the dismemberment of the Whig party," also expected the worst. So did Edward Everett, but for reasons quite different than those voiced by Winthrop and Dexter. Whereas the latter blamed Webster for mounting party woes, Everett thought the *Atlas* and other antislavery Whig papers were the main culprits. As for Schouler, he and his associates still sought to patch together some consensus among the party's warring factions. To pacify "country whigs" who "said they could not possibly stand their ground without distinct expressions of anti-slavery feeling," the Schoulerites passed resolutions at the state convention declaring the Fugitive Slave Act unacceptable in its present form. At the same time, they tried to explain to Websterites what they were doing in the hope that the secretary's followers would understand the need for such action.[34]

Some Websterites may have, but the great man was not among them. Increasingly preoccupied with dreams of forming a Union party committed to upholding the Compromise, Webster had no time for Whigs, "*afraid* to act a manly part, lest they should lose the State Government." Indeed, he may have been the only Whig in Massachusetts who did not seem alarmed by recent developments. In a letter to Millard Fillmore that November, he made the astonishing claim that antislave-law discontent was "fast subsiding" in the state. His Boston supporters knew better. Between mid-October and election day, the *Advertiser* devoted ten editorials to a defense of the measure. It is unlikely that they changed many opinions. When the votes were finally tallied, Massachusetts had a new government, as a coalition of Free Soilers and Democrats captured the governorship and both houses of the legislature.[35]

Defeat widened the fissures within party ranks. In his analysis of the debacle, Schouler observed that about twenty thousand of the state's twenty-seven thousand Free Soilers had been Whigs several years earlier. He believed they would still be Whigs if Fillmore's administration had adopted Taylor's dual statehood plan and abandoned the Fugitive Slave Act. Any northern party that remained indifferent to slavery "will surely go down," he added. "It cannot stand because it is false to the sympathies and moral and religious culture of the people." Not surprisingly, Websterite organs saw things differently. According to the *Advertiser*, it was not Fillmore or Webster, but irresponsible critics such as Schouler who had dragged the party down. Massachusetts Whigs needed to recognize their obligations to party members in other states, which required their accepting the Compromise in its entirety. When elite Bostonians organized a union meeting in late November, the *Advertiser* applauded this initiative to allay "the feeling of anxiety and alarm which has been excited in the Southern States by the apparent determination of the people of Massachusetts to prevent the execution of the Fugitive Slave Law."[36]

Whatever assurance southerners derived from the meeting did not last long. As Schouler stated, the Fugitive Slave Act represented an affront to regional conceptions of justice and morality. No gathering of Boston notables, however wealthy and powerful, could change that fact. Two events in early 1851 confirmed Schouler's judgment. The first occurred in mid-February and involved a fugitive named Shadrach Minkins. Apprehended in Boston where he worked as a waiter at the Cornhill Coffee House, Minkins was hauled in front of slave law commissioner George Ticknor Curtis, who granted the fugitive's lawyer a three-day delay to prepare his case. The hearing never took place. After the courtroom had been cleared, local blacks forced their way into the chamber, seized Minkins from his captors, and spirited him to Canada.[37]

The rescue aroused strong feelings on all sides. While Websterites raged about the triumph of mob law, Free Soilers used the occasion to comment on the moral and political failings of elite Bostonians. "Who are the 'leading men' who are so indignant at the violation of law?" William S. Robinson asked: "State-street brokers and Milk-street jobbers," people more concerned about preserving "the good understanding between the planters and the manufacturers" than in defending the rights and interests of New Englanders. The sight of "Boston Hunkers prating of justice" infuriated the *Worcester Spy* editor John Milton Earle, who wished Shadrach "a fleet horse, a pleasant journey, and a safe deliverance from such justice" as he was likely to have received from state slave law commissioners. To other observers, the rescue showed that Massachusetts still retained some sense of honor. As one of Mann's correspondents wrote, "The action & spirit of such a mob gives one more courage, some hope that everything is not given over to the Devil & Danl Webster."[38]

Though Webster may not have grasped the full import of what this writer was trying to say, he certainly recognized that his position had been challenged. Humiliated that such an event could occur in Boston, he initiated proceedings to prosecute those responsible for the escape, vowing that it would never happen again. In early April, the capture of another fugitive, Thomas Sims, gave him an opportunity to make good on that resolve. This time local authorities surrounded the courthouse with chains and adopted other security measures designed to prevent the Boston Vigilance Committee from reenacting the Shadrach rescue. Thus foiled, antislavery activists were forced to watch helplessly when an armed guard of three hundred men escorted Sims to the brig that would return him to bondage. Needless to say, Webster did not share their gloom. "On this occasion all Boston people appear to have behaved well," he wrote to Fillmore. Could Shadrach's rescuers be convicted and imprisoned, he added, everything would be as it should.[39]

The secretary's Boston supporters would have been surprised to hear this. The flood of invective unleashed by Sims's capture and return so alarmed Samuel A. Eliot—the only Massachusetts congressman to vote for the Fugitive Slave Act—that he feared local antislavery activists sought "a direct issue of force" with those city leaders committed to upholding the law. Taking the lead, Theodore Parker enunciated a message that no one could misunderstand: "Boston is now a shop, with the aim of a shop, and the morals of a shop, and the politics of a shop." When Eliot returned from Washington after voting for the bill, Parker declared, he was warmly greeted by two groups of men: "those whom money makes 'respectable' and prominent" and "those whom money makes servile and contemptible." The latter group included most of the city's ministers, who during the current crisis had again placed social position before social justice. "Poor and in chains, the government of the nation against him, [Sims] sent round to the churches his petition for their prayers." It was to no avail. "The New England church of commerce said: 'Thy name is Slave. I baptize thee in the name of the golden eagle, and of the silver dollar, and of the copper cent.'" Never at a loss for a Revolutionary era parallel, Parker hoped that Bay Staters would "remember the Boston Kidnapping, as our fathers kept the memory of the Boston Massacre."[40]

Outside Boston, Free Soil publicists echoed many of the same themes in editorials urging Bay Staters to make amends for the metropolis's iniquity. Writing from Lowell, William Robinson did not blame all Bostonians for Sims's return; the city's "money and Websterism" were most responsible. But these were powerful forces, and subduing the "mercenary spirit of Boston" would require moral and political pressure from "other parts of the State where people love liberty more than money." In central Massachusetts, Worcester's John Milton Earle took a similar tack. Though Boston was "disgraced forever," he wrote, voters elsewhere in the commonwealth could use their ballots to "redeem the Puritan State from the domination of the soulless merchants and demagogues who have murdered American Liberty in the home of her youth, and desecrated the first altars reared to freedom in the new world, with the blood of human sacrifice." Lynn *Bay State* editor Lewis Josselyn also looked outside the metropolis for redemption. "Sims has been sent back," he observed, "not because Bostonians cherish the Constitution and love the Union, but because '*their pockets began to suffer*—Then *their dormant patriotism awoke*'!" Fortunately, Josselyn added, "Boston is not Massachusetts." In Lynn and other cities where "the old Puritan leaven still prevails," one could yet find people who, despite southern threats to boycott local products, "will never consent to compromise their principles and consider their pockets of more value than their souls."[41]

Free Soilers were not the only Bay Staters who thought elite Bostonians had lost their way. Although they expressed their dissatisfaction in more muted tones, "country" Whigs had grievances of their own. The most prominent of these critics was John Davis, a Worcester attorney and former governor now serving in the U.S. Senate. In a May 1852 letter to Robert Winthrop, Davis complained that Bostonians "seem to imagine themselves as being in a day which is past without the power to recognize the present. They cannot understand that the sun has gone beyond the equator and the winter of discontent has come." He only hoped "they will not when the calm comes *wonder at the wreck they have made*." Coming from a longtime Whig stalwart of Davis's stature, such sentiments indicated a serious breakdown in party affairs.[42]

What made Davis's discontent so significant was that few party members better embodied the popular conservatism on which Massachusetts Whigs based their appeal. Although the ever acerbic Charles Francis Adams characterized Davis as "a good, plodding, yankee minded rather thick headed man who under the guise of great plainness is as selfish as any politician agoing," most Bay Staters held him in higher regard. To them he was "Honest John," a straightforward, unpretentious lawyer from "the heart of the commonwealth" who could always be counted on to do the right thing. Like George Briggs, another popular Whig governor of the period from the Berkshire hilltown of Lanesboro, Davis was someone party leaders could trot out to refute Democratic charges of aristocratic elitism. His success at the polls shows that he made the most of this assigned role.[43]

More important, Davis consistently upheld the party's image as advocate of free labor and defender of New England civilization. Two decades earlier, standing beside Nathan Appleton on the floor of Congress, he had helped forge a party ideology that linked industrialization, protectionism, and interclass prosperity in a stirring defense of regional interests. But while

Appleton and other Associates grew increasingly fearful about antagonizing the South, Honest John never retreated from that position; while they
displayed "a timidity about public affairs" that Davis once described as a
weakness of Boston's elite, he remained committed to those principles that
made Worcester County the state's main center of antislavery agitation. On
the stump, he emphasized the differences between free and slave labor in
his appeals to Bay State voters. In Congress, he aided John Quincy Adams's
petition campaign and supported other initiatives that bolstered northern
Whiggery's antislavery credentials. As a private citizen, he helped raise
funds to liberate slaves whom he deemed capable of becoming productive
members of free society.[44]

In 1850, Davis endorsed Taylor's dual statehood plan. Adamantly opposed to slave expansionism, he believed that the president's proposal best
protected northern interests. He also voted against the fugitive slave bill
and later backed efforts by Bay State Whigs to amend the enacted measure.
That Webster demanded total acceptance of the Compromise and sought
to use his cabinet position to proscribe dissenting party members enraged
Davis. His anger stemmed in part from long-standing tensions between
the two men. They had never been close, and when Honest John became a
Lawrence ally in intraparty disputes, Webster turned against his colleague,
on one occasion working to sabotage his candidacy for the vice-presidential
spot on the national ticket; Davis's disgust at the Seventh of March speech
reinforced his poor opinion of a man whom he already had ample reason
to dislike. As a party loyalist of the first order, Davis could put all this
behind him should electoral considerations require a show of unity. What
he could not do was approve a course of action that cast aside state and
regional concerns for the sake of pacifying the slave power. "Must a man
bow down to slavery to be national?" he asked Schouler. "Must he pray for
its triumph morning and night to be fit to be a senator?"[45]

Davis could never adopt such a position. To do so would mean abandoning everything he stood for as a public figure. "The great mass of the
Whig party have always been the unswerving advocates of the interests of
free labor," he told one correspondent, and those interests were now being
sacrificed to maintain slaveholder ascendancy. Although the "union savers"
talked much about abolitionist agitation and runaway slaves, these were
only side issues. The real question was "whether a policy should be pursued
[that is] adapted to promote the success of slave labor to the prejudice of
free labor." In his view, the present conflict could best be seen as a continu-
ation of the tariff disputes of the past two decades. "Slavery," he explained,
"works for a foreign trade beginning with exports and ending with imports,
while free labor struggles to support its own country with its wants and

to give it a character of independence." Whereas protectionists sought "to encourage & secure prosperity to free labor," their free-trade adversaries "had the opposite objective of giving a greater impulse to the productions of slavery." The 1846 tariff provided Davis all the evidence he needed for these assertions. "The cotton planters stretched their arms across the Atlantic Ocean and shook hands with the spinner of Europe," he declared in a congressional speech on the Compromise. "The cry was 'cheap labor and cheap goods'; money was at the bottom of the whole of it. Who," he asked, "can help seeing that this combination exerted its great power against the free laborers of the country?"[46]

That Davis chose to frame the midcentury crisis in these terms explains much about Whiggery's past successes in Massachusetts. To him and those party leaders who shared his views, protectionism was never simply a "matter of dollars and cents." A more important consideration, he told delegates to the 1849 state convention, was "whether the industrial portion of this community, which constitutes nearly the whole of it, shall be respected; shall be enlightened; shall pursue its business with success; or shall go down the scale of social order, until it falls into the condition of the people of Europe." Davis's inability to move beyond this frame of reference also tells us much about the dilemma Bay State Whigs then faced. Not only had slavery-related issues displaced Jacksonian-era economic questions as the focus of debate, but the efforts of "union savers" to link tariff reform to support for the Compromise had transformed the meaning of protectionism in ways that undermined its traditional appeal. By hitching an issue that had long symbolized regional progress and assertiveness to the oxcart of slavery, the Websterites had unwittingly destroyed whatever political utility protectionism still retained.[47]

Davis himself provided one of the better commentaries we have on this transformation. "The mercenary passions have also been addressed," he wrote in a June 1851 letter describing Websterite tactics: "The contest about slavery it is said occasions loss of business, and every man who has failed to realize all he has hoped for can find a ready & satisfactory solution of his misfortune in the cunning suggestions. Others are made to believe that the only course to obtain a tariff is to humiliate themselves by admitting and lamenting all the gross calumnious charges of aggression which are brought against the north." As these remarks indicate, Davis was hardly naive or unobservant. But like many Whigs of his generation, background, and perspective, he had trouble coming to grips with what he saw happening around him. Appalled by Websterite conduct but afraid of deepening intraparty divisions, Davis was unwilling to take a forthright public stand on what he called "the vexed national questions of the day." At home, he counseled party leaders "to make none but state issues and leave other topics" to a more appropriate time when they could be addressed in a "manly independent way"; in Congress, he tried to shift debate to those economic matters with which he felt most comfortable.[48]

That the marginalization of protectionist appeals occurred at a time when political adversaries were beginning to mount serious attacks on the Whig doctrine of social interdependence no doubt deepened the Worcester senator's gloom. Bay Staters, a Free Soil editor declared, wanted no part of an economic system that placed "small owners at the mercy of large ones" and that enabled corporate managers to "combine and conspire for the purpose of depressing the price of labor" whenever it suited their needs. Not all workers "are thus at the mercy of the capitalists," this writer conceded, yet "such is the tendency of this system, that if it be suffered to expand and enlarge as it has done for a few years, no man can tell but the middling and lower classes will be thus situated." When the emergence of such fears are linked to other developments of the period, one can easily understand the frustration and anger felt by party veterans such as Davis, who saw a lifetime of political accomplishments collapsing around them with no means at hand to ward off the disaster. The chapter's final section examines how this new threat to Whig dominance contributed to the party's eventual destruction.[49]

IT WAS NOT an unusual sight—three men strolling around Boston Common on a fine spring day in 1850 discussing the major political issues of the moment. But this was no ordinary conversation. Each of the men held seats in the legislature, and what they had to say to one another would have far-reaching consequences for state politics. Doing most of the talking was "the Natick Cobbler" Henry Wilson, a self-educated shoe manufacturer who had risen from poverty to become a prominent Free Soiler and respected figure in the General Court. His two companions, Nathaniel Banks and George Boutwell, hailed from similar backgrounds and occupied comparable positions in the state's Democratic Party. Wilson, who had been trying without success to push a set of stiff anticompromise resolutions through the legislature, had just read Daniel Webster's Seventh of March speech. As much as the address angered him, he had not asked Banks and Boutwell to join him simply to let off steam. A shrewd political strategist with many antislavery acquaintances within the commonwealth's dominant party, Wilson recognized immediately that Bay State Whiggery would never be quite the same again. Nor would there ever be a better time, he contended, for Massachusetts Democrats and Free Soilers to combine forces against their mutual foe.[50]

What Wilson proposed was not new. The previous summer, Franklin County Free Soilers had publicized a six-plank platform designed to provide a basis on which the two parties might work together, and in the fall elections, there had been uncoordinated efforts to form joint tickets. Although the Whigs once again triumphed, the results were promising. Many contests had been decided by the narrowest of margins, and there was every reason to expect success from a better-organized and more energetic initiative. The foundation for a more effective combination certainly existed. On one side, Webster's speech had considerably enhanced Free Soilism's appeal among anticompromise Whigs. On the other, coalition offered something to Democrats of all persuasions. Whereas antislavery Jacksonians welcomed a chance to speak freely about the slave power, their more Hunkerish party colleagues coveted the perquisites of power. As one cynical but observant Whig leader later put it, certain Democrats would never participate in such a union, "yet there are enough of them who will submit to *any* terms to secure their portion of the spoils, and you may rely upon their not letting this opportunity slip from antiquated scruples about principle or conscience." Wilson knew this better than anyone. In approaching Banks and Boutwell, he had singled out two men whose well-earned reputations for opportunism surpassed even his own.[51]

As it turned out, the strongest resistance Wilson encountered came from members of his own party. To former Conscience Whigs such as Charles Francis Adams and John Gorham Palfrey, union with the Democrats represented an unconscionable surrender of independence and principle that could end only in disaster for the antislavery cause. But these dissenting voices could be largely ignored. Even some of their fellow subelites thought them too fastidious. If forced to choose between a Whig and a Democrat, Charles Sumner told Palfrey, "let me vote for the Democrat because in that way we may secure the *balance of power.*" Thanks to Wilson's efforts, the coalition did just that in November, capturing substantial majorities in both houses of the legislature. When it did so again by a smaller margin the following year, elite consternation turned to alarm. Writing from London, Abbott Lawrence no doubt spoke for many of his class when he observed that "the whole country appears to be turned upside down."[52]

Lawrence's observation was more accurate than even he probably realized. In supporting coalition candidates, Bay Staters were not simply rejecting Whiggery. Many of these votes represented a conscious repudiation of a social class as well as a political party. Some observers had seen it coming at the 1849 Free Soil Convention, where delegate condemnation of elite rule threatened to overshadow concerns about slavery. "The soreness of feeling about corporations is greater than I had imagined," Adams said of the proceedings, "yet considering the tyrannical manner in which they have ruled, it is not surprising." Convention resolutions flaying "the Money-Power" and calling for electoral reforms to curb its political might embodied these feelings. Such sentiments were particularly strong in Middlesex County, where Free Soilers declared that "it has been too much the tendency of legislation in this Commonwealth to consolidate wealth in Corporations, thus enabling comparatively few men to wield the vast power inherent in millions of combined wealth, over the political affairs of the State, and the business and financial operations of the people."[53]

That Middlesex proved to be fertile ground for Free Soil assaults on elite political and economic hegemony was an ominous portent for Massachusetts Whiggery. A large, sprawling county, located between Suffolk and Essex to its east and Worcester to its west, Middlesex sent six senators to a forty-member upper house and generally elected more Whig representatives than any other county in the commonwealth. It was also home to Lowell, the state's leading textile center and the county's most populous urban locale. Whigs had long relied on support from the city's voters. As Webster once observed, party dominance statewide depended on the steady majorities obtained there and in other major cities. For some Whig leaders, Lowell had symbolic as well as practical significance. To Robert Winthrop, it was "the very soul and centre of our manufacturing interests." If Whigs could no longer control "the headquarters of [their] American System," he said after the 1851 election, they were "doomed to defeat under almost any imaginable circumstances."[54]

As Winthrop knew, Whigs had fared badly in Middlesex during the previous two years. Where the party had narrowly retained a majority of the county's house delegation in 1849, it lost by decisive margins in 1850 (39–25) and 1851 (37–23); it did even worse in senate races, where opponents captured the county's six seats in all three contests. In effect, Middlesex functioned as a swing county in the critical 1850 and 1851 elections. If the Whigs could have repeated their mediocre 1849 performance in house races, they would have more than halved the coalition majority in 1850 and regained control of that body the following year when the party staged a solid comeback in neighboring Essex, another traditionally Whig county with a large house delegation.[55]

As much as anyone, the person responsible for this turnabout was William S. Robinson, editor of the *Lowell American*. A former Whig and assistant to William Schouler at the *Lowell Courier* during the mid-1840s, Robinson was a gifted editorialist whose knowledge of Massachusetts politics, adept use of invective, and talent for exposing the inconsistencies in an adversary's argument or conduct made him one of the state's most respected political writers. His strongly worded articles on the slave power had given the *Courier* an otherwise undeserved reputation for antislavery during Schouler's tenure. When the latter departed for Boston in 1847, Robinson remained at the newspaper, where his anti-Taylor editorials brought him into conflict with local elites during the following year's presidential campaign. Told by two corporation agents to moderate his stance or move on, he left Lowell in June 1848 and worked briefly for Boston's two Free Soil papers before founding the *American* in early 1849.[56]

An outline of the course Robinson intended to pursue at Lowell can be found in a post-election analysis that appeared in the *Boston Republican* during his short stint there as chief editorial writer and that was almost certainly his work. Prior to 1848, he observed, elite Bostonians had acted with restraint, being careful not to set "themselves in resistance to the moral sentiments of the State." This was no longer the case; their heavy-handed efforts to influence voters during the recent presidential contest amply demonstrated as much. Although Robinson had no desire to interfere "with the just rights of property," something had to be done. "Regret it as we may," he said, ". . . the question is gradually narrowing itself down to this—shall State street rule Massachusetts?—shall a money influence dictate to her the terms of her own degradation, making her the mere football of the South, shall her independent, honest yeomanry who are not linked in with the combinations of associated wealth, make one effort to unite upon a system of counteraction which shall replace her in the position in which they were once proud to have her stand?"[57]

Building on these questions, Robinson went on to introduce a theme that would appear again in various contexts over the next half-dozen years: the view that Bay State politics had become "a contest between the City of Boston and the Country," a struggle "between the property holders in that city and neighborhood, together with all the connexions they can influence throughout the State, and the great mass of the industrial classes." Wherever one went outside of Boston, he said of the recent election, "the threads which still hold men to Taylorism in the interior towns are nearly all found to run into city hands." These ties were particularly strong in areas surrounding the city, in those manufacturing centers that Webster identified as the mainstays of Whig hegemony. With his subsequent decision to establish operations in the "City of Spindles," Robinson signaled his determination to confront the money power in the most formidable of these party strongholds. As a Free Soil colleague later told him: "You bearded the lion in his very den; for, if there was one spot in Massachusetts where it was more dangerous than in any other to follow independent convictions, that spot was Lowell."[58]

The first major question Robinson faced as editor of the *American* was what to do about proposals for some form of union between Free Soilers and Democrats. As a onetime Whig stalwart who still viewed Democrats with suspicion, he was initially leery. At the same time, however, he wanted to see Whiggery defeated and knew his party could not do it alone. Putting aside whatever reservations he had, Robinson decided that Free Soilers could support such a movement without "*dishonor*," so long as cooperation stopped short of actual merger. When union candidates performed well in the 1849 election, Robinson's enthusiasm for coalition increased, although he continued to assure readers that interparty cooperation was "*for local and temporary purposes only.* There is no pretence . . . that these coalitions are *fusions* of parties."[59]

In at least one respect, Robinson was as well prepared as any Free Soiler to engage in coalition politics. Like most rank-and-file Democrats, he had no love for corporations. He also recognized that many Lowell voters shared his aversion. Several years earlier, when told that John Allen planned to turn the *Voice of Industry* into a Fourierist journal, he predicted that it would soon fail, "for those who patronize it, do so, on account of its abuse of the corporations & the agents." As editor of the *American*, Robinson acted often on this insight. His former employer, William Schouler, provided one opening when in an unguarded moment Schouler observed that the General Court had spent much of the 1849 session legislating "to build up capital and capitalists." Taking advantage of the gaffe, Robinson declared it "high time that these children of the state were *weaned* and allowed to go alone and make their way in the world after the best fashion." After all, he remarked: "The *Labor* of the State has had to look out for itself." Too often, its "just demand[s]" went unaddressed in order "that '*capital and capitalists*' might be built up."[60]

In linking corporate lobbying to labor's inability to secure needed reform legislation, Robinson was not simply trying to score points with Lowell wage earners. More so than most Free Soil editors, he evinced a genuine concern for working people, particularly those who toiled in local mills. The period around midcentury was not an especially happy time for Massachusetts textile workers. As effects of the overproduction crisis lingered, pressure to reduce labor costs mounted. In a December 1850 letter to Nathan Appleton, Abbott Lawrence said that he believed the time had come when "labor should be made to bear its proportion of the loss sustained by" manufacturers. "I know the troubles and difficulty in the reduction of labor," he added. "Yet it must come down unless some improvement takes place in the general manufacturing interest of the Country." Although no comprehensive pay cut occurred during these years, individual mills

slashed both worker wages and executive salaries. There were also continuing efforts to intensify the pace of work. Between 1835 and 1855, Lowell's
Lawrence Company maintained the same level of output with basically the
same machinery despite a one-third reduction in unit labor inputs.[61]

Under the circumstances, it was no surprise that when ten-hour agitation revived in 1849 under the leadership of Charlestown's James M. Stone,
Lowell operatives quickly reclaimed their place in the movement's van-
guard. As they did, Robinson emerged as one of their most active supporters. Having been Schouler's assistant during the mid-1840s campaign,
this was a new role for the Free Soil editor. But he made the most of it. In
addition to reprinting Stone's reports and articles in the *American*, he urged
readers to attend local meetings, kept them informed of the movement's
progress in other locales, and added his own arguments on behalf of shorter
hours; that Middlesex Free Soilers regularly included a ten-hour plank in
their campaign platforms doubtless owed much to his intervention. Stone
certainly appreciated Robinson's contributions. When the Charlestown activist's *Democratic Standard* folded in 1851, he transferred its subscription list
to the *American*.[62]

Robinson had various reasons for taking the stance that he did. On one
level, his involvement stemmed from a general conviction that the corporate elite could no longer be trusted to uphold the interests of other Bay
Staters. Its role in the Taylor campaign and Compromise struggle removed
any illusions he might have had about its benign influence. Assertions about
the paternalistic intentions of mill owners now seemed much less persuasive
than they had when he was writing editorials for Schouler. On a related
matter, he recognized that conditions were changing in Lowell and other
manufacturing centers. As it had been in the mid-1840s, the contention
that long hours made the creation of a permanent operative class inevitable
by depriving workers of time required for self-improvement remained an
integral part of the reformers' critique; the need, Stone contended, was
particularly acute among Irish immigrants who lacked the common school
education enjoyed by the Yankee women they were replacing in regional
mills. Thus, when Schouler regaled a house committee considering ten-
hour legislation with tales about the salutary effects of his own youthful
experience in a textile mill, Robinson hastened to set the record straight.
"The Colonel and his father have no doubt 'worked in the factory' and
found it profitable," he told readers, "but the attempt to make the Legislature believe their case was at all parallel to the day-laborers in the Lowell
mills, strikes us as disingenuous."[63]

Robinson further realized that supporting shorter-hours legislation was
good politics in Lowell. Whereas city elites and petty entrepreneurs with

ties to local mills were unlikely to court manufacturer disapproval by deserting Whiggery, Lowell working people had demonstrated a capacity for independent political action on issues affecting their class interests. Their patronage had made the *Voice of Industry* New England's most successful labor journal of the mid-1840s, and their votes had helped defeat Schouler's reelection bid after he sabotaged the 1845 ten-hour bill. While many of them would have backed coalition candidates for antislavery reasons alone, promises of a shorter workday all but guaranteed their support. Robert Winthrop at least saw it that way. In 1851, as local voters prepared to cast their ballots in a second trial for state representative, he predicted: "The *ten hour system* will carry Lowell."[64]

Although the shorter-hours question did not arouse the same intense feelings statewide that it did in Lowell, its influence on Massachusetts politics was not confined to the Merrimack Valley textile center. To be sure, no Free Soil editor championed ten-hour legislation as ardently as Robinson did in 1850 and 1851, and with the possible exception of Lawrence, no local election elsewhere in the commonwealth turned on the issue during those years. But unlike the mid-1840s when Whig legislators successfully buried the question, in the 1850s it refused to go away. One difference was the greater tenacity and organization of labor reformers, who recruited a substantial number of new supporters from other manufacturing districts in 1852 and 1853. By the latter year, they claimed, one of every ten house members owed his election to the support of shorter-hours advocates. More important, the issue had already become closely linked to ongoing disputes about voter protection.[65]

The controversy initially centered on an 1839 law requiring voters to submit unfolded ballots. Although complaints about voter intimidation began soon afterward, few people took them seriously until the 1848 presidential election. In that contest, Free Soilers charged, Whig leaders instructed Boston businesspeople to close their establishments on election day so that they could monitor voter behavior at local polling places. In Lowell, overseers from major mills performed like services for the party by taking "a position around the ballot box where they could and did see what kinds of ballots each and every man deposited." According to the *Republican*, this was the first time Boston's "desperate money aristocracy" had—to any appreciable extent—deemed it necessary to use "the power of influence and money" at the polls. When Whigs subjected voters to similar pressure in succeeding years, enactment of a secret ballot law that would give "every man the right to utter his sentiments through the ballot-box without fear of being overawed by his purse-proud employer" became a central demand of coalitionists. They were particularly outraged by a letter circulated shortly before the 1850 election in which the Whig state chairman George Morey urged every good citizen "To Use The Full Influence He Can Over Those In His Employ, Or In Any Way Under His Control, in order to persuade them to go and vote on the side of our old Commonwealth at the present crisis." Armed with Morey's letter and enjoying substantial majorities in both houses of the 1851 legislature, coalitionists had little trouble passing a law to protect Bay State voters from employer intimidation.[66]

Despite claims that the measure was not directed at corporate power alone, concerns about the growing concentration of capital among Boston's monied elite were nevertheless an important factor in its enactment. "Wealth is so rapidly accumulating in few hands, in this State," Robinson said of the bill's passage, "that it became evident that before many years, with the open system of voting, under the restraint of men eminent for nothing but gold or brass, it would be wholly impossible to procure a fair and unbiased expression of the popular will." In the same editorial, he informed readers of a recent conversation with a leading Whig legislator who told him that "if you carry Lowell [in the 1851 election], you will establish the necessity for that law; but you will not carry it; you will be beaten and the law repealed." The prediction proved half right, though in ways that could hardly have gladdened Robinson's acquaintance. Coalition forces once again defeated local Whigs at the polls, but the Lowell contest focused unprecedented attention on the voter protection issue, in the process raising serious questions about the political role of corporate power in a democratic society.[67]

Boston's elite had much at stake in the 1851 Lowell election. Not only did Whig prospects of recapturing the legislature depend on a good showing there, but local coalition candidates were the state's most vocal proponents of a ten-hour law. This latter circumstance particularly concerned the Boston Associates, whose mills had only begun to recover from the overproduction crisis of the later 1840s, and who wanted desperately to put that issue to rest. Although critics never proved that they instructed local mill executives to coerce voters in their employ, evidence that such intimidation occurred was too extensive to be dismissed. The charges centered on Linus Child, a former state legislator who in addition to his duties as agent at the Boott Mills performed a variety of political tasks on behalf of the Associates. Child, of course, denied the accusations, but in doing so he did little to remove suspicions about his conduct. Adoption of the ten-hour system, he explained in a public letter, would have destroyed at least one-sixth of Boott's capital stock. He thus felt "that any party who would resort to such means to awaken the prejudices of laborers, could not expect that those whose interests were thus assailed, would sit quietly by and make no effort to avert the blow aimed at their very existence." In light of these views, which he doubtless conveyed to Boott overseers, it is easy to understand why Robinson considered the mill agent's denial "a Falsehood And A Fraud."[68]

The *American* editor's party colleagues shared his anger. Informed that Child had threatened to discharge any worker who supported the coalition ticket, Alpheus R. Brown had earlier declared "that if a single man was turned off, for that reason, he, as a member of the House, would introduce a bill *for taking away the charter of the Boott Corporation*." Though unable to make good on that promise, Brown did add to the Associates' discomfort by initiating a legislative investigation of the Lowell election. When Whigs tried to kill the probe, Robinson lashed out at legislators "who implicitly believe it to be in the nature of sacrilege to make any inquiry into the doings of a corporation, and who worship the Agent of a Cotton Factory with a reverence far more awful than that with which they bend before God." Listening to them, one would think that corporations were "at least equal to the Commonwealth in all the attributes of sovereignty." Fortunately, he added, voters recognized the threat and had begun asking "whether it was profitable to create or continue such irresponsible powers in the State."[69]

"Heretofore," said a Boston Free Soil editor on the eve of Lowell's second election in 1851, "the favor of the Whig party has been regarded as the life of the laboring classes." That had now changed, though leading Whigs were apparently unwilling to accept the fact. "The first dismissal of an operative for voting against the dictation of his employer," this commentator warned, "will sound the death-knell of chartered monopolies in Massachusetts." For reasons to be examined more fully in the next chapter, coalitionists and other political dissidents had little intention of destroying the material bases of elite rule. But the reputation of Bay State Whiggery had certainly been tarnished, and not only among the laboring classes. Moreover, it had been damaged largely because of the party's close ties to major industrial corporations. For nearly two decades, Whigs had drawn strength from claims that a seamless web of interdependence linked the interests of state manufacturers to those of citizens throughout the commonwealth. These claims could no longer be sustained in a world where protectionism had lost its appeal and where mill agents used their positions to dictate the political choices of workers. "For the past week," Robinson observed shortly after the 1851 election, "this question of Personal Freedom became the most important one of the whole contest." As John Quincy Adams demonstrated during the petition campaign of the 1830s, no party on the wrong side of this issue could hope to be successful in Massachusetts politics. If Whiggery was to survive the crisis, its leaders would need to exhibit considerably more forbearance, ingenuity, and sagacity than they had in recent years.[70]

CHAPTER SEVEN

The Final Years of Bay State Whiggery

*T*HOUGH BADLY WOUNDED, Bay State Whiggery was not yet dead. Despite its mounting troubles, the party returned to power in 1852 and retained its hold on the statehouse and legislature through the following year's elections. It did so, however, more because of coalition weaknesses than its own strengths. From the outset, many Free Soilers had expressed reservations about Democratic reliability. Some, such as Charles Francis Adams and John Gorham Palfrey, considered any movement toward interparty cooperation morally objectionable; others hoped that state Jacksonians could be turned into dependable antislavery allies. Similar divisions existed among Democrats. Whereas people such as Lynn's Lewis Josselyn and Worcester's J. S. C. Knowlton combined a principled opposition to slavery with a strong commitment to reform, party Hunkers worried that coalition would isolate them from the planter-dominated national organization. Sooner or later, something had to give. When in 1852 the Democrats nominated Franklin Pierce for president on a pro-Compromise platform, the nomination exacerbated these tensions and made further cooperation increasingly problematic.

With the coalition's collapse, Massachusetts Whigs regained control of state government. But they did so without addressing equally serious problems within their own ranks. Although Webster's death in the fall of 1852 removed one source of disruption, neither the great man's followers nor their anti-Compromise adversaries had forgotten or forgiven past slights. Worse, the party's Boston leaders acted as if nothing had changed. Oblivious to the declining appeal of major party organs and uncertain what to do about the withdrawal of important party figures from active politics, they paid little attention to the reform proposals of concerned party members who recognized that Bay State Whiggery was losing touch with growing segments of the populace. When the Kansas-Nebraska Act reignited antislavery agitation, they were ill-prepared to deal with the resulting turmoil. Despite their strong condemnation of the measure, fears of disunionism prevented them from providing the aggressive defense of regional interests that the public demanded.

Meanwhile, a new coalition was gathering force under the guise of Know-Nothingism. As much a reform party as a nativist organization, the Know-Nothings took up where the coalition had left off. Their crushing victory in 1854 destroyed Whiggery as an organized entity. A party that had long directed state government from elite drawing rooms could now seat its entire membership in one of those spacious chambers. The death of the second party system in Massachusetts not only transformed state politics, it also ended an era of upper-class rule that stretched back to the Federalist period.

GIVEN THE TRADITIONAL proslavery stance of Democrats, Nathan Appleton observed in a January 1851 letter to the *Boston Advertiser*, the coalition was "a combination of opposing elements, like oil and water. It had no principle in common but the spoils of office to be wrenched from the Whigs." Such a union could not be sustained, Appleton said, and when it collapsed, as surely it must, Whiggery would return to power. It was a comforting message that many in his intended audience eagerly embraced. After the thrashing they took in the 1850 state elections, Whigs needed assurance that the contest's outcome was a perverse anomaly that could not be repeated. The industrialist told them exactly what they wanted to hear.[1]

Yet, Appleton's observations represented more than the wishful thinking of a defeated party leader. There were, indeed, tensions within the coalition, and they surfaced shortly after the election when a group of Democratic legislators refused to honor their party's pledge to support Charles Sumner for U.S. senator. Although Sumner ultimately obtained the seat after a long and wearisome contest, the ordeal left bad feelings, particularly among Free Soilers already suspicious of Democratic intentions. A good example was Samuel Gridley Howe, a South Boston reformer and antislavery activist whose grudging support of the coalition rested entirely on his close ties to Sumner. "We must fight the Democrats before long," he later wrote to Sumner. "They have not—the masses have not—intelligence enough to overcome their prejudices about colour." Were it not for Webster's baleful influence, he believed, the Whigs would make much "better allies." Though more hopeful, Sumner also expressed concern about where the alliance was heading, on one occasion complaining that the "half-Hunkerism" of Democratic governor George Boutwell prevented Free Soilers "from consolidating a permanent party in Massachusetts,—

not by coalition, but by fusion of all who are truly liberal, humane, and democratic."[2]

Sumner was not the only Free Soiler who hoped that the alliance could be turned into a new, more broadly based antislavery party. "I trust there is a good time coming when we can dispense with all combinations to which you" might object, the East Walpole paper manufacturer and coalition organizer Francis W. Bird wrote to Charles Francis Adams in an October 1851 letter discussing Norfolk County politics. Writing again a week later, he confidently predicted that as soon as the national Democratic convention formally endorsed the Compromise, "we shall make a heavy drain on their ranks." Why Bird felt so optimistic is difficult to understand. In the seven days separating the two letters, Norfolk Democrats had held their annual convention. Nearly equally divided between those who supported and those who opposed coalition, the delegates engaged in a rancorous dispute that ended when national Democrats walked out. Across the state, similar strife erupted among Hampden County Democrats, with much the same result. Although such divisions contributed to the organizational purity sought by Bird and Sumner, they hardly betokened long-term electoral success.[3]

Meanwhile, Essex Free Soilers had their own debate about preserving the coalition. Here the main issue was the Democratic state convention's endorsement of the fugitive slave law. Led by the Unitarian minister Thomas Wentworth Higginson, a group of delegates to the county Free Soil convention demanded that Essex Democrats repudiate the stand taken by their state organization. "We can only do good by making our alliance conditional & dependent on [Democratic] virtue," said Higginson, who believed that Free Soilers had "nothing to live on but moral power. Take that away & we are inevitably extinct within two years." Like the national Democrats who bolted the Norfolk and Hampden county conventions, Higginson represented a minority faction of his party, which voted to continue the coalition despite his warnings. But the dissension surrounding the incident helps explain why Essex Whigs made such a strong comeback in the 1851 state elections. Whereas coalition candidates occupied 28 of 41 seats in the county's 1850 House delegation, Whigs captured 23 of 43 seats the following year.[4]

Less substantive matters also threatened coalition unity. Few Democrats ever forgot that most Free Soilers had been Whigs, and even the most ardent coalitionists among them remained distrustful of their one-time political adversaries. The ease with which their suspicions could be aroused can perhaps best be seen in a vituperative exchange involving the *Dedham Gazette*'s Free Soil editor, Edward L. Keyes, and James M. Stone of the *Democratic Standard*. When Keyes attacked Stone for criticizing John

Gorham Palfrey and reprinting a speech by New York Democrat John Van Buren, the Charlestown labor reformer responded by raising questions about the distribution of patronage within the coalition. He particularly objected to Keyes's contention that Free Soilers deserved a larger share of offices because they had formerly held prominent positions in the Whig Party, while most Democratic coalitionists were from "the rank and file— men never who were leaders in their own party" and who had no aspirations of assuming such roles. After assuring Keyes that this was not true, Stone ended his rebuttal on a harshly personal note that revealed the ongoing influence of prior controversies. "His innate and unqualified contempt of *democrats and democracy,* and the facility with which he could apply his extensive fish market vocabulary," he wrote of the Dedham editor, "caused him to be regarded favorably for a time by his former whig associates, although they finally were glad to have him run away from them, when they found that by his continual use of Billingsgate he was a standing contradiction to the claim of the whig party that it possessed 'all the morality and decency.'"[5]

What made Stone's display of temper so noteworthy was his place among the highly factionalized Bay State Democrats, where he stood in the front ranks of a group of staunch antislavery party members. Few Democrats had so completely embraced the coalition or had greater reservations about the national party. Democrats, he declared early in 1851, needed an organization that "shall boldly meet the conservative principles, which the whig party under the false flag of 'Unionism' would set up in behalf of the false claims of property, as against the rights of man." Only then would they be ready to combat the "slavery propagandists, and the monied interests of all parts of the country," who were "banding together to put down true democratic principles, and elevate an oligarchy of the wealthy classes, to be sustained by the power and patronage of the federal government." By summer of that year, he had abandoned hopes of saving the Democracy and urged his readers to follow the example of Ohio's Salmon P. Chase, who was trying to erect an independent antislavery party on Democratic foundations. Not long afterward, Stone merged the *Standard* with William S. Robinson's *Lowell American,* "the only *live* paper in this State, which advocates consistently the cause of freedom, and also democratic measures of progress and reform."[6]

If someone of Stone's convictions could be so easily angered by former Whigs such as Keyes, it is safe to assume that the bulk of Democrats were at least as sensitive about such matters. As things stood at midcentury, the Bay State Democracy comprised two main factions: a group of state-oriented, Van Burenite "country" Democrats who had long resented slaveholder dictation of national party policy; and a group of "customhouse" Democrats whose access to federal patronage rested on unswerving adherence to the national organization. According to the *Worcester Palladium* editor J. S. C. Knowlton, the customhouse faction's "respect for the state government, state laws, and state institutions, bears and has borne, about the same proportion to their regard for the general government which two-and-six-pence bear to a hundred dollars; and perhaps the reason is that what is paid by the one is about in that sort of proportion to what is paid by the other." Knowlton further claimed that the country faction numbered some forty thousand members, while its customhouse adversaries had no more than five thousand followers. It would be rash to accept these figures at face value. As a leading country spokesman, Knowlton hardly qualified as an objective commentator. Yet the inability of national Democrats to impose their will on county conventions does suggest the numerical dominance of their country foes, who because of their antiplanter animus and greater concern with what happened in Massachusetts looked favorably on the Free Soil alliance. Knowlton, for one, consistently supported the coalition.[7]

Not everybody followed the Worcester editor's lead, however. Perhaps the most notable exception was Marcus Morton, a two-time governor and former member of the state's Supreme Judicial Court, who considered customhouse leaders "a burden and a disgrace to any party." Having voted against the Missouri Compromise as a young congressman three decades earlier, Morton opposed slave expansionism throughout his long career. And believing that most Democratic problems could be traced to the party's "great fraternity with Slavery," he had supported Van Buren's Free Soil candidacy in 1848. If Democrats really wanted to revive their fortunes, he wrote after the election, "[l]et them cast off this incubus, discard the dough faces, who constitute the slave influence, for the patronage it can bestow, and return to the doctrines of Washington, Jefferson, and the patriots of the Revolution."[8]

Given these sentiments, Morton should have welcomed an alliance with state Free Soilers. But this was not the case. After reluctantly assenting to the union, he quickly turned against it, in part because he feared Free Soil radicalism. For all his anti-aristocratic rhetoric, Morton was at heart a conservative who opposed any fundamental changes in the existing social order. As he once put it, "I have made up my mind never for any office, to vote for a *Whig*, a *Socialist*, an *Abolitionist*, a *Slavery Extensionist*, or a *transcendentalist*." Despite his commitment to Van Buren in 1848, he refused to work with Conscience Whigs and Libertyites in the state campaign. Just as important was Morton's preoccupation with patronage matters, which had long been a source of conflict with party Hunkers. Reading his correspondence, one gets the impression that he sometimes felt the republic's fate hinged on such questions as who received the collectorship at New Bedford. In 1850, the polls had barely closed before he was complaining that a self-aggrandizing Whig minority, "which has shut out all democratic influence," controlled the coalition. It was almost exactly the same language Morton had earlier used to condemn his customhouse foes, and in the months ahead he repeatedly informed correspondents that coalition leaders were every bit as greedy and corrupt as the worst Hunker Democrat.[9]

It would be easy to dismiss Morton's remarks as the cranky fulminations of an aging party leader whose career was then in eclipse. One can only do so, however, by ignoring an important fact of antebellum political life: Democrats rarely possessed the material resources that Whigs did. This was especially so in Massachusetts, where more than one jobless Whig politician found employment in the Lowell mills, and where no Democrat could match Abbott Lawrence's capacity for assuring defeated candidates who loyally followed party dictates that they "will be provided for." This meant that patronage assumed a much larger role in Democratic thinking, particularly among party operatives who relied on some form of organizational assistance. A dedicated reformer such as James M. Stone could put such considerations behind him; many other Democrats could not.[10]

Nobody knew this better than the men who headed the party's customhouse faction. At midcentury, they included Caleb Cushing, a prosouthern former Whig who later served as Franklin Pierce's attorney general; Benjamin F. Hallett, a one-time Antimason and political ally of John Quincy Adams whose early antislavery convictions had long since succumbed to the demands of party orthodoxy; and Charles G. Greene, editor of the *Boston Post*. Country Democrats often accused the customhouse faction of placing national concerns above state concerns and of pursuing policies designed to keep the party "conveniently small" in order to reduce competition for federal patronage. The charges were only half-true. While giving primary loyalty to the national organization, customhouse leaders did show some interest in state party building. Aware that a flat rejection of coalition proposals could result in massive defections, their initial response was not entirely negative. Although Cushing opposed the arrangement from the outset, Greene counseled *Post* readers to support coalition candidates nominated at regular party gatherings. "There is no reason," he observed, "why the opposition in Massachusetts should be kept in a perpetual minority because they don't agree on national matters."[11]

Such statements notwithstanding, even Greene had little real enthusiasm for the coalition, as became apparent the following year. Whereas Knowlton and other country Democrats roundly condemned the Norfolk bolters, the *Post* editor found their anticoalition resolutions "pertinent and forcible." And while Knowlton's *Palladium* continued to trumpet the need for state reform after the election, Greene looked forward to the 1852 presidential contest, "when standing on indisputable national ground" a united Democratic Party would fulfill its appointed mission of saving "the Union from the perils of sectional strife." This hardly pleased state Free Soilers, who were already upset by Democratic unwillingness to repudiate the Compromise. As Lynn's John B. Alley remarked, "It seems to me that the coalition next autumn must be blown sky high."[12]

Although too pessimistic, Alley's observation was nevertheless well taken. The 1852 elections exposed all of the coalition's numerous contradictions to pitiless scrutiny. At the county level, the Hunker revolt spread form Norfolk to neighboring Middlesex, where more than one hundred delegates from eighteen towns bolted the Democratic convention. In resolutions issued shortly afterward, they declared preservation of the Union more important than any reforms that might be achieved through coalition with another party. The defectors were led by the Lowell senator Ithamar W. Beard, a well-known political hack whose aggressive opportunism had disrupted the county coalition on at least two previous occasions. "Those of us who love democratic principles better than office and power," he shamelessly asserted in a public letter condemning coalition efforts to enact a personal liberty law, must combat all disunionist measures "or be content to be swallowed by the vile sectional party now called the 'free soil party.' Count on me as one who own will resist to the death." Such rank demagoguery did not escape the notice of William Robinson, who said everyone knew that Beard would "take any National office, and if he cannot get anything else will put up with any old clothes or cold victuals the party may have to spare." It was a wonderfully apt retort that fully confirmed Robinson's reputation for well-chosen invective. But as the Lowell editor almost certainly understood, the threat Beard's insurrection posed to coalition prospects was no laughing matter. If it could not carry Middlesex, the alliance had no hope of retaining its hold on state government.[13]

What happened in Middlesex had already occurred at the Democratic state convention in Fitchburg. There several weeks earlier a group of about 150 delegates, contending that the Massachusetts Democracy "must not be Abolitionized, for the sake of Abolition support," had withdrawn to hold their own meeting. To J. S. C. Knowlton, the walkout represented a desperate attempt on the part of customhouse leaders to reclaim their once dominant position in the party. "It is the old spirit of *Boston dictation*," he wrote in the *Palladium*, "clamoring for its lost ascendancy; and *literally* scolding the country democracy for presuming to have any thoughts, any opinion, or any purposes as a party, except such as have been measured out to them in Boston, custom-house measure." Not surprisingly, Charles Greene viewed the bolt in a much different light. Now claiming that he had always opposed the coalition, his only complaint was that the protesters should have confined their anti-Free Soil activities to county and town gatherings.[14]

However great their differences on state questions, Knowlton and Greene did have one thing in common. Both editors fully supported the presidential candidacy of Franklin Pierce, a New Hampshire doughface who could be expected to do the South's bidding as chief executive. So did most other Democratic coalitionists, including such antislavery stalwarts as Lynn's Lewis Josselyn. The only exception was the *Fall River News* editor John C. Milne, who resigned his position because he could not endorse the national party's pro-Compromise Baltimore platform. "Whatever may betide me," Milne wrote in a valedictory column, "I resist the gag, and shall act as a freeman, with convictions strengthened, that *true* Democracy does not consist in aiding to return a Freeman to bondage without a trial by jury, or in adoration of the Finality of the Compromise as the chief corner stone of the Republican Edifice!" That more Democrats did not voice similar sentiments placed further strains on coalition unity. "I find that our friends here talk in a spirit of enmity to Pierce," Adams observed in an August letter to Sumner. "How this is to be accommodated to any phase of the coalition I am at a loss to see." None of this surprised Adams, who had long anticipated such conduct on the part of Democrats. But it was a rude awakening to others. As noted, many Free Soilers had hoped to transform the coalition into a genuine antislavery party. They were now learning that this was not to be.[15]

One final source of coalition divisiveness was the temperance issue. Following the lead of Maine prohibitionists, the Massachusetts legislature had enacted a stringent antisaloon law during its 1852 session. Though popular with Free Soilers, many of whom had been inspired by evangelical teachings, the measure violated the libertarian precepts of state Democrats. The resulting disputes proved particularly disruptive in the coalition's Worcester stronghold, which had been a hotbed of temperance agitation since the 1830s. "In all the towns it is thought impossible for the Free Soilers and Democrats to unite on a man for representative," one Worcester Whig reported to his party's county committee. This was so, he explained, because "Free Soilers insist on having a Maine law man or they wont vote for him, and the Democrats as a body are as radically opposed to any friend of the law and *swear* they wont vote for one." Similar disagreements marred efforts to select coalition candidates for representative elsewhere in the state, and more than one commentator later attributed the alliance's defeat to the "rum question."[16]

To make matters worse, these developments occurred at a time when Bay State Whiggery was showing signs of returning life under the shrewd and energetic leadership of State Central Committee chairman George Morey. To prevent additional Compromise-related defections, Morey worked hard to minimize Websterite influence on the central committee, and to maintain some measure of party cohesion, he tried to do so without needlessly antagonizing the secretary of state's followers. At one point, he even assured Fletcher Webster that he had long been one of his father's staunchest allies—as brazen a lie as any politician ever uttered in the service of party. Morey also spent considerable time attempting to mobilize material and human resources for the upcoming election. He was particularly concerned about reforging ties with the party's middling and working-class base. In a letter urging gubernatorial candidate John H. Clifford to secure Robert Winthrop's active participation in the campaign, he thus wrote: "Let him go to Natick or any such town, stop with a shoe maker or any other one of the class of *common folks.*"[17]

Having Clifford at the head of the state ticket further enhanced Whig prospects. One of the commonwealth's most respected lawyers, the New Bedford attorney had somehow managed to escape involvement in intraparty squabbles, despite his contempt for Webster. "I believe I can assure you of the full & cordial respect of all cliques, divisions & wings of the whig party," said one Springfield supporter, who believed this as "good [a] negative qualification" as one could possess in those acrimonious times. An open-minded man who refused to let his dislike of Free Soilism prevent him from congratulating Richard Henry Dana, Jr., on his defense of Shadrach's rescuers, Clifford also mixed well with people from a variety of social backgrounds. Whether conversing with Robert Winthrop or addressing a group of mechanics, he invariably hit the right note. At a ten-hour anniversary banquet organized by workers from South Boston's Globe and Mattapan Works, he offered a toast to "The Machinists—first and foremost in ranks of reform; sure indications that they are inspired with the spirit of our forefathers." His manners and appearance added yet another dimension to Clifford's appeal. Dana's father found it hard to believe that someone with his pleasing personality and "kind-hearted" face could have achieved such distinction in so disputatious a profession.[18]

Despite Morey's effort and Clifford's virtues, Whigs received 20 percent fewer votes than they had a year earlier. But the party triumphed nevertheless. Unable to find common ground on the temperance question, a badly divided coalition was further hampered by insurgent Hunker tickets and Free Soil uncertainty about Democratic constancy on slavery-related issues. As the historian Kevin Sweeney has written, "The Whigs did not really win: the coalition lost."[19]

Although beaten, coalitionists could take some consolation in the election's outcome. Constitutional revision had long been a major concern of coalition leaders, and in 1852 voters narrowly approved a convention resolution. After securing a comfortable majority at delegate elections held the following March, coalition forces focused their energies on reforming the commonwealth's system of representation. The current system, they claimed, gave Boston and other urban Whig strongholds in eastern Massachusetts an unfair advantage in state electoral contests. To correct these alleged inequities, coalition delegates pushed through proposed changes that would have substantially increased rural and small-town representation in the General Court. In so doing, however, they overreached. The suggested reforms were not only complicated and unwieldy, but they also revealed a blatant anti-urban bias that opponents compellingly exploited with ridiculous ease. That November, both the constitution and its coalition advocates went down to defeat.[20]

Although the dual setback formally ended the coalition, it was hardly the main cause of its demise. Even if Bay State voters had approved the new constitution, the alliance would have faced a problematic future. With the prosouthern Pierce administration setting Democratic policy, there was little chance of closing the breach between the state party's country and customhouse factions. How far the two groups had drifted apart can perhaps best be seen in the derisive manner in which coalition delegates responded to Benjamin F. Hallett's "Union-Saving speeches" at the convention. "One day," Dana recounted, the Boston attorney "reproached the House for laughing at him, & they laughed the more. Then he told them that men who wd. laugh then wd. laugh at the day of Judgment, which made them worse than ever." One reason the delegates treated Hallett so contemptuously was that they knew he and his associates held them in similar regard. Throughout the ensuing campaign, Greene reminded *Post* readers that their activities were being "closely scanned" by national leaders in editorials warning state Democrats "to avoid so fatal an error as an alliance with the free soil party."[21]

Pierce's attorney general, Caleb Cushing, removed any doubts as to whether Greene truly spoke for the national party when, shortly before the election, he issued his infamous "ukase," banning cooperation between state Democrats and Free Soilers. Though delighting Greene, Cushing's action enraged country Democrats. If the decree was indeed genuine, Lynn's Lewis Josselyn wrote, then the attorney general "is a traitor to the Democracy of Massachusetts, and will receive a traitor's reward." Worcester's J. S. C. Knowlton was even more upset. The new constitution that would have "restored to the people the power, of which they have been largely robbed by associated wealth," he declared in an editorial addressed to Cushing, "has been prostrated; and mainly, as I am constrained to believe, by the factitious influence of your letter." No longer sure what the Democratic Party represented, Knowlton afterward urged progressives from all existing organizations to join hands in forming a constitutional reform party. Thus it was that in helping to cripple the coalition, Cushing had also destroyed what little effectiveness state Democrats still possessed as an electoral body.[22]

The election left most Free Soil coalitionists equally embittered. In several instances, they too turned their rage inward. Here the main targets of editorial wrath were John Gorham Palfrey and Charles Francis Adams, each of whom had issued statements criticizing the new constitution during the campaign. As William Robinson saw it, both men knew better. It was not opposition to the constitution but "pure and unadulterated malice towards [Henry] Wilson" that prompted their intervention; in Palfrey's case, "an intense desire to 'get his legs again under Whig mahogany'" provided additional motivation. Writing to Adams not long afterward, the normally even-tempered Lowell editor gave vent to long-building resentments that—like the reference to Wilson above—suggested the existence of heretofore concealed class tensions within Bay State Free Soilism. For the past four and a half years, Robinson stated, he had devoted every dollar he possessed to the struggle against slavery. "If you have *done* more, of which I entertain considerable doubt," he told Adams, "you have not *sacrificed* more."[23]

Adams, of course, had never supported the coalition. Its collapse left him perfectly satisfied, as it did other subelites such as Theodore Parker and Samuel Gridley Howe who shared his aversion to any initiative that might involve some compromise of principle. More significant was the reaction of Francis Bird. The East Walpole manufacturer had entered the coalition with high hopes and had worked hard to bring them to fruition. By the spring of 1854, he wondered if it had been worth the effort. "We have always professed to believe," he wrote to Sumner, "that the coalition was a temporary thing: That we were indoctrinating the democratic party with our views, & when then the day of separation should come, we should take the best part of the party with us." That day had come and passed: "It came when Frank Pierce delivered his Inaugural; but the humbug of State Reform had kept up the pretext for the Coalition; it came again when [Cushing's] 'crushing out' letter appeared." It was now time, he concluded, to withdraw from this "degrading alliance," which he later told Adams had been a "terrible mistake" from the beginning.[24]

Not all Free Soil coalitionists viewed what had happened in the same dark light that Bird did. Like J. S. C. Knowlton, William Robinson and other antislavery activists who championed a broad-ranging reform agenda continued to hope that some new alliance could be formed. But Bird was not alone; other Free Soilers were similarly disillusioned. This, coupled with the ever-deepening divisions within Democratic ranks, all but ensured that should any new coalition emerge, it would be much different than the one now expiring. Meanwhile, Bay State Whigs could not have been happier—or so it appeared.

FOR MASSACHUSETTS WHIGS, the 1853 elections could not have turned out better. In addition to defeating constitutional reform, they captured the statehouse and legislature for the second year in a row. At one of the many gatherings organized to celebrate this dual triumph, Abbott Lawrence told Worcester Whigs: "The occasion is worthy of a Jubilee, and I hope that all who compose the meeting may be thankful, (as I am) for our merciful deliverance from the *most extraordinary combination of political adventurers* that ever afflicted our beloved Commonwealth." The aging industrialist had come out of retirement to spearhead opposition to the constitution, and he now looked forward to an extended period of business as usual. Many others did as well. A good example was a *Lowell Courier* postelection editorial reminding readers of the dominating role that coalitionists had so recently assumed in city politics. But that day had thankfully passed, the paper's editor proclaimed: "By thus electing ten staunch Whigs [to the legislature], Lowell has solemnly and emphatically affixed her seal of condemnation on those deluders of the people who have so long clamored for secret ballot laws, ten hour laws, new constitutions, and all the *et ceteras* in the schedule of the proposed 'State Reforms.'" With the coalition dead and Whiggery back in power, these celebrants seemed to be saying, nothing more needed to be done. Bay State voters had returned to their senses and all was well.[25]

In reality, the political situation in postelection Massachusetts was not nearly as simple or trouble-free as Lawrence and the *Courier* editor believed. For one thing, the grievances that had fueled coalition politics had not gone away. If Whigs did nothing to address them, someone else would. James M. Stone was one of many coalitionists who thought Whig arrogance was "consolidating our ranks & fixing the determination of Free Democrats more firmly than ever. . . . Depend upon it," he told Sumner, "this constitutional battle has got to be fought over." Just as important, state Whigs remained seriously divided. Even with Webster's death in October 1852, his followers continued to harass party members who refused to embrace the Compromise, much to the disgust of John Davis and others who understood the baneful effect their intolerance was having on Massachusetts Whiggery. As the Fillmore administration prepared to leave office early in 1853, Davis said that it could not do so soon enough to suit him. "This saving of the Union," he wrote to Winthrop, "has become a by word a mere clap trap to help break down our party." John H. Clifford, whose contempt for Websterites nearly equaled that of Davis, felt much the same way. While still in office, he observed that "if fortune is to favor the deserving, and the Gods are to help those who help themselves, the Whig party has little comfort in store for it for a long time to come." Why a sitting governor would make such comments about his own party is a question worthy of further examination.[26]

Perhaps the best place to begin is with Boston's Whig press. At midcentury, the *Advertiser, Atlas,* and *Courier* set the tone for party discourse, as they had for a generation or more. Of the three newspapers, the *Advertiser* had changed least. Still controlled by the Hale family, it remained a "conservative, respectable, high-toned" sheet whose elite readers could scan its columns each morning with every assurance that they would find nothing there to upset them. Given its select audience and generally bland content, the *Advertiser* could do only so much to shape public opinion. As the elite's paper of choice, its influence could not be dismissed. But because so few people outside the metropolitan upper class noticed or cared about what its editors had to say, it was manifestly ill-equipped to mobilize the general populace.[27]

This vital task was left to the *Atlas* and *Courier,* each of which tended to adopt a more aggressive stance on major political issues of the day. For many years, the *Atlas* had been Webster's most steadfast journalistic champion in Boston. This changed in 1847, when William Schouler assumed control of the paper. As the Boston Associates' leading political operative in Lowell, where he led the fight against ten-hour legislation, Schouler had developed close ties to Abbott Lawrence, who appreciated his able work on behalf of elite interests and Middlesex Whiggery. He was so appreciative, in fact, that he had mixed feelings about the Lowell editor moving to the capital. Although he certainly welcomed the increased support that a Boston editorship would enable Schouler to provide in intraparty squabbles with Webster, the industrialist feared that he might not be able to find an adequate replacement for the critically important Lowell post.[28]

That Lawrence thought so highly of Schouler was not surprising. The industrious former calico printer possessed a number of strengths as an editor, not the least of which was an outgoing personality that most people found engaging. Richard H. Dana, Jr., described him as "a good-natured, pleasant, easy speaker, never rising above the personals of politics, the trash-bin & gossip, but is clever at that." Such qualities may not have earned the *Atlas* editor an invitation to dine at Dana's table, but they did make him a good journalist. On taking pen in hand, Schouler rarely exhibited the skills of a William Robinson; nevertheless, he could when the occasion demanded write as forcefully as any of his peers. Under his editorship, said Winthrop, the *Atlas* was "a thoroughgoing Whig paper, energetic & impulsive. Not always prudent, but always courageous." It was, in short, just the kind of party organ needed to reach voters unreceptive to the *Advertiser*'s more staid appeal.[29]

Winthrop's assessment comes from a September 1852 letter in which he sought restoration of the government printing contracts Schouler lost after Webster became secretary of state. "The *Atlas* is too important a paper to put under ban," he told John Pendleton Kennedy, "& it was a paltry thing to take away its crumbs as a punishment for its independence." Whether Winthrop succeeded is unclear; whether it would have made any difference at that point is equally unclear. By the following spring, Schouler had left Massachusetts for Ohio, where he took over the *Cincinnati Gazette*. His departure weakened Bay State Whiggery on at least two counts. The bitter memories of close associates such as the State Executive Committee secretary Ezra Lincoln, who never forgot the shabby treatment Schouler had received, obstructed subsequent efforts to close intraparty divisions. And the ineptitude of Schouler's successor at the *Atlas*, Charles Hudson, further detracted from party effectiveness. Taking note of what Lincoln derisively referred to as "Hudson's ponderous wisdom," Robinson subjected the new editor to some of his most inventive taunts, on one occasion relating how a famous linguist had "died of confusion of the brain" after a fruitless struggle to make sense of the former congressman's leaden prose. "There may be some dispute whether a blockhead or a knave is the greater nuisance," he wrote of Hudson a week later, "but a compound of both is certainly worse than either, alone." This was not the kind of language one directed toward a respected member of the editorial fraternity, and as strongly as he sometimes disagreed with his one-time employer, Robinson never spoke of Schouler in such terms.[30]

As much as these developments hurt Bay State Whiggery, they were rel-atively innocuous compared to what transpired at the *Courier* during these years. Founded in 1824 by Joseph T. Buckingham, the *Courier* was the lead-ing voice of popular conservatism in Boston for nearly a quarter-century. To understand its special contribution to party successes, one need look no further than Buckingham's 1848 valedictory, which artfully combined those appeals to regional pride and social inclusiveness that made Whig ideology so compelling. "Born and bred in New-England," he wrote, "my affections and sympathies centre there; if I forgot *her*, may my right hand forget its cunning!" He rarely did. Nor did he forget the men and women for whom the *Courier* spoke. His major aim, he told readers, had been to make his paper "the advocate of what may be called, without reproach, the 'Middling Interest,' and to that class of people it was chiefly indebted for such measure of prosperity as it finally attained." The same might have been said for the party he had so ably served during his long editorship.[31]

Buckingham's retirement came several days after Zachary Taylor's nomination for president, an event that also prompted Buckingham's withdrawal from the Whig party. As someone who regularly opened the *Courier*'s columns to all sides of a controversy, he had initially tried to maintain a staunch opposition to slave expansionism without completely alienating those local elites seeking a compromise position. But the Louisiana slaveholder's selection as Whig standard-bearer was more than he could endure. Every vote that supported Taylor or the party he represented, Buckingham wrote of the 1848 election, was "equivalent to a vote to sustain the odious prepotency of the Slave Power in our national councils" and to delay "that political equality . . . which rightfully belongs to the free states." In acting as he did, Buckingham said, he had not deserted Whiggery; rather, "the party left me."[32]

Finding a suitable replacement for the veteran editor would not have been easy under the best of circumstances. As it turned out, the course taken by the *Courier* following Buckingham's departure could scarcely have been more destructive. Adopting a rigid Websterite stance, the paper heaped invective on everyone who questioned the Compromise, in one instance calling for a boycott of all businesspeople and professionals who refused to endorse the fugitive slave law. Though particularly harsh on the *Atlas*, whose patronage it acquired after Webster entered Fillmore's cabinet, the *Courier* also flayed prominent country journals such as Samuel Bowles's *Springfield Republican,* frequently using language that was as condescending as it was abusive. In this and other attacks, it seemed to be suggesting that anyone who resided outside Boston lacked the sophistication and experience needed to participate intelligently in public affairs. This was unspeakably foolhardy behavior at a time when resentment of elite dominance—often clothed in a more generalized antimetropolitan rhetoric—was on the rise throughout the commonwealth. And it did not go unnoticed. As one self-described country Whig wrote to Schouler, the *Courier* had lost whatever effectiveness it once possessed as a party organ:

"It is the 'Journal of Commerce' of Boston & should be no longer regarded as a Whig print."[33]

The *Courier's* campaign of divisiveness reached its peak during the 1852 presidential contest, when according to the *Republican* it was the only Whig sheet in New England that refused to accept Winfield Scott's nomination. Long after it had become clear that Webster had no chance of election, the paper continued to champion his candidacy in editorials questioning Scott's Whig credentials. Nor did it show any greater enthusiasm for the party's regular nominee following Webster's death in October. On election day, more than a thousand Bostonians cast their ballots for a dead man. By this point, many Whig jaws reflexively tightened at the very thought of the *Courier* and its Websterite readers. "All I can say," wrote the Worcester lawyer Emory Washburn, is "if that is the way they honor deceased great men, I wonder what they do when they try to disgrace them!" His correspondent, governor-elect John H. Clifford, no doubt wondered as well.[34]

These and related events took a heavy toll on party morale. Of those affected, few were more distressed than Robert C. Winthrop, the state's most respected Whig leader. An aristocrat by birth, Winthrop embodied everything that Brahmin society felt a politician should be: intelligent, well mannered, of good family, and without any of the ethical baggage that had long darkened Webster's reputation. Many elite Bostonians looked forward to the day when he would replace the Marshfield orator as their leading representative in Washington, and it appeared for a while that he would do just that. Despite "a certain native *hauteur*" that prevented his becoming a popular figure in the Davis or Briggs mold, Winthrop moved ahead with almost effortless ease during the early years of his political career. After graduating from Harvard and studying law in Webster's office, he won election to the General Court, where he served six terms before securing Suffolk's congressional seat in 1840. Only thirty-one at the time, he seemed well on his way to meeting the expectations of his Brahmin well-wishers. By midcentury, however, the still youthful Winthrop was deeply disillusioned. His falling out with Webster after the Seventh of March speech came on the heels of a series of unpleasant incidents that had already sapped his enthusiasm for political life.[35]

The first of these occurred in 1846 when his support for Polk's Mexican War bill prompted a withering attack from Conscience Whigs. The bitter disputes about slavery in the Mexican cession that afterward tore Congress apart were no less disagreeable to a man who "hate[d] controversy, & most of all, sectional controversy." By 1849, Winthrop had seen enough and would have returned to private life had Nathan Appleton and other party leaders not convinced him that duty required his remaining in Washington.

He soon regretted the decision, as his involvement that winter in a bruising contest for House speaker left him more disenchanted than ever. That he lost did not bother him nearly as much as how he had lost. Though not surprised by the opposition of antislavery activists such as John Gorham Palfrey and Ohio's Joshua Giddings, Winthrop had anticipated the backing of southern Whigs. When they turned on him as well, he began to wonder whether anything could be done to halt the drift toward disunion. The dismay and sense of betrayal that he and other Brahmins felt was perhaps best expressed by Edward Everett, who believed that "the South ought to be both proud & happy to support a man of your principles. What in the name of Heaven do they expect northern men to do? They declare against the fanaticism of northern abolitionists, & join them in pulling down moderate & reasonable men!"[36]

The question was well put. What could "moderate and reasonable men" do at a time when moderation and reason—as they defined those terms— appeared to be in short supply? To the extent that Winthrop's correspondence furnishes an answer, it seemed to be: not much. Had Winthrop been elected Speaker, Everett told him, he would have been placed in an impossible position with no clear guidelines as to where "the path of duty" lay. "From the embarrassment and danger of these situations, you are saved and . . . without having shrunk from them, and consequently without loss of credit." Samuel A. Eliot, who would soon take Winthrop's place in Congress, made the same point in another letter to the defeated candidate. "We are fully absolved now; & on the Locos & recreants rests the absolute responsibility for public measures. Whatever we may suffer in fortune, therefore, our character will be untouched; & it is more important to deserve success than to achieve it." All this was well and good, but it hardly provided a basis for ongoing political engagement. That many elite Bostonians held such views—views with which Winthrop heartily concurred— helps explain why they were so ill-prepared to control Websterite excesses. It was during this period of confusion that Webster delivered his Seventh of March speech.[37]

Winthrop had known the senator a long time and considered him a good friend. Aware that an address was coming, he had no idea what his former mentor would say. His initial reaction was mixed: on one hand, pleased that Webster's criticism of northern antislavery radicalism had undercut southern extremists who were planning to meet at Nashville in June; on the other, worried that he had gone too far in his fulsome endorsement of fugitive slave legislation. Like Schouler, Winthrop further believed that Zachary Taylor's dual-statehood plan offered the best solution to the territorial crisis. Although he carefully avoided saying anything that might be interpreted as a personal slight, his position did not satisfy Webster, who expected nothing less than total support from a younger colleague with whom he had worked so closely in the past; he especially resented Winthrop's later vote against the fugitive slave law. The accumulating tensions came to a head the following year when Webster went out of his way to disassociate himself from Winthrop's unsuccessful gubernatorial bid. "My friends say 'better luck next time,'" Winthrop wrote to Clifford afterward, "but between ourselves there is not likely to be any next time for me." Nor was there. Asked to run again, he refused; he also turned down a subsequent opportunity to fill a senate vacancy, declaring that he had could accomplish little in a body now filled with so many extremists. Still the target of attacks from diehard Websterites, he found them "even less endurable than the Free Soilers ever were."[38]

Winthrop's experience is significant for several reasons. Of particular importance is the light it sheds on relations between Boston's elite and the Webster movement. When most Bay Staters looked toward Boston at midcentury, they saw a cohesive social and ideological bloc whose various parts functioned in perfect unison. From this perspective, Websterite initiatives proceeded with the local aristocracy's full approval and had a single underlying aim: to bolster metropolitan elite influence within the commonwealth. In reality, the situation was much more complicated. Although most upper-class Bostonians hailed the Seventh of March speech, their support for Webster later receded. By 1851, there were clear signs of disaffection. Commenting on one Webster appearance in the city, Amos A. Lawrence quipped, "Old Daniel is here, apparently prepared with an oily speech to smooth over matters at home." Nathan Appleton was equally unenthusiastic. "What a mistake," he said of Webster's last presidential bid, "to suppose that honour can be obtained by personal seeking." When Webster later refused to back Winthrop for governor, elite disillusionment turned to anger. Abbott Lawrence doubtless spoke for many of his social peers when he told the former congressman that he could attribute his loss "to a *malign* influence that has too often defeated the honest purposes of the Whigs of Massachusetts."[39]

In light of the foregoing, it is easy to understand why a reporter attending an 1852 Websterite convention held in the wake of Scott's nomination found that "[n]one of the old leaders of the Whig party of Boston and of Massachusetts were even in the hall." Those who did attend included people such as the former *Atlas* publisher William Hayden, clergymen Hubbard Winslow and Matthew Hale Smith, merchant Arthur Chickering, banker Pliney Cutler, and attorney George T. Curtis. With the exception of Curtis, few if any of these individuals moved in upper-class circles. Although well-to-do, they lacked the wealth and prestige that set families such as the Appletons, Lawrences, Winthrops, and Lowells apart from the rest of Boston society. Had local elites wished to do so, they could easily have marshaled their vast resources to quash the Websterite insurrection.[40]

Why didn't they? Lingering attachment to Webster was one reason. However much they disapproved of the secretary's course, some upper-class Bostonians found old loyalties hard to shed. Richard H. Dana told of one wealthy contributor to Webster's subscription fund who called the great man a "dam'd scoundrel" while endorsing a note to finance his activities. A more important reason was their inability to come to grips with the evolving sectional crisis. In a September 1851 diary entry concerning Winthrop, Charles Francis Adams observed: "The real objection to him was his vacillation of mind which rendered him not trustworthy by any side." He could have said much the same thing about most elite Bostonians. Many saw clearly what Webster was doing to their party, but they shared too many of his disunionist fears to confront him or his followers openly. Despite growing evidence that southern Whigs considered intersectional issues nonnegotiable, they continued to hope that reason would prevail among their elite counterparts in the region. Mounting a public assault on the Webster movement at this juncture might undermine or alienate southern moderates who needed every assurance that northern leaders understood their delicate situation. Under the circumstances, a do-nothing policy had much to recommend it.[41]

Winthrop's withdrawal from active politics highlights another dilemma then facing Boston's elite. As noted earlier, leading Associates were aging rapidly and would soon need an infusion of new blood to continue the tradition of social and political leadership they had inherited from their Federalist forebears. By midcentury, that time had come. Now in his seventies, Nathan Appleton could no longer be expected to step forward and champion elite interests in Washington as he had done so capably during several prior crises. Although younger, Abbott Lawrence was in failing health and wanted "if possible to keep out of political partisan warfare—which," he told Appleton, "has been carried on in our State to an absurd extent." The same combination of advancing age and physical debilitation had hobbled many of their longtime business partners. And having lost so many potential replacements in the Conscience Whig revolt, they hoped all the more that Winthrop would assume the role for which he had been groomed. His unwillingness to shoulder that burden made a bad situation serious indeed.[42]

The adverse consequences of this failure to develop a new generation of political talent had become all too apparent after midcentury. William

Appleton, who succeeded Samuel Eliot in Boston's congressional seat, provides one example. A wealthy investor who felt most at ease discussing movements in stock prices, Appleton had never been particularly concerned about public affairs. He was even less so now. "I wish you success," he wrote to Amos A. Lawrence of an 1854 plan to settle "the right sort of people" in Kansas, but "getting old with many things to occupy my mind I do not feel the lively interest in the politics of the day that you and others should." Voiced during the midst of the period's most heated political controversy, this was an astonishing admission from someone chosen to represent New England's leading city in Congress. In fairness to Appleton, he knew he was not the right man for the job and did not really want it. That November, however, he reluctantly consented when party leaders placed heavy pressure on him to run again. They may not have had much choice.[43]

Whatever his shortcomings, Appleton never gave party leaders any reason to regret having supported him. Their selection of Edward Everett to fill a U.S. Senate seat that opened up in 1853 proved considerably more problematic. At first glance, Everett seemed a logical choice for the position. A former congressman, governor, president of Harvard College, ambassador to Great Britain, and secretary of state, the sixty-year-old orator had as impressive a resume as any major politician of the period. But something was missing. For all his experience, Everett lacked assertiveness. Faced with a difficult decision, his first impulse was to equivocate, and when he finally spoke, he typically did so at great length without ever engaging the point at issue. In the words of his brother-in-law, Charles Francis Adams, he was made of "stuff not good enough to wear in rainy weather, though bright enough in sunshine."[44]

The debate over the Kansas-Nebraska Act brought all of Everett's weaknesses to the fore. Submitted by the Illinois senator Stephen A. Douglas in early 1854, the measure repealed the Missouri Compromise and threatened slave expansionism in western territories that most northerners had long assumed would remain forever free. Though opposed to the initiative, Everett vacillated from the start. "Can you not give me some information," he asked John H. Clifford, "as to the light in which the Nebraska bill will be regarded in Massachusetts by the judicious part of the community?" Apparently sensing that the senator's backbone needed stiffening, Clifford responded in the strongest possible terms: everyone he knew believed that "if the South cannot stand upon the Compromise of 1820, which she extorted from us at the sacrifice of nearly every northern man who aided its passage, the issue may as well be met now as ever." He added that in his personal opinion, "the moral element involved in this question is too serious to be made any further or any longer subordinate to the political exigencies arising out of it."[45]

Clifford did not overstate elite opposition to the Kansas-Nebraska Act. To most upper-class Bostonians, the Missouri Compromise represented a binding contract between the sections. That southerners and their northern Democratic allies would even consider repealing it shocked and angered them. At a February meeting in Faneuil Hall, Winthrop, Abbott Lawrence, and George Ticknor urged regional congressmen to do whatever they could to defeat Douglas's pernicious measure. When Congress passed the bill in early March, Boston's normally reserved aristocracy made no effort to conceal its displeasure. "You wd suppose from the looks of our people that they had all been drinking," said Amos A. Lawrence. "We went to bed one night old fashioned, conservative, compromise, Union Whigs & waked up stark mad Abolitionists." Although Lawrence exaggerated, it is easy to understand why he did so. Even staunch Websterites, Winthrop noted, considered Kansas-Nebraska "an act of political perfidy." And for a moment at least, others began thinking the unthinkable. According to George Morey, Nathan Appleton was so disturbed that he felt it time to start discussing "dissolution[,] for the question may be forced upon us."[46]

Everett's response to these developments could not have been more different. Despite Clifford's advice, he continued to look for compromise positions that no longer existed. In a February speech designed to conciliate both sides, he evoked hostile comment from Bay State critics without doing anything to reduce tensions in Congress. Noting the careful, "timid" manner in which Everett "weigh[ed] his words," a *Commonwealth* editorialist declared that the state would have enjoyed much more forceful representation "had the Coalition prevailed; for the power of the commercial aristocracy, the sceptre of the Boston oligarchy, would have been broken, and Massachusetts would have spoken, as it became the sons of '76 to speak." Worse followed. Not only was Everett absent when the act finally came up for a vote in the Senate, but his tepid presentation of an anti-Nebraska remonstrance signed by three thousand New England ministers upset his one-time colleagues in the clergy.[47]

In poor health at the time, Everett had a plausible excuse for missing the Nebraska Act vote. But nobody wanted to hear it. Most Bay Staters were thinking only of Everett's reputation for evading hard decisions. "His name is pronounced with derision & contempt by all men," Henry Wilson wrote to Sumner. Another correspondent told the senator that he was fortunate to have such a colleague, as Everett's "servility & meanness make a strong contrast to anything like manhood & magnanimity." That Massachusetts Free Soilers felt this way was hardly surprising; that many elite Bostonians shared their assessment was less expected and showed how deeply they felt about the Nebraska question. "People who are very prudent generally," said Amos A. Lawrence, "condemn Mr. Everett's course in violent terms."

When the denunciations stopped, ridicule took over. At an elite dinner party attended by Richard Henry Dana, Jr., guests entertained each other by mimicking "poor Everett's attempt to compliment & conciliate both parties without offending either."[48]

Thus it happened that elite opposition to the Kansas-Nebraska Act went largely unacknowledged. Outside Boston, most Bay Staters mistook Everett's vacillating conduct for the will of his aristocratic patrons. Not privy to what transpired in upper-class circles, they were disinclined to challenge the disparaging commentary of Free Soil editors. And in light of elite Boston's avid embrace of the Compromise and other "Union-saving" initiatives, there was little reason why they should have. Since the late 1840s, critics had repeatedly questioned the integrity of elite Bostonians, charging that they were incapable of placing principle before profit and unwilling to subordinate personal considerations to the common good. These assaults continued. In a major address on the Nebraska question, Theodore Parker contended that there was no difference between the two major parties. Democrats may have proposed the measure, but the moral vacuity of Whigs made them equally culpable. "The dollar," he declared in building toward his main argument, "is the germinal dot of the Whig party; its motive is pecuniary; its motto should be, to state it in Latin, *pecunia pecuniata*, money moneyed, money made." Thus it was, and thus it would always be. "Everything must yield to money; that is to have the universal right of way. Down with mankind! The dollar is coming!" There was little new here. Parker had been saying much the same thing for years. What had changed was that the loss of moral authority such attacks inevitably exacted was now being felt. Public indifference to what the elite actually thought about Kansas-Nebraska established a pattern that would repeat itself on at least two critical occasions in the months ahead.[49]

The first involved Anthony Burns, a Virginia fugitive who found employment in a Boston clothing store after his recent escape from bondage. His apprehensions on May 24 and return to slavery ten days later inflamed public opinion throughout the commonwealth. Unlike 1851, when they had gone out of their way to assist Thomas Sims's captors, most elite Bostonians shared the outrage of other Bay Staters. No one better exemplified this change of sentiment than Amos A. Lawrence, who three years earlier had been among the first "to volunteer to shoot the abolitionists & free soilers" obstructing Sims's return. But that was before Kansas-Nebraska. He now felt that elite opinion on the slavery question was "the same as it is in the country towns thro. N. England." More important, he was willing to act on that belief. Upon hearing of Burns's seizure, Lawrence immediately arranged to provide Richard Henry Dana, Jr., any assistance he might need in conducting the fugitive's defense. "He said," Dana wrote of the offer, that "he was authorized to do this by a number of active 1850 men, who determined it shd. be known that it was not the Free Soilers only who were in favor of the liberty of the Slaves, but the conservative, compromise men." Nearly three thousand of these same "conservative, compromise men" later signed a Merchants' Exchange petition demanding repeal of the Fugitive Slave Act.[50]

As it turned out, the initiative angered southern leaders without producing any appreciable change in popular perceptions of the elite. In another major address, Theodore Parker noted—in one brief sentence—that local "merchants feel as they never did before." But the bulk of his remarks showed that he still had grave doubts about where they stood. Confirming Boston's reputation as a place where no foul deed ever goes unremembered, Parker gave his listeners a history lesson, reminding them of such moral travesties as Everett's 1826 proslavery speech in Congress, Garrison's mobbing a decade later by "an assembly of 'respectable gentlemen,'" and the way in which "[m]en of property and standing all over New England supported the apostasy of Daniel Webster" in 1850. Even the elite-sponsored anti-Nebraska gathering at Faneuil Hall—"a meeting of icebergs" that "must have been an encouragement to the men at Washington who advocated the bill"—came in for harsh comment. Although Parker again said little that he had not said before, people who might have been expected to adopt a more charitable view of elite conduct seemed to agree with him. One of them was Dana's father, a retired lawyer and one-time literary figure of some distinction who knew as much as anyone about upper-class society. Deeply "mortified" by Burns's return, he told his good friend William Cullen Bryant that he had lost all "hope that we should be roused to be men." Nothing good, he lamented, could be expected of a community where commerce played so dominant a role: "We are trading creatures; and so shall we continue. Where the calling of a class is *direct* gain, it will drain honor and wear away the pride." Like Parker, Dana was no doubt thinking about the ardent backing elite Bostonians had given the Fugitive Slave Act. They were not alone. By evoking such memories, Henry Wilson later observed, Burns's rendition made a major contribution to the destruction of Bay State Whiggery.[51]

Another instance of elite inability to reclaim the moral high ground occurred that August when Whigs met for their annual state convention. Nearly everyone agreed that the party needed to take a strong stand on Kansas-Nebraska and slave expansionism. The only question was how strong. Ezra Lincoln, who was enjoying the "confusions" of Union-saving colleagues and who wanted "a resolution declaring our eternal hostility to the institution of Slavery as a *political engine,*" found party leaders unwilling to go quite that far. "I have been blowing about for a few days in favor of plain talk," he wrote to Schouler, "but the State Committee are at their old tactics of qualifying the resolutions so as to suit the most delicate, organized minds." Lincoln's discontent notwithstanding, the convention took firm ground on slavery-related issues, condemning Kansas-Nebraska, demanding revision or repeal of the Fugitive Slave Act, and asking party members "to give such aid and direction to the great tide of Western emigration as shall secure our new and unoccupied territories to the dominion of free labor and free institutions, and thus thwart the efforts of the present national administration to bring them under the dominion of slavery." While the platform may have displeased Websterite diehards, there is little reason to question elite support for the resolutions. Not only did the *Advertiser* defend them, but the plank on western settlement could have been lifted from the correspondence of Amos A. Lawrence, who would soon play a major role in financing the New England Emigrant Aid Society's Kansas operations.[52]

Again, however, their political adversaries refused to acknowledge that anything had changed. Unable to criticize the Whig platform, they focused instead on party leadership, asking why the "solid men" of Boston had not attended the convention. Bay State Whiggery, the *Commonwealth* said, "is controlled by a very few persons—men of gravity or eminent wealth. The man that can pay the largest assessment, has the most influence. That man is Abbott Lawrence." But Lawrence apparently wanted nothing to do with a convention committed to combating the spread of slavery, and neither did Everett, Choate, Winthrop, and other party notables who "took good care to keep out of sight of sectionalism."[53]

Considering the source, it is unlikely that these comments occasioned any loss of sleep in Boston's better neighborhoods. Much more worrisome was an editorial on the convention that appeared in William Schouler's *Cincinnati Gazette.* Still in touch with Lincoln and other Whig dissidents, the former *Atlas* editor remained well informed about Massachusetts politics. When he wrote of the "moneyed insolence of the first men of Boston," who "a few years ago considered the fugitive slave law as next in importance to making money and supporting the Union," it was not simply—as the *Courier* observed—evidence of his "hyena-like vindictiveness towards Daniel Webster." Rather, he was speaking for a group of disenchanted party operatives who had played a critical role in Whiggery's revival and belonged to what Lincoln later called the "old clique" that had gathered around the *Atlas.* Without their active support, state Whigs had no hope of retaining power, and at least some of them were now looking elsewhere. As Lincoln wrote to Schouler shortly before the election, "This is to be a year of abortions in every walk of life, & I propose to lie low, study the gospels and enjoy myself as well as I can."[54]

That people of Lincoln's background chose to sit out the 1854 election hammered the final few nails into the coffin of Bay State Whiggery. For that reason alone, it is well worth asking why they did so. In Lincoln's case, the decision doubtless stemmed from resistance to the antislavery resolutions he had proposed inserting in the party platform; like his good friend Schouler, he may have also supported the formation of a broad anti-Nebraska coalition—an initiative that Bay State party leaders adamantly opposed. But these were only proximate causes. As a longtime party regular who lacked the prestige and power that went with an elite pedigree, Lincoln had almost certainly met similar rebuffs on other occasions. Moreover, the platform did take a strong stand on slavery, even if it did not go as far as he wished; he was also as well positioned as anyone to know that elite sentiment on the slavery question was changing. Such differences of opinion as still existed had narrowed considerably during the previous year. Why, then, did he choose this particular moment to desert a party he had served so long and so well?[55]

A large part of the answer can be found in the Kansas-Nebraska Act's effect on state politics. For the past decade, there had been increasing talk of a slave power conspiracy to eliminate northern influence in national councils. With the passage of Kansas-Nebraska, it became considerably harder to dismiss these claims as the paranoid ranting of abolitionist fanatics. By opening the territories to slavery, Douglas's measure cast recent developments in an entirely new light for many Bay Staters. Rather than isolated incidents, the annexation of Texas, the Mexican War, and related events now appeared to be interconnected elements in a broader pattern of slaveholder aggression. At the same time, Kansas-Nebraska destroyed public tolerance for compromise, in the process discrediting all those who had advocated such a course and establishing new standards for regional leadership. In an 1851 response to a letter decrying the oppressive features of Puritan rule, Richard H. Dana conceded that his ancestors had often acted in much too heavy-handed a fashion. Yet, he added, "they had manly adventure, steady endurance, & a stiff & obstinate spirit" that "however misdirected it then was, I should rejoice in my heart to see a little more in the present New England, in this present cause." After Kansas-Nebraska, many others began looking for those same qualities in their political leaders.[56]

For all the vehemence with which they condemned Douglas's bill, elite Bostonians did not fully grasp the magnitude of this shift in public sentiment. Despite their own anger and sense of betrayal, many continued to believe that intersectional harmony could by restored, and that antislavery activists posed as great a threat to national well-being as slave expansionists. The predicament in which they found themselves can perhaps best be seen in an *Advertiser* editorial published shortly before the Whig state convention. In it, the paper's editor complained about Free Soil "ridicule of 'Union-savers.'" The notion that the Union might truly be endangered, he lamented, "is scouted as a bug-bear by men who are constantly stigmatizing the citizens of Boston at the present day for having degenerated from the heroic standard of '76, and calling upon us to imitate the example of Samuel Adams and James Otis." It was a revealing statement that sheds considerable light on why Ezra Lincoln acted as he did. If the former party secretary did not read it, he certainly encountered some expression of it at the convention. More important, no one had to tell him what it meant: in the present crisis, a ruling elite that feared comparison with Adams, Otis, and other revolutionary heroes had plainly lost its moral mandate. Attitudes that had been barely acceptable a few years earlier could no longer be endured.[57]

As significant as these developments were, they do not entirely account for Whiggery's demise. The Know-Nothing insurrection of 1854 also drew on other, equally powerful anti-elite impulses. To understand their effect on Bay State politics, we need to take a brief look at the "country" critique of metropolitan domination.

TENSIONS BETWEEN CITY and country have been a recurring theme throughout much of American history. In Massachusetts, they can be traced at least as far back as the currency debates of the early eighteenth century, which pitted Atlantic traders against proponents of internal development. With the emergence of political parties after the American Revolution, the tradition took on new life in the anti-aristocratic rhetoric that Jeffersonians and Democrats used to lash their Federalist and Whig foes. The midcentury country critique employed similar language. Like the Republicans and Democrats before them, these critics were most concerned about the excessive economic political power of metropolitan elites. What had changed was the political dynamics of dissent. Whereas earlier Democratic assaults on Whig elitism helped bolster party loyalty in a relatively stable two-party system, the midcentury critique contributed to the system's destruction.[58]

Signs of impending dissolution appeared well before the critical 1854 election. One such sign was the breakdown of relations between country Democrats and their customhouse adversaries. Although the two factions had been feuding since the mid-1830s, their mutual detestation of

Whiggery and hunger for office had enabled them to close ranks at election time. But this could only go on for so long. Loathing and opportunism have never been the most enduring bases for cooperation, and by the early 1850s they no longer sufficed. As noted, a major turning point was the coalition's 1852 defeat, which leading country Democrats attributed to customhouse treachery. In a postelection editorial claiming that at least half of Boston's Democrats *"went over to the whigs,"* Worcester's J. S. C. Knowlton condemned *Boston Post* editors for welcoming a political turnabout that placed *"capital,* instead of *men,"* in control of state government. If this meant the coalition's end, then "what follows as a matter of course from its termination?" asked the *Palladium* editor. "A failure of the constitutional convention; the election of a majority of its delegates by Boston and a few other cities and towns that are mere echoes of Boston; and a consequent centralization of all the civil and political power of the state in that place— in the hands of the whigs; and that, it is fair to presume, would also give 'a great deal of pleasure' to the Post."[59]

As it turned out, proponents of reform controlled the convention, and the *Post* gave them consistent editorial backing. But the outcome of the campaign—an effort to make "MEN, and not MONEY," the dominant power in the commonwealth—only added to Knowlton's bitterness. That voters rejected the new constitution was bad enough; that Caleb Cushing's ukase contributed to its defeat confirmed his already low opinion of customhouse leaders. By this point, Knowlton could see no appreciable difference between them and their Whig counterparts. When the party held its 1854 convention in Lowell, he claimed it did so to exclude country Democrats from western areas of the state. The latter nevertheless made their presence felt, and the gathering "was any thing but a harmonious one," as they adamantly opposed resolutions "to bring the general government to the aid of the slaveholders in extending slavery beyond the bounds assigned to it by the founders of the republic." The convention's general neglect of state reform left them all the more discontented and ready to support the Know-Nothing insurrection. Though sharing their anger, Knowlton did not follow them. Repelled by nativism, but no longer a Democrat, he eventually found a new home in the Republican Party.[60]

When country Democrats assailed metropolitan elitism, they drew on a rhetorical tradition that stretched back to the party's Jeffersonian origins. The political heritage of most Free Soilers was much different. As former Whigs, many of them had once been the targets of such attacks. Their adoption of the country critique stemmed from elite resistance to their antislavery activities. The more obstacles they encountered, the more convinced they became that the unchecked power of Boston's ruling elite threatened democratic government in Massachusetts. The realization came at different times to different people. But at one point or another, most of them reached the same conclusion as Samuel Downer, who in an 1850 letter told Horace Mann: "It seems to me, there has grown up amongst us, from our manufacturers, an all controlling Aristocracy, who from some fatal infatuation, are determined to break down all agitation either in regard to the extension or restraining of Slavery—& they control enough of the money, talent & Character of the Community, to render all other opposition abortive."[61]

Like country Democrats, Free Soilers looked to constitutional reform as a means of checking elite dominance. The fact that many of them were thoroughgoing urbanites did not prevent their making full use of the country critique at the convention. "Whatever may be said to the contrary," declared Lynn shoe manufacturer John B. Alley, "I nevertheless believe that the country does need protection against the cities and large towns." What made that influence so pernicious was the role money played in urban life. Where accumulation dwarfed all other concerns, basic issues of justice and morality could never receive a fair hearing. "Put wealth in one scale and the question of human freedom in the other," said Worcester's Henry Chapin, "and see, in a community devoted to trade, which will soonest kick the beam. Where do you find the rights of man most sacredly regarded?" he asked. "Is it in that spot where the whole atmosphere breathes of nothing but of making money, or where the blue sky shines above us, where the fresh breezes are blowing over the hills, and where the great moral eye of public virtue looks in upon wrong and rebukes it[?]" No country Democrat or Free Soiler had to think twice before answering that question. And the effectiveness of such rhetoric could afterward be seen in the strong anti-urban bias of the convention's proposals for reforming the state's system of representation.[62]

That same bias largely explained the constitution's defeat. Not surprisingly, proponents of reform did not see it that way. Although their post-election analyses took various factors into account, the influence of Boston money loomed large in all of them. They devoted particular attention to the conspicuous role played by Abbott Lawrence. "We shall have his money to fight and also those who think 'his hand feeds them,'" Henry Wilson wrote several months before the election. But that was just as well, he added: "As the head of the corporation interests he will be objectionable to the Democrats." Wilson and others adopted a much different view of the industrialist's intervention after voters rejected the new constitution. "Abbott Lawrence going about the state drenching his pocket-handkerchief with tears at the bare idea of being disfranchised was," said William Robinson, "a subject of mirth, to be sure; but Abbott Lawrence dragging his wallet and contents out to 'feed' forty-one perambulating Whig orators formed quite another picture." Worcester's John Milton Earle, who had been as ardent an advocate of constitutional reform as any editor in the commonwealth, no doubt had just such a picture in mind when he told *Worcester Daily Spy* readers: "The money power has been brought to bear and now sits enthroned over the State, chuckling in the belief that its permanent reign is secured."[63]

Whatever elite Bostonians may have thought, other Whigs recognized that the questions raised by proponents of reform had not been answered and needed to be taken much more seriously than party leaders realized. Their main spokesman was Samuel Bowles, the enterprising editor of the *Springfield Republican,* which in recent years had emerged as the party's most influential country sheet. Writing to Henry Dawes in May 1853, Bowles observed: "Now is the time to start new; the old issues are gone, we can't live under them. We are beaten out." By taking an advanced position on constitutional reform, he believed, Bay State Whigs could refurbish their image and establish a solid foundation for future electoral successes. For a variety of reasons, Bowles found the new constitution unacceptable. But this did not diminish his commitment to reform. Rather than gloating over its defeat—as Lawrence and others did—he continued to urge Whig leaders to make the issue their own.[64]

Their response proved disappointing. Although Boston's "eminent hunker Whigs" made no effort "to 'crush out' the reformatory notions of the Springfield Republican & Company," as the *Worcester Spy* predicted they would after the election, they gave equally little indication that they were listening to Bowles. Indeed, since returning to power the party's only initiative on a reform-related measure was to emasculate the secret-ballot law by making the use of sealed envelopes optional in elections—an action that the *Republican* characterized as "a great blunder of a blundering" legislative session. This issue also received attention at the convention, where delegates furnished extensive evidence of voter intimidation in various manufacturing centers. In so doing, they depicted a chain of dependency that extended downward from corporate offices to the most menial occupation in the state's industrial workplaces. As Henry Wilson described the situation: "The men who control the hundred of millions of corporate and individual wealth, employed in the immense manufacturing and mechanical interest of this State, and their agents, overseers, clerks, and master workmen who are dependent upon them for positions of influence and pecuniary value, are very apt to think that the policy of the government [a]ffects that interest, and that the laborers and mechanics dependent upon that interest, should vote, not according to their own convictions, but according to their supposed interests, or the interests of their employers."[65]

Wilson's remarks, which go to the heart of the country critique, tell us much about why it seemed so compelling. In Whig ideology, the manufacturing interest comprised one group in an interdependent socioeconomic system and provided the material foundation for a harmonious society in which everyone benefited from industrial growth and expansion. If Wilson was right, something had gone terribly wrong: The world created by the Boston Associates had become one of class oppression, not social harmony—one of dependence rather than interdependence. By midcentury, increasing numbers of people had reason to take such rhetoric seriously. In addition to the state's burgeoning industrial labor force, their ranks included farmers, shopkeepers, and small producers. Caught up in the market revolution that transformed antebellum society, these petty entrepreneurs had learned—often the hard way—that the managerial hierarchies of Lowell textile mills were not the only chains of dependency that threatened the autonomy of Massachusetts citizens. By putting a face on their fears and grievances, the country critique crystallized worker and middling-class discontent, in the process turning it into a powerful force for political change.[66]

The growing acceptance of these views completed the destruction of Bay State Whiggery's ideological foundations. By 1854, a once compelling political appeal had lost whatever power it had to sway voters. In the wake of Kansas-Nebraska, nothing could be done to repair the damage to the party's reputation as a defender of New England civilization; with the spreading embrace of the country critique, its claims to represent a much cherished harmony of interests appeared equally suspect. Along the way, the party had experienced a gradual hollowing-out that began with the Conscience Whig revolt of 1848, worsened under the strains of Websterite factionalism, and ended in the defection of its most able political operatives. These developments, coupled with a dawning realization that no moderate solution existed to the sectional crisis, even affected some of the elite Bostonians who dictated party policy, stripping them of the confidence needed to continue the struggle. A shell of its former self, with leaders who no longer possessed the moral authority to mount a comeback, Bay State Whiggery passed from the scene, thus ending the second party system in Massachusetts.

Conclusion

$\mathcal{N}$EARLY A CENTURY and a half later, the Know-Nothing triumph of 1854 continues to occupy a unique place in Massachusetts electoral history. The party not only captured the governorship and every congressional seat, but the entire state senate and all but three seats in a 379-member lower house as well. Edward Everett, who had taken comfort in the fact that "[n]o person of standing in the political world" had enlisted in the new organization, could barely contain his astonishment afterward. "The overwhelming completeness of the revolution, the novelty, the uncertain character of the disturbing force," he wrote, "have produced a sort of paralysis in the minds of men." Even people whose hatred of Whiggery left them much better prepared for such a turnabout expressed surprise at the election's outcome. Using language very similar to that of Everett, Charles Francis Adams observed, "There has been no revolution so compete since the organization of government."[1]

How could this have happened to a party that had dominated state politics since its inception two decades earlier? That Whigs everywhere experienced defeat in 1854 is certainly significant, and the national party's inability to regroup afterward partly explains the subsequent demise of Bay State Whiggery. No one wants to be the last person on the deck of a sinking ship. But this had happened before—in 1815 when Federalism succumbed as a national party—and Boston's political elite had weathered the storm. What was so different about 1854? And why were Massachusetts Whigs so resoundingly repudiated?

One important change was a growing perception that the activities of elite Bostonians threatened rather than reinforced interclass harmony. With the emergence of a broad-based country critique that incorporated and extended dissident views first expressed by labor radicals, increasing numbers of Bay Staters began to look more closely at the political and economic ramifications of elite power. As they did, they wondered whether the Boston Associates still shared their commitment to the doctrine of social interdependence. What they concluded was less significant than the fact that such questions were being asked. That people had any doubts at all undercut a major ideological prop of Federalist-Whig rule.

The rise of Conscience Whiggery marked another major difference between late antebellum politics and the Federalist era. During the earlier period, a group of young Federalists took over for party elders and revived a deteriorating organization that seemed destined for an early end. Whereas these young men of the elite brought new life to a party in decline, their counterparts in the late 1840s helped destroy a still vigorous organization that appeared ready to dominate national as well as state affairs. When Boston's elite later sought an infusion of new political blood, the pool of suitable donors was much smaller than it otherwise would have been. Had Bay State Whiggery survived, the social composition of its leadership still would have changed.

Even more important than the foregoing was the inability of elite Bostonians to uphold their reputation as defenders of New England civilization. When they lost that, they also lost the moral authority on which their rule rested. "The political creed was Whig," Henry Adams once wrote of antebellum Brahmin politics, "if creed that were which consisted mainly of an unlimited respect for the status quo, and left its disciples quite wild when confronted with, or called upon for anything like a principle." Given the often abusive treatment Adams's father and grandfather received at the hands of these people, his malice is certainly understandable; forgiving and forgetting were never conspicuous elements of the Adams ethos. Yet for all the ill feeling that prompted the remark, there was an uncomfortable amount of truth in it. As sectional differences deepened and the nation moved toward war, elite Bostonians spoke often of law and order, the need for moderation and reason, respect for the Constitution, and above all property rights, which according to George Ticknor formed "the great bond of society" everywhere. "I wonder how we should feel," said Robert Winthrop, "if *our* property was at stake, here in New England."[2]

Absent in all this was any hint of the assertive regionalism that had made Whiggery and Federalism before it so appealing. Bay Staters continued to cherish all the values mentioned above; they had, Theodore Parker observed, "profound respect for social unity, represented by General Law." But these values formed part of a broader constellation of beliefs that gave them an abiding sense of what it meant to be a New Englander. "I am, as a public man, a child of Massachusetts," John Clifford wrote to Winthrop in an 1856 letter explaining why he could no longer tolerate southern arrogance:

"I think the time has come when the Slave States of this Union must understand that the political power of this government is, and of right ought to be with the Free States, and that by the blessing of God we mean to exercise it." These sentiments, though voiced by a longtime friend who was in most respects just as conservative as the former congressman, made no impression on Winthrop. He and other elite Bostonians consistently rejected requests that they join the newly formed Republican Party, choosing instead to back Millard Fillmore's 1856 American candidacy. Four years later, the final presidential contest of the antebellum era completed their political marginalization, as they regrouped under the banner of Constitutional Unionism—a party that, in the words of one wag, drew its membership from "a class of simple people who believe that the sun rises in Chelsea, comes up over State Street, hovers above the State House, and sinks into the waters of the Back Bay."[3]

Throughout, the Associates' materialistic view of historical processes limited their ability to comprehend the deep passions fueling the sectional conflict. They never really understood their southern counterparts. Eminently prudent people themselves, they could not believe a ruling elite would be so reckless as to gamble everything on secession when it had so much to gain from preserving the status quo. "What can be more advantageous than the intercourse between South Carolina and Massachusetts?" asked Nathan Appleton in a public letter written shortly after the Palmetto State seceded from the Union. "You furnish us with cotton, which we manufacture, and supply you with many wholesome 'notions.'" It was a sad but fitting commentary on the death of Bay State Whiggery. Three decades earlier, during another sectional crisis, the great industrialist had helped lay the ideological foundation for a generation of party dominance with his defense of regional interests; he now demonstrated why that "creed" and those who espoused it had been cast aside.[4]

As it turned out, the Associates' political isolation did not last long. When Confederate forces bombarded Fort Sumter in April 1861, they immediately rallied to the flag, declaring their willingness to do whatever they could to aid the Union cause. Assisted by Governor John A. Andrew, who went out of his way to promote elite support for the war effort, they gradually reentered the mainstream of public life. With the formation of the Boston Union Club and the New England Loyal Publication Society in 1863, their political reintegration was nearly complete. By the following year, William Robinson could report that "[t]he best part of the old conservative Whig section is with the Republican party now."[5]

Many of them probably wondered why they had not made the move sooner. Though led by longtime political adversaries, the party they joined had much in common with antebellum Whiggery. Its commitment to economic development and a free labor ideology that emphasized the interdependence of capital and labor made most elite Bostonians feel right at home. Where doubts remained, Republican wartime policies quickly dispelled them. As early suspicions of corporate influence faded, party legislators pushed through an economic program that one historian aptly dubbed a "second American System." Its escalating tariff rates, munificent grants to railroad companies, and general openness to manufacturers' concerns gave the Associates all the assurance they needed about the soundness of Republican doctrine.[6]

One should not conclude from all this that little had changed. Nothing could be farther from the truth. As Union armies gathered to destroy the last remnant of the slave power in April 1865, it was easy to forget how improbable such an event seemed only a decade earlier. In an 1851 letter complaining about the Free Soilers' inability to make themselves heard, Samuel Downer observed: "It is the first time, when I have ever noticed the controlling part of both parties, bent on debauching the nation & it makes one restless & unhappy, a sort of nightmare feeling." He wanted to "cry out" but could not, as resistance "appears to give new forces of power to their energy & they trample all the more."

While this work has focused on the major public figures who helped shatter that wall of indifference, the contributions made by many ordinary men and women should not be forgotten. "Every where the characters are the same," Charles Francis Adams said of the typical audience at early Free Soil meetings. "A union of the middling classes of the three parties, farmers, mechanics, and working men." It was they who inspired Channing, helped Adams's father defend the right of petition, brought down Whiggery, and filled Bay State regiments in the Civil War. Living in a world where media and party routinely assert that hopes for human betterment must be subordinated to market dictates—in the process creating that same "nightmare feeling" of which Downer spoke—we too should draw inspiration from them.[7]

Notes

Introduction

1. Kinley J. Brauer, *Cotton versus Conscience: Massachusetts Whig Politics and Southwestern Expansion, 1843–1848* (Lexington: University of Kentucky Press, 1967), 5. The term "Boston Associates" was coined by Vera Shlakman, *Economic History of a Factory Town: A Study of Chicopee, Massachusetts* (1934–1935; repr. New York: Octagon Books, 1969), 28–47.

2. John Mayfield, *Rehearsal for Republicanism: Free Soil and the Politics of Anti-Slavery* (Port Washington, N.Y.: Kennikat Press, 1980), 51.

3. For more on the significant role of the middling classes in antebellum politics, see two articles by Bruce Laurie: "'Spavined Ministers, Lying Toothpullers, and Buggering Priests': Third-Partyism and the Search for Security in the Antebellum North," in *American Artisans: Crafting Social Identity, 1750–1850*, ed. Howard B. Rock, Paul A. Gilje, and Robert Asher (Baltimore: Johns Hopkins University Press, 1995), 98–119; and "The 'Fair Field' of the 'Middle Ground': Abolitionism, Labor Reform, and the Making of an Antislavery Bloc in Antebellum Massachusetts," in *Labor Histories: Class, Politics, and the Working-Class Experience,* ed. Eric Arnesen, Julie Greene, and Bruce Laurie (Urbana: University of Illinois Press, 1998), 45–70.

Chapter One

1. Christopher Gore to Rufus King, 10 March 1805, Rufus King, *The Life and Correspondence of Rufus King: Comprising His Letters, Private and Official, His Public Documents and His Speeches,* ed. Charles R. King, 6 vols. (New York: G. P. Putnam's Sons, 1894–1900), 4: 448.

2. David Hackett Fischer, *The Revolution of American Conservatism: The Federalist Party in the Era of Jeffersonian Democracy* (New York: Harper & Row, 1965). As the chapter title suggests, I have leaned heavily on Fischer's work. His book not only provides an able description of the Federalists' efforts to create a popular

conservatism, but contains perceptive observations on the broader significance of their achievement.

3. Ibid., 245–77.

4. Richard E. Welch, Jr., *Theodore Sedgwick, Federalist: A Political Portrait* (Middletown, Conn.: Wesleyan University Press, 1965), 136; Fischer, *Revolution of American Conservatism*, 3–5; James M. Banner, Jr., *To the Hartford Convention: The Federalists and the Origins of Party Politics in Massachusetts, 1789–1815* (New York: Alfred A. Knopf, 1970), 53–58.

5. Thomas Wentworth Higginson, *Life and Times of Stephen Higginson* (Boston: Houghton Mifflin, 1907), 42; William T. Whitney, Jr., "The Crowninshields of Salem, 1800–1808: A Study in the Politics of Commercial Growth, Part I," *Essex Institute Historical Collections* 94 (January 1958): 31; William Bentley, *Diary of William Bentley, D.D., Pastor of the East Church, Salem, Massachusetts*, 4 vols. (Salem, Mass.: The Essex Institute, 1905–1914), 4: 387.

6. Christopher Clark, *The Roots of Rural Capitalism: Western Massachusetts, 1780–1860* (Ithaca, N.Y.: Cornell University Press, 1990), 50–55; Banner, *To the Hartford Convention*, 183; George Cabot to Caleb Strong, 6 June 1796, Henry Cabot Lodge, *Life and Letters of George Cabot* (Boston: Little, Brown, 1877), 96.

7. David H. Fisher, "The Myth of the Essex Junto," *William and Mary Quarterly* 21 (April 1964): 197–99; Peter Dobkin Hall, "Family Structure and Class Consolidation among the Boston Brahmins" (Ph.D. diss., State University of New York at Stony Brook, 1973), 7–8, 26–31; Winfred E. A. Bernhard, *Fisher Ames: Federalist and Statesman, 1758–1808* (Chapel Hill: University of North Carolina Press, 1965), 72; Fisher Ames, "Equality: No. II," November 1801, Fisher Ames, *Works of Fisher Ames: With a Selection from His Speeches and Correspondence*, ed. Seth Ames, 2 vols. (Boston: Little, Brown, 1854), 2: 211.

8. George Cabot to Christopher Gore, 2 May 1799, Lodge, *Cabot*, 231. See also Cabot to Timothy Pickering, 7 November 1798, ibid., 181; and Banner, *To the Hartford Convention*, 81–83.

9. Stephen Higginson to Nathan Dane, 3 March 1787, "Letters of Stephen Higginson, 1783–1804," ed. J. Franklin Jameson, *Annual Report of the American Historical Association*, 2 vols. (Washington, D.C.: Government Printing Office, 1897), 1: 754.

10. Bentley, *Diary*, 4: 17; Theodore Sedgwick to Rufus King, 20 March 1799, King, *Correspondence*, 2: 582; Paul Goodman, *The Democratic-Republicans of Massachusetts: Politics in a Young Republic* (Cambridge: Harvard University Press, 1964), 70, 75–77; Henry Adams, *History of the United States during the Administrations of Jefferson and Madison*, 9 vols. (New York: Charles Scribner's Sons, 1889–1891), 2: 206.

11. Fischer, "Myth of the Essex Junto," 204–9.

12. [Stephen Higginson], *Ten Chapters in the Life of John Hancock: The Writings of Laco* (1789; repr. New York: n.p., 1857), 10–11, 20–21, 24–26.

13. Fisher Ames to Oliver Wolcott, 9 July 1795, Oliver Wolcott, *Memoirs of the Administrations of Washington and John Adams, Edited from the Papers of Oliver Wolcott, Secretary of the Treasury*, ed. George Gibbs, 2 vols. (New York: n.p., 1846), 1: 210; Paul A. Varg, *New England and Foreign Relations, 1789–1850* (Hanover, N.H.:

University Press of New England, 1983), 24–27; George Cabot to Timothy Picker-
ing, 21 February 1799, Lodge, *Cabot,* 219–20; Cabot to Wolcott, 22 February 1799,
Wolcott, *Memoirs,* 2: 183. Additional expressions of old-school disappointment con-
cerning the merchant response to Jay's Treaty can by found in Cabot to Rufus King, 25
July 1795, King, *Correspondence,* 2: 17; and Cabot to Wolcott, 24 August 1795, Wolcott,
Memoirs, 1: 227.

14. Stephen Higginson to Oliver Wolcott, 25 June 1799, Wolcott, *Memoirs,* 2:
243–44.

15. Stephen Higginson to Samuel Adams, 20 May, 10 June 1783, *Letters of Members of the Continental Congress,* ed. Edmund C. Burnett, 8 vols. (Washington, D.C.:
Carnegie Institution of Washington, 1921–1936), 7: 107, 184; Higginson to Alexander
Hamilton, 11 November 1789, Alexander Hamilton, *The Papers of Alexander Hamilton,*
ed. Harold C. Syrett et al., 27 vols. (New York: Columbia University Press, 1961–
1987), 5: 510–11.

16. Stephen G. Kurtz, *The Presidency of John Adams: The Collapse of Federalism,
1795–1800* (Philadelphia: University of Pennsylvania Press, 1957), 359–66, 380; Stanley
Elkins and Eric McKitrick, *The Age of Federalism: The Early American Republic, 1788–
1800* (New York: Oxford University Press, 1993), 714–19, 726–40.

17. George Cabot to Oliver Wolcott, 3 April 1797, Wolcott, *Memoirs,* 1: 489;
Lodge, *Cabot,* 575.

18. Bentley, *Diary,* 3: 370–71; Fisher Ames to Thomas Dwight, 31 December 1792;
Ames to Timothy Pickering, 5 November 1799; Ames to George R. Minot, 27 May
1789, Ames, *Works,* 1: 126, 263, 44.

19. Fisher Ames to Christopher Gore, 14 December 1801, Ames, *Works,* 1: 311;
Bernhard, *Fisher Ames,* 289; Ames, "Falkland. No. III," February 1801, Ames, *Works,*
2: 137; Fischer, *Revolution,* 59; Ames to Gore, 13 December 1802, Ames, *Works,* 1: 311;
"He that robs me" quotation in Ames to Thomas Dwight, 29 November 1803, ibid.,
1: 335; Ames to George R. Minot, 27 May 1789, 16 February 1792, ibid., 1: 45, 112; Ames
to Timothy Pickering, 28 April 1804, Timothy Pickering Papers, Massachusetts
Historical Society, Boston, Massachusetts (MHS), microfilm ed., reel 27.

20. Fisher Ames to Oliver Wolcott, 12 January 1800, Wolcott, *Memoirs,* 2: 319;
Ames to Theodore Dwight, 19 March 1801, Ames, *Works,* 1: 294; Fisher, *Revolu-
tion,* 135–36; Banner, *To the Hartford Convention,* 134–35; quotations from Ames to
Jeremiah Smith, 14 December 1802, Ames, *Works,* 1: 316.

21. Banner, *To the Hartford Convention,* 258–60; Fisher Ames, "The Dangers of
American Liberty," 1805, Ames, *Works,* 2: 344–99, quotations from pp. 357, 380.

22. Fisher Ames to Timothy Pickering, 17 January 1807, Ames, *Works,* 1: 386;
George Cabot to Pickering, 14 February 1804, *Documents Relating to New-England
Federalism, 1800–1815,* ed. Henry Adams (Boston: Little, Brown, 1877), 347–48. Cabot
was not the only old-schooler to voice such sentiments. See Theodore Sedgwick to
Alexander Hamilton, 27 January 1803, Hamilton, *Papers,* 26: 79.

23. Banner, *To the Hartford Convention,* 216–67; Fischer, *Revolution,* 59, 65; Samuel Eliot Morison, *The Life and Letters of Harrison Gray Otis, Federalist, 1765–1848,*
2 vols. (Boston: Houghton Mifflin, 1913), 1: 286–320. The phrase "Headquarters

of good principles" is from Josiah Dwight to Harrison Gray Otis, 16 March 1808, Morison, *Otis*, 1: 334.

24. W. J. Rorabaugh, *The Craft Apprentice: From Franklin to the Machine Age in America* (New York: Oxford University Press, 1986), 17–20, 22–23, 26–29; Joseph T. Buckingham, *Specimens of Newspaper Literature: With Personal Memoirs, Anecdotes, and Reminiscences,* 2 vols. (Boston: Charles C. Little and James Brown, 1850), 2: 5, 77.

25. Buckingham, *Specimens,* 2: 57, 45, 110, quotation from p. 110; Buckingham, *Annals of the Massachusetts Charitable Mechanic Association* (Boston: Crocker and Brewster, 1853), 6.

26. John Quincy Adams, *Memoirs of John Quincy Adams, Comprising Portions of His Diary from 1795 to 1848,* ed. Charles Francis Adams, 12 vols. (Philadelphia: J. B. Lippincott, 1874–1877), 1: 259–60; *Columbian Centinel,* 5 February 1803. It should be added that Adams, who was then a member of the state senate, also objected to the proposed charter. When James Lloyd asked that he support the measure, Adams refused, stating that he intended to submit a bill opening stock subscriptions to all comers. See J. Q. Adams, *Memoirs,* 1: 261. The bank conflict is also examined in Goodman, *Democratic-Republican,* 171–73; and Robert A. East, "Economic Development and New England Federalism, 1803–1814," *New England Quarterly* 10 (September 1937): 434–36.

27. Naomi Lamoreaux, *Insider Lending: Banks, Personal Connections, and Economic Development in Industrial New England* (Cambridge: Cambridge University Press, 1994), 1–30; *Columbian Centinel,* 9 and 16 February 1803.

28. *Columbian Centinel,* 20 April 1803, 25 June 1805.

29. Morison, *Otis,* 1: 262–63, 270; Stephen Higginson to Timothy Pickering, 22 November 1803, "Higginson Letters," 1: 837–38; Leverett Saltonstall to Nathaniel Saltonstall, 23 July 1803, "The Saltonstall Papers, 1607–1815," ed. Robert E. Moody, *Collections of the Massachusetts Historical Society,* 80–81 (1972–1974), 81: 158; *Columbian Centinel,* 13, 16, and 23 July 1803.

30. George Cabot to Timothy Pickering, 14 February 1804, *Documents,* ed. Adams, 349.

31. Samuel Taggart to John Taylor, 13 January 1804, "Letters of Samuel Taggart, Representative in Congress, 1803–1814," ed. George Henry Haynes, *Proceedings of the American Antiquarian Society,* 33 (11 April–17 October 1923): 123.

32. Bradford Perkins, *Prologue to War: England and the United States, 1805–1812* (Berkeley: University of California Press, 1961), 79–82; Christopher Gore to Rufus King, 7 October 1805, King, *Correspondence,* 4: 457; *Annals of Congress,* 9th Cong., 2d sess., Appendix, 890–99, quotation from p. 899.

33. Christopher Gore to Rufus King, 14 August 1806, 25 November 1805, King, *Correspondence,* 4: 537, 467–68. It should be noted that not all New England Federalists adopted so mercenary a view of the European war. Leverett Saltonstall, a young Federalist from Salem, expressed regret that regional merchants had become "careless to the honor of the nation" as they profited from the "calamities" of others. See Leverett Saltonstall to Nathaniel Saltonstall, 7 February 1807, "Saltonstall Papers," 81: 360.

34. Perkins, *Prologue to War,* 101–56.

35. George Cabot to Timothy Pickering, 31 December 1807, Pickering Papers, MHS, reel 28; Benjamin Goodhue to Pickering, 31 March 1806, Pickering Papers, reel 27.

36. Samuel Taggart to John Taylor, 22 December 1807, "Taggart Letters," 224; Thomas Jefferson to J. C. Cabell, 2 February 1816, quoted in Dumas Malone, *Jefferson the President: Second Term, 1805–1809* (Boston: Little, Brown, 1974), 613.

37. George Cabot to Timothy Pickering, 31 December 1807, Pickering Papers, MHS, reel 28; *Columbian Centinel,* 6 January 1808; Merchants and Others of the Town of Boston to Thomas Jefferson, 4 March 1808, Thomas Jefferson Papers, Library of Congress (LC), microfilm ed., reel 40; Samuel Eliot Morison, *The Maritime History of Massachusetts, 1783–1860* (Boston: Houghton Mifflin, 1921), 188–89; *Columbian Centinel,* 30 March 1808.

38. George Cabot to Timothy Pickering, 31 December 1807, Pickering Papers, MHS, reel 28; Merchants and Others of the Town of Boston to Thomas Jefferson, 4 March 1808, Jefferson Papers, LC, reel 40; *Salem Gazette,* 6 September 1808. Given the sentiments expressed in these and numerous other memorials from Bay State communities, it is little wonder that Jefferson soon grew weary of reading Massachusetts petitions. Malone, *Jefferson the President: Second Term,* 608–9.

39. The letters from "Timothy" and "Curtius" are both in *Massachusetts Spy,* 30 March 1808. Also, see the letter from "A Farmer" in *Hampshire Gazette* (Extra), 30 March 1808, and the Lancaster and Petersham petitions in *Massachusetts Spy,* 14 September 1808.

40. J. E. Crowley, *This Sheba, Self: The Conceptualization of Economic Life in Eighteenth-Century America* (Baltimore: Johns Hopkins University Press, 1974), 111–16; both the Lancaster and Northborough petitions are in *Worcester Spy,* 14 September 1808. As with much that occurred during the period, George Cabot anticipated the renewed regard for merchant contributions to society. See Cabot to Timothy Pickering, 31 March 1806, Pickering Papers, MHS, reel 27.

41. *Columbian Centinel,* 20 January, 23 March, 29 June 1808.

42. An Elector of Plymouth District to Congressman Joseph Barker, *Columbian Centinel,* 30 April 1808; *Hampshire Gazette* (Extra), 23 March 1808; *Massachusetts Spy,* 30 March 1808. A particularly comprehensive discussion of the sectional jealousy theme can be found in the series of articles by "Falkland" in *Columbian Centinel,* September–October 1808. The belief that southerners envied New England's commercial achievements was not new. See Stephen Higginson to John Adams, 30 December 1785, "Higginson Letters," 1: 728–29. It should also be noted that Jeffersonian economic views were more complex than most Federalists believed, as Drew McCoy shows in *The Elusive Republic: Political Economy in Jeffersonian America* (Chapel Hill: University of North Carolina Press, 1980).

43. *Columbian Centinel,* 3 April, 16 July 1808. Various expressions of the Virginia tyranny theme can be found in the communications of "Thousands," *Hampshire Gazette,* 8 May 1808; "Every Patriot of New England," *New England Palladium,* 30 August 1808; "Hampden," *Columbian Centinel,* 7 September 1808; "Boston," *New*

England Palladium, 9 September 1808; and "Sentinel," *New England Palladium,* 29 November 1808.

44. *Independent Chronicle,* 3 November, 12 September 1808.

45. Joseph Story to Samuel P. P. Fay, 9 January 1809, William W. Story, *Life and Letters of Joseph Story, Associate Justice of the Supreme Court, and Dane Professor of Law at Harvard University,* 2 vols. (Boston: Charles C. Little and James Brown, 1851), 1: 182; Orchard Cook to John Quincy Adams, 10 and 28 November 1808, Adams Family Papers, MHS, microfilm ed., reel 406. It took some time before Story himself reached this conclusion; he initially believed that most southern politicians were "vehement opposers" of commerce. Story to William Fettyplace, 28 February 1808, Story, *Life and Letters of Story,* 1: 165. Addressing the sectional issue from a partisan perspective, the Federalist congressman Samuel Taggart observed that northern Republicans feel "the encroachments of Virginia, tho I do not find that they have been possessed of honesty, and independence enough to state the same to their constituents." Taggart to John Taylor, 17 November 1804, "Taggart Letters," 132.

46. *Independent Chronicle,* 31 December 1807, 4 January, 26 May 1808. In fairness to the *Chronicle*'s editor, it should be noted that he doubtless scored a few points when he added the following to the statement quoted in the text: "If the industrious merchant and tradesman are pressed by a set of harpies, who distress the needy in the loan of money at" exorbitant interest rates, "we expect such *usury laws* will be passed to check the *internal commercial depredation* which is daily made by a few who prowl the Exchange." This does not, however, contradict my broader point: Massachusetts Republicans had no effective response to Federalist charges that the embargo was crippling merchants, farmers, and mechanics.

47. Josiah Quincy to Harrison Gray Otis, 26 November 1811, Quincy, Wendell, Holmes, and Upham Papers (QWHU Papers), MHS, microfilm ed., reel 35.

48. Josiah Quincy, *Figures of the Past: From the Leaves of Old Journals* (Boston: Roberts Brothers, 1884), 324–25; Timothy Pickering to Henry Pickering, 1810, Octavius Pickering and Charles W. Upham, *The Life of Timothy Pickering,* 4 vols. (Boston: Little, Brown, 1874), 4: 201; Fischer, "Myth of the Essex Junto," 197. The best biography of Pickering is Gerard H. Clarfield, *Timothy Pickering and the American Republic* (Pittsburgh: University of Pittsburgh Press, 1980).

49. James Morton Smith, *Freedom's Fetters: The Alien and Sedition Laws and American Civil Liberties* (Ithaca, N.Y.: Cornell University Press, 1956), 182–83, 186–87; Bentley, *Diary,* 2: 457; 3: 29; Clarfield, *Pickering,* 165–79.

50. Thomas Jefferson to Levi Lincoln, 23 March 1808, Jefferson Papers, LC, reel 41. The letter to which Jefferson refers can be found in *Columbian Centinel,* 12 March 1808; it is as good an example as any of Pickering's tendency to go overboard in his defense of British policy. Between 1804 and 1809, the proportion of adult white males voting in Massachusetts rose from 42 percent to 63.9 percent. Banner, *To the Hartford Convention,* 359–60.

51. *Columbian Centinel,* 31 March 1810; *Independent Chronicle,* quoted in Helen R. Pinkney, *Christopher Gore, Federalist of Massachusetts, 1758–1827* (Waltham, Mass.: Gore Place Society, 1969), 116.

52. Ronald P. Formisano, *The Transformation of Political Culture: Massachusetts Politics, 1790s–1840s* (New York: Oxford University Press, 1983), 68–72; Stephen Higginson to John Adams, 24 March 1790, "Higginson Letters," 1: 177; Timothy Williams to Timothy Pickering, 9 January 1808, Pickering Papers, MHS, reel 28. Following Sullivan's advice, the seamen afterward submitted a relief petition to Boston selectmen. *Independent Chronicle,* 21 January 1808.

53. Perkins, *Prologue to War,* 160–61; Burton Spivak, *Jefferson's English Crisis: Commerce, Embargo, and the Republican Revolution* (Charlottesville: University Press of Virginia, 1979), 166; John D. Forbes, "Boston Smuggling, 1807–1815," *American Neptune* 10 (April 1950): 146.

54. James Sullivan to Thomas Jefferson, 21 and 23 July 1808, Jefferson Papers, LC, reel 41. Evidence supporting Sullivan's contention about Bay State smuggling traditions can be found throughout Thomas C. Barrow's fine work on British commercial policy during the colonial era, *Trade and Empire: The British Customs Service in Colonial America* (Cambridge: Harvard University Press, 1967).

55. Albert Gallatin to Thomas Jefferson, 17 August, 16 September 1808, *The Writings of Albert Gallatin,* ed. Henry Adams, 3 vols. (Philadelphia: J. B. Lippincott, 1879), 1: 406, 418; Malone, *Jefferson the President: Second Term,* 595–96. Despite his lack of confidence in Sullivan, Jefferson was nevertheless alarmed by the governor's reports concerning the potential for Federalist insurrection in Massachusetts. See Jefferson to Henry Dearborn, 9 August 1808, Thomas Jefferson, *The Writings of Thomas Jefferson,* ed. Paul Leicester Ford, 10 vols. (New York: G. P. Putnam's Sons, 1892–1899), 9: 201–2.

56. *Massachusetts Spy,* 28 December 1808; *Salem Gazette,* 3 January 1809; "Coaster," *Columbian Centinel,* 3 December 1808; Christopher Gore to Rufus King, 26 December 1808, King, *Correspondence,* 5: 112; Harrison Gray Otis to Josiah Quincy, 15 December 1808, QWHU Papers, MHS, reel 36. The efforts of Otis and other Federalist leaders to moderate popular radicalism are described in Banner, *To the Hartford Convention,* 302–6.

57. Quotations from *Salem Gazette,* 17 and 20 January 1809. Extracts from memorials are reprinted in *Columbian Centinel* and *Salem Gazette,* January–February 1809. Also see Banner, *To the Hartford Convention,* 299–301; and Perkins, *Prologue to War,* 163–65.

58. John Quincy Adams to Ezekiel Bacon, 17 November, 21 December 1808; Adams to Orchard Cook, 19 December 1808, Adams Family Papers, MHS, reel 135; Bacon to Adams, 11 December 1808; Cook to Adams, 4 December 1808, Adams Family Papers, reel 406. Goodman, *Democratic-Republicans,* 194–95; Spivak, *Jefferson's English Crisis,* 163–72, 181–85, 191–92, 198–203; Cook to Adams, 4 December 1808, Adams Family Papers, MHS, reel 406; Cook to Adams, 1 January 1809, Adams Family Papers, reel 407; Perkins, *Prologue to War,* 228–29; Story, *Life and Letters of Story,* 1: 187. Federalist congressman Samuel Taggart offered a characteristically less charitable view of Republican actions. In a late December letter, he observed that regional Jeffersonians were scurrying for cover, in search of "a hole by which they may make an honorable retreat after scourging the nation with their

folly for more than a year." Taggart to John Taylor, 30 December 1808, "Taggart Letters," 329.

59. Leverett Saltonstall Diary (4 April 1808), "Saltonstall Papers," 81: 438; George Cabot to Timothy Pickering, 9 April 1808, Pickering Papers, MHS, reel 28.

60. Perkins, *Prologue to War,* 231–33.

61. Ibid., 245–49; Ralph Ketcham, *James Madison: A Biography* (Charlottesville: University Press of Virginia, 1990), 504–6.

62. Adams, *History,* 6: 116–81; Perkins, *Prologue to War,* 315–19; Reginald Horsman, *The Causes of the War of 1812* (Philadelphia: University of Pennsylvania Press, 1962), 245–58.

63. For examples of the continuing vitality of the sectional theme in Federalist electioneering appeals during the post-embargo period, see: "A Middlesex Farmer," *Columbian Centinel,* 30 March 1811; "Massachusetts," *New England Palladium,* 16 April 1811; "The Crisis in Massachusetts," *Columbian Centinel,* 27 April 1811.

64. Formisano, *Transformation of Political Culture,* 62–63; Fisher Ames to Christopher Gore, 5 March 1800, quoted in Banner, *To the Hartford Convention,* 223; William Sullivan, *Familiar Letters on Public Characters, and Public Events; from the Peace of 1783 to the Peace of 1815* (Boston: Russell, Odiorne, and Metcalf, 1834), 369.

65. *Salem Gazette,* 7 July 1812; *New England Palladium,* 30 June 1812.

66. *Massachusetts Spy,* 19 August 1812; *Salem Gazette,* 10 July 1812; "G," "Inordinate Ambition of Virginia," *Salem Gazette,* 13 October 1812; "Letters on National Affairs, No. V," *New England Palladium,* 4 November 1812.

67. J. C. A. Stagg, *Mr. Madison's War: Politics, Diplomacy, and Warfare in the Early American Republic, 1783–1830* (Princeton: Princeton University Press, 1983), 363–64, 381, 383–84; Banner, *To the Hartford Convention,* 313–18; Samuel Eliot Morison, "Dissent in the War of 1812," in Samuel Eliot Morison, Frederick Merk, and Frank Freidel, *Dissent in Three American Wars* (Cambridge: Harvard University Press, 1970), 10–12.

68. "Camillus," *Columbian Centinel,* 12 February 1814.

69. Josiah Quincy to John Adams, 14 December 1808; Quincy to Harrison Gray Otis, 8 November 1811, QWHU Papers, MHS, reel 36.

70. Samuel Taggart to John Taylor, 2 December 1811, "Taggart Letters," 367–68.

71. Philip J. Greven, Jr., *Four Generations: Population, Land, and Family in Colonial Andover, Massachusetts* (Ithaca, N.Y.: Cornell University Press, 1970); Stephen Innes, *Creating the Commonwealth: The Economic Culture of Puritan New England* (New York: W. W. Norton, 1995), 271–306; Winifred Barr Rothenberg, *From Market-Places to Market Economy: The Transformation of Rural Massachusetts, 1750–1850* (Chicago: University of Chicago Press, 1992), 80–111; *Hampshire Gazette,* 8 July 1812.

72. Richard L. Bushman, *King and People in Provincial Massachusetts* (Chapel Hill: University of North Carolina Press, 1985), 190–210; Bushman, "Massachusetts Farmers and the Revolution," in *Society, Freedom, and Conscience: The Coming of the Revolution in Virginia, Massachusetts, and New York,* ed. Richard M. Jellison (New York: W. W. Norton, 1976), 77–124; James L. Huston, *Securing the Fruits of Labor: The American Concept of Wealth Distribution, 1765–1900* (Baton Rouge: Louisiana State University Press, 1998), 14–19.

73. Nathan Dane to Thomas Dwight, 11 February 1786, *Letters of Members of the Continental Congress*, 8: 302; Newburyport *Herald*, 13 March 1798, quoted in Benjamin W. Labaree, *Patriots & Partisans: The Merchants of Newburyport, 1764–1815* (New York: W. W. Norton, 1975), 126; Abijah Bigelow to Hannah Bigelow, 17 October 1814, "Letters of Abijah Bigelow, Member of Congress, to His Wife, 1810–1815," ed. C.S.B., *Proceedings of the American Antiquarian Society* 40 (6 April–15 October 1930): 393–94; Linda Kerber, *Federalists in Dissent: Imagery and Ideology in Jeffersonian America* (Ithaca, N.Y.: Cornell University Press, 1970), 23–32.

74. *Columbian Centinel*, 2 February 1814. New Englanders' use of Virginia as a counterimage was hardly new. It began during the seventeenth century with John Winthrop. Innes, *Creating the Commonwealth*, 83–85.

75. *Salem Gazette*, 25 January, 25 February 1814.

76. Morison, "Dissent in the War of 1812," 16–17; Harrison Gray Otis to Josiah Quincy, 15 December 1808, QWHU Papers, MHS, reel 36; Otis to Christopher Gore, 3 December 1814, Harrison Gray Otis Papers, MHS, microfilm ed., reel 5. For a particularly able examination of efforts by Otis and other moderate Federalists to restrain popular radicalism after Madison's embargo, see Banner, *To the Hartford Convention*, 317–32.

77. Banner, *To the Hartford Convention*, 333–43; Theodore Dwight, *History of the Hartford Convention: With a Review of the Policy of the United States Government Which Led to the War of 1812* (New York: N. & J. White, 1833), 370–78.

78. Morison, "Dissent in the War of 1812," 22–25; Banner, *To the Hartford Convention*, 104–15; Kerber, *Federalists in Dissent*, 50–51; John Rutledge to Harrison Gray Otis, 17 July 1803, Otis Papers, MHS, reel 3. In this letter, Rutledge commends Otis for providing one of the runaway's pursuers with a particularly careful description of the slave.

79. Banner, *To the Hartford Convention*, 108–9. Quincy's tendency to follow his own counsel is examined at some length in Matthew H. Crocker, "'The Magic of the Many That Sets the World on Fire': Boston Elites and Urban Political Insurgents during the Early Nineteenth Century" (Ph.D. diss., University of Massachusetts at Amherst, 1997).

Chapter Two

1. Daniel Messinger et al. to Harrison Gray Otis, 1 March 1831; Otis to Committee of Artists and Mechanics, 2 March 1831, Harrison Gary Otis Papers, Massachusetts Historical Society (MHS), microfilm ed., reel 9. A perceptive discussion of the persistence of older patterns of deference can be found in Ronald P. Formisano, *The Transformation of Political Culture: Massachusetts Parties, 1790s–1840s* (New York: Oxford University Press, 1983), 130–40.

2. Christopher Gore to Rufus King, 26 January 1817, Rufus King, *The Life and Correspondence of Rufus King: Comprising His Letters, Private and Official, His Public Documents and His Speeches*, ed. Charles R. King, 6 vols. (New York: G. P. Putnam

& Sons, 1894–1900), 6: 48; Shaw Livermore, Jr., *The Twilight of Federalism: The Disintegration of the Federalist Party, 1815–1830* (Princeton: Princeton University Press, 1962), 23–24; Richard E. Ellis, "The Market Revolution and the Transformation of American Politics, 1801–1837," in *The Market Revolution in America: Social, Political, and Religious Expressions, 1800–1880,* ed. Melvyn Stokes and Stephen Conway (Charlottesville: University Press of Virginia, 1996), 160–61.

3. Samuel Eliot Morison, *The Life and Letters of Harrison Gray Otis, Federalist, 1765–1848,* 2 vols. (Boston: Houghton Mifflin, 1913), 2: 206–9; Harry Ammon, *James Monroe: The Quest for National Identity* (Charlottesville: University Press of Virginia, 1990), 374–77; Formisano, *Transformation of Political Culture,* 118–19.

4. Although marred by the author's uncritical acceptance of Republican assertions that Federalist partisanship was the main source of anti-Compromise sentiment, Glover Moore's *The Missouri Controversy, 1819–1821* (Lexington: University of Kentucky Press, 1953) remains the standard treatment of the subject.

5. First quotation is from the Berkshire County meeting in *Berkshire Star,* 20 January 1820. The resolutions of other Missouri meetings can be found in *Columbian Centinel,* 4 December 1819; *Salem Gazette,* 10 December 1819; and *Massachusetts Spy,* 15 December 1819. The remaining quotations are in *Columbian Centinel,* 24 November 1819; *New England Palladium & Commercial Advertiser,* 8 February 1820; and *Boston Daily Advertiser,* 6 March 1820.

6. Moore, *Missouri Controversy,* 195, 200; *Annals of Congress,* 15th Cong., 2d sess., 1179–84; Edward Dowse to his wife, 3 March 1820, in Edmund Quincy, *Life of Josiah Quincy of Massachusetts* (Boston: Fields, Osgood, 1869), 389; Charles Warren, *Jacobin and Junto: or Early American Politics as Viewed in the Diary of Dr. Nathaniel Ames, 1758–1822* (1931; repr. New York: Benjamin Blom, 1968), 324.

7. William W. Story, *Life and Letters of Joseph Story, Associate Justice of the Supreme Court of the United States, and Dane Professor of Law at Harvard University,* 2 vols. (Boston: Charles C. Little and James Brown, 1851), 1: 187, 359–60; quotations from Joseph Story to Edward Everett, 7 March 1820, ibid., 1: 366–67.

8. Harrison Gray Otis to James Prince, 1 April 1820, Otis Papers, MHS, reel 7.

9. Harrison Gray Otis to William Sullivan, 19 January 1822, Otis papers, MHS, reel 8; Moore, *Missouri Controversy,* 85; quotation from Otis to Sullivan, 7 February 1820, in Morison, *Otis,* 2: 227; *Annals of Congress,* 16th Cong., 1st sess., 238–55. Otis himself viewed the January speech as a clear departure from his previous course, writing to William Sullivan that "I feel as I had been working hard again for my old friends and old principles, and my last exertions are not calculated to help me with my new friends—But I know the satisfaction of feeling well upon the occasion, and that is about as much of a reward as any federalist in our Country is entitled to expect." Otis to Sullivan, 7 February 1820, Otis Papers, MHS, reel 7.

10. Harrison Gray Otis to William Sullivan, 13 February 1820, in Morison, *Otis,* 2: 226–27.

11. Helen R. Pinkney, *Christopher Gore, Federalist of Massachusetts, 1758–1827* (Waltham, Mass.: Gore Place Society, 1969), 142–43; Christopher Gore to Jeremiah Mason, 24 January 1820, in George S. Hillard, *Memoir, Autobiography and Corre-*

spondence of Jeremiah Mason (1873; repr. Boston: Boston Law Book, 1917), 230–31; first quotation in Gore to Rufus King, 28 January 1820, King, *Correspondence*, 6: 260; second quotation in Gore to Mason, 25 June 1820, Hillard, *Mason Correspondence*, 240.

12. Robert Stanley Rich, "Politics and Pedigrees: The Wealthy Men of Boston, 1798–1852" (Ph.D. diss., University of California, Los Angeles, 1975), 55–56, 84–87; Moore, *Missouri Controversy*, 198–99, 216–17; *Boston Daily Advertiser*, 7 and 28 March, 21 April 1820. Technically, four Bay State representatives voted for the compromise. Two of them, however, were from the Maine district, which became an independent state as a result of the measure.

13. William Tudor to Rufus King, 12 February 1820, King, *Correspondence*, 6: 274; *Salem Gazette*, 10 March 1820; *New England Galaxy and Masonic Magazine* 3 (10 March 1820): 85; Harlow W. Sheidley, *Sectional Nationalism: Massachusetts and the Transformation of America, 1815–1836* (Boston: Northeastern University Press, 1998), 20–21. All in all, the attacks on Mason were relatively mild compared to the harsh public pummeling administered to Henry Shaw, the other Bay State representative to vote for the compromise. As a resident of Berkshire County, where the moderate stance of Boston's Federalist elite had little influence on local politics, Shaw was exposed to the full fury of anti-Compromise sentiment. *Berkshire Star*, 3 February, 23 March, 20 April, 24 August 1820. Nor was Shaw's vote soon forgotten. Although he later achieved some prominence in the state legislature, the fact that he had been a "doughface in 1819" prevented his being seriously considered for high office. See Charles P. Curtis to Daniel Webster, 26 January 1833, Daniel Webster, *The Papers of Daniel Webster: Correspondence*, ed. Charles M. Wiltse and Harold D. Moser, 7 vols. (Hanover, N.H.: University Press of New England, 1974–1986), 4: 21.

14. Andrew A. L. Cayton, "The Fragmentation of 'A Great Family': The Panic of 1819 and Rise of the Middling Interest in Boston," *Journal of the Early Republic* 2 (Summer 1982): 145–51.

15. This and the next three paragraphs draw heavily on the analyses in Matthew H. Crocker, " 'The Magic of the Many That Sets the World on Fire': Boston Elites and Urban Political Insurgents during the Early Nineteenth Century" (Ph.D. diss., University of Massachusetts at Amherst, 1997), 118–48, 163–80; Clayton, "The Fragmentation of 'A Great Family,' " 152–67; and Formisano, *Transformation of Political Culture*, 138–40, 182–87. Cayton does, however, overstate the extent to which the insurgency represented a break with the past and is too quick to dismiss the continuing popularity of political appeals framed in organic terms. My reasons for these objections will become clearer in the chapter's concluding section, where I examine the ways in which a new manufacturing elite used the tariff issue to revive the popular conservatism of the embargo and war years.

16. *Columbian Centinel*, 2 March 1822.

17. *New England Galaxy* 5 (1 February 1822).

18. Ibid., 5 (24 May 1822); 5 (17 May 1822).

19. Cayton, "The Fragmentation of 'A Great Family,' " 145; Gary J. Kornblith, "Becoming Joseph T. Buckingham: The Struggle for Artisanal Independence in Early-Nineteenth-Century Boston," in *American Artisans: Crafting Social Identity,*

1750–1850, ed. Howard B. Rock, Paul A. Gilje, and Robert Asher (Baltimore: Johns Hopkins University Press, 1995), 124–27; Kornblith, "From Artisans to Businessmen: Master Mechanics in New England, 1789–1850" (Ph.D. diss., Princeton University, 1983), 292–325.

20. *New England Galaxy* 5 (5 July 1822); 4 (12 October 1821); *New England Galaxy and Masonic Magazine* 3 (28 January 1820); Joseph T. Buckingham, *Personal Memoirs and Recollections of Editorial Life*, 2 vols. (Boston: Ticknor, Reed, and Fields, 1852), 1: 121–22. For a particularly abusive commentary on Russell's personal idiosyncrasies and political inconsistencies, see *New England Galaxy* 5 (24 May 1822).

21. *New England Galaxy* 7 (16 April 1824). For a fuller statement of Buckingham's views on class relations, see his observations in *Personal Memoirs*, 2: 154–57; also see Kornblith, "From Artisans to Businessmen," 497–501. I will return to this topic later in the study.

22. *Boston Daily Courier*, 12 June, 22 and 24 July 1824.

23. Formisano, *Transformation of Political Culture*, 173–96, quotation on p. 187; Bruce Laurie, "'Spavined Ministers, Lying Toothpullers, and Buggering Priests': Third-Partyism and the Search for Security in the Antebellum North," in *American Artisans*, ed. Rock, Gilje, and Asher, 98–119.

24. The phrase "Headquarters of good principles" is from Northampton Federalist Josiah Dwight in Morison, *Otis*, 1: 334; Crocker, "'The Magic of the Many That Sets the World on Fire,'" 283–305; Formisano, *Transformation of Political Culture*, 120–25.

25. Christopher Gore to Rufus King, 2 June 1822, King, *Correspondence*, 6: 473; Isaac Parker to Daniel Webster, 19 February 1825, Webster, *Correspondence*, 2: 27.

26. Daniel Webster to Samuel A. Bradley, 21 April 1816, Webster, *Correspondence*, 1: 197; Robert Varnum Spalding, "The Boston Mercantile Community and the Promotion of the Textile Industry in New England, 1813–1860" (Ph.D. diss., Yale University, 1963), 21; Robert F. Dalzell, Jr., "The Rise of the Waltham-Lowell System and Some Thoughts on the Political Economy of Modernization in Ante-Bellum Massachusetts," *Perspectives in American History* 9 (1975): 236.

27. *Columbian Centinel*, 21 August 1811. This argument could still be heard a decade later. See, for example, the observations of "A Farmer" in *Columbian Centinel*, 4 October 1820.

28. *Salem Gazette*, 1 February 1820; Peter Dobkin Hall, "Family Structure and Class Consolidation among the Boston Brahmins" (Ph.D. diss., State University of New York at Stony Brook, 1973), 43–46; Spalding, "Boston Mercantile Community," 17–18; Frances W. Gregory, *Nathan Appleton: Merchant and Entrepreneur, 1779–1861* (Charlottesville: University Press of Virginia, 1975), 70–71, 142, 146, 149–50. The Salem memorial can also be found in *Annals of Congress*, 16th Cong., 1st sess., Appendix, 2335–48.

29. Israel Thorndike to A. J. Dallas, 23 October 1815, Timothy Pickering Papers, MHS, microfilm ed., reel 30; Thorndike to Timothy Pickering, 20 March, 1 April 1816, Pickering Papers, reel 31; George Cabot to Pickering, 20 December 1815, Pickering Papers, reel 30. For additional merchant opinion on the 1816 tariff, see

Nathaniel Bowditch to Pickering, 24 February 1816; Dudley L. Pickman to Pickering, 21 March 1816; William Read to Pickering, 26 March 1816, Pickering Papers, reel 31; and *one among your numerous friends* to Pickering, 20 February 1816, Pickering Papers, reel 55.

30. Whitman quotation in *Annals of Congress,* 16th Cong., 1st sess., 1999; "A Mechanic," *Boston Daily Advertiser,* 13 June 1820; Salem memorial, *Annals of Congress,* 16th Cong., 1st sess., Appendix, 2346, 2348; *New England Palladium & Commercial Advertiser,* 3 October 1820. The Boston resolutions are also reprinted in *Report of a Committee of Citizens of Boston and Vicinity, Opposed to a Further Increase of Duties on Importations* (Boston: From the Press of Nathan Hale, 1827), 94–95.

31. "The Tariff—No. I," *Boston Daily Advertiser,* 4 September 1820; Edward Stanwood, *American Tariff Controversies in the Nineteenth Century,* 2 vols. (Boston: Houghton Mifflin, 1903), 1: 174; Israel Thorndike to Timothy Pickering, 1 April 1816, Pickering Papers, MHS, reel 31.

32. Carl F. Prince and Seth Taylor, "Daniel Webster, the Boston Associates, and the U.S. Government's Role in the Industrializing Process, 1815–1830," *Journal of the Early Republic* 2 (Fall 1982): 288; Robert F. Dalzell, Jr., *Enterprising Elite: The Boston Associates and the World They Made* (Cambridge: Harvard University Press, 1987), 39–40; Thomas R. Gold to Nathan Appleton, 5 April 1816; *Boston Daily Advertiser,* 15 January 1828, in Nathan Appleton scrapbooks, both items in Appleton Family Papers, MHS. In his autobiography, Appleton noted that Lowell's views on the tariff "were much more moderate" than those of other regional manufacturers. "Autobiography," 13, Appleton Family Papers, MHS.

33. Nathan Appleton's name also appeared on the Boston tariff resolutions, but he later insisted that it had been placed there without his authorization. Nathan Appleton to Isaac Winslow, 16 and 31 August 1831, Appleton Family Papers, MHS.

34. Nathan Appleton to Ezra S. Gannett, 24 January 1828, Appleton Family Papers, MHS. Appleton's role as a defender of manufacturer interests would continue for another four decades. See, for example, Robert Varnum Spalding's insightful analysis of Appleton's motives for writing *The Introduction of the Power Loom and Origin of Lowell* (1858) in "Boston Mercantile Community," 1–4.

35. The articles, which appeared in July 1821, are in Nathan Appleton scrapbooks, Appleton Family Papers, MHS.

36. *Boston Daily Advertiser,* 15 January 1828; *Annals of Congress,* 18th Cong., 1st sess., Appendix, 3079–92; Dalzell, "Waltham-Lowell System," 236–38.

37. Stanwood, *Tariff Controversies,* 1: 238; *Boston Daily Advertiser,* 15 January 1828; Gregory, *Appleton,* 179–80; Stanwood, *Tariff Controversies,* 1: 256. Lawrence's lobbying efforts on behalf of the 1828 tariff are discussed in Abbott Lawrence to Amos Lawrence, 2, 11, and 14 February 1828, Amos Lawrence Papers, MHS.

38. Henry Lee to William Huskisson, 21 December 1827, in *Henry and Mary Lee: Letters and Journals with Other Family Letters, 1802–1860,* ed. Frances Rollins Morse (Boston: n.p., 1926), 250; *Register of Debates,* 20th Cong., 1st sess., 2136. Daniel Webster used the same argument to explain his shift from free-trade advocate to protectionist. See Webster to William Coleman, 23 February 1827, Webster, *Correspondence,*

2: 162–63; and *Register of Debates,* 20th Cong., 1st sess., 750–51, 759. In a speech op-posing the 1820 bill, Harrison Gray Otis had predicted that passage of a protective tariff would significantly affect investor behavior. Anticipating the later assertions of Reed, Webster, and others, he further asserted that once enacted, such a measure "cannot be repealed without a breach of the public faith." *Annals of Congress,* 16th Cong., 1st sess., 667, 670–71.

39. *New England Galaxy* 7 (9 April 1824). The uneven progress of political amal-gamation in Massachusetts following the demise of Federalism is ably surveyed in Sheidley, *Sectional Nationalism,* chap. 3.

40. *Report of a Committee of the Citizens Opposed to a Further Increase of Duties on Importations* (1827); *Boston Daily Courier,* 17 January 1828.

41. *Boston Daily Courier,* 2 January 1828. Also, see the observations of "Clarendon" in ibid., 8 January, 8 February 1828.

42. *Boston Daily Courier,* 2 and 8 February, 17 and 23 January 1828. Although Buckingham did not have close ties to BMC-Lowell promoters, he had received financial aid from several small woolen manufacturers whose marginal enterprises depended on tariff protection. Buckingham, *Personal Memoirs,* 2: 5–9.

43. *Boston Daily Courier,* 14 and 1 January 1828. Also see Buckingham's editorial, "Trade and Commerce," and an article on the interdependence of agriculture and manufactures from the *Worcester Spy* ibid., 8 and 23 November 1827.

44. The lonely and embattled position of elite defenders of protectionism during the early 1820s is mentioned in H. W. Dwight to Harrison Gray Otis, 10 January 1830, Otis Papers, MHS, reel 9.

45. *Boston Daily Courier,* 18, 21, 25, 28, and 29 October 1830; quotations are from the 28 October and 21 October editions.

46. *Boston Patriot,* 19 October 1830, in Nathan Appleton scrapbooks, Appleton Family Papers, MHS; *Boston Daily Courier,* 20 and 22 October 1830.

47. *Boston Daily Advertiser,* 29 October 1830; Daniel Webster to Theophilus Par-sons, 2 January 1841, Webster, *Correspondence,* 5: 79; *Boston Daily Courier,* 5 January 1828; Nathan Hale to Henry Lee, 3 March 1832, Lee Family Papers, MHS, microfilm ed., reel 3; *Boston Daily Advertiser,* 2 June 1832. The financial assistance Hale subse-quently received from Boston manufacturers no doubt influenced his increasingly favorable view of protectionism. See George Bond to Nathan Appleton, 26 January 1832, Appleton Family Papers, MHS.

48. *Boston Daily Courier,* 1 November 1830.

49. William W. Freehling, *Prelude to Civil War: The Nullification Controversy in South Carolina, 1816–1836* (New York: Harper Torchbooks, 1968), 36–39; John Niven, *John C. Calhoun and the Price of Union: A Biography* (Baton Rouge: Louisiana State University Press, 1988), 158–64.

50. Freehling, *Prelude to Civil War,* 146, 192–96.

51. Abbott Lawrence to Daniel Webster, 7 May 1828, Webster, *Correspondence,* 2: 342–43; Abbott Lawrence to Nathan Appleton, 30 December 1831; Amos Lawrence to Appleton, 31 January 1832; Peter O. Thacher to Appleton, 14 March 1832, Appleton Family Papers, MHS.

52. *Boston Daily Advertiser,* 15 January 1828; Appleton, "Autobiography," 24; J. E. Colhoun (?) to Appleton, 7 February 1832, Appleton Family Papers, MHS. Appleton's Bay State colleagues also doubted that tariff reduction would do much to help hard-pressed Carolinians. "Will the destruction of manufactures," John Davis asked, "make the poor exhausted lands of South Carolina as productive as the virgin soils of the Southwest?" *Register of Debates,* 22d Cong., 1st sess., 3313.

53. Gregory, *Appleton,* 173–74, 185, 192–93, 196, 199, quotation from p. 196; Harrison Gray Otis to George Harrison, 5 March 1833, Otis Papers, MHS, reel 9. Also see William Appleton, Diary, 1 January 1833, typescript, Appleton Family Papers, MHS.

54. Paul A. David, "Learning by Doing and Tariff Protectionism: A Reconsideration of the Case of the Ante-Bellum United States Cotton Textile Industry," *Journal of Economic History* 30 (September 1970): 521–601; Lance E. Davis, "Sources of Industrial Finance: The American Textile Industry, A Case Study," *Explorations in Entrepreneurial History* 9 (April 1957): 198–203; Harrison Gray Otis to George Harrison, 5 March 1833, Otis Papers, MHS, reel 9.

55. Appleton, *Gregory,* 261–62; George Morey to Harrison Gray Otis, 11 June 1832, Otis Papers, MHS, reel 9; Gregory, *Appleton,* 203, 255; Spalding, "Boston Mercantile Community," 43–62, 178.

56. Nathan Appleton to Harrison Gray Otis, 26 February 1832, Otis Papers, MHS, reel 9; Appleton, "Autobiography," 25–26; *Register of Debates,* 22d Cong., 1st sess., 3191–92, 3197, 3209. Although it is unlikely that northerners paid much attention to Appleton's attack on the forty-bale theory, many southerners did. Writing to Appleton shortly afterward, a South Carolina unionist said that "your speech is a masterly refutation of McDuffies wild doctrine—all parties are calling on me for a copy. I shall have it published in our Union papers." J. E. Colhoun (?) to Appleton, 9 July 1832, Appleton Family Papers, MHS.

57. *Register of Debates,* 22d Cong, 1st sess., 3204–5. Also see Edward Everett's observations ibid., 3760.

58. Ibid., 3309.

59. The expression "new class" is from Appleton's article "The New Tariff—No. III," *Boston Daily Advertiser,* July 1821, in Nathan Appleton scrapbooks, Appleton Family Papers, MHS.

60. Abbott Lawrence to Nathan Appleton, 15 January 1833, Letters to Nathan Appleton by or about Abbott Lawrence, bMS Am 1557 (7–71), Houghton Library, Harvard University, Cambridge, Massachusetts (HL).

61. *Hampshire Gazette,* 13 June 1832. See also the resolutions of the Worcester and Middlesex County meetings in *Boston Daily Courier,* 8 and 15 June 1832, and the Springfield meeting in *Boston Daily Advertiser,* 23 May 1832.

62. Memorial of the Association of Mechanics, Farmers, and other Working Men, in the towns of Amesbury and Salisbury, 6 June 1832, House Executive Doc. No. 258. According to the petition, most of the Amesbury and Salisbury memorialists worked in local textile mills.

63. J. E. Colhoun (?) to Nathan Appleton, 9 July 1832, Appleton Family Papers, MHS; Freehling, *Prelude to Civil War,* 260–64.

64. *Boston Daily Advertiser,* 17 December 1832; Joseph Story to Judge Fay, 11 February 1833, Story, *Life and Letters of Story,* 2: 122; William Sullivan to Nathan Appleton, 25 January 1833, Appleton Family Papers, MHS; Samuel Eliot Morison, "Dissent in the War of 1812," in Morison, Frederick Merk, and Frank Freidel, *Dissent in Three American Wars* (Cambridge: Harvard University Press, 1970), 20–24; John Lowell to Appleton, 23 January 1833, Appleton Family Papers, MHS.

65. *Boston Daily Courier,* 2 February 1833, 27 November and 27 December 1832, 11 and 16 January 1833.

66. John Quincy Adams, *Life in a New England Town, 1787, 1788: Diary of John Quincy Adams, While a Student in the Office of Theophilus Parsons at Newburyport,* ed. Charles Francis Adams (Boston: Little, Brown, 1903), 65; Henry Adams to Brooks Adams, 18 February 1909, in *Henry Adams: Selected Letters,* ed. Ernest Samuels (Cambridge: Harvard University Press, 1992), 511–13; Thomas W. Ward to Joshua Bates, 7 April 1848, copy, Thomas Wren Ward Papers, MHS; Peter C. Brooks to Edward Everett, 17 January 1832, Edward Everett Papers, MHS, microfilm ed., reel 5; Samuel Flagg Bemis, *John Quincy Adams and the Union* (New York: Alfred A. Knopf, 1956), 8–10, 161–76; Leonard L. Richards, *The Life and Times of Congressman John Quincy Adams* (New York: Oxford University Press, 1986), 32–35; Sheidley, *Sectional Nationalism,* 74–82

67. Harrison Gray Otis to Nathan Appleton, 11 February 1832, Appleton Family Papers, MHS; Bemis, *John Quincy Adams,* 25–26, 241–47; John Quincy Adams, *Memoirs of John Quincy Adams, Comprising Portions of His Diary from 1795 to 1848,* ed. Charles Francis Adams, 12 vols. (Philadelphia: J. B. Lippincott, 1874–1877), 8: 460, 510; Adams to Samuel L. Southard, 5 December 1832, copy, Adams Family Papers, MHS, microfilm ed., reel 151.

68. Clayton quotation in Bemis, *John Quincy Adams,* 266; *Register of Debates,* 22d Cong., 2d sess., 1613–15. Adams expanded on his remarks in a minority report for the Committee on Manufactures that he prepared with Lewis Condict. See *Register of Debates,* 22d Cong., 2d sess., Appendix, 41–60.

69. Bemis, *John Quincy Adams,* 267; *Boston Daily Courier,* 25 February 1833; *Northampton Courier,* 27 February 1833; Benjamin F. Hallett to John Quincy Adams, 26 February 1833, Adams Family Papers, MHS, reel 497.

70. John Quincy Adams to Charles Francis Adams, 13 March 1833; Adams to Benjamin F. Hallett, 6 March 1833, copies, Adams Family Papers, MHS, reel 151.

71. Merrill D. Peterson, *Olive Branch and Sword—The Compromise of 1833* (Baton Rouge: Louisiana State University Press, 1982), 69; Marcus Morton to John C. Calhoun, 7 March 1829, John C. Calhoun, *The Papers of John C. Calhoun,* ed. Robert L. Meriwether et al., 23 vols. to date (Columbia: University of South Carolina Press, 1959–), 12: 7; Arthur B. Darling, *Political Changes in Massachusetts, 1824–1848: A Study of Liberal Movements in Politics* (New Haven: Yale University Press, 1925), 146; Martin Van Buren to Thomas Ritchie, 13 January 1827, quoted in Robert V. Remini, *Martin Van Buren and the Making of the Democratic Party* (New York: Columbia University Press, 1959), 131; John Davis, "The Influence of Slavery upon Free Labor," ms. speech, 1840, John Davis Papers, American Antiquarian Society, Worcester, Massachusetts

(AAS); Abbott Lawrence to Leverett Saltonstall, 10 August 1841, "The Papers of Leverett Saltonstall, 1816–1845," ed. Robert E. Moody, *Collections of the Massachusetts Historical Society* 82–86 (1978–1992), 84: 165; Amos Lawrence to his son, 16 January 1831, in *Extracts from the Diary and Correspondence of the Late Amos Lawrence with a Brief Account of Some Incidents in His Life*, ed. William R. Lawrence (Boston: Gould and Lincoln, 1855), 104.

72. The political disarray during this transitional period within Massachusetts is well documented in Sheidley, *Sectional Nationalism*, 132–66.

Chapter Three

1. *Columbian Centinel*, 20 April 1825, in John R. Commons et al., eds., *A Documentary History of American Industrial Society*, 10 vols. (Cleveland: Arthur H. Clark Company, 1910–1911), 6: 76.

2. Christopher Tomlins, *Law, Labor, and Ideology in the Early American Republic* (Cambridge: Cambridge University Press, 1993), 111–12; Bruce Laurie, *Artisans into Workers: Labor in Nineteenth-Century America* (New York: Noonday Press, 1989), 35–46, 64; Gary John Kornblith, "From Artisans to Businessmen: Master Mechanics in New England, 1789–1850" (Ph.D. diss., Princeton University, 1983), 87, 213–17.

3. *Boston Daily Courier*, 28 August 1830, in Commons et al., eds., *Documentary History*, 5: 188; *Columbian Centinel*, 15 February 1832, ibid., 5: 192.

4. Norman Ware, *The Industrial Worker, 1840–1860* (1924; repr. Chicago: Quadrangle Books, 1964).

5. *Boston Daily Courier*, 28 August 1830, in Commons et al., eds., *Documentary History*, 5: 188; *New England Artisan*, 10 January, 8 August 1833; *Young America*, 31 January 1846.

6. Laurie, *Artisans into Workers*, 63.

7. David Hackett Fischer, *Albion's Seed: Four British Folkways in America* (New York: Oxford University Press, 1989), 158–61; Stephen Innes, *Creating the Commonwealth: The Economic Culture of Puritan New England* (New York: W. W. Norton, 1995), 9–16, 139–48; Paul Leicester Ford, ed., *The New England Primer* (New York: Teachers College, Columbia University, 1962); Russell B. Nye, *George Bancroft: Brahmin Rebel* (New York: Alfred A. Knopf, 1945), 69.

8. W. J. Rorabaugh, *The Craft Apprentice: From Franklin to the Machine Age in America* (New York: Oxford University Press, 1986), 16–130; Kornblith, "From Artisans to Businessmen," 523–27; William F. Hartford, *Working People of Holyoke: Class and Ethnicity in a Massachusetts Mill Town, 1850–1960* (New Brunswick, N.J.: Rutgers University Press, 1990), 11; *Springfield Republican*, quoted in *Boston Daily Courier*, 17 September 1830. The fragmentary records of the Hampden Mechanics' Association are at the Connecticut Valley Historical Museum, Springfield, Massachusetts.

9. Quotation from *The Mechanic* (January 1834): 15; *Young Mechanic* (August 1832): 122–23; Teresa Anne Murphy, *Ten Hours' Labor: Religion, Reform, and Gender in Early New England* (Ithaca, N.Y.: Cornell University Press, 1992), 60–61; *Boston*

Mechanic (July 1835): 131; *The Mechanic* (August 1834): 262; (March 1834): 102; (May 1834): 167; Rex Burns, *Success in America: The Yeoman Dream and the Industrial Revolution* (Amherst: University of Massachusetts Press, 1976), 94–104.

10. Larcom quotation in Claudia L. Bushman, *"A Good Poor Man's Wife": Being a Chronicle of Harriet Hanson Robinson and Her Family in Nineteenth-Century New England* (Hanover, N.H.: University Press of New England, 1981), 16; Benita Eisler, "Introduction," *The Lowell Offering: Writings by New England Mill Women (1840–1845)*, ed. Eisler (Philadelphia: J. B. Lippincott Company, 1977), 29–36; Harriet H. Robinson, *Loom & Spindle: Or Life among the Early Mill Girls* (1898; repr. Kailua, Hawaii: Press Pacifica, 1976), 59–78.

11. *New England Artisan,* 11 April, 9 November 1833; Richard D. Brown, *The Strength of a People: The Idea of an Informed Citizenry in America, 1650–1870* (Chapel Hill: University of North Carolina Press, 1996), 164–65.

12. *Lowell Offering,* ed. Eisler, 63–65, 66–73; *Voice of Industry,* 29 May 1846, in *The Factory Girls,* ed. Philip S. Foner (Urbana: University of Illinois Press, 1977), 170–72. Major documents from the dispute are reprinted with commentary ibid., 57–73, quotation from p. 61. Also see the harshly critical *Voice* editorial of January 1846, "Lowell Offering." In fairness to Farley, it should be noted that the *Offering* did sometimes attempt to stake out an independent position. See, for example, Farley's editorial, "The Ten-Hour Movement," and Betsey Chamberlain's essay, "A New Society," in *Lowell Offering,* ed. Eisler, 201–3, 208–10.

13. Murphy, *Ten Hours' Labor,* 61; *Young Mechanic* (November 1832): 167; *The Mechanic* (October 1834): 309. In making a distinction between radicals and those who believed in the sufficiency of self-improvement, I have been influenced by David A. Zonderman's insightful discussion of social mobility and worker consciousness in *Aspirations and Anxieties: New England Workers and the Mechanized Factory System, 1815–1850* (New York: Oxford University Press, 1992), 272–75, 288–301. Teresa Anne Murphy provides a more extensive examination of the "knowledge is power" theme in *Ten Hours' Labor,* 58–69.

14. *New England Artisan,* 5 January 1832; also see the observations of "W.A.F." in Lynn *Awl,* 7 December 1844, who declared that "[k]nowledge will elevate us far above the worldly and purse-proud aristocrat."

15. *New England Artisan,* 11 October 1832; Lynn *Awl,* 8 March 1845.

16. Carl Bridenbaugh, *Vexed and Troubled Englishmen, 1590–1642* (New York: Oxford University Press, 1967), chap. 10; Fischer, *Albion's Seed,* 199–205.

17. Stanley K. Schultz, *The Culture Factory: Boston Public Schools, 1789–1860* (New York: Oxford University Press, 1973), 3–68; Henry F. May, *The Enlightenment in America* (New York: Oxford University Press, 1976), 180, 235–36; *Common School Journal* 1 (November 1838): 6; Seth Luther, *An Address to the Workingmen of New England on the State of Education and on the Condition of the Producing Classes in Europe and America* (Boston: Published by the Author, 1832), 6, 29; *Voice of Industry,* 7 November 1845, in *Factory Girls,* ed. Foner, 112.

18. William Manning, *The Key of Liberty: The Life and Democratic Writings of William Manning, "A Laborer," 1747–1814,* ed. Michael Merrill and Sean Wilentz

(Cambridge: Harvard University Press, 1993), 125, 138; *New England Artisan*, 5 April 1832.

19. *New England Artisan*, 5 April, 23 February 1832.

20. David R. Roediger and Philip S. Foner, *Our Own Time: A History of American Labor and the Working Day* (London: Verso, 1989), 7; *The Man*, 13 May 1835, in Commons et al., eds., *Documentary History*, 6: 95; *New England Artisan*, 15 March 1832.

21. *Factory Tract No. 1*, in *Factory Girls*, ed. Foner, 134; *Voice of Industry*, 16 January, 6 February 1846, ibid., 224, 227. The origins and early development of the "Republican Motherhood" theme are examined in Linda K. Kerber, *Women of the Republic: Intellect and Ideology in Revolutionary America* (Chapel Hill: University of North Carolina Press, 1980), 11–12, 199–200, 228–31, 283–87.

22. *New England Artisan*, 22 March 1832; *Harbinger*, 7 August 1847.

23. *Lowell Offering*, ed. Eisler, 201–3; Lucy Larcom, *A New England Girlhood* (Boston: Houghton Mifflin, 1889), 228. Another champion of self-improvement who supported shorter hours was George W. Light, a close associate of Timothy Claxton, with whom he coedited several mechanics' journals. *Boston Mechanic* (December 1835): 238–41. Rex Burns provides insightful commentary on Light's career in *Success in America*, 103–5.

24. "A Workingmen's Evening School," Fall River *Mechanic*, 30 November 1844; *New England Artisan*, 25 October 1832; "To our Patrons," Fall River *Mechanic*, 27 April 1844.

25. Bruce Laurie, "'Spavined Ministers, Lying Toothpullers, and Buggering Priests': Third-Partyism and the Search for Security in the Antebellum North," in *American Artisans: Crafting Social Identity, 1750–1850*, ed. Howard B. Rock, Paul A. Gilje, and Robert Asher (Baltimore: Johns Hopkins University Press, 1995), 98–106; *The Man*, 30 May 1834, in Commons et al., eds., *Documentary History*, 6: 92–93.

26. Luther, *Address*, 5.

27. Address of Boston Mechanics and Laborers, in *Working Man's Advocate*, 2 November 1844; Hewitt quotation in "Journal of an Early Labor Organizer," ed. Philip S. Foner, *Labor History* 10 (Spring 1969): 221; *Voice of Industry*, 31 July 1845.

28. Murphy, *Ten Hours' Labor*, chap. 3; *The Factory Girl*, in *Factory Girls*, ed. Foner, 76; Stephen Foster, *Their Solitary Way: The Puritan Social Ethic in the First Century of Settlement in New England* (New Haven: Yale University Press, 1971), 120–26; Innes, *Creating the Commonwealth*, 122–25; Lynn *Awl*, 18 September 1844.

29. Laurie, *Artisans into Workers*, 44–45; Jama Lazerow, *Religion and the Working Class in Antebellum America* (Washington, D.C.: Smithsonian Institution Press, 1995), 196–98.

30. Harrison Gray Otis to George Harrison, 6 June 1836, Harrison Gray Otis Papers, Massachusetts Historical Society, Boston, Massachusetts (MHS), microfilm ed., reel 10; William Sullivan to Nathan Appleton, 29 February 1832, Appleton Family Papers, MHS.

31. William Sullivan, *Familiar Letters on Public Characters and Public Events; from the Peace of 1783 to the Peace of 1815* (Boston: Russell, Odiorne, and Metcalf, 1834), 227;

Benjamin Merrill to Leverett Saltonstall, 16 August 1841, "The Papers of Leverett Saltonstall, 1816–1845," ed. Robert E. Moody, *Collections of the Massachusetts Historical Society* 82–86 (1978–1992), 84: 174.

32. Harrison Gray Otis to Benjamin Pickman, 5 February 1834; Otis to George Harrison, 11 March 1834, 11 January 1837, Otis Papers, MHS, reel 10; Robert J. Haws, "Massachusetts Whigs, 1833–1854" (Ph.D. diss., University of Nebraska, 1973), 60–62.

33. Sullivan, *Familiar Letters,* 307; [Henry Adams], review of *Life, Letters, and Journals of George Ticknor,* in *North American Review* 123 (July 1876): 210; second quotation in Adams, *History of the United States during the Administrations of Jefferson and Madison,* 9 vols. (New York: Charles Scribner's Sons, 1889–1891), 1: 97.

34. William Lawrence, *Life of Amos A. Lawrence, with Extracts from His Diary and Correspondence* (Boston: Houghton Mifflin, 1889), 23–24; Robert F. Dalzell, Jr., *Enterprising Elite: The Boston Associates and the World They Made* (Cambridge: Harvard University Press, 1987), 71–73, 79–112, 233–38; Frances W. Gregory, *Nathan Appleton: Merchant and Entrepreneur, 1779–1861* (Charlottesville: University Press of Virginia, 1975), 212; Vera Shlakman, *Economic History of a Factory Town: A Study of Chicopee, Massachusetts* (1934–1935; repr. New York: Octagon Books, 1969), 28–47; Betty G. Farrell, *Elite Families: Class and Power in Nineteenth-Century Boston* (Albany: State University of New York Press, 1993), 39–69; Daniel Walker Howe, *The Political Culture of the American Whigs* (Chicago: University of Chicago Press, 1979), 101–2.

35. Amos Lawrence to his son, 16 January 1831, in *Extracts from the Diary and Correspondence of the Late Amos Lawrence with a Brief Account of Some Incidents in His Life,* ed. William R. Lawrence (Boston: Gould and Lincoln, 1855), 103–4; Edward Everett, "Lecture on the Workingmen's Party," October 1830, in *Orations and Speeches on Various Occasions,* 4 vols. (Boston: Little, Brown, 1865–1872), 1: 283–306; *Springfield Republican,* quoted in *Boston Daily Courier,* 17 September 1830. Also see the definition of the laboring classes in *New England Farmer* (9 September 1840): 78.

36. *The Diary of Christopher Columbus Baldwin, 1829–1835* (Worcester, Mass.: American Antiquarian Society, 1901), 91, 328; Joseph T. Buckingham to Daniel Webster, 11 May 1832, in Daniel Webster, *The Papers of Daniel Webster: Correspondence,* ed. Charles M. Wiltse and Harold D. Moser, 7 vols. (Hanover, N.H.: University Press of New England, 1974–1986), 3: 169–70.

37. Buckingham, *Personal Memoirs and Recollections of Editorial Life,* 2 vols. (Boston: Ticknor, Reed, and Fields, 1852), 2: 155; *Boston Daily Courier,* 2 June 1832.

38. *Boston Daily Advertiser,* 4 June 1832; *Boston Daily Courier,* 7 June 1832; *New England Artisan,* 28 June 1832; *Boston Daily Courier,* 3 January 1833; Tomlins, *Law, Labor, and Ideology,* 186–90; Joseph T. Buckingham to Nathan Appleton, 17 April 1834, Appleton Family Papers, MHS. In describing himself as a "watchman on the walls of our political Zion," Buckingham appropriated an expression traditionally used to describe the New England clergy's role as defenders of social order. Donald M. Scott, *From Office to Profession: The New England Ministry, 1750–1850* (Philadelphia: University of Pennsylvania Press, 1978), xi.

39. Gary J. Kornblith, "Becoming Joseph T. Buckingham: The Struggle for Artisanal Independence in Early Nineteenth-Century Boston," in *American Artisans,*

ed. Rock, Gilje, and Asher, 129–32; Joseph T. Buckingham, *Personal Memoirs,* 2: 145–46, 154–57, quotation from p. 157. Buckingham's attachment to the doctrine of stewardship was more than rhetorical. He never forgot the assistance that concerned neighbors provided his mother during the hard times she experienced following his father's death. See ibid., 1: 10–14.

40. William Appleton, Diary, January 1835, typescript, Appleton Family Papers, MHS; Octavius Brooks Frothingham, *Boston Unitarianism, 1820–1850: A Study of the Life and Work of Nathaniel Langdon Frothingham* (1890; repr. Hicksville, N.Y.: Regina Press, 1975), 104, 118. The author was Brooks's grandson.

41. Daniel Walker Howe, *The Unitarian Conscience: Harvard Moral Philosophy, 1805–1861* (Cambridge: Harvard University Press, 1970), 43–144; Frederic Cople Jaher, *The Urban Establishment: The Upper Strata in Boston, New York, Charleston, Chicago, and Los Angeles* (Urbana: University of Illinois Press, 1982), 62–63; *Diary and Correspondence of Amos Lawrence,* 81, 197, 311, quotations from pp. 197, 81; Dalzell, *Enterprising Elite,* 143–48.

42. Ronald Story, *The Forging of an Aristocracy: Harvard & the Boston Upper Class, 1800–1870* (Middletown, Conn.: Wesleyan University Press, 1980), 6–19, 160–67; Dalzell, *Enterprising Elite,* 113–15, 123–39; quotations in Howe, *Unitarian Conscience,* 144, 254.

43. Paul Goodman, "Ethics and Enterprise: The Values of a Boston Elite, 1800–1860," *American Quarterly* 18 (Fall 1966): 446; [Samuel A. Eliot], "Public and Private Charities in Boston," *North American Review* 61 (1845): 141–47; Jaher, *Urban Establishment,* 59; *New England Farmer* (16 January 1826): 190; *Boston Courier,* 29 January 1845; Dalzell, *Enterprising Elite,* 148–51.

44. Fisher Ames to George R. Minot, 3 September, 31 May 1789, Fisher Ames, *Works of Fisher Ames: With a Selection from His Speeches and Correspondence,* ed. Seth Ames, 2 vols. (Boston: Little, Brown, 1854), 1: 69, 51; David Hackett Fischer, "The Myth of the Essex Junto," *William and Mary Quarterly* 21 (April 1964): 210; Webster, quoted in Frank Tracy Carlton, *Economic Influences upon Educational Progress in the United States, 1820–1850* (1908; repr. New York: Teachers College Press, Columbia University, 1965), 64; George Ticknor to Maria Edgeworth, 6 March 1839, George Ticknor, *Life, Letters, and Journals of George Ticknor,* ed. George S. Hillard, 2 vols. (Boston: James R. Osgood and Company, 1876), 2: 188.

45. [Eliot], "Public and Private Charities in Boston," 155–56.

46. *Boston Courier,* 4 October 1845.

47. Editorial criticism of protectionist arguments can be found in *New England Artisan,* 19 April, 3 May, 20 December 1832, 2 January 1833. The views of correspondents who disagreed with Douglas are ibid., 17 May and 27 December 1832, 2 January, 11 April, 8 August 1833; also see the protariff sentiments expressed by Essex County textile workers in Memorial of the Association of Mechanics, Farmers, and other Working Men, in the towns of Amesbury and Salisbury, 6 June 1832, House Executive Doc. No. 258. Gary J. Kornblith discusses earlier instances of mechanic support for protective tariffs in "From Artisans to Businessmen," 57–61, 65–67, 75–78, 81–82.

48. Barbara M. Tucker, *Samuel Slater and the Origins of the American Textile In-dustry, 1790–1860* (Ithaca, N.Y.: Cornell University Press, 1984), 139–47; *New England Artisan*, 23 February 1832; Thomas Dublin, *Women at Work: The Transformation of Work and Community in Lowell, Massachusetts, 1826–1860* (New York: Columbia University Press, 1979), 72–74, 86–107; Roediger and Foner, *Our Own Time*, 45–49.

49. Dalzell, *Enterprising Elite*, 52; Kenneth Wiggins Porter, *The Jacksons and the Lees: Two Generations of Massachusetts Merchants, 1765–1844*, 2 vols. (Cambridge: Harvard University Press, 1937), I: 125–26; Dublin, *Women at Work*, 108–13; Roediger and Foner, *Our Own Time*, 49–52.

50. John Davis to Fall River Association of Industry, 20 October 1842, John Davis Papers, American Antiquarian Society, Worcester, Massachusetts (AAS). Davis's most popular Democratic counterpart, Marcus Morton, responded to demands for ten-hour legislation in much the same way. See Arthur B. Darling, *Political Changes in Massachusetts, 1824–1848: A Study of Liberal Movements in Politics* (New Haven: Yale University Press, 1925), 264–65.

51. Dublin, *Women at Work*, 113–15.

52. Abbott Lawrence to William Schouler, 28 March 1845, William Schouler Papers, MHS; Massachusetts General Court, House of Representatives, *House Documents, No. 50*, 1845, in *Factory Girls*, ed. Foner, 241–42. For evidence that Lowell mill owners expected Schouler to help protect the reputation of their local establishments, see Samuel Lawrence to Schouler, 9 January 1844, William Schouler Papers, MHS. Discussing a proposed article by Horace Greeley, Lawrence told Schouler that the *New York Tribune* editor would be best advised "to show off statistical information of various kinds to prove the virtue of the system but not the profits of the Lowell mills."

53. *Voice of Industry*, 12 June 1845; ibid., 9 January 1846, 8 November 1845, in *Factory Girls*, ed. Foner, 243, 246; Dublin *Women at Work*, 115–16.

54. *Lowell Daily Courier*, 11 November 1845; *Voice of Industry*, 28 August and 21 November 1845, 2 October 1846, 25 September 1845, 6 November 1846, 25 June 1847.

55. Daniel Webster to Edward Everett, 30 November 1843, Webster, *Correspondence*, 5: 322; Charles E. Persons, "The Early History of Factory Legislation in Massachusetts: From 1825 to the Passage of the Ten Hour Law in 1874," in *Labor Laws and Their Enforcement*, ed. Susan M. Kingsbury (New York: Longmans, Green, 1911), 69–74.

56. John A. Lowell, *Memoir of Patrick Tracy Jackson* (New York: Press of Hunt's Merchants' Magazine, 1848); Robert V. Spalding, "The Boston Mercantile Community and the Promotion of the Textile Industry in New England, 1813–1860" (Ph.D. diss., Yale University, 1963), 3; Thomas W. Ward to Joshua Bates, 24 September 1850, copy, Ward Papers, MHS; John Quincy Adams, *Memoirs of John Quincy Adams, Comprising Portions of His Diary from 1795 to 1848*, ed. Charles Francis Adams, 12 vols. (Philadelphia: J. B. Lippincott, 1874–1877), 10: 43; Abbott Lawrence to Amos Lawrence, 2 February 1828, Amos Lawrence Papers, MHS; Joshua Bates to Thomas W. Ward, 4 October 1850, copy, Ward Papers, MHS; fourth quotation from Abbott Lawrence to T. B. Curtis et al., 25 March 1837, in Hamilton Andrews Hill, *Memoir*

of Abbott Lawrence (Boston: n.p., 1883), 15; Lawrence to Leverett Saltonstall, 28 January 1842, "Saltonstall Papers," 85: 23; Lawrence to John Davis, 17 March 1842, Davis Papers, AAS; fifth quotation from Lawrence to Nathan Appleton, 15 January 1833, Letters to Nathan Appleton by or about Abbott Lawrence, bMS Am 1557 (7–71), Houghton Library, Harvard University, Cambridge, Massachusetts (HL); Lawrence to Robert C. Winthrop, 8 April 1850, Winthrop Family Papers, MHS, microfilm ed., reel 26.

57. Nathan Appleton, "Labor, Its Relations in Europe and the United States, Compared," *Hunt's Merchants' Magazine* 11 (September 1844): 217–23. Also see Appleton's clarification of his land argument in Appleton to Andrews Norton, 23 November 1844, Appleton Family Papers, MHS. James L. Huston examines the broader intellectual context from which Appleton's thought arose in *Securing the Fruits of Labor: The American Concept of Wealth Distribution, 1765–1900* (Baton Rouge: Louisiana State University Press, 1998), 50–53, 153–56, 167–83, 245–51.

58. Andrews Norton to Nathan Appleton, 11 November 1844; James S. Amory to Appleton, 5 October 1844, Appleton Family Papers, MHS. Two of the better studies of antebellum communitarianism are Carl J. Guarneri, *The Utopian Alternative: Fourierism in Nineteenth-Century America* (Ithaca, N.Y.: Cornell University Press, 1991); and Christopher Clark, *The Communitarian Moment: The Radical Challenge of the Northampton Association* (Ithaca, N.Y.: Cornell University Press, 1995).

59. Anne C. Rose, *Transcendentalism as a Social Movement, 1830–1850* (New Haven: Yale University Press, 1981), 154; *Voice of Industry,* 25 September, 18 September 1846. Allen was not the only writer who singled out Lawrence for criticism; on at least one occasion, the manufacturer's nephew felt compelled to refute charges that he was deliberately seeking to reduce the wages of factory operatives. See Amos A. Lawrence to John T. Gibbs, editor of the *Dover Gazette,* 1847, Amos A. Lawrence Letterbook, MHS.

60. Jean V. Matthews, *Rufus Choate: The Law and Civic Virtue* (Philadelphia: Temple University Press, 1980), 74–75.

Chapter Four

1. *Liberator,* 1 January 1831.

2. Samuel Eliot Morison, *The Life and Letters of Harrison Gray Otis, 1765–1848,* 2 vols. (Boston: Houghton Mifflin, 1913), 2: 259–64, 276–80; quotation from p. 262.

3. William Lloyd Garrison to *Salem Gazette,* 11 June, 6 August 1824; Garrison to Frances M. L. Garrison, 26 May 1823, in *The Letters of William Lloyd Garrison,* ed. Walter M. Merrill and Louis Ruchames, 6 vols. (Cambridge: Harvard University Press, 1971–1981), 1: 16, 29, 10; quotation in John L. Thomas, *The Liberator, William Lloyd Garrison: A Biography* (Boston: Little, Brown, 1963), 66.

4. Thomas, *The Liberator,* 370–71; *Liberator,* 1 and 29 January, 5 February 1831; *New England Artisan,* 15 August 1833; Fall River *Mechanic,* 24 April 1844; final two quotations in *Voice of Industry,* 25 February, 7 May 1847.

236 ⌒ NOTES TO PAGES 93-98

5. Nathan Appleton to J. N. Danforth, 11 August 1848, Appleton Family Papers, Massachusetts Historical Society, Boston, Massachusetts (MHS); Morison, *Otis*, 2: 219; Nathan Appleton, Journal, 8 January, 4 February 1805, Appleton Family Papers, MHS.

6. William Ellery Channing, "Remarks on the Slavery Question, in a Letter to Jonathan Phillips, Esq.," 1839, in William Ellery Channing, *The Works of William Ellery Channing*, 6 vols. (Boston: American Unitarian Association, n.d.), 5: 77; John Hope Franklin, *A Southern Odyssey: Travelers in the Antebellum North* (Baton Rouge: Louisiana State University Press, 1976), 1-112; Edward L. Pierce, *Memoir and Letters of Charles Sumner*, 4 vols. (Boston: Roberts Brothers, 1877-1894), 3: 6.

7. Daniel Jenifer to Nathan Appleton, 25 June 1834; second quotation in Appleton to J. N. Danforth, 11 August 1848; Appleton to Rev. M. M. Dillon, 23 August 1854, Appleton Family Papers, MHS; Leverett Saltonstall to Mary Saltonstall, 6 January 1839, "The Papers of Leverett Saltonstall, 1816-1845," ed. Robert E. Moody, *Collections of the Massachusetts Historical Society* 82-86 (1978-1992), 83: 155.

8. Morison, *Otis*, 2: 262-64; *Boston Daily Advertiser*, 5 April 1832; Harrison Gray Otis to Daniel Webster, 11 April 1832; Otis to Theodore Sedgwick, 3 January 1833, Harrison Gray Otis Papers, MHS, microfilm ed., reel 9.

9. Leonard L. Richards, *"Gentlemen of Property and Standing": Anti-Abolition Mobs in Jacksonian America* (New York: Oxford University Press, 1970), 50-52; *Boston Daily Atlas*, 31 July 1835; *Boston Daily Advocate*, 9 March 1836; Daniel Webster, *The Papers of Daniel Webster: Correspondence*, ed. Charles M. Wiltse and Harold D. Moser, 7 vols. (Hanover, N.H.: University Press of New England, 1974-1986), 4: 48-49.

10. *Boston Daily Advertiser*, 22 August 1835; Theodore M. Hammett, "Two Mobs of Jacksonian Boston: Ideology and Interest," *Journal of American History* 62 (March 1976): 864-65; Harrison Gray Otis to George Harrison, 10 September 1835, Otis Papers, MHS, reel 10; John Quincy Adams, *Memoirs of John Quincy Adams, Comprising Portions of His Diary from 1795 to 1848*, ed. Charles Francis Adams, 12 vols. (Philadelphia: J. B. Lippincott, 1874-1877), 9: 253.

11. *Boston Daily Advertiser*, 19 September 1835; *Boston Courier*, 11 September 1835; final two quotations ibid., 9 and 15 September 1835.

12. Henry E. Benson to Amos A. Phelps, 27 August 1835, Antislavery Collection, Boston Public Library, Boston, Massachusetts (BPL); Thomas, *The Liberator*, 37-38; Morison, *Otis*, 2: 246, 273-74; *Liberator*, 5, 12, and 19 September 1835, quotation from 5 September edition.

13. Richards, *"Gentlemen of Property and Standing,"* 51, 62-71; Thomas, *The Liberator*, 200-204; *Boston Daily Atlas*, 30 September, 16 October 1835.

14. *Hampshire Gazette*, 28 October 1835; *Salem Landmark*, in *Liberator*, 21 November 1835; "A Working Man" quotation ibid., 31 November 1835; "A Democrat" and William Comstock quotations ibid., 14 November 1835.

15. William L. Garrison to Helen E. Garrison, 9 November 1835, Garrison, *Letters*, 1: 552; Henry Wilson, *History of the Rise and Fall of the Slave Power in America*, 3 vols. (Boston: James R. Osgood and Company, 1872-1877), 1: 321-22; *Fifth Annual Report of the Board of Managers of the Massachusetts Anti-Slavery Society* (Boston, 1837),

65–70; Thomas, *The Liberator*, 215–16; *Boston Daily Advocate*, 18 March 1836; *Boston Courier*, 10 March 1836; Samuel J. May, *Some Recollections of Our Antislavery Conflict* (Boston: Fields, Osgood, 1869), 185–202; Bond quotation in *Liberator*, 26 March 1836. Abolitionist testimony before the committee is reprinted ibid., 19 and 26 March 1836.

16. *Boston Daily Advocate*, 1 April 1836; *Fifth Annual Report of the Massachusetts Anti-Slavery Society*, 70.

17. Leonard L. Richards, *The Life and Times of Congressman John Quincy Adams* (New York: Oxford University Press, 1986), 115–28.

18. Benjamin Waterhouse to John Quincy Adams, 10 May 1836, Adams Family Papers, MHS, microfilm ed., reel 503; "the new folk hero" is from the title to chapter four of Richards, *John Quincy Adams;* Morton Eddy to Adams, 26 December 1837; Samuel Osgood to Adams, 20 December 1837, Adams Family Papers, MHS, reel 507.

19. Fisher A. Kingsbury to John Quincy Adams, 10 January 1836, Adams Family Papers, MHS, reel 503; Ichabod M. Morton to Adams, 11 January 1837; William S. Wilder to Adams, 4 February 1837; Elbridge B. Howe to Adams, 7 February 1837; Joseph Paine to Adams, 6 February 1837; William Lee to Adams, 22 February 1837; John Marston to Adams, 25 February 1837, Adams Family Papers, reel 505; Anthony Collamore to Adams, 10 March 1837, Adams Family Papers, reel 506; quotations in Cyrus P. Grosvenor to Adams, 10 February 1837; and William B. Clark to Adams, 29 January 1837, Adams Family Papers, reel 505.

20. Richard L. Bushman, *King and People in Provincial Massachusetts* (Chapel Hill: University of North Carolina Press, 1985), 46–54; Ellis G. Loring to William Ellery Channing, 17 March 1838, William Ellery Channing Papers, MHS, microfilm ed., reel 3; *Sixth Annual Report of the Board of Managers of the Massachusetts Anti-Slavery Society* (Boston, 1838), 16–20.

21. Anne W. Weston to Mary Weston, 27 October 1835, Weston Papers, BPL: Wendell Phillips Garrison and Francis Jackson Garrison, *William Lloyd Garrison, 1805–1879: The Story of His Life, Told by His Children*, 4 vols. (New York: Century, 1885–1889), 1: 496; 2: 188.

22. First quotation in Timothy Pickering to John Marshall, 7 January 1829; Pickering to Elijah H. Mills, 15 April 1826; Pickering to John Lowell, 25 April 1826, Timothy Pickering Papers, MHS, reel 16; *Salem Gazette*, April 1826, Pickering Papers, reel 55; Peter C. Brooks to Edward Everett, 17 December 1832, Edward Everett Papers, MHS, microfilm ed., reel 5; final quotation in *Liberator*, 10 November 1837; *Boston Daily Atlas*, 4 November 1837. For a particularly vicious survey of Everett's conduct over a thirty-five-year period, see Theodore Parker to Caroline Thayer, 10 June 1860, copy, Theodore Parker Papers, MHS, microfilm ed., reel 2.

23. *Boston Daily Atlas*, 18 February 1836; *Boston Atlas*, 3 March 1837; *Boston Daily Advertiser*, 3 March, 1 April 1837; *Boston Atlas*, 10 April 1837. Haughton's political idol doubtless influenced his own changing views. During these years, Webster was developing a healthy respect for antislavery sentiment. See, for example, Webster to Benjamin D. Silliman, 29 January 1838, Webster, *Correspondence*, 4: 265.

24. Leonard L. Richards, "The Jacksonians and Slavery," in *Antislavery Reconsidered: New Perspectives on the Abolitionists*, ed. Lewis Perry and Michael Fellman (Baton Rouge: Louisiana State University Press, 1979), 109–12; John Niven, *Martin Van Buren: The Romantic Age of American Politics* (New York: Oxford University Press, 1983), 410–11; Arthur B. Darling, *Political Changes in Massachusetts, 1824–1848: A Study of Liberal Movements in Politics* (New Haven: Yale University Press, 1925), 156; quotation from Lydia Maria Child to Ellis G. Loring, 5 December 1838, Lydia Maria Child Letters, 1838–56, Manuscripts and Archives Division, New York Public Library, Astor, Lenox and Tilden Foundations, in Lydia Maria Child, *The Collected Correspondence of Lydia Maria Child*, ed. Patricia G. Holland and Milton Meltzer (Millwood, N.Y.: Kraus Microform, 1980), microfiche ed., card 6.

25. Edmund Quincy to John Quincy Adams, 31 January 1842, Quincy, Wendell, Holmes and Upham Papers (QWHU Papers), MHS, microfilm ed., reel 46.

26. Thomas, *The Liberator*, 289–93; Debra Gold Hansen, *Strained Sisterhood: Gender and Class in the Boston Female Anti-Slavery Society* (Amherst: University of Massachusetts Press, 1993), 93–117; Thomas, *The Liberator*, 328–33.

27. Ellis G. Loring to William Ellery Channing, 17 March 1838, Channing Papers, MHS, reel 3; Loring to Lydia Maria Child, 29 April 1841, Ellis Gray Loring Letterbook, bMS Am 1554, Houghton Library, Harvard University, Cambridge, Massachusetts (HL), in Child, *Collected Correspondence*, card 9; Edmund Quincy to Richard Webb, 30 January 1844, QWHU Papers, MHS, reel 47.

28. Edmund Quincy to Richard D. Webb, 29 March 1845, QWHU Papers, MHS, reel 48; John Greenleaf Whittier to Gerrit Smith, 8 March 1840, John Greenleaf Whittier, *The Letters of John Greenleaf Whittier*, ed. John B. Pickard, 3 vols. (Cambridge: Harvard University Press, 1975), 1: 388.

29. William Ellery Channing to Joseph Tuckerman, 13 May 1835, Channing Papers, MHS, reel 3; William Henry Channing, *The Life of William Ellery Channing, D.D.* (Boston: American Unitarian Association, 1880), 456; Lydia Maria Child to Henrietta Sargent, 13 November 1836, in *Lydia Maria Child: Selected Letters, 1817–1880*, ed. Milton Meltzer and Patricia G. Holland (Amherst: University of Massachusetts Press, 1982), 56; final quotation in Channing, *Life of Channing*, 456.

30. Chapman quotation in Jack Mendelsohn, *Channing: The Reluctant Radical* (Boston: Little, Brown, 1971), 237; Lydia Maria Child to Louisa Loring, 19 July 1836, Loring Family Papers, A-115: 20, Schlesinger Library, Radcliffe Institute, Harvard University, Cambridge, Massachusetts, in Child, *Collected Correspondence*, card 4.

31. William Ellery Channing to Daniel Webster, 14 May 1828, Webster, *Correspondence*, 2: 347–48.

32. Deborah Pickman Clifford, *Crusader for Freedom: A Life of Lydia Maria Child* (Boston: Beacon Press, 1992), 103, 129; Lydia Maria Child to Lucy and Mary Osgood, 11 May 1856, Lydia Maria Child Papers, Anti-Slavery Collection, Cornell University Libraries, Ithaca, New York, in Child, *Collected Correspondence*, card 33; May, *Recollections*, 172–75; Channing, *Life of Channing*, 269–70, 421, 531–32; quotation from Channing, *Slavery* (1835), in Channing, *Works*, 2: 141.

33. First quotation in Channing, *Life of Channing*, 533; William Ellery Channing to Blanco White, 27 February 1841, Channing Papers, MHS, reel 3; Edmund Quincy to Richard D. Webb, 22 September 1844, QWHU Papers, MHS, reel 48; Donald Yacovone, *Samuel Joseph May and the Dilemmas of the Liberal Persuasion, 1797–1871* (Philadelphia: Temple University Press, 1991), 79; final quotation in Channing, *Life of Channing*, 373. Also see Douglas C. Stange, *Patterns of Antislavery among American Unitarians, 1831–1860* (Rutherford, N.J.: Fairleigh Dickinson University Press, 1977).

34. Harrison Gary Otis to George Harrison, 22 January 1836, Otis Papers, MHS, reel 10; William Ellery Channing to John C. Warren, 19 August 1835, Channing Papers, MHS, reel 3; final quotation in Channing, *Slavery*, in Channing, *Works*, 2: 145.

35. Channing, *Slavery*, in Channing, *Works*, 2: 98, 106–10, 126–30, quotation from pp. 127–28.

36. First quotation in *Fourth Annual Report of the Board of Managers of the Massachusetts Anti-Slavery Society*, 30; J. Q. Adams, *Memoirs*, 9: 268; *Liberator*, 27 February 1836; William Lloyd Garrison to Samuel J. May, 5 December 1835, in Garrison, *Letters*, 1: 572.

37. William Ellery Channing to Noah Worcester, 16 December 1835, Channing Papers, MHS, reel 3; *Boston Daily Atlas*, 9 December 1835; Harrison Gray Otis to George Harrison, 22 January 1836, Otis Papers, MHS, reel 10. Haughton reprinted Austin's pamphlet in the *Atlas* during March and April 1836; the Austin quotations are from the April 7 edition of the papers.

38. Yacovone, *May*, 63. These suppositions concerning Bond are based on his remarks at an antislavery meeting held the following year in Faneuil Hall. See *Liberator*, 15 December 1837.

39. First quotation in Samuel E. Sewall to William Ellery Channing, 25 November 1837, Channing Papers, MHS, reel 3; Channing to Sewall, 25 November 1837, Garrison Papers, BPL; response of mayor and aldermen quoted in *Sixth Annual Report of the Board of Managers of the Massachusetts Anti-Slavery Society*, 40; Channing's letter to the citizens of Boston is reprinted in *Liberator*, 8 December 1837, and *Boston Courier*, 9 December 1837.

40. *Boston Atlas*, 6 December 1837; *Boston Daily Advertiser*, 2 and 11 December 1837; *Fitchburg Courier* quoted in *Liberator*, 29 December 1837; Charles Francis Adams, *Diary of Charles Francis Adams*, ed. Aida DiPace Donald et al., 8 vols. (Cambridge: Harvard University Press, 1964–1986), 7: 353–54; *Sixth Annual Report of the Massachusetts Anti-Slavery Society*, 45–47, final quotation from p. 46.

41. *Sixth Annual Report of the Massachusetts Anti-Slavery Society*, 47–50; James Brewer Stewart, *Wendell Phillips: Liberty's Hero* (Baton Rouge: Louisiana State University Press, 1986), 58–63; Bond quotation in *Liberator*, 15 December 1837.

42. William Ellery Channing to Joanna Baillie, 12 July 1831, in Channing, *Life of Channing*, 509; C. F. Adams, *Diary*, 7: 358; final quotation in Deborah Weston to Anne W. Weston, 6 June 1836, Weston Papers, BPL; Channing, *Life of Channing*, 570–71.

43. Lydia Maria Child to Louisa and Ellis Gray Loring, 16 August 1838, Loring Family Papers, A-115: 22, Schlesinger Library, Radcliffe Institute, Harvard University, in Child, *Collected Correspondence,* card 6; second quotation in Channing, *Life of Channing,* 542; final quotation in *Liberator,* 27 December 1837.

44. First quotation in William Ellery Channing, "Remarks on the Slavery Question," in Channing, *Works,* 5: 29; ibid., 5:77; Channing, "The Present Age," 11 May 1841, ibid., 6: 177; Channing, "An Address Delivered at Lenox, on the First of August, 1842, Being the Anniversary of Emancipation in the British West-Indies," ibid., 6: 418; Channing to William Rathbone, 23 August 1837, in Channing, *Life of Channing,* 586.

45. William Ellery Channing to George Combe, 19 March 1840; quotations in Channing to Harmanus Bleecker, 7 February 1842, both items in Channing, *Life of Channing,* 594, 519.

46. Channing, *Life of Channing,* 542; "prejudices of property" segment of Quincy quotation from *Sixth Annual Report of the Massachusetts Anti-Slavery Society,* xiv; Edmund Quincy to Richard D. Webb, 27 November 1843, QWHU Papers, MHS, reel 47.

47. William Ellery Channing, "Ministry for the Poor," 9 April 1835, in Channing, *Works,* 4: 270–71; Channing, "A Discourse on the Life and Character of the Rev. Joseph Tuckerman, D.D.," 31 January 1841, ibid., 6: 102–4, "moral care" quotation from p. 102; Channing to J. C. L. Simonde de Sismondi, 10 September 1841, in Channing, *Life of Channing,* 518; Channing, "Lectures on the Elevation of the Labouring Portion of the Community," 11 February 1840, in Channing, *Works,* 5: 203, 207–8, final quotation from pp. 207–8.

48. William Ellery Channing, *Slavery,* in Channing, *Works,* 2: 109–10; second quotation from Channing, "Remarks on the Slavery Question," ibid., 5: 60; third quotation from Channing, "Emancipation," 15 November 1840, ibid., 6: 35; Channing, "The Present Age," ibid., 6: 171–74, final quotation from p. 174.

49. J. Q. Adams, *Memoirs,* 10: 40; Pierce, *Sumner,* 3: 119–20; final quotation in Charles Sumner to Nathan Appleton, 22 August 1846, Appleton Family Papers, MHS.

50. William Ellery Channing, "The Duty of the Free States," Part II, 1842, in Channing, *Works,* 6: 349.

51. Kinley J. Brauer, *Cotton versus Conscience: Massachusetts Whig Politics and Southwestern Expansion, 1843–1848* (Lexington: University of Kentucky Press, 1967), 30–36; Jean V. Matthews, *Rufus Choate: The Law and Civic Virtue* (Philadelphia: Temple University Press, 1980), 69–70; Henry Wilson to William Schouler, 16 April 1844, William Schouler Papers, MHS.

52. Brauer, *Cotton versus Conscience,* 68–75; Hamilton Andrews Hill, *Memoir of Abbott Lawrence* (Boston: n.p., 1883), 21; Amos Lawrence to Mrs. Appleton, 15 November 1844, in *Extracts from the Diary and Correspondence of the Late Amos Lawrence with a Brief Account of Some Incidents from His Life,* ed. William R. Lawrence (Boston: Gould and Lincoln, 1855), 192.

53. Leverett Saltonstall to Stephen C. Phillips, 29 January 1845; Saltonstall to Robert C. Winthrop, 20 December 1844, in "Saltonstall Papers," 86: 315, 286.

54. Brauer, *Cotton versus Conscience*, 115–25, 149–54; Pierce, *Sumner*, 3: 101–2; quotation in *Boston Courier*, 19 November 1845.

55. The letters, which were written in January and February 1846, are reprinted in Hill, *Memoir of Abbott Lawrence*, 137–67; they also appeared in *Boston Courier*, 20, 30, and 31 January, 13 March 1846, as well as numerous other newspapers of the period.

56. Louis S. Gerteis, *Morality and Utility in American Antislavery Reform* (Chapel Hill: University of North Carolina Press, 1987), 68–71, quotation from p. 69; Paul Conkin, *Prophets of Prosperity: America's First Political Economists* (Bloomington: Indiana University Press, 1980), 275–76. Unlike most elite Bostonians, Sumner did not accept Carey's argument that slavery could be abolished through the "working of natural causes." Pierce, *Sumner*, 3: 59–60.

57. George Ticknor to Charles Lyell, 14 December 1843, in Ticknor, *Life, Letters, and Journals*, 2 vols. (Boston: James R. Osgood, 1876), 2: 218; Nathan Appleton to J. N. Danforth, 11 August 1848, Appleton Family Papers, MHS; Abbott Lawrence to Edward Everett, 18 March 1850, Everett Papers, MHS, reel 13A.

58. *Lowell Daily Courier*, 27 January 1846.

59. *Boston Daily Whig*, 17 June, 14 and 23 August 1846; Charles Sumner to Nathan Appleton, 31 August 1848, copy, Appleton-Sumner Correspondence, BPL; Joseph T. Buckingham, *Personal Memoirs and Recollections of Editorial Life*, 2 vols. (Boston: Ticknor, Reed, and Fields, 1852), 2: 104–5; Buckingham to Charles Sumner, 30 September, 1 October 1846, Charles Sumner Papers, bMS Am 1, HL, quotation from 30 September letter; Charles Francis Adams, Diary, 3 August 1846, Adams Family Papers, MHS, reel 68; Martin B. Duberman, *Charles Francis Adams, 1807–1886* (Boston: Houghton Mifflin, 1961), 110–11.

60. Quotations in *Boston Daily Whig*, 26 June, 19 June, 3 July, 23 August 1846.

61. Ibid., 10 July and 3 July 1846.

62. Ibid., 18 September, 21 July 1846; Pierce, *Sumner*, 3: 123.

63. Abbott Lawrence to John P. Bigelow, 27 December 1850, John P. Bigelow Papers, bMS Am 801.2 (820–60), HL; Lawrence to Nathan Appleton, 15 January 1833, Letters to Nathan Appleton by or about Abbott Lawrence, bMS Am 1557 (7–71), HL.

64. Shaw Livermore, Jr., *The Twilight of Federalism: The Disintegration of the Federalist Party, 1815–1830* (Princeton: Princeton University Press, 1962); Thomas Brown, *Politics and Statesmanship: Essays on the American Whig Party* (New York: Columbia University Press, 1985), 175–79, 184–87.

65. Abbott Lawrence to John Davis, 3 February 1849, John Davis Papers, American Antiquarian Society, Worcester, Massachusetts (AAS); second quotation in Lawrence to Edward Everett, 18 March 1850, Everett Papers, MHS, reel 13A; Lawrence to Nathan Appleton, December 1850, Letters to Nathan Appleton by or about Abbott Lawrence, bMS Am 1557 (7–71), HL. On the growing national orientation of other Associates during the period, see Frances W. Gregory, *Nathan Appleton:*

Merchant and Entrepreneur, 1779–1861 (Charlottesville: University Press of Virginia, 1975), 225–26; Arthur M. Johnson and Barry Supple, *Boston Capitalists and Western Railroads: A Study in the Nineteenth-Century Investment Process* (Cambridge: Harvard University Press, 1967), 67–70, 81–191; and William Gates, *Michigan Copper and Boston Dollars: An Economic History of the Michigan Copper Mining Industry* (Cambridge: Harvard University Press, 1951), 32–35.

66. Abbott Lawrence to Henry Clay, 26 March 1833, in Henry Clay, *Works of Henry Clay: Comprising His Life, Correspondence, and Speeches,* ed. Calvin Colton, 7 vols. (New York: Henry Clay Publishing, 1897), 4: 358; Channing, *Slavery,* in Channing, *Works,* 2: 7.

Chapter Five

1. David Herbert Donald, *Charles Sumner and the Coming of the Civil War* (1960; repr. Chicago: University of Chicago Press, 1981), 143–46; Kinley J. Brauer, *Cotton versus Conscience: Massachusetts Whig Politics and Southwestern Expansion, 1843–1848* (Lexington: University of Kentucky Press, 1967), 170–78; first quotation in Robert C. Winthrop to Edward Everett, 7 June 1846, Edward Everett Papers, Massachusetts Historical Society, Boston, Massachusetts (MHS), microfilm ed., reel 12A; Winthrop to John H. Clifford, 9 September 1846, copy, Winthrop Family Papers, MHS, microfilm ed., reel 39.

2. Brauer, *Cotton versus Conscience,* 183–94; Robert C. Winthrop to John H. Clifford, 27 September 1846, copy, Winthrop Family Papers, MHS, reel 39; *Boston Daily Whig,* 1 October 1846. This was not the first time the expression "Cotton Whig" had been used to describe party members who represented the manufacturing interest; its origin can be traced to a state senate debate earlier that year in which E. Rockwood Hoar declared "it quite as desirable that the Legislature should represent the conscience as the cotton of the Commonwealth." George F. Hoar, *Autobiography of Seventy Years,* 2 vols. (New York: Charles Scribner's Sons, 1903), 1: 134.

3. Brauer, *Cotton versus Conscience,* 204–5, 212–19, 238–39.

4. Ibid., 238–39; *Boston Daily Whig,* 6 July 1848.

5. Nathan Appleton to Charles Sumner, 1 July 1848; Sumner to Appleton, 12 August 1848; Appleton to Sumner, 17 August 1848; Sumner to Appleton, 31 August 1848, copies, Appleton-Sumner Correspondence, Boston Public Library, Boston, Massachusetts (BPL).

6. Nathan Appleton to Charles Sumner, 4 September 1848, copy, Appleton-Sumner Correspondence, BPL; Edward L. Pierce, *Memoir and Letters of Charles Sumner,* 4 vols. (Boston: Roberts Brothers, 1877–1894), 2: 4–10, 338–42; Ronald Story, *The Forging of an Aristocracy: Harvard and the Boston Upper Class, 1800–1870* (Middletown, Conn: Wesleyan University Press, 1980), 124–34.

7. *Boston Daily Whig,* 18 September 1846.

8. Samuel Gridley Howe to Theodore Parker, 28 November 1854, in Samuel

Gridley Howe, *Letters and Journals of Samuel Gridley Howe*, ed. Laura Richards, 2 vols. (Boston: Dana Estes & Company, 1909), 2: 406.

9. Charles Francis Adams to Theodore Parker, 24 March 1853, copy, Theodore Parker Papers, MHS, microfilm ed., reel 4; Adams to C. H. Dillaway, 14 July 1857, copy, Adams Family Papers, MHS, microfilm ed., reel 162; *Boston Courier*, 18 July 1843; John Quincy Adams to Charles Francis Adams, 28 November 1840, copy, Adams Family Papers, MHS, reel 154.

10. Charles Francis Adams, *Diary of Charles Francis Adams*, ed. Aida DiPace Donald et al., 8 vols. (Cambridge: Harvard University Press, 1964–1986), 3: 29; Martin B. Duberman, *Charles Francis Adams, 1807–1886* (Boston: Houghton Mifflin, 1961), 26–32, 35–36.

11. C. F. Adams, *Diary*, 2: 172; 6: 123–24; quotation in 4: 362 (13 September 1832); 3: 270; 4: 152; Paul C. Nagel, *Descent from Glory: Four Generations of the John Adams Family* (New York: Oxford University Press, 1983), 161–62, 174–79; C. F. Adams, *Diary* 6: 22; 5: 322; Peter C. Brooks to Edward Everett, 15 February 1836, Everett Papers, MHS, reel 6.

12. Quotations in C. F. Adams, *Diary*, 4: 338 (30 July 1832); 5: 186–87 (6 October 1833); 4: 30 (17 April 1831); 4: 49 (15 May 1831).

13. Ibid., 3: 371, 381; 5: 99; first quotation in 6: 202–3 (24 August 1835); second quotation in 7: 320 (24 September 1837).

14. Quotations ibid., 1: 312 (4 September 1824); 5: 366 (23 August 1834); Charles Francis Adams, Diary, 16 July 1850, Adams Family Papers, MHS, reel 71.

15. C. F. Adams, *Diary*, 7: 124; Leonard L. Richards, *The Life and Times of Congressman John Quincy Adams* (New York: Oxford University Press, 1986), 32–37, 43–51; final quotation in C. F. Adams, *Diary*, 6: 190 (3 August 1835); Charles Francis Adams to John Quincy Adams, 28 May 1836, Adams Family Papers, MHS, reel 3; Duberman, *Charles Francis Adams*, 44–51, 53–55.

16. Duberman, *Charles Francis Adams*, 61–62; quotation in *Boston Daily Advocate*, 24 June 1836; C. F. Adams, *Diary*, 7: 353.

17. Duberman, *Charles Francis Adams*, 63–65; *Boston Daily Advocate*, 25 June 1836; manuscript article titled "Political Speculations, No. 1," ca. 1838, Adams Family Papers, MHS, reel 320.

18. Duberman, *Charles Francis Adams*, 60–61, 65, 69–70; C. F. Adams, *Diary*, 8: 43; first quotation in 8: 138 (12 November 1838); second quotation in Charles Francis Adams, Diary, 10 November 1840, Adams Family Papers, MHS, reel 65; final quotation in C. F. Adams, *Diary*, 7: 297 (18 August 1837).

19. Charles Francis Adams, Diary, 16 March 1844, Adams Family Papers, MHS, reel 67; quotations from entries for 20 March 1843, 7 March 1842, Adams Family Papers, reel 66; 10 April 1844, Adams Family Papers, reel 67.

20. Richards, *John Quincy Adams*, 151–72; Duberman, *Charles Francis Adams*, 84–45, 87–89.

21. Charles Francis Adams, Diary, 21 March 1844, Adams Family Papers, MHS, reel 67; *Boston Courier*, 13 December 1844, Adams Family Papers, reel 323; *Boston Daily Whig*, 7 August 1846; Duberman, *Charles Francis Adams*, 89–92.

22. *Boston Daily Whig*, 17 June 1846; William Slade to Charles Francis Adams, 24 December 1845, Adams Family Papers, MHS, reel 533.

23. Charles Francis Adams, Diary, 13 November 1841, Adams Family Papers, MHS, reel 66; Adams to E. A. Stansbury, 24 September 1853, copy, Adams Family Papers, reel 161; *Boston Daily Whig*, 1 June 1847.

24. Quotation in Charles Francis Adams to O. W. Albee, 14 October 1846; Adams to T. G. Cary, 22 September 1846; Adams to J. T. Stevenson, 7 October 1846, copies, Adams Family Papers, MHS, reel 158; Adams, Diary, 3 October 1846, Adams Family Papers, MHS, reel 68.

25. Charles Francis Adams, Diary, 20 July 1846, Adams Family Papers, MHS, reel 68; *Boston Courier*, 23 July 1842, Adams Family Papers, MHS, reel 323; tariff quotation in *Boston Daily Whig*, 10 July 1846; final quotation in Adams, Diary, 18 September 1846, Adams Family Papers, MHS, reel 68.

26. Robert C. Winthrop, Jr., "Memoir of the Hon. David Sears, A.M.," *Proceedings of the Massachusetts Historical Society* 2, 2d ser. (1885–1886): 415; G. H. Snelling to Horace Mann, 21 February 1849, Horace Mann Papers, MHS, microfilm ed., reel 13; David Sears to John Quincy Adams, 15 November 1843, Sears Family Papers, MHS; second quotation in Sears to Adams, 3 March 1847, Adams Family Papers, MHS, reel 536; *Boston Courier*, 11 March 1847.

27. *Boston Daily Whig*, 8 January 1847, 24 November, 14 December 1846; *Boston Courier*, December–March 1846; Henry Lee to Theodore Parker, 8 July 1848, copy, Parker Papers, MHS, reel 3.

28. Charles Francis Adams, Diary, 12 October 1847, Adams Family Papers, MHS, reel 69; Adams to Joshua R. Giddings, 18 October, 30 December 1847; Adams to John Gorham Palfrey, 17 December 1847; second quotation in Adams to Giddings, 24 January 1848; Adams to Gamaliel Bailey, 7 August 1847, copies, Adams Family Papers, reel 159.

29. Abbott Lawrence to Robert C. Winthrop, 4 February 1848, Winthrop Family Papers, MHS, reel 25; second quotation in Charles Francis Adams, Diary, 12 June 1848, Adams Family Papers, MHS, reel 70; Adams to Joshua R. Giddings, 15 June 1848, copy, Adams Family Papers, reel 159; final quotation in Adams, Diary, 14 September 1848, Adams Family papers, reel 71.

30. Charles Francis Adams to John Gorham Palfrey, 12 December 1848, copy, Adams Family Papers, MHS, reel 160; Adams, Diary, 31 December 1848, Adams Family Papers, reel 71; Duberman, *Charles Francis Adams*, 139–57.

31. William S. Robinson, *"Warrington" Pen-Portraits: A Collection of Personal and Political Reminiscences from 1848 to 1876, from the Writings of William S. Robinson*, ed. Mrs. W. S. Robinson (Boston: Mrs. W. S. Robinson, 1877), 419; Charles Francis Adams, Diary, 19 September 1848, Adams Family Papers, MHS, reel 71.

32. Nathan Appleton to Ezra S. Gannett, 24 January 1828; Gannett to Appleton, 20 November 1833, Appleton Family Papers, MHS.

33. Nathan Appleton to John Gorham Palfrey, 15 October 1846; Palfrey to Appleton, 17 October 1846, Appleton Family Papers, MHS. The comments that prompted Appleton's letter can be found in John Gorham Palfrey, *Papers on the Slave Power*,

First Published in the "Boston Whig" (Boston: Merrill, Cobb, 1846), 25–27, 33–35, 77–79. Also see the Appleton-Sumner correspondence, July–August 1848, BPL, for further evidence of subelite sensitivity to the imperious tone of elite language. As a younger man, Palfrey had consciously deferred to elite opinion and expectations. Harlow Elizabeth Walker Sheidley, "Sectional Nationalism: The Culture and Politics of the Massachusetts Conservative Elite, 1815–1836" (Ph.D. diss., University of Connecticut, 1990), 37–38, 206–7.

34. Harrison Gray Otis to Nathan Appleton, 26 November 1846, Appleton Family Papers, MHS; Choate quotation in Jean V. Matthews, *Rufus Choate: The Law and Civic Virtue* (Philadelphia: Temple University Press, 1980), 226; Theodore Parker, "The Chief Sins of the People," 10 April 1851, in Theodore Parker, *The Collected Works of Theodore Parker, Minister of the Twenty-Eighth Congregational Society at Boston, U.S.*, ed. Frances Power Cobbe, 14 vols. (London: Trubner, 1863–1879), 7: 264–65. For a description of Parker's pulpit style, see *Boston Daily Bee*, 26 November 1845.

35. Theodore Parker to Frances Cobbe, 31 August 1859; first quotation in Parker to James F. Clarke, 9 November 1859, in Theodore Parker, *Life and Correspondence of Theodore Parker*, ed. John Weiss, 2 vols. (New York: D. Appleton, 1864), 2: 348, 386; Samuel Bowles to Miss Whitney, 20 September 1862, George S. Merriam, *The Life and Times of Samuel Bowles*, 2 vols. (New York: Century, 1885), 1: 381; Parker to Samuel J. May, 23 September 1853, copy, Parker Papers, MHS, reel 2. In his will, Parker bequeathed the two muskets to the commonwealth, asking that they be placed in the senate chamber. Parker, *Life and Correspondence*, 2: 443.

36. Parker, *Life and Correspondence*, 2: 475–76; Theodore Parker, "The Slave Power," 29 May 1850, in Theodore Parker, *The Slave Power*, ed. James K. Hosmer (n.d.; repr. New York: Arno Press & the New York Times, 1969), 279; quotations in Parker, *Life and Correspondence*, 1: 197.

37. Theodore Parker, "A Discourse of the Transient and Permanent in Christianity," 19 May 1841, in Parker, *Collected Works*, 8: 1–30, quotation from p. 24.

38. "Parker's Experience as a Minister," in Parker, *Life and Correspondence*, 2: 470–75.

39. Robert C. Albrecht, *Theodore Parker* (New York: Twayne Publishers, 1971), 19–20; Robert C. Winthrop to John P. Kennedy, 23 April 1851, copy, Winthrop Family Papers, MHS, reel 39.

40. Theodore Parker to Joseph H. Allen, 12 August 1844, copy, Parker Papers, MHS, reel 4; Parker to Ezra S. Gannett, 19 December 1846, copy, Parker Papers, reel 2; Parker to Charles Sumner, 21 March 1846, in Parker, *Life and Correspondence*, 1: 317.

41. First quotation from Theodore Parker to Chandler Robbins, 29 January 1845, in Parker, *Life and Correspondence*, 1: 251; John Pierpont to Parker, 22 March 1845, copy, Parker Papers, MHS, reel 4; second quotation in "Parker's Experience as a Minister," Parker, *Life and Correspondence*, 2: 467; Parker to Samuel J. May, 5 March 1853, copy, Parker Papers, MHS, reel 2.

42. First quotation from Theodore Parker to his brother, 22 January 1840, in Parker, *Life and Correspondence*, 1: 144; second quotation in Parker to Joseph H. Allen,

12 August 1844, copy, Parker Papers, MHS, reel 2; Parker, *Life and Correspondence,* 2: 478.

43. Henry Steele Commager, *Theodore Parker: Yankee Crusader* (1936; repr. Boston: Beacon Press, 1947), 100–116; Parker, *Life and Correspondence,* 1: 264; 2: 469, 479–80; Albrecht, *Parker,* 69–72, 132.

44. Thomas Wentworth Higginson, *Cheerful Yesterdays* (Boston: Houghton Mifflin, 1898), 98; *Boston Daily Bee,* 26 November 1845. Parker's own observations on his speaking style can be found in Parker, *Life and Correspondence,* 2: 504–6; and Parker to Joseph H. Allen, 24 November 1849, copy, Parker Papers, MHS, reel 2; also see Octavius Brooks Frothingham, *Theodore Parker: A Biography* (Boston: James R. Osgood, 1874), 334–43.

45. Theodore Parker, "The Mercantile Classes," 22 November 1846, in Theodore Parker, *Social Classes in a Republic,* ed. Samuel A. Eliot (Boston: American Unitarian Association, n.d.), 5, 8–11, 22–24, 29–32, quotation from pp. 23, 29; newspaper clipping, ca. 1846, in Nathan Appleton scrapbook, Appleton Family Papers, MHS.

46. Theodore Parker to John L. Manley, 4 August 1859, in Parker, *Life and Correspondence,* 2: 329; first quotation in Parker to George Cabot, 3 November 1859, copy, Parker Papers, MHS, reel 2; Parker, "The State of the Nation," 1850, in Theodore Parker, *The Rights of Man in America,* ed. F. B. Sanborn (1911; repr. New York: Negro Universities Press, 1969), 95; Parker, *Life and Correspondence,* 2: 339–40, 487–88, second quotation from p. 487; final quotation from Parker, "Moral Conditions," 11 February 1849, in Parker, *Social Classes in a Republic,* 274.

47. Parker, *Life and Correspondence,* 1: 71, 396; 2: 493–95; Theodore Parker to Samuel P. Andrews, 12 December 1837, copy, Parker Papers, MHS, reel 1; Parker, "A Sermon of Slavery," 31 January 1841, in Parker, *The Slave Power,* 1–20; Parker to Samuel J. May, 15 July 1846, copy, Parker Papers, MHS, reel 2; Douglas C. Stange, *Patterns of Antislavery among American Unitarians, 1831–1860* (Rutherford, N.J.: Fairleigh Dickinson University Press, 1977), 194–203.

48. First quotation in Theodore Parker, "A Sermon of War," 7 June 1846, in Parker, *Collected Works,* 4: 24–25; Parker to Horace Mann, 6 August 1848, Mann Papers, MHS, reel 11; Parker to John G. Palfrey, 9 September 1850, Palfrey Family Papers, bMS Am 1704 (694), Houghton Library, Harvard University, Cambridge, Massachusetts (HL); Parker, "The Slave Power," 29 May 1850, in Parker, *The Slave Power,* 272; final quotation in Parker, "The Rights of Man in America," 1854, in Parker, *Rights of Man,* 371.

49. Robinson, *"Warrington" Pen-Portraits,* 507; *Boston Investigator,* 19 February 1845; *Harbinger,* 22 May 1847; *Voice of Industry,* 27 February 1846; Thomas G. Minnis to Theodore Parker, 29 July 1851; E. D. Linton to Parker, 10 September 1855, copies, Parker Papers, MHS, reel 3.

50. Richard H. Dana, Jr., *The Journal of Richard Henry Dana, Jr.,* ed. Robert F. Lucid, 3 vols. (Cambridge: Harvard University Press, 1968), 1: 334–36.

51. Samuel Gridley Howe to Horace Mann, 4 August 1857, in "Samuel G. Howe to Horace Mann," ed. Robert L. Straker, *New England Quarterly* 16 (September 1943): 495; Horace Mann, *Third Annual Report of the Board of Education Together with*

the *Third Annual Report of the Secretary of the Board* (Boston: Dutton and Wentworth, 1840), 64; final quotation in Mary Mann, *Life of Horace Mann* (Boston: Willard Small, 1888), 495.

52. Theodore Parker to Samuel Gridley Howe, 26 August 1859, in Parker, *Life and Correspondence*, 2: 342.

53. Quotation in Mann, *Life of Mann*, 10; Jonathan Messerli, *Horace Mann: A Biography* (New York: Alfred A. Knopf, 1972), 3–137, quotation from p. 114.

54. Messerli, *Mann*, 138–75; Horace Mann, Journal, 27–31 July 1837, Mann Papers, MHS, reel 33.

55. Messerli, *Mann*, 165, 175–76, 249–50.

56. Ibid., 188–250; quotations in Mann, *Life of Mann*, 90, 132.

57. Horace Mann to Theodore Parker, 17 June 1848, Mann Papers, MHS, reel 10; Mann, Journal, 4 July 1837, Mann Papers, reel 33. William Ellery Channing was the only person who offered his congratulations.

58. Horace Mann, Journal, 19 August 1838, 28 August 1841, Mann Papers, MHS, reel 33.

59. Horace Mann, *An Oration Delivered before the Authorities of the City of Boston, July 4, 1842* (Boston: W. B. Fowle and N. Capen, 1842), 11, 18–21, 24, first quotation from p. 24; Mann, *First Annual Report* (1838), 49–55, second quotation from p. 50; third quotation in *Fourth Annual Report* (1841), 41; final quotation in Mann, *Life of Mann*, 92.

60. Messerli, *Mann*, 103, 246, 299–300, 437–38; comments on Dwight in Horace Mann to Mary Mann, 26 March 1850, Mann Papers, MHS, reel 16; Mann, Journal, 15 and 27 September 1837, in Mann, *Life of Mann*, 87–88.

61. Daniel Walker Howe, *The Political Culture of the American Whigs* (Chicago: University of Chicago Press, 1979), 32–37; Horace Mann, Journal, 26 May 1838, Mann Papers, MHS, reel 33; Mann, *Eleventh Annual Report* (1848), 125–26.

62. Messerli, *Mann*, 385–92; Mann, *Life of Mann*, 176–77, 183–84, 196, 202, 216.

63. Messerli, *Mann*, 404–24; *Lowell Tri-Weekly American*, 1 November 1852; Mann, *Seventh Annual Report* (1844), 191–98, quotation from p. 197.

64. Horace Mann, *Tenth Annual Report* (1847), 111–27, quotations from pp. 111, 113, 118–19, 126–27, 132.

65. Oscar Handlin and Mary Flug Handlin, *Commonwealth: A Study of the Role of Government in the American Economy, Massachusetts, 1774–1861* (Cambridge: Harvard University Press, 1969), 229–43; Messerli, *Mann*, 246, 299–301, 437–38; Horace Mann to Mary Mann, 22 June 1848, Mann Papers, MHS, reel 11; Mann, *Twelfth Annual Report* (1849), 53–60, quotations from pp. 57, 59.

66. Horace Mann to Mary Mann, 14 June 1848, Mann Papers, MHS, reel 11; Robert C. Winthrop to John H. Clifford, 24 March 1848, copy, Winthrop Family Papers, MHS, reel 39; Mann to George Combe, 26 January 1851, copy, Mann Papers, MHS, reel 26; last two quotations in Mann to Mary Mann, 6 September, 18 August 1850, Mann Papers, reels 18, 17; Mann, *Slavery: Letters and Speeches* (1851; repr. Miami: Mnemosyne Publishing, 1969), 524–32. For an excellent critique of the limitations of Mann's social thought that is also appreciative of its strengths, see Christopher Lasch,

The Revolt of the Elites and the Betrayal of Democracy (New York: W. W. Norton, 1995), chap. 8.

Chapter Six

1. *Boston Daily Advertiser,* 21 September 1850.

2. David Potter, *The Impending Crisis, 1848–1861* (New York: Harper & Row, 1976), 90–140; Horace Mann to Mary Mann, 12 September 1850, Horace Mann Papers, Massachusetts Historical Society, Boston, Massachusetts (MHS), microfilm ed., reel 18; Edward Everett to Robert C. Winthrop, 21 March 1850, Winthrop Family Papers, MHS, microfilm ed., reel 26.

3. George F. Hoar, *Autobiography of Seventy Years,* 2 vols. (New York: Charles Scribner's Sons, 1903), 1: 134, 142; Richard Henry Dana, Jr., *The Journal of Richard Henry Dana, Jr.,* ed. Robert F. Lucid, 3 vols. (Cambridge: Harvard University Press, 1968), 1: 68; 2: 515.

4. Historians have offered numerous interpretations of Webster's motivation. Robert F. Dalzell, Jr., probably came closest to the truth when he wrote that the address "stood as the ultimate expression of Webster's nationalism, and whatever lay uppermost in his mind that day in the Senate—his own interests or those of the nation—nationalism for him had always been an amalgam of both." *Daniel Webster and the Trial of American Nationalism, 1843–1852* (Boston: Houghton Mifflin, 1972), 192–93.

5. Harlow Elizabeth Walker Sheidley, "Sectional Nationalism: The Culture and Politics of the Massachusetts Conservative Elite, 1815–1836" (Ph.D. diss., University of Connecticut, 1990), 350–51, 379–99, 403–8; Robert V. Remini, *Daniel Webster: The Man and His Time* (New York: W. W. Norton, 1997), 178–87, 247–52, 317–31; Daniel Webster, *The Writings and Speeches of Daniel Webster,* 18 vols. (Boston: Little, Brown, 1930), 10: 57–96, quotations from pp. 64, 86.

6. Boston *Semi-Weekly Republican,* 13 March 1850; Theodore Parker, "Reply to Webster," 25 March 1850, in Theodore Parker, *The Slave Power,* ed. James K. Hosmer (n.d.; repr. New York: Arno Press & the New York Times, 1969), 243; Charles Francis Adams to John G. Palfrey, 9 June 1850, copy, Adams Family Papers, MHS, microfilm ed., reel 160; James S. Pike to William Schouler, 12 April 1850, William Schouler Papers, MHS.

7. Horace Mann to E. W. Clap, 11 March 1850, Mann Papers, MHS, reel 16; Mann, *Slavery: Letters and Speeches* (1851; repr. Miami: Mnemosyne Publishing, 1969), 250–75, 282–337, 516–21; Charles Francis Adams, Diary, 27 July 1850, Adams Family Papers, MHS, reel 71; Jonathan Messerli, *Horace Mann: A Biography* (New York: Alfred A. Knopf, 1972), 512–17.

8. Webster, *Writings and Speeches of Daniel Webster,* 10: 64; Thomas M. Brewer to William Schouler, 8 March 1850, Schouler Papers, MHS; *Boston Daily Atlas,* 11 March 1850.

NOTES TO PAGES 153-155 ~~~ 249

9. William S. Robinson, *"Warrington" Pen-Portraits: A Collection of Personal and Political Reminiscences from 1848 to 1876, from the Writings of William S. Robinson,* ed. Mrs. W. S. Robinson (Boston: Mrs. W. S. Robinson, 1877), 529; *Lowell Daily Courier,* 27 and 28 January 1846.

10. Edward L. Pierce, *Memoir and Letters of Charles Sumner,* 4 vols. (Boston: Roberts Brothers, 1877–1894), 3: 204; *Lowell Tri-Weekly American,* 14 November 1849; *Boston Atlas,* 11 March 1849; Holman Hamilton, *Zachary Taylor: Soldier in the White House* (Indianapolis: Bobbs-Merrill, 1951), 175–83, 285, 379–84; Michael F. Holt, *The Rise and Fall of the American Whig Party: Jacksonian Politics and the Onset of the Civil War* (New York: Oxford University Press, 1999), 435–39, 461–66, 474–76.

11. *Boston Daily Atlas,* 6 May 1850; William Schouler to Horace Mann, 6 May 1850; George Morey to Mann, 6 May 1850, Mann Papers, MHS, reel 16; Edward Everett to Robert C. Winthrop, 8 May 1850, Winthrop Family Papers, MHS, reel 26. For more on *Atlas* strategy, see Everett's account of a conversation he later had with Schouler associate Ezra Lincoln in Everett to Daniel Webster, 5 October 1850, Daniel Webster, *The Papers of Daniel Webster: Correspondence,* ed. Charles M. Wiltse and Harold D. Moser, 7 vols. (Hanover, N.H.: University Press of New England, 1974–1986), 7: 156–57. Mann's observation that commercial considerations strongly influenced the way merchants responded to slavery apparently struck a nerve among elite Bostonians. See E. Winston to Mann, 6 May 1850, Mann Papers, MHS, reel 16; and Benjamin Seaver to Mann, 31 July 1850, Mann Papers, reel 17. His remarks can be found in Mann, *Slavery,* 275–79.

12. Samuel Downer to Horace Mann, 17 March 1850, Mann Papers, MHS, reel 16; Thomas H. Perkins et al. to Daniel Webster, 21 March 1850, Webster, *Correspondence,* 7: 44–45; John H. Clifford to Robert C. Winthrop, 5 May 1850; Edward Everett to Winthrop, 10 April, 8 May 1850, Winthrop Family Papers, MHS, reel 26; Everett to Abbott Lawrence, 29 April 1850, Edward Everett Papers, MHS, microfilm ed., reel 29.

13. David Sears to Robert C. Winthrop, 8 January 1850; Winthrop to Sears, 13 January 1850; Sears to Thomas B. Curtis, 27 October 1850, Sears Family Papers, MHS; Gerald T. White, *A History of the Massachusetts Hospital Life Insurance Company* (Cambridge: Harvard University Press, 1955), 81.

14. Nathan Appleton to Henry W. Hilliard, 22 December 1849, Appleton Family Papers, MHS; Samuel A. Eliot to William Schouler, 10 June 1850, Schouler Papers, MHS; final quotation in George Morey to Horace Mann, 8 August 1850, Mann Papers, MHS, reel 17; Appleton to Robert C. Winthrop, 29 July 1850, Winthrop Family Papers, MHS, reel 26.

15. John H. Clifford to Robert C. Winthrop, 15 June 1850, Winthrop Family Papers, MHS, reel 26; Daniel Webster to Franklin Haven, 11 July 1850, Webster, *Correspondence,* 7: 123; Horace Mann to Mary Mann, 21 July 1850; final quotation in Mann to Charles Sumner, 1 August 1850, Mann Papers, MHS, reel 17. As it turned out, Fillmore prevented Webster from replacing anti-Compromise officeholders in Massachusetts with his own supporters. Holt, *Rise and Fall of the American Whig Party,* 547–49, 580, 583.

16. Dalzell, *Daniel Webster and the Trial of American Nationalism*, 64–78, 158–59; Robert J. Haws, "Massachusetts Whigs, 1833–1854" (Ph.D. diss., University of Nebraska, 1973), 142–49, 154–69, 203–5; Robert C. Winthrop, Jr., *A Memoir of Robert C. Winthrop* (Boston: Little, Brown, 1897), 86–87.

17. George Morey to Horace Mann, 4 April 1850, Mann Papers, MHS, reel 16, 8 August 1850, reel 17; quotation in Abbott Lawrence to Leverett Saltonstall, 29 October 1842, "The Saltonstall Papers, 1816–1845," Robert E. Moody, ed., *Collections of the Massachusetts Historical Society* 82–86 (1978–1992), 85: 291; Samuel A. Eliot to Daniel Webster, 12 June 1850; Samuel Lawrence to Webster, 19 June 1850; Abbott Lawrence to Edward Everett, 16 August 1850, all three items in Webster, *Correspondence*, 7: 116, 120, 147–48; Lawrence to Everett, 6 August, 31 October 1850, Everett Papers, MHS, reel 13A; Lawrence to Nathan Appleton, December 1850, Letters to Nathan Appleton by or about Abbott Lawrence, bMS Am 1557 (7–71), Houghton Library, Harvard University, Cambridge, Massachusetts (HL); Dalzell, *Daniel Webster and the Trial of American Nationalism*, 216–17.

18. *Boston Daily Advertiser*, 20 November 1850.

19. Robert Varnum Spalding, "The Boston Mercantile Community and the Promotion of the Textile Industry, 1813–1860" (Ph.D. diss., Yale University, 1963), 165–71.

20. Ibid., 169–78, 192–95; Nathan Appleton, *Introduction of the Power Loom, and Origins of Lowell* (Lowell: B. H. Penhallow, 1858), 31; Thomas W. Ward to John G. Ward, 26 January 1848, 15 December 1850; Thomas W. Ward to George C. Ward, 26 July 1848; Ward to Joshua Bates, 2 February 1849, copies, Thomas Wren Ward Papers, MHS; memorandum, "Causes of overproduction of coarse goods," 1851, Amos A. Lawrence Papers, MHS; White, *History of the Massachusetts Hospital Life Insurance Company*, 89–98; Paul F. McGouldrick, *New England Textiles in the Nineteenth Century: Profits and Investment* (Cambridge: Harvard University Press, 1968), 29–30, 42.

21. This paragraph is based largely on my reading of Spalding's "Boston Mercantile Community," which focuses on the Associates' promotional activities. Although the Associates did not initiate all the major mill-building projects, they did come to dominate them. See Francois Weil, "Capitalism and Industrialization in New England, 1815–1845," *Journal of American History* 86 (March 1986): 1342–54. The "sorry history" of the Lawrence project is also examined in Frances W. Gregory, *Nathan Appleton: Merchant and Entrepreneur, 1779–1861* (Charlottesville: University Press of Virginia, 1975), 204–8. For more on Holyoke, see Constance McLaughlin Green, *Holyoke, Massachusetts: A Case Study of the Industrial Revolution in America* (New Haven: Yale University Press, 1939), chap. 2.

22. Nathan Appleton to William M. Meredith, 1 November 1849, Appleton Family Papers, MHS; Abbott Lawrence to Nathan Appleton, 10 August 1842, 18 June 1850, Letters to Nathan Appleton by or about Abbott Lawrence, bMS Am 1557 (7–71), HL; Amos A. Lawrence to Samuel A. Eliot, 20 September 1850, Amos A. Lawrence Letterbook, MHS. Appleton had earlier urged that Lawrence be appointed secretary of the treasury because he was "better qualified" to resolve the tariff

question "than any other man in the United States." Appleton to Millard Fillmore, 6 February 1849, Appleton Family Papers, MHS.

23. Amos A. Lawrence to Amos Lawrence, 13 February 1850; Lawrence to Robert C. Winthrop, 20 August 1850, Amos A. Lawrence Letterbook, MHS; Joshua Bates to Thomas W. Ward, 22 February 1849, copy, Ward Papers, MHS.

24. Amos A. Lawrence to N. Silsbee, 19 November 1849; Lawrence to J. B. Francis, 19 November 1849, Amos A. Lawrence Letterbook, MHS; [Lawrence], "The Condition and Prospects of American Cotton Manufactures in 1849," *Hunt's Merchants' Magazine* 21 (December 1849): 628–33; 22 (January 1850): 26–35; Herbert Collins, "The Southern Industrial Gospel before 1860," *Journal of Southern History* 12 (August 1946): 388–89; Amos Lawrence to Robert Rhett, 12 December 1849, in *Extracts from the Diary and Correspondence of the Late Amos Lawrence with a Brief Account of Some Incidents in His Life,* ed. William R. Lawrence (Boston: Gould and Lincoln, 1855), 275.

25. Amos A. Lawrence to William Appleton, 5 March 1852; Lawrence to Abbott Lawrence, 19 December 1850, Amos A. Lawrence Letterbook, MHS; William Phillips, *Propositions Concerning Protection and Free Trade* (Boston: Charles C. Little and James Brown, 1850), 204–9; final quotation in Amos A. Lawrence to Freeman Hunt, 3 December 1850, Amos A. Lawrence Letterbook, MHS. Also see Lawrence to Robert C. Winthrop, 20 August 1850; Lawrence to Charles Richards, 12 December 1850; Lawrence to Samuel Eliot, 27 January 1851; and Lawrence to Dr. Watson, 29 January 1852, Amos A. Lawrence Letterbook, MHS. Lawrence's uncle agreed that product diversification was necessary but added that such changes would likely "prove expensive" and something first had to be done to halt "the excessive importations of foreign merchandise." Abbott Lawrence to Amos A. Lawrence, 9 January 1851, Amos A. Lawrence Papers, MHS.

26. Patrick J. Hearden, *Independence and Empire: The New South's Cotton Mill Campaign, 1865–1901* (Dekalb: Northern Illinois University Press, 1982), 12; William Gregg to Amos A. Lawrence, 2 September 1850, in Thomas P. Martin, ed., "The Advent of William Gregg and the Graniteville Company," *Journal of Southern History* 11 (August 1945): 422–23.

27. First quotation in Daniel Webster to Peter Harvey, 29 May 1850; Webster to Harvey, 15 April, 2 June 1850; Webster to Franklin Haven, 18 May 1850; Webster to Edward Everett, 26 September 1850, in Webster, *Correspondence,* 7: 103, 69, 107–8, 100, 154; George Morey to Horace Mann, 8 August 1850; Samuel Downer to Mann, 7 August 1850; final quotation in E. W. Clap to Mann, 12 August 1850, Mann Papers, MHS, reel 17.

28. First quotation in Horace Mann, *Slavery,* 137; Mann to Mary Mann, 20 September 1850, Mann Papers, MHS, reel 18; Mann to Mary Mann, 13 June 1850, Mann Papers, reel 17; Mann to George Combe, 15 November 1850, 6 January 1851, copies, Mann Papers, reel 26; quotation from letter to his wife in Mann to Mary Mann, 17 September 1850, Mann Papers, reel 18; Mann to Charles Sumner, 5 August

1850, Mann Papers, reel 17; final quotation in Mann to Mary Mann, 17 September 1850, Mann Papers, reel 18.

29. Samuel Downer to Horace Mann, 14 September 1850, Mann Papers, MHS, reel 18; *Boston Daily Republican,* 6 and 12 October 1849; *Lowell Tri-Weekly American,* 8 June 1849, 20 May 1850.

30. First quotation in Mann, *Slavery,* 341; Mann to Mary Mann, 24 September 1850, Mann Papers, MHS, reel 18; *Boston Daily Whig,* 10 July 1846; Mann to John Murray Forbes, 30 January 1851, Mann Papers, MHS, reel 19.

31. C. L. Knapp to Horace Mann, 17 October 1851, Mann Papers, MHS, reel 19; Mann, *Slavery,* 383–84, 524–32, quotation from pp. 383–84.

32. Boston *Commonwealth,* 17 November 1851; James Thurston to Horace Mann, 4 May 1851, Mann Papers, MHS, reel 19.

33. *Boston Daily Atlas,* 1 May, 14 September 1850; *Northampton Courier,* 15 October 1850.

34. Robert C. Winthrop to J. P. Kennedy, 18 October 1850, copy, Winthrop Family Papers, MHS, reel 39; Franklin Dexter to John Davis, 17 September 1850, John Davis Papers, American Antiquarian Society, Worcester, Massachusetts (AAS); Edward Everett to Robert C. Winthrop, 23 September 1850, Winthrop Family Papers, MHS, reel 26; final quotation is from the state party secretary Ezra Lincoln in Everett to Daniel Webster, 5 October 1850, Webster, *Correspondence,* 7: 156–57; Dalzell, *Daniel Webster and the Trial of American Nationalism,* 218–19.

35. Daniel Webster to Peter Harvey, 2 October 1850; Webster to Millard Fillmore, 24 October, 5 November 1850, Webster, *Correspondence,* 7: 155–56, 165, 178, first quotation in October 24 letter to Fillmore; *Boston Daily Advertiser,* 14, 19, 21, 22, 23, 24, 26, and 30 October, 2 and 4 November 1850.

36. *Boston Atlas,* 21 November 1850; *Boston Daily Advertiser,* 15, 23, and 26 November 1850; Haws, "Massachusetts Whigs," 221–22.

37. Gary Collinson, *Shadrach Minkins: From Fugitive Slave to Citizen* (Cambridge: Harvard University Press, 1977), 110–33.

38. Ibid., 135–36; Robinson, ed., *"Warrington" Pen-Portraits,* 191; *Worcester Daily Spy,* 18 February 1851; Charles C. Sewall to Horace Mann, 9 March 1851, Mann Papers, MHS, reel 19.

39. Dalzell, *Daniel Webster and the Trial of American Nationalism,* 229–30; Stanley W. Campbell, *The Slave Catchers: Enforcement of the Fugitive Slave Law, 1850–1860* (New York: W. W. Norton, 1972), 117–20; Daniel Webster to Millard Fillmore, 13 April 1851, Webster, *Correspondence,* 7: 232–33.

40. Eliot quotation in Charles Francis Adams, Diary, 26 April 1851, Adams Family Papers, MHS, reel 72; Theodore Parker, "The Boston Kidnapping," 12 April 1852, in Parker, *The Slave Power,* 316–85, quotations on pp. 369, 334, 323, 326. Although Parker delivered this address on the first anniversary of Sims's return, it was similar in tone to that of various speeches he made during the ordeal, when he spoke before crowds on the Common and elsewhere in the city.

41. Robinson, ed., *"Warrington" Pen-Portraits,* 193–94; *Lowell Tri-Weekly American,* 14 April 1851; *Worcester Daily Spy,* 9 April 1851; Lynn *Bay State,* 24 April 1851.

42. John Davis to Robert C. Winthrop, 8 May 1852, Winthrop Family Papers, MHS, reel 27.

43. Charles Francis Adams, Diary, 9 January 1841, Adams Family Papers, MHS, reel 69; Claude M. Fuess, "John Davis," *Dictionary of American Biography*, 20 vols. (New York: Charles Scribner's Sons, 1928–1936), 5: 134; Ronald P. Formisano, *The Transformation of Political Culture: Massachusetts Parties, 1790s–1840s* (New York: Oxford University Press, 1983), 253, 300–301. The sharp distinction Formisano makes between Briggs and Davis is overdrawn. Although Briggs rose from much humbler origins than Davis, the latter's public manner was every bit as unassuming as that of his Berkshire counterpart. It may have been an act—as Adams suggested—but Bay State voters bought it.

44. John Davis to Levi Lincoln [?], 19 January 1835; Davis, "Distribution of Political Power," ms. speech, 1836; Davis, "The Influence of Slavery upon Free Labor," ms. speech, 1840, Davis Papers, AAS; Davis to John Quincy Adams, 25 February 1837, Adams Family Papers, MHS, reel 505; Davis to Daniel Waldo, 16 November 1838, Davis Papers, AAS.

45. *Congressional Globe*, 31st Cong., 1st sess., Appendix, 879–86; Daniel Webster to Thomas Corwin, 13 November 1850; Webster to Millard Fillmore, 15 November 1850; Webster to Franklin Haven, 9 May 1851, Webster, *Correspondence*, 7: 180–81, 248; *Boston Daily Atlas*, 4 April 1851; Haws, "Massachusetts Whigs," 156, 219–20, 227–28; Dalzell, *Daniel Webster and the Trial of American Nationalism*, 66, 71–72, 89–90, 100; John Davis to William Schouler, 23 January 1851, Schouler Papers, MHS.

46. John Davis to My Dear Col., June 1851, Davis Papers, AAS; *Congressional Globe*, 31st Cong., 1st sess., Appendix, 886.

47. *Boston Daily Advertiser*, 5 October 1849.

48. John Davis to My Dear Col., 13 June 1851, Davis Papers, AAS; Davis to Robert C. Winthrop, 6 September 1851, Winthrop Family Papers, MHS, reel 27; *Congressional Globe*, 32d Cong., 1st sess., Appendix, 131–34.

49. *Boston Daily Republican*, 7 November 1849.

50. Henry Wilson, *History of the Rise and Fall of the Slave Power*, 3 vols. (Boston: James R. Osgood and Company, 1872–1877), 2: 247–52, 341–42; Ernest A. McKay. "Henry Wilson and the Coalition of 1851," *New England Quarterly* 36 (September 1963): 341–42.

51. Kevin Sweeney, "Rum, Romanism, Representation, and Reform: Coalition Politics in Massachusetts, 1847–1853," *Civil War History* 22 (June 1976): 120–21; Anson Burlingame to Robert C. Winthrop, 8 August 1850, Winthrop Family Papers, MHS, reel 26; quotation in John H. Clifford to Winthrop, 14 December 1850, copy, Winthrop Family Papers, MHS, reel 39.

52. McKay, "Henry Wilson and the Coalition of 1851," 339–40, 343–48; Charles Sumner to John G. Palfrey, 15 October 1850, Palfrey Family Papers, bMS 1704 (886), HL; Abbott Lawrence to John P. Bigelow, 28 November 1851, John P. Bigelow Papers, bMS Am 801.2 (820–60), HL.

53. Charles Francis Adams, Diary, 12 September 1849, Adams Family Papers, MHS, reel 71; *Lowell Tri-Weekly American*, 28 September, 12 October 1849.

54. Daniel Webster to Edward Everett, 30 November 1843, Webster, *Correspondence*, 5: 322; Robert C. Winthrop to John P. Kennedy, 24 December 1851, copy, Winthrop Family Papers, MHS, reel 39.

55. *Lowell Tri-Weekly American*, 14 November 1849; *Boston Daily Atlas*, 12 November 1850; *Springfield Republican* in *Boston Courier*, 27 November 1851.

56. Robinson, *"Warrington" Pen Portraits*, 32, 36–37, 41; Henry Greenleaf Pearson, *The Life of John Andrew: Governor of Massachusetts, 1861–1865*, 2 vols. (Boston: Houghton Mifflin, 1904), 1: 59; Paul Goodman, "The Politics of Industrialization: Massachusetts, 1830–1870," in *Uprooted Americans: Essays to Honor Oscar Handlin*, ed. Richard L. Bushman et al. (Boston: Little, Brown, 1979), 181; *Boston Daily Whig*, 20 June, 29 July 1848. Although Robinson hoped Schouler would "recover his old anti-slavery position," he did not believe that *Atlas* readers would "bear such strong anti-slavery doses as we helped him put into the Lowell Courier." *Lowell Tri-Weekly American*, 14 September 1849.

57. *Boston Daily Republican*, 13 December 1848.

58. Ibid.; final quotation from Francis W. Bird in Robinson, *"Warrington" Pen Portraits*, 122.

59. *Lowell Tri-Weekly American*, 17 October 1849, 30 October 1850.

60. William S. Robinson to William Schouler, 14 June 1846, Schouler Papers, MHS; *Lowell Tri-Weekly American*, 2 November 1849.

61. Abbott Lawrence to Nathan Appleton, December 1850, Letters to Nathan Appleton by or about Abbott Lawrence, bMS Am 1557 (7–71), HL; Amos A. Lawrence to Pliny Lawton, 19 September 1850, Amos A. Lawrence Letterbook, MHS; Memorandum, 23 September 1850, Amos A. Lawrence Papers, MHS; McGouldrick, *New England Textiles in the Nineteenth Century*, 41, 147–48. Although McGouldrick contends that "it is doubtful whether the pace of work increased appreciably after 1845," he does not explain why such changes would have been confined largely to the earlier period. With regard to wages, it should be noted that other major investors expressed concerns about labor costs much earlier than Lawrence did. See Thomas W. Ward to John G. Ward, 10 July 1847, 4 July 1848, copies, Ward Papers, MHS.

62. Charles E. Persons, "The Early History of Factory Legislation in Massachusetts: From 1825 to the Passage of the Ten Hour Law in 1874," in *Labor Laws and Their Enforcement*, ed. Susan M. Kingsbury (New York: Longmans, Green, 1911), 60–62, 65–66; *Lowell Tri-Weekly American*, 14 January, 17 May, and 14 November 1850, 3 November 1851, 10 June 1850, 10, 29, and 31 October 1851, 12 October 1849, 1 August 1851.

63. Massachusetts *House Document*, no. 153, 1850, in John R. Commons et al., eds., *A Documentary History of American Industrial Society*, 10 vols. (Cleveland: Arthur H. Clark, 1910–1911), 8: 158–60, 170–73; *Lowell Tri-Weekly American*, 29 April 1850.

64. Persons, "Early History of Factory Legislation in Massachusetts," 69–70; Robert C. Winthrop to John H. Clifford, 15 November 1851, Winthrop Family Papers, MHS, reel 27.

65. Persons, "Early History of Factory Legislation in Massachusetts," 65–66, 70; *Lowell Tri-Weekly American*, 3 January 1853; David R. Roediger and Philip S. Foner,

Our Own Time: A History of American Labor and the Working Day (London: Verso, 1989), 67–69.

66. *Official Report of the Debates and Proceedings of the State Convention, Assembled May 4, 1853, to Revise and Amend the Constitution of the Commonwealth of Massachusetts,* 3 vols. (Boston: White and Potter, 1853), 1: 593–97; *Boston Daily Republican,* 6 November 1848; first quotation in *Official Report of the Debates and Proceedings of the State Convention,* 1: 756; *Boston Daily Republican,* 7 November 1848; "every man" quotation from Lynn *Bay State,* 17 October 1850; *Lowell Tri-Weekly American,* 15 November 1850. The Morey letter was uncovered by Elizur Wright and first appeared in his *Chronotype.*

67. *Lowell Tri-Weekly American,* 12 November 1850.

68. *Lowell Tri-Weekly American,* 3 November, 12 and 26 December 1851; *Official Report of the Debates and Proceedings of the State Convention,* 1: 657–64; Persons, "Early History of Factory Legislation in Massachusetts," 70–73; Child quotation and Robinson observation in *Lowell Tri-Weekly American,* 17 December 1851.

69. *Lowell Tri-Weekly American,* 24 November 1851; Persons, "Early History of Factory Legislation in Massachusetts," 73–74; *Official Report of the Debates and Proceedings of the State Convention,* 1: 657–64; final quotation in *Lowell Tri-Weekly American,* 18 February 1852.

70. Boston *Commonwealth,* 24 November 1851; *Lowell Tri-Weekly American,* 26 November 1851.

Chapter Seven

1. *Boston Daily Advertiser,* 7 January 1851, in Nathan Appleton scrapbooks, Appleton Family Papers, Massachusetts Historical Society, Boston, Massachusetts (MHS).

2. Richard H. Dana, Jr., to Edmund T. Dana, 2 March 1851, Dana Family Papers, MHS; Harold Schwartz, *Samuel Gridley Howe: Social Reformer, 1801–1876* (Cambridge: Harvard University Press, 1956), 170–76; Samuel G. Howe to Charles Sumner, 12 December 1851, in Samuel Gridley Howe, *Letters and Journals of Samuel Gridley Howe,* ed. Laura E. Richards, 2 vols. (Boston: Dana Estes, 1909), 2: 353; Sumner to John Bigelow, 2 May 1851, in Edward L. Pierce, *Memoir and Letters of Charles Sumner,* 4 vols. (Boston: Roberts Brothers, 1877–1894), 3: 247.

3. Francis W. Bird to Charles Francis Adams, 10 and 17 October 1851, Adams Family Papers, MHS, microfilm ed., reel 540; *Boston Daily Courier,* 15 and 24 October 1851.

4. *Boston Daily Courier,* 15 October 1851; quotation from Thomas W. Higginson to Charles Sumner, 6 September 1851, Charles Sumner Papers, bMS Am 1, Houghton Library, Harvard University, Cambridge, Massachusetts (HL); *Springfield Republican,* in *Boston Courier,* 27 November 1851.

5. Boston *Democratic Standard,* 28 June 1851.

6. Boston *Democratic Standard,* 8 February, 19 April, 21 June, 26 July 1851, quotations from February 8 and July 21 editions. For more on Chase's activities during these years, see John Niven, *Salmon P. Chase: A Biography* (New York: Oxford University Press, 1995), 99–152.

7. *Worcester Palladium,* 4 October 1854; George S. Boutwell, *Reminiscences of Sixty Years in Public Affairs,* 2 vols. (New York: McClure, Phillips, 1902), 1: 114. Although Marcus Morton claimed that country Democrats outnumbered their customhouse foes by a margin similar to that stated by Knowlton, he had even less reason than the Worcester editor to offer an objective accounting, given his long-standing rivalry with David Henshaw and other customhouse leaders. Morton to John Fairfield, 23 January 1846; Morton to Benjamin Tappan, 23 April 1846, copies, Marcus Morton Papers, MHS.

8. Arthur B. Darling, *Political Changes in Massachusetts, 1824–1848: A Study of Liberal Movements in Politics* (New Haven: Yale University Press, 1925), 44, 81, 149–50, 349–51; first quotation in Marcus Morton to John Fairfield, 23 January 1846; Morton to George Bancroft, 26 December 1845; Morton to Jesse D. Bright, 4 August 1848; final quotations in Morton to F. A. Hildreth, 11 May, 18 August 1849, copies, Morton Papers, MHS.

9. Ernest A. McKay, "Henry Wilson and the Coalition of 1851," *New England Quarterly* 36 (September 1963): 342, 344, 354; first quotation in Marcus Morton to Frederick Gourgar, 18 January 1852, copy, Morton Papers, MHS; Darling, *Political Changes,* 352–56; second quotation in Morton to B. V. French, 22 November 1850; Morton to Benjamin Tappan, 23 April 1846; Morton to John Fairfield, 23 January 1846; Morton to William C. Bryant, 8 January 1852, copies, Morton Papers, MHS. Morton's direct involvement in patronage matters had increased substantially during the Polk administration, when he served as collector of the port of Boston.

10. Francis J. Grund, *Aristocracy in America: From the Sketch-book of a German Nobleman* (1839; repr. New York: Harper Torchbooks, 1959), 132–33; *Lowell Tri-Weekly American,* 6 October 1853; Abbott Lawrence to Robert C. Winthrop, 12 January 1849, Winthrop Family Papers, MHS, microfilm ed., reel 26. The defeated candidate whom Lawrence agreed to aid was not Winthrop but Charles Hudson; Winthrop did not need material assistance from anyone.

11. *Worcester Palladium,* 1 December 1852, 4 October 1854; Claude H. Fuess, *The Life of Caleb Cushing,* 2 vols. (New York: Harcourt, Brace, 1923), 2: 98–104; *Boston Post,* 28 October, 4 November 1850, quotation from November 4 edition.

12. *Worcester Palladium,* 22 October 1851; *Fall River News,* 13 November 1851; *Boston Post,* 16 October, 12 November 1851; John B. Alley to Charles Sumner, 3 January 1852, Sumner Papers, bMS Am 1, HL.

13. Boston *Commonwealth,* 5 October 1852; *Lowell Tri-Weekly American,* 9, 21 October 1850; *Boston Daily Courier,* 6 and 8 October 1851; quotations in *Lowell Tri-Weekly American,* 27 September 1852.

14. *Boston Daily Courier,* 9 September 1852; first quotation in *Boston Post,* 7 October 1852; *Worcester Palladium,* 15 September, 13 October 1852, quotation from 13 October edition; *Boston Post,* 12 October 1852.

15. Lynn *Bay State,* 7 and 28 October, 4 November 1852; *Fall River News,* 7 October 1852; Bernard Mandel, *Labor: Free and Slave: Workingmen and the Anti-Slavery Movement in the United States* (New York: Associated Authors, 1955), 143–45; Charles Francis Adams to Charles Sumner, 1 August 1852, copy, Adams Family Papers, MHS, reel 161.

16. Ian R. Tyrell, *From Temperance to Prohibition in Antebellum America, 1800–1860* (Westport, Conn.: Greenwood Press, 1979), 92–115, 260–62; Kevin Sweeney, "Rum, Romanism, Representation, and Reform: Coalition Politics in Massachusetts, 1847–1853," *Civil War History* 22 (June 1976): 128–33; S. Stone to the County Committee, 20 September 1852, Emory Washburn Papers, MHS; *Worcester Palladium,* 1 December 1852; Boston *Commonwealth,* 25 November 1852; Lynn *Bay State,* 2 December 1852; *Northampton Courier,* 30 November 1852.

17. Robert James Haws, "Massachusetts Whigs, 1833–1854" (Ph.D. diss., University of Nebraska, 1974), 233–37; George Morey to John H. Clifford, 19 April, 5 August 1851, John H. Clifford Papers, MHS; Daniel F. Webster to Daniel Webster, 30 October 1851, *Papers of Daniel Webster,* ed. Charles M. Wiltse (Ann Arbor, Mich.: University Microfilm in collaboration with Dartmouth College Library, 1971), microfilm ed., reel 25; George Morey to John H. Clifford, 7 September 1852, Clifford Papers, MHS.

18. John H. Clifford to Robert C. Winthrop, 15 June, 14 November 1850, Winthrop Family Papers, MHS, reel 26; first quotation in Reuben A. Chapman to John H. Clifford, 20 August 1852, Clifford Papers, MHS; John H. Clifford to Richard H. Dana, Jr., 6 March 1851, Dana Family Papers, MHS; South Boston and Dorchester *Gazette and Chronicle,* 9 October 1852; Richard H. Dana to Richard H. Dana, Jr., 12 July 1851, Dana Family Papers, MHS.

19. Sweeney, "Rum, Romanism, Representation, and Reform," 132–33, quotation from p. 132; John R. Mulkern, *The Know-Nothing Party in Massachusetts: The Rise and Fall of a People's Movement* (Boston: Northeastern University Press, 1990), 39–40.

20. Sweeney, "Rum, Romanism, Representation, and Reform," 133–35; Mulkern, *Know-Nothing Party in Massachusetts,* 40–59; Samuel Shapiro, "The Conservative Dilemma: The Massachusetts Constitutional Convention of 1853," *New England Quarterly* 33 (June 1960): 207–24; *Discussions on the Constitution Proposed to the People of Massachusetts by the Convention of 1853* (Boston: Little, Brown, 1854), 24–26, 214–17.

21. Richard Henry Dana, Jr., *Journal of Richard Henry Dana, Jr.,* ed. Robert F. Lucid, 3 vols. (Cambridge: Harvard University Press, 1968), 2: 566; *Boston Post,* 7 September, 2 November 1853.

22. Fuess, *Caleb Cushing,* 2: 139–44; *Boston Post,* 3 November 1853; Lynn *Bay State,* 3 November 1853; *Worcester Palladium,* 30 November 1853, 15 March 1854.

23. *Lowell Tri-Weekly American,* 1 and 17 November 1853, first two quotations from 17 November edition; William S. Robinson to Charles Francis Adams, 21 November 1853, Adams Family Papers, MHS, reel 542. For Palfrey's disturbed response to these and similar allegations from other sources, see John G. Palfrey to Richard H. Dana, 15 March 1854, Palfrey Family Papers, bMS Am 1704.1 (75), HL. Adams, who never let such criticism bother him, laconically noted in his diary that "the feeling of our

political friends [is] very bitter against Mr. Palfrey and myself." Adams, Diary, 19 November 1853, Adams Family Papers, MHS, reel 73.

24. Charles Francis Adams, Diary, 15 November 1853, Adams Family Papers, MHS, reel 73; Theodore Parker to Charles Ellis, 20 November 1853, Theodore Parker, *Life and Correspondence of Theodore Parker*, ed. John Weiss, 2 vols. (New York: D. Appleton & Company, 1864), 2: 233–34; Samuel Gridley Howe to Horace Mann, 16 December 1853, Howe, *Letters and Journals*, 2: 306; Francis W. Bird to Charles Sumner, 15 April 1854, Sumner Papers, bMS Am 1, HL; Bird to Charles Francis Adams, 1 September 1854, Adams Family Papers, MHS, reel 542.

25. Quotations in *Lowell Tri-Weekly American*, 2 and 15 December 1853.

26. James M. Stone to Charles Sumner, 20 December 1853, Sumner Papers, bMS Am 1, HL; John Davis to William Schouler, 4 November 1852, William Schouler Papers, MHS; Davis to Robert C. Winthrop, 15 January 1853; John H. Clifford to Winthrop, 5 and 16 September 1853, Winthrop Family Papers, MHS, reel 27, quotation from 16 September letter.

27. Quotation from Samuel Bowles to Charles Allen, 9 April 1857, in George S. Merriam, *The Life and Times of Samuel Bowles*, 2 vols. (New York: Century, 1885), 1: 292.

28. Abbott Lawrence to William Schouler, 28 March 1845, Schouler Papers, MHS.

29. Dana, *Journal*, 2: 568; Robert C. Winthrop to John P. Kennedy, 7 September 1852, copy, Winthrop Family Papers, MHS, reel 39.

30. Robert C. Winthrop to John P. Kennedy, 7 September 1852, copy, Winthrop Family Papers, MHS, reel 39; Ezra Lincoln to John H. Clifford, 16 November 1854, Clifford Papers, MHS; *Lowell Tri-Weekly American*, 4 and 11 June 1853.

31. Joseph T. Buckingham, *Personal Memoirs and Recollections of Editorial Life*, 2 vols. (Boston: Ticknor, Reed, and Fields, 1852), 2: 217–18, 221.

32. Robert C. Winthrop to John H. Clifford, 2 August 1846, copy, Winthrop Family Papers, MHS, reel 39; Charles Sumner to John Gorham Palfrey, 21 December 1847, Palfrey Family Papers, bMS Am 1704 (886), HL; Buckingham, *Personal Memoirs*, 2: 226–28.

33. Elbert D. Smith, *The Presidencies of Zachary Taylor & Millard Fillmore* (Lawrence: University Press of Kansas, 1988), 235; Robert C. Winthrop to John P. Kennedy, 7 September 1852, copy, Winthrop Family Papers, MHS, reel 39; *Boston Daily Courier*, 5 and 8 September 1851, 18 September 1852, 18, 19, and 21, October, 8 November 1852, 9 September 1851, 2 October 1852; J. P. Fairbanks to William Schouler, 14 July 1852, Schouler Papers, MHS.

34. *Springfield Republican*, 1 September 1852; *Boston Daily Courier*, 9, 15, and 16 October, 1 and 3 November 1852; Charles T. Russell to John H. Clifford, 24 November 1852; Emory Washburn to Clifford, 8 November 1852, Clifford Papers, MHS.

35. Robert C. Winthrop, Jr., *A Memoir of Robert C. Winthrop* (Boston: Little, Brown, 1897), 8–9, 19, 126, quotation from p. 126.

36. Kinley J. Brauer, *Cotton versus Conscience: Massachusetts Whig Politics and Southwestern Expansion, 1843–1848* (Lexington: University of Kentucky Press, 1967),

170–78; first quotation in Robert C. Winthrop to John P. Kennedy, 18 October 1850, copy, Winthrop Family Papers, MHS, reel 39; Winthrop, *Memoir of Winthrop*, 83–85; Brauer, *Cotton versus Conscience,* 219–22; Nathan Appleton to Winthrop, 10 and 20 December 1849; Edward Everett to Winthrop, 15 December 1849, Winthrop Family Papers, MHS, reel 26.

37. Edward Everett to Robert C. Winthrop, 7 January 1850; Samuel A. Eliot to Winthrop, 8 January 1850; Winthrop to Eliot, 13 January 1850, Winthrop Family Papers, MHS, reel 26.

38. Robert C. Winthrop to John H. Clifford, 10 March 1850; Winthrop to George Morey, 1 May 1850, Winthrop Family Papers, MHS, reel 26; Robert F. Dalzell, Jr., *Daniel Webster and the Trial of American Nationalism, 1843–1852* (Boston: Houghton Mifflin, 1973), 232–34; Daniel Webster to Edward Everett, 3 September 1851, *The Papers of Daniel Webster: Correspondence,* ed. Charles M. Wiltse and Harold D. Moser, 7 vols. (Hanover, N.H.: University Press of New England, 1974–1986), 7: 270; Michael F. Holt, *The Rise and Fall of the American Whig Party: Jacksonian Politics and the Onset of the Civil War* (New York: Oxford University Press, 1999), 642–44, 770; Winthrop, *Memoir of Winthrop,* 151, 162, first quotation from p. 162; final quotation in Winthrop to John H. Clifford, 14 October 1853, Winthrop Family Papers, MHS, reel 27.

39. Amos A. Lawrence to D. R. Green, 15 April 1851, Amos A. Lawrence Letterbook, MHS; Nathan Appleton to Robert C. Winthrop, 30 June 1851, Winthrop Family Papers, MHS, reel 26; Abbott Lawrence to Winthrop, 5 November 1851, Winthrop Family Papers, reel 27.

40. *Springfield Republican,* 15 September 1852.

41. Richard H. Dana to William C. Bryant, 6 March 1851, Dana Family Papers, MHS; Charles Francis Adams, Diary, 24 September 1851, Adams Family Papers, MHS, reel 72.

42. Abbott Lawrence to Nathan Appleton, 27 July 1852, Letters to Nathan Appleton by or about Abbott Lawrence, bMS Am 1557 (7–71), HL.

43. William Appleton to Amos A. Lawrence, 27 June 1854, Amos A. Lawrence Papers, MHS; *Boston Daily Courier,* 3 November 1854.

44. Adams quotation in Paul Revere Frothingham, *Edward Everett: Orator and Statesman* (Boston: Houghton Mifflin, 1925), 334.

45. Edward Everett to John H. Clifford, 10 January 1854; Clifford to Everett, 20 January 1854, Clifford Papers, MHS. Everett also sought advice on the matter from Winthrop, Appleton, Lawrence, and other prominent Bay Staters. Frothingham, *Edward Everett,* 345–46.

46. Pierce, *Sumner,* 3: 364–65; Amos A. Lawrence to Giles Richards, 1 June 1854, Amos A. Lawrence Letterbook, MHS; Robert C. Winthrop to John P. Kennedy, June 1854, copy, Winthrop Family Papers, MHS, reel 39; George Morey to Emory Washburn, 12 June 1854, Washburn Papers, MHS.

47. Boston *Commonwealth,* 13 February 1854; Holt, *Rise and Fall of the American Whig Party,* 816–17; Frothingham, *Edward Everett,* 356–58; Edward Everett to Mrs. Charles Eames, 21 March 1854, copy, Edward Everett Papers, MHS, reel 15A.

48. Frothingham, *Edward Everett,* 350–54; Henry Wilson to Charles Sumner, 15 March 1854; Amasa Walker to Sumner, 25 April 1854, Sumner Papers, bMS Am 1, HL; Amos A. Lawrence to J. W. Edwards, 16 March 1854, Amos A. Lawrence Letterbook, MHS; Dana, *Journal,* 2: 624–25.

49. Theodore Parker, "The Nebraska Question: Some Thoughts on the New Assault upon Freedom in America, and the General State of the Country in Relation Thereunto," 12 February 1854, in Theodore Parker, *The Collected Works of Theodore Parker,* ed. Frances Power Cobbe, 14 vols. (London: Trubner & Co., 1863–1879), 5: 266–69, quotation on p. 266. For a particularly good example of country Whig misunderstanding of the Boston elite's position on this and later slavery-related matters, see *Worcester Weekly Transcript,* 25 November 1854.

50. Amos A. Lawrence to S. H. Walley, 12 May 1854; Lawrence to Mr. Andrews, 26 May 1854, Amos A. Lawrence Letterbook, MHS; Dana, *Journal,* 2: 628; Pierce, *Sumner,* 3: 375.

51. Boston *Daily Commonwealth,* 28 June 1854; Theodore Parker, "The New Crime Against Humanity," 1854, in Theodore Parker, *The Rights of Man in America,* ed. F. B. Sanborn (1911; repr. New York: Negro Universities Press, 1969), 250–332, quotations from pp. 323, 269, 273, 282; Samuel Shapiro, *Richard Henry Dana, Jr., 1815–1882* (East Lansing: Michigan State University Press, 1961), 4; Richard H. Dana to Henry J. Raymond, 5 June 1854; Dana to William C. Bryant, 6 June 1854, Dana Family Papers, MHS; Albert J. Von Frank, *The Trials of Anthony Burns: Freedom and Slavery in Emerson's Boston* (Cambridge: Harvard University Press, 1998), 238–39.

52. Ezra Lincoln to William Schouler, 14 and 17 August 1854, Schouler Papers, MHS; quotation from resolution in *Boston Daily Courier,* 17 August 1854; *Boston Daily Advertiser,* 31 August 1854; Richard H. Abbott, *Cotton & Capital: Boston Businessmen and Antislavery Reform, 1854–1868* (Amherst: University of Massachusetts Press, 1991), chap. 2. For evidence that Websterites would have preferred a more conciliatory approach to the slavery question, see *Boston Daily Courier,* 14 August 1854.

53. *Worcester Palladium,* 30 August 1854; Boston *Daily Commonwealth,* 24 August 1854.

54. Schouler quotation from *Boston Daily Courier,* 24 August 1854; Ezra Lincoln to William Schouler, 30 June 1856, 26 October 1854, Schouler Papers, MHS.

55. Holt, *Rise and Fall of the American Whig Party,* 842, 862–63, 865.

56. Eric Foner, *Free Soil, Free Labor, Free Men: The Ideology of the Republican Party before the Civil War* (New York: Oxford University Press, 1970), 87–102; William E. Gienapp, *The Origins of the Republican Party, 1852–1856* (New York: Oxford University Press, 1987), 76–77, 357–65; Holt, *Rise and Fall of the American Whig Party,* 843–44; Richard H. Dana to William Corbin, 31 December 1851, Dana Family Papers, MHS.

57. *Boston Daily Advertiser,* 5 August 1854; Holt, *Rise and Fall of the American Whig Party,* 890.

58. Margaret Ellen Newell, *From Dependency to Independence: Economic Revolution in Colonial New England* (Ithaca, N.Y.: Cornell University Press, 1998), chaps. 8–9, 11; Ronald P. Formisano, *The Transformation of Political Culture: Massachusetts Politics, 1790s–1840s* (New York: Oxford University Press, 1983), 149–54, 255–57, 268–301.

59. Formisano, *Transformation of Political Culture,* 257–61; Darling, *Political Changes; Worcester Palladium,* 1 December 1852.

60. *Worcester Palladium,* 30 November 1853, 4 October 1854.

61. Samuel Downer to Horace Mann, 12 September 1850, Horace Mann Papers, MHS, microfilm ed., reel 18.

62. *Official Report of the Debates and Proceedings of the State Convention, Assembled May 4th, 1853, to Revise and Amend the Constitution of the Commonwealth of Massachusetts,* 3 vols. (Boston: White & Potter, 1853), 2: 145, 230. Alley and Chapin were not the only convention delegates who drew on the country critique. See ibid., 1: 924, 938, 948–49; 2: 146–51, 163–64, 418.

63. Henry Wilson to Charles Sumner, 1 September 1853, Sumner Papers, bMS Am 1, HL; William S. Robinson, *"Warrington" Pen-Portraits: A Collection of Personal and Political Sketches from 1848 to 1876, from the Writings of William S. Robinson,* ed. Mrs. W. S. Robinson (Boston: Mrs. W. S. Robinson, 1877), 204; *Worcester Daily Spy,* 15 November 1853. Further editorial condemnation of Lawrence's role in the campaign can be found in the Boston *Daily Commonwealth,* 4 November 1853; *Dedham Gazette,* 12 November 1853; and *Northampton Courier,* 22 November 1853. When Wilson and Robinson spoke of people being fed by Lawrence's hand, they were referring to a comment made by Boston Whig George Hillard at the convention, where he told Richard Henry Dana, Jr.: "As the bread that he and I both eat comes from the business community of Boston; from men, some of whom are rich and all of whom hope to be rich, it does not become us, like forward children, to strike at the hand that feeds us." Critics of Boston's elite long remembered the remark. *Official Report of the Debates and Proceedings of the State Convention,* 2: 129–30.

64. First quotation in Michael F. Holt, *The Political Crisis of the 1850s* (New York: W. W. Norton, 1983), 130; *Springfield Republican,* 3 and 16 September, 16 November 1853.

65. *Worcester Daily Spy,* 26 November 1853; *Springfield Republican,* 2 September 1853; Michel Brunet, "The Secret Ballot Issue in Massachusetts Politics from 1851 to 1853," *New England Quarterly* 25 (September 1952): 357–59; *Official Report of the Debates and Proceeding of the State Convention,* 1: 582–83, 593–97, 615–16, 657–62, 756–57, Wilson quotation from p. 583.

66. There is a growing literature on the market revolution of the antebellum period. Among the more important works are Charles Sellers, *The Market Revolution: Jacksonian America, 1815–1846* (New York: Oxford University Press, 1991); and Melvyn Stokes and Stephen Conway, eds., *The Market Revolution in America: Social, Political, and Religious Expressions, 1800–1880* (Charlottesville: University Press of Virginia, 1996).

Conclusion

1. John Mulkern, *The Know-Nothing Party in Massachusetts: The Rise and Fall of a People's Movement* (Boston: Northeastern University Press, 1990), 76; Edward Everett to Mrs. Charles Eames, 30 September, 16 November 1854, copies, Edward

Everett Papers, Massachusetts Historical Society, Boston, Massachusetts (MHS), microfilm ed., reel 15A; Charles Francis Adams, Diary, 14 November 1854, Adams Family Papers, MHS, microfilm ed., reel 73.

2. [Henry Adams], review of *Life, Letters, and Journals of George Ticknor, North American Review* 123 (July 1876): 213; George Ticknor to Charles Lyell, 27 November 1860, George Ticknor, *Life, Letters, and Journals of George Ticknor,* ed. George Hillard, 2 vols. (Boston: James R. Osgood, 1876), 2: 430; Robert C. Winthrop, Jr., *A Memoir of Robert C. Winthrop* (Boston: Little, Brown, 1897), 172–75, 178, 211, quotation from p. 211.

3. Theodore Parker to Dr. Flint, 31 December 1859, in Theodore Parker, *Life and Correspondence of Theodore Parker,* ed. John Weiss, 2 vols. (New York: D. Appleton, 1864), 2: 398; John H. Clifford to Robert C. Winthrop, 10 June 1856, copy, Winthrop Family Papers, MHS, microfilm ed., reel 39; William E. Gienapp, *The Origins of the Republican Party, 1852–1856* (New York: Oxford University Press, 1987), 215–16; final quotation in Richard H. Abbott, *Cotton & Capital: Boston Businessmen and Antislavery Reform, 1854–1868* (Amherst: University of Massachusetts Press, 1991), 65.

4. Nathan Appleton to South Carolina correspondent, 15 December 1860, *National Intelligencer,* in Nathan Appleton scrapbooks, Appleton Family Papers, MHS.

5. Henry Greenleaf Pearson, *The Life of John A. Andrew: Governor of Massachusetts, 1861–1865,* 2 vols. (Boston: Houghton Mifflin, 1904), 1: 195–96, 199, 242–44; Edith Ellen Ware, *Political Opinion in Massachusetts during the Civil War and Reconstruction* (New York: Columbia University, 1916), 67–68, 122–26; Abbott, *Cotton & Capital,* 100–105; William S. Robinson, *"Warrington" Pen-Portraits: A Collection of Personal and Political Reminiscences from 1848 to 1876, from the Writings of William S. Robinson,* ed. Mrs. W. S. Robinson (Boston: Mrs. W. S. Robinson, 1877), 302.

6. Abbott, *Cotton & Capital,* 57; Eric Foner, *Free Soil, Free Labor, Free Men: The Ideology of the Republican Party before the Civil War* (New York: Oxford University Press, 1970), 11–39, 176–79; Phillip Shaw Paludan, *"A People's Contest": The Union and Civil War, 1861–1865* (New York: Harper & Row, 1988), chap. 6.

7. Samuel Downer to Horace Mann, 24 March 1851, Horace Mann Papers, MHS, microfilm ed., reel 19; Charles Francis Adams to John G. Palfrey, 23 July 1848, copy, Adams Family Papers, MHS, reel 159. For a good example of the type of work needed to illuminate the contributions made by ordinary people, see Julie Roy Jeffrey, *The Great Silent Army of Abolition: Ordinary Women in the Antislavery Movement* (Chapel Hill: University of North Carolina Press, 1998).

Bibliography

Primary Sources

MANUSCRIPT COLLECTIONS

Boston, Mass., Boston Public Library. Antislavery Collection.
———. Appleton-Sumner Correspondence.
———. George Bond Papers.
———. Garrison Papers.
———. Weston Papers.
Boston, Mass., Massachusetts Historical Society. Adams Family Papers. Microfilm ed.
———. Appleton Family Papers.
———. William Ellery Channing Papers. Microfilm ed.
———. John H. Clifford Papers.
———. Dana Family Papers.
———. Edward Everett Papers. Microfilm ed.
———. Amos Lawrence Papers.
———. Amos A. Lawrence Papers.
———. Lee Family Papers. Microfilm ed.
———. Horace Mann Papers. Microfilm ed.
———. Marcus Morton Papers.
———. Harrison Gray Otis Papers. Microfilm ed.
———. Theodore Parker Papers. Microfilm ed.
———. Timothy Pickering Papers. Microfilm ed.
———. Quincy, Wendell, Holmes, and Upham Papers. Microfilm ed.
———. William Schouler Papers.
———. Sears Family Papers.
———. Amasa Walker Papers.
———. Thomas Wren Ward Papers.
———. Emory Washburn Papers.
———. Winthrop Family Papers. Microfilm ed.

Cambridge, Mass., Houghton Library, Harvard University. Letters to Nathan Appleton by or about Abbott Lawrence.
———. John P. Bigelow Papers.
———. Samuel Gridley Howe Papers.
———. Ellis Gray Loring Letterbook.
———. Palfrey Family Papers.
———. Charles Sumner Papers.
Washington, D.C., Manuscript Division, Library of Congress. Thomas Jefferson Papers. Microfilm ed.
Worcester, Mass., American Antiquarian Society. John Davis Papers.

BOOKS AND ARTICLES

Adams, Charles Francis. *Diary of Charles Francis Adams.* Edited by Aida DiPace Donald et al. 8 vols. to date. Cambridge: Harvard University Press, 1964–1986.
Adams, Henry, ed. *Documents Relating to New-England Federalism, 1800–1815.* Boston: Little, Brown, 1877.
Adams, John Quincy. *Life in a New England Town, 1787, 1788: Diary of John Quincy Adams, While a Student in the Office of Theophilus Parsons at Newburyport.* Edited by Charles F. Adams. Boston: Little, Brown, 1903.
———. *Memoirs of John Quincy Adams, Comprising Portions of His Diary from 1795 to 1848.* Edited by Charles F. Adams. 12 vols. Philadelphia: J. B. Lippincott, 1874–1877.
Ames, Fisher. *Works of Fisher Ames: With a Selection from His Speeches and Correspondence.* Edited by Seth Ames. 2 vols. Boston: Little, Brown, 1854.
Amory, Thomas C. *Life of James Sullivan: With Selections from His Writings.* 2 vols. Boston: Phillips, Sampson, 1859.
Appleton, Nathan. *Introduction of the Power Loom, and Origin of Lowell.* Lowell: B. H. Penhallow, 1858.
———. "Labor, Its Relations in Europe and the United States, Compared." *Hunt's Merchants' Magazine* 11 (September 1844): 217–23.
———. *Remarks on Currency and Banking: Having Reference to the Present Derangement of the Circulating Medium in the United States.* Boston: Charles C. Little and James Brown, 1841.
Baldwin, Christopher C. *The Diary of Christopher Columbus Baldwin.* Worcester: American Antiquarian Society, 1901.
Bancroft, George. *The Life and Letters of George Bancroft.* Edited by M. A. DeWolfe Howe. 2 vols. New York: Charles Scribner's Sons, 1908.
Batchelder, Samuel. *Introduction and Early Progress of the Cotton Manufacture in the United States.* Boston: Little, Brown, 1863.
Bentley, William. *Diary of William Bentley, D.D., Pastor of the East Church, Salem, Massachusetts.* 4 vols. Salem, Mass.: The Essex Institute, 1905–1914.
Bigelow, Abijah. "Letters of Abijah Bigelow, Member of Congress, to His Wife,

1810–1815." Edited by C.S.B. *Proceedings of the American Antiquarian Society* 60 (6 April–15 October 1930): 305–406.

Boutwell, George S. *Reminiscences of Sixty Years in Public Affairs.* 2 vols. New York: McClure, Phillips, 1902.

Buckingham, Joseph T. *Personal Memoirs and Recollections of Editorial Life.* 2 vols. Boston: Ticknor, Reed, and Fields, 1852.

———. *Specimens of Newspaper Literature: With Personal Memoirs, Anecdotes, and Reminiscences.* 2 vols. Boston: Charles C. Little and James Brown, 1850.

Burnett, Edmund C., ed. *Letters of Members of the Continental Congress.* 8 vols. Washington, D.C.: Carnegie Institution of Washington, 1921–1936.

Butler, Benjamin F. *Butler's Book: Autobiography and Personal Reminiscences of Major-General Benjamin F. Butler.* Boston: A. M. Thayer, 1892.

Channing, William Ellery. *The Works of William Ellery Channing.* 6 vols. Boston: American Unitarian Association, 1903.

Child, Lydia Maria. *The Collected Correspondence of Lydia Maria Child, 1817–1880.* Edited by Patricia G. Holland and Milton Meltzer. Millwood, N.Y.: Kraus Microform, 1980.

———. *Lydia Maria Child: Selected Letters, 1817–1880.* Edited by Milton Meltzer and Patricia G. Holland. Amherst: University of Massachusetts Press, 1982.

Clay, Henry. *Works of Henry Clay: Comprising His Life, Correspondence and Speeches.* Edited by Calvin Colton. 7 vols. New York: Henry Clay Publishing Company, 1897.

Commons, John R., et al., eds. *A Documentary History of American Industrial Society.* 10 vols. Cleveland: Arthur H. Clark Company, 1910–1911.

Curtis, Benjamin R. *A Memoir of Benjamin Robbins Curtis, LL.D., with Some of His Professional and Miscellaneous Writings.* 2 vols. Boston: Little, Brown, 1879.

Dana, Richard H., Jr. *The Journal of Richard Henry Dana, Jr.* Edited by Robert F. Lucid. 3 vols. Cambridge: Harvard University Press, 1968.

Dwight, Theodore. *History of the Hartford Convention: With a Review of the Policy of the United States Government Which Led to the War of 1812.* New York: N. & J. White, 1833.

Eisler, Benita, ed. *The Lowell Offering: Writings by New England Mill Women (1840–1845).* New York: J. B. Lippincott, 1977.

Emerson, George B., et al. *Memoir of Samuel J. May.* Boston: Roberts Brothers, 1874.

Everett, Edward. *Orations and Speeches on Various Occasions.* 4 vols. Boston: Little, Brown, 1865–1872.

Foner, Philip S., ed. *The Factory Girls.* Urbana: University of Illinois Press, 1977.

Forbes, John Murray. *Letters and Recollections of John Murray Forbes.* Edited by Sarah Forbes Hughes. 2 vols. Boston: Houghton Mifflin, 1899.

Garrison, William L. *The Letters of William Lloyd Garrison.* Edited by Walter M. Merrill and Louis Ruchames. 6 vols. Cambridge: Harvard University Press, 1971–1981.

Grund, Francis J. *Aristocracy in America: From the Sketch-Book of a German Nobleman.* 1839; repr. New York: Harper Torchbooks, 1959.

Hamilton, Alexander. *The Papers of Alexander Hamilton.* Edited by Harold C. Syrett et al. 27 vols. New York: Columbia University Press, 1961–1987.

[Higginson, Stephen]. "Letters of Stephen Higginson, 1783–1804." Edited by J. Franklin Jameson. *Annual Report of the American Historical Association for the Year 1896.* 2 vols. Washington, D.C.: Government Printing Office, 1897.

———. *Ten Chapters in the Life of John Hancock: The Writings of Laco.* 1789; repr. New York: n.p., 1857.

Higginson, Thomas W. *Cheerful Yesterdays.* Boston: Houghton Mifflin, 1898.

———. *Contemporaries.* Boston: Houghton Mifflin, 1899.

Hillard, George S. *Memoir, Autobiography and Correspondence of Jeremiah Mason.* 1873; repr. Boston: Boston Law Book, 1917.

Hoar, George F. *Autobiography of Seventy Years.* 2 vols. New York: Charles Scribner's Sons, 1903.

Howe, Samuel G. *Letters and Journals of Samuel Gridley Howe.* Edited by Laura E. Richards. 2 vols. Boston: Dana Estes, 1909.

Hudson, Charles. "The Protective System—Its Character and Constitutionality." *Hunt's Merchants' Magazine* 8 (June 1843): 512–23.

King, Rufus. *The Life and Correspondence of Rufus King: Comprising His Letters, Private and Official, His Public Documents and His Speeches.* Edited by Charles H. King. 6 vols. New York: G. P. Putnam's Sons, 1894–1900.

Larcom, Lucy. *A New England Girlhood.* Boston: Houghton Mifflin, 1889.

Lawrence, Amos. *Extracts from the Diary and Correspondence of the Late Amos Lawrence with a Brief Account of Some Incidents in His Life.* Edited by William B. Lawrence. Boston: Gould and Lincoln, 1855.

Lee, Henry, and Mary Lee. *Henry and Mary Lee: Letters and Journals with Other Family Letters, 1802–1860.* Edited by Frances Rollins Morse. Boston: n.p., 1926.

Lodge, Henry Cabot. *Life and Letters of George Cabot.* Boston: Little, Brown, 1877.

Luther, Seth. *An Address to the Workingmen of New England, on the State of Education, and on the Condition of the Producing Classes in Europe and America.* Boston: n.p., 1832.

Mann, Horace. *An Oration Delivered before the Authorities of the City of Boston, July 4, 1842.* Boston: W. B. Fowle and N. Capen, 1842.

———. *Slavery: Letters and Speeches.* 1851; repr. Miami: Mnemosyne Publishing, 1969.

Mann, Mary. *Life of Horace Mann.* Boston: Willard Small, 1888.

Manning, William. *The Key of Liberty: The Life and Democratic Writings of William Manning, "A Laborer," 1747–1814.* Edited by Michael Merrill and Sean Wilentz. Cambridge: Harvard University Press, 1993.

May, Samuel J. *Some Recollections of Our Antislavery Struggle.* Boston: Fields, Osgood, 1869.

Palfrey, John G. *Papers on the Slave Power, First Published in the "Boston Whig."* Boston: Merrill, Cobb, 1846.

Parker, Theodore. *The Collected Works of Theodore Parker, Minister of the Twenty-Eighth Congregational Society at Boston, U.S.* Edited by Frances Power Cobbe. 14 vols. London: Trubner, 1863–1879.

⸻. *Life and Correspondence of Theodore Parker.* Edited by John Weiss. 2 vols. New York: D. Appleton, 1864.

⸻. *The Rights of Man in America.* Edited by F. B. Sanborn. 1911; repr. New York: Negro Universities Press, 1969.

⸻. *The Slave Power.* Edited by James K. Hosmer. N.d.; repr. New York: Arno Press & the New York Times, 1969.

⸻. *Social Classes in a Republic.* Edited by Samuel A. Eliot. Boston: American Unitarian Association, n.d.

Phillips, Wendell. *Speeches, Lectures, and Letters.* Series One. Boston: Lee and Shepard, 1884.

⸻. *Speeches, Lectures, and Letters.* Series Two. Boston: Lee and Shepard, 1891.

Phillips, Willard. *A Manual of Political Economy with Particular Reference to the Institutions, Resources and Condition of the United States.* Boston: Hilliard, Gray, Little, and Wilkins, 1828.

⸻. *Propositions Concerning Protection and Free Trade.* Boston: Charles C. Little and James Brown, 1850.

Pickering, Octavius, and Charles W. Upham. *The Life of Timothy Pickering.* 4 vols. Boston: Little, Brown, 1873.

Pierce, Edward L. *Memoir and Letters of Charles Sumner.* 4 vols. Boston: Roberts Brothers, 1877–1984.

Quincy, Edmund. *Life of Josiah Quincy of Massachusetts.* Boston: Fields, Osgood, 1869.

Richards, William C. *Great in Goodness: A Memoir of George N. Briggs, Governor of the Commonwealth of Massachusetts, from 1844 to 1851.* Boston: Gould and Lincoln, 1866.

Robinson, Harriet H. *Loom & Spindle: or Life Among the Early Mill Girls.* 1898; repr. Kailua, Hawaii: Press Pacifica, 1976.

Robinson, William S. *"Warrington" Pen-Portraits: A Collection of Personal and Political Reminiscences from 1848 to 1876, from the Writings of William S. Robinson.* Edited by Mrs. W. S. Robinson. Boston: Mrs. W. S. Robinson, 1877.

Saltonstall, Leverett. "The Papers of Leverett Saltonstall, 1816–1845." Edited by Robert E. Moody. *Collections of the Massachusetts Historical Society* 82–86 (1978–1992).

Story, William W. *The Life and Letters of Joseph Story, Associate Justice of the Supreme Court of the United States, and Dane Professor of Law at Harvard University.* 2 vols. Boston: Charles C. Little and James Brown, 1851.

Sullivan, William. *Familiar Letters on Public Characters, and Private Events; from the Peace of 1783 to the Peace of 1815.* Boston: Russell, Odiorne, and Metcalf, 1834.

Sumner, Charles. *The Selected Letter of Charles Sumner.* Edited by Beverly Wilson Palmer. 2 vols. Boston: Northeastern University Press, 1990.

Taggart, Samuel. "Letters of Samuel Taggart, Representative in Congress, 1803–1814." Edited by George Henry Haynes. *Proceedings of the American Antiquarian Society* 33 (11 April–17 October 1923): 113–226, 297–438.

Ticknor, George. *Life, Letters, and Journals of George Ticknor.* Edited by George S. Hillard. 2 vols. (Boston: James R. Osgood, 1876).

Webster, Daniel. *The Papers of Daniel Webster: Correspondence.* Edited by Charles M. Wiltse and Harold D. Moser. 7 vols. Hanover, N.H.: University Press of New England, 1974–1986.

Whittier, John G. *The Letters of John Greenleaf Whittier.* Edited by John B. Pickard. 3 vols. Cambridge: Harvard University Press, 1975.

Wilson, Henry. *History of the Rise and Fall of the Slave Power in America.* 3 vols. Boston: James R. Osgood, 1872–1877.

Wolcott, Oliver. *Memoirs of the Administrations of Washington and John Adams, Edited from the Papers of Oliver Wolcott, Secretary of the Treasury.* Edited by George Gibbs. 2 vols. New York: n.p., 1846.

Secondary Sources

BOOKS AND ARTICLES

Abbott, Richard H. *Cobbler in Congress: The Life of Henry Wilson, 1812–1875.* Lexington: University Press of Kentucky, 1972.

———. *Cotton & Capital: Boston Businessmen and Antislavery Reform, 1854–1868.* Amherst: University of Massachusetts Press, 1991.

Adams, Henry. *History of the United States during the Administrations of Jefferson and Madison.* 9 vols. New York: Charles Scribner's Sons, 1889–1891.

Albrecht, Robert C. *Theodore Parker.* New York: Twayne Publishers, 1971.

Ammon Harry. *James Monroe: The Quest for National Identity.* 1971; repr. Charlottesville: University Press of Virginia, 1990.

Anbinder, Tyler. *Nativism and Slavery: The Northern Know Nothings and the Politics of the 1850s.* New York: Oxford University Press, 1992.

Ashworth, John. *"Agrarians" & "Aristocrats": Party Political Ideology in the United States, 1837–1846.* London: Royal Historical Society, 1983.

———. *Slavery, Capitalism, and Politics in the Antebellum Republic: Commerce and Compromise, 1820–1850.* Cambridge: Cambridge University Press, 1995.

Banner, James M., Jr. *To the Hartford Convention: The Federalists and the Origins of Party Politics in Massachusetts, 1789–1815.* New York: Alfred A. Knopf, 1970.

Barrow, Thomas C. *Trade and Empire: The British Customs Service in Colonial America.* Cambridge: Harvard University Press, 1967.

Bartlett, Irving H. *Daniel Webster.* New York: W. W. Norton, 1978.

———. *Wendell & Ann Phillips: The Community of Reform, 1840–1860.* New York: W. W. Norton, 1979.

———. *Wendell Phillips: Brahmin Radical.* Boston: Beacon Press, 1961.

Baum, Dale. *The Civil War Party System: The Case of Massachusetts, 1848–1876.* Chapel Hill: University of North Carolina Press, 1984.

Baxter, Maurice C. *Henry Clay and the American System.* Lexington: University Press of Kentucky, 1995.

Bemis, Samuel Flagg. *John Quincy Adams and the Union.* New York: Alfred A. Knopf, 1956.

Bernhard, Winfred E. A. *Fisher Ames: Federalist and Statesman, 1758–1808.* Chapel Hill: University of North Carolina Press, 1965.

Blue, Frederick J. *The Free Soilers: Third Party Politics, 1848–1854.* Urbana: University of Illinois Press, 1973.

Brant, Irving. *James Madison: Commander in Chief, 1812–1816.* Indianapolis: Bobbs-Merrill, 1961.

———. *James Madison: The President, 1809–1812.* Indianapolis: Bobbs-Merrill, 1956.

Brauer, Kinley J. *Cotton versus Conscience: Massachusetts Whig Politics and Southwestern Expansion, 1843–1848.* Lexington: University of Kentucky Press, 1967.

Brooke, John J. *The Heart of the Commonwealth: Society and Political Culture in Worcester County, Massachusetts, 1713–1861.* 1989; repr. Amherst: University of Massachusetts Press, 1992.

Brown, Richard D. *The Strength of a People: The Idea of an Informed Citizenry in America, 1650–1870.* Chapel Hill: University of North Carolina Press, 1996.

Brown, Roger H. *The Republic in Peril: 1812.* New York: Columbia University Press, 1964.

Brown, Thomas. *Politics and Statesmanship: Essays on the American Whig Party.* New York: Columbia University Press, 1985.

Burns, Rex. *Success in America: The Yeoman Dream and the Industrial Revolution.* Amherst: University of Massachusetts Press, 1976.

Bushman, Claudia L. *"A Good Poor Man's Wife": Being a Chronicle of Harriet Hanson Robinson and Her Family in Nineteenth-Century New England.* Hanover, N.H.: University Press of New England, 1981.

Bushman, Richard L. *King and People in Provincial Massachusetts.* Chapel Hill: University of North Carolina Press, 1985.

Carlton, Frank Tracy. *Economic Influences upon Educational Progress in the United States, 1820–1850.* 1908; repr. New York: Teachers College Press, Columbia University, 1965.

Cayton, Andrew R. L. "The Fragmentation of 'A Great Family': The Panic of 1819 and the Rise of the Middling Interest in Boston, 1818–1822." *Journal of the Early Republic* 2 (Summer 1982): 143–67.

Chadwick, John White. *Theodore Parker: Preacher and Reformer.* Boston: Houghton Mifflin, 1900.

Channing, William Henry. *The Life of William Ellery Channing, D.D.* Boston: American Unitarian Association, 1880.

Clarfield, Gerard H. *Timothy Pickering and the American Republic.* Pittsburgh: University of Pittsburgh Press, 1980.

Clark, Christopher. *The Communitarian Moment: The Radical Challenge of the Northampton Association.* Ithaca, N.Y.: Cornell University Press, 1995.

————. *The Roots of Rural Capitalism: Western Massachusetts, 1780–1860.* Ithaca, N.Y.: Cornell University Press, 1990.

Clifford, Deborah Pickman. *Crusader for Freedom: A Life of Lydia Maria Child.* Boston: Beacon Press, 1992.

Collins, Herbert. "The Southern Industrial Gospel before 1860." *Journal of Southern History* 12 (August 1946): 386–402.

Collinson, Gary. *Shadrach Minkins: From Fugitive Slave to Citizen.* Cambridge: Harvard University Press, 1997.

Combs, Jerald A. *The Jay Treaty: Political Battleground of the Founding Fathers.* Berkeley: University of California Press, 1970.

Commager, Henry Steele. *Theodore Parker: Yankee Crusader.* 1936; repr. Boston: Beacon Press, 1947.

Conkin, Paul K. *Prophets of Prosperity: America's First Political Economists.* Bloomington: Indiana University Press, 1980.

Crouch, Barry A. "Amos A. Lawrence and the Formation of the Constitutional Union Party: The Conservative Failure in 1860." *Historical Journal of Massachusetts* 9 (June 1980): 46–58.

Crowley, J. F. *This Sheba, Self: The Conceptualization of Economic Life in Eighteenth-Century America.* Baltimore: Johns Hopkins University Press, 1974.

Dalzell, Robert F., Jr. *Daniel Webster and the Trial of American Nationalism, 1843–1852.* Boston: Houghton Mifflin, 1973.

————. *Enterprising Elite: The Boston Associates and the World They Made.* Cambridge: Harvard University Press, 1987.

————. "The Rise of the Waltham-Lowell System and Some Thoughts on the Political Economy of Modernization in Ante-Bellum Massachusetts." *Perspectives in American History* 9 (1975): 229–68.

Darling, Arthur B. *Political Change in Massachusetts, 1824–1848: A Study of Liberal Movements in Politics.* New Haven: Yale University Press, 1925.

David, Paul A. "Learning by Doing and Tariff Protection: A Reconstruction of the Case of the Ante-Bellum United States Cotton Textile Industry." *Journal of Economic History* 30 (September 1970): 521–601.

Donald, David H. *Charles Sumner and the Coming of the Civil War.* 1960; repr. Chicago: University of Chicago Press, 1981.

Duberman, Martin B. *Charles Francis Adams, 1807–1886.* Boston: Houghton Mifflin, 1961.

Dublin, Thomas. *Women at Work: The Transformation of Work and Community in Lowell, Massachusetts, 1826–1860.* New York: Columbia University Press, 1979.

Dubofsky, Melvyn. "Daniel Webster and the Whig Theory of Economic Growth: 1828–1848." *New England Quarterly* 42 (December 1969): 551–72.

Edelstein, Tilden. *Strange Enthusiasm: A Life of Thomas Wentworth Higginson.* New Haven: Yale University Press, 1968.

Elkins, Stanley, and Eric McKitrick. *The Age of Federalism: The Early American Republic, 1788–1800.* New York: Oxford University Press, 1993.

Ellis, Richard E. *The Union at Risk: Jacksonian Democracy, States' Rights, and the Nullification Crisis.* New York: Oxford University Press, 1987.

Farrell, Betty G. *Elite Families: Class and Power in Nineteenth-Century Boston.* Albany: State University of New York Press, 1993.

Field, Peter S. *The Crisis of the Standing Order: Clerical Intellectuals and Cultural Authority in Massachusetts, 1780–1833.* Amherst: University of Massachusetts Press, 1998.

Fischer, David Hackett. *Albion's Seed: Four British Folkways in America.* New York: Oxford University Press, 1989.

———. "The Myth of the Essex Junto." *William and Mary Quarterly* 21 (April 1964): 191–235.

———. *The Revolution of American Conservatism: The Federalist Party in the Era of Jeffersonian Democracy.* New York: Harper & Row, 1965.

Foner, Eric. *Free Soil, Free Labor, Free Men: The Ideology of the Republican Party before the Civil War.* New York: Oxford University Press, 1970.

Foner, Philip S. *Business & Slavery: The New York Merchants & the Irrepressible Conflict.* 1941; repr. New York: Russell & Russell, 1968.

Forbes, J. B. *Israel Thorndike, Federalist Financier.* New York: Exposition Press, 1953.

Formisano, Ronald P. *The Transformation of Political Culture: Massachusetts Parties, 1790s–1840s.* New York: Oxford University Press, 1983.

Foster, Stephen. *Their Solitary Way: The Puritan Social Ethic in the First Century of Settlement in New England.* New Haven: Yale University Press, 1971.

Franklin, John Hope. *A Southern Odyssey: Travelers in the Antebellum North.* Baton Rouge: Louisiana State University Press, 1976.

Freehling, William W. *Prelude to Civil War: The Nullification Controversy in South Carolina, 1816–1836.* 1965; repr. New York: Harper Torchbooks, 1968.

———. *The Road to Disunion: Secessionists at Bay, 1776–1854.* New York: Oxford University Press, 1990.

Frothingham, Octavius Brooks. *Boston Unitarianism, 1820–1850: A Study of the Life and Work of Nathaniel Langdon Frothingham.* 1890; repr. Hicksville, N.Y.: Regina Press, 1975.

———. *Theodore Parker: A Biography.* Boston: James R. Osgood and Company, 1874.

Frothingham, Paul Revere. *Edward Everett: Orator and Statesman.* Boston: Houghton Mifflin, 1925.

Fuess, Claude M. *The Life of Caleb Cushing.* 2 vols. New York: Harcourt, Brace, 1923.

Garrison, Wendell Phillips, and Francis Jackson Garrison. *William Lloyd Garrison, 1805–1879: The Story of His Life, Told by His Children.* 4 vols. New York: Century, 1885–1889.

Gerteis, Louis S. *Morality and Utility in American Antislavery Reform.* Chapel Hill: University of North Carolina Press, 1987.

Gienapp, William E. *The Origins of the Republican Party, 1852–1856.* New York: Oxford University Press, 1987.

Goodheart, Lawrence B. *Abolitionist, Actuary, Atheist: Elizur Wright and the Reform Impulse.* Kent, Ohio: Kent State University Press, 1990.

Goodman, Paul. *The Democratic-Republicans of Massachusetts: Politics in a Young Republic.* Cambridge: Harvard University Press, 1964.

———. "Ethics and Enterprise: The Values of a Boston Elite, 1800–1860." *American Quarterly* 18 (Fall 1966): 437–51.

———. *Of One Blood: Abolitionism and the Origins of Racial Equality.* Berkeley: University of California Press, 1998.

———. "The Politics of Industrialization: Massachusetts, 1830–1870." In *Uprooted Americans: Essays to Honor Oscar Handlin,* ed. Richard L. Bushman et al., 161–207. Boston: Little, Brown, 1979.

———. *Towards a Christian Republic: Antimasonry and the Great Transition in New England, 1826–1836.* New York: Oxford University Press, 1988.

Gregory, Frances W. *Nathan Appleton: Merchant and Entrepreneur, 1779–1861.* Charlottesville: University Press of Virginia, 1975.

Guarneri, Carl J. *The Utopian Alternative: Fourierism in Nineteenth-Century America.* Ithaca, N.Y.: Cornell University Press, 1991.

Hall, Van Beck. *Politics without Parties: Massachusetts, 1780–1791.* Pittsburgh: University of Pittsburgh Press, 1964.

Hamilton, Holman. *Zachary Taylor: Soldier in the White House.* Indianapolis: Bobbs-Merrill, 1951.

Hammett, Theodore M. "Two Mobs of Jacksonian Boston: Ideology and Interest." *Journal of American History* 62 (March 1976): 845–68.

Handlin, Oscar, and Mary Flug Handlin. *Commonwealth: A Study of the Role of Government in the American Economy, 1774–1861.* Rev. ed. Cambridge: Harvard University Press, 1969.

Hartz, Louis. "Seth Luther: The Story of a Working-Class Rebel." *New England Quarterly* 13 (September 1940): 401–18.

Higginson, Thomas Wentworth. *The Life and Times of Stephen Higginson.* Boston: Houghton Mifflin, 1907.

Hill, Hamilton A. *Memoir of Abbott Lawrence.* Boston: n.p., 1883.

Holt, Michael F. *The Political Crisis of the 1850s.* New York: John Wiley & Sons, 1978.

———. *The Rise and Fall of the American Whig Party: Jacksonian Politics and the Onset of the Civil War.* New York: Oxford University Press, 1999.

Horsman, Reginald. *The Causes of the War of 1812.* Philadelphia: University of Pennsylvania Press, 1962.

Howe, David Walker. *The Political Culture of the American Whigs.* Chicago: University of Chicago Press, 1979.

———. *The Unitarian Conscience: Harvard Moral Philosophy, 1805–1861.* 1970; repr. Middletown, Conn.: Wesleyan University Press, 1988.

Huston, James L. *Securing the Fruits of Labor: The American Concept of Wealth Distribution, 1765–1900.* Baton Rouge: Louisiana State University Press, 1998.

Innes, Stephen. *Creating the Commonwealth: The Economic Culture of Puritan New England.* New York: W. W. Norton, 1995.

Jackson, Sidney L. "Labor, Education, and Politics in the 1830s." *Pennsylvania Magazine of History and Biography* 66 (July 1942): 279–91.

Jaher, Frederic Cople. "Businessman and Gentleman: Nathan and Thomas Gold Appleton—An Exploration in Intergenerational History." *Explorations in Entrepreneurial History* 4 (Fall 1966): 17–39.

———. *The Urban Establishment: Upper Strata in Boston, New York, Charleston, and Los Angeles.* Urbana: University of Illinois Press, 1982.

Johannsen, Robert W. *Stephen A. Douglas.* 1973; repr. Urbana: University of Illinois Press, 1997.

Johnson, Arthur W., and Barry F. Supple. *Boston Capitalists and Western Railroads: A Study in the Nineteenth-Century Railroad Investment Process.* Cambridge: Harvard University Press, 1967.

Johnson, Reinhard O. "The Liberty Party in Massachusetts, 1840–1848: Antislavery Third Party Politics in the Bay State." *Civil War History* 28 (September 1982): 237–65.

Karcher, Carolyn L. *The First Woman in the Republic: A Cultural Biography of Lydia Maria Child.* Durham, N.C.: Duke University Press, 1994.

Kerber, Linda F. *Federalists in Dissent: Imagery and Ideology in Jeffersonian America.* Ithaca, N.Y.: Cornell University Press, 1970.

———. *Women of the Republic: Intellect and Ideology in Revolutionary America.* Chapel Hill: University of North Carolina Press, 1980.

Ketcham, James. *James Madison: A Biography.* 1971; repr. Charlottesville: University Press of Virginia, 1990.

Kurtz, Stephen G. *The Presidency of John Adams: The Collapse of Federalism, 1795–1800.* Philadelphia: University of Pennsylvania Press, 1957.

Lamoreaux, Naomi B. *Insider Lending: Banks, Personal Connections, and Economic Development in Industrial New England.* Cambridge: Cambridge University Press, 1994.

Lasch, Christopher A. *The Revolt of the Elites and the Betrayal of Democracy.* New York: W. W. Norton, 1995.

Laurie, Bruce. *Artisans into Workers: Labor in Nineteenth-Century America.* New York: Noonday Press, 1989.

———. "The 'Fair Field' of the 'Middle Ground': Abolitionism, Labor Reform, and the Making of an Antislavery Bloc in Antebellum Massachusetts." In *Labor Histories: Class, Politics, and the Working-Class Experience,* ed. Eric Arnesen et al., 45–70. Urbana: University of Illinois Press, 1998.

———. "'Spavined Ministers, Lying Toothpullers, and Buggering Priests': Third-Partyism and the Search for Security in the Antebellum North." In *American Artisans: Crafting Social Identity, 1750–1850,* ed. Howard B. Rock et al., 98–119. Baltimore: Johns Hopkins University Press, 1995.

Lazerow, Jama. "Religion and Labor Reform in Antebellum America: The World of William Field Young." *American Quarterly* 38 (Summer 1986): 265–86.

———. *Religion and the Working Class in Antebellum America.* Washington: Smithsonian Institution Press, 1995.

Livermore, Shaw, Jr. *The Twilight of Federalism: The Disintegration of the Federalist Party, 1815–1830*. Princeton, N.J.: Princeton University Press, 1962.

Magdol, Edward. *The Antislavery Rank and File: A Social Profile of the Abolitionists' Constituency*. Westport, Conn.: Greenwood Press, 1986.

Malone, Dumas. *Jefferson the President: First Term, 1801–1805*. Boston: Little, Brown, 1970.

———. *Jefferson the President: Second Term, 1805–1809*. Boston: Little, Brown, 1974.

Mandel, Bernard. *Labor: Slave and Free: Workingmen and the Anti-Slavery Movement in the United States*. New York: Associated Authors, 1955.

Matthews, Jean V. *Rufus Choate: The Law and Civic Virtue*. Philadelphia: Temple University Press, 1980.

May, Henry F. *The Enlightenment in America*. New York: Oxford University Press, 1977.

Mayfield, John. *Rehearsal for Republicanism: Free Soil and the Politics of Anti-Slavery*. Port Washington, N.Y.: Kennikat Press, 1980.

McCaughey, Robert A. *Josiah Quincy, 1772–1864: The Last Federalist*. Cambridge: Harvard University Press, 1974.

McCoy, Drew R. *The Elusive Republic: Political Economy in Jeffersonian America*. Chapel Hill: University of North Carolina Press, 1980.

McDonald, Forrest. *Alexander Hamilton: A Biography*. New York: W.W. Norton, 1982.

McGouldrick, Paul F. *New England Textiles in the Nineteenth Century: Profits and Investment*. Cambridge: Harvard University Press, 1968.

McKay, Ernest A. "Henry Wilson and the Coalition of 1851." *New England Quarterly* 36 (September 1963): 338–57.

———. *Henry Wilson: Practical Radical*. Port Washington, N.Y.: Kennikat Press, 1971.

Mendelsohn, Jack. *Channing: The Reluctant Rebel*. Boston: Little, Brown, 1971.

Merriam, George S. *The Life and Times of Samuel Bowles*. 2 vols. New York: Century, 1885.

Merrill, Walter M. *Against Wind and Tide: A Biography of William Lloyd Garrison*. Cambridge: Harvard University Press, 1963.

Messerli, Jonathan. *Horace Mann: A Biography*. New York: Alfred A. Knopf, 1972.

Morison, Samuel Eliot. *The Life and Letters of Harrison Gray Otis*. 2 vols. Boston: Houghton Mifflin, 1913.

Morris, Thomas D. *Free Men All: The Personal Liberty Laws of the North, 1780–1861*. Baltimore: Johns Hopkins University Press, 1974.

Mulkern, John R. *The Know-Nothing Party in Massachusetts: The Rise and Fall of a People's Movement*. Boston: Northeastern University Press, 1990.

Murphy, Teresa Anne. *Ten Hours' Labor: Religion, Reform, and Gender in Early New England*. Ithaca, N.Y.: Cornell University Press, 1992.

Nagel, Paul C. *Descent from Glory: Four Generations of the John Adams Family*. New York: Oxford University Press, 1983.

Newell, Margaret Ellen. *From Dependency to Independence: Economic Revolution in Colonial New England.* Ithaca, N.Y.: Cornell University Press, 1998.

Niven, John. *John C. Calhoun and the Price of Union: A Biography.* Baton Rouge: Louisiana State University Press, 1988.

———. *Martin Van Buren: The Romantic Age of American Politics.* New York: Oxford University Press, 1983.

———. *Salmon P. Chase: A Biography.* New York: Oxford University Press, 1995.

Nye, Russel B. *Fettered Freedom: Civil Liberties and the Slavery Controversy, 1830–1860.* 1963; repr. Urbana: University of Illinois Press, 1972.

———. *George Bancroft: Brahmin Rebel.* New York: Alfred A. Knopf, 1945.

O'Connor, Thomas H. *Lords of the Loom: The Cotton Whigs and the Coming of the Civil War.* New York: Charles Scribner's Sons, 1968.

Paludan, Phillip S. *"A People's Contest": The Union and Civil War, 1861–1865.* New York: Harper & Row, 1988.

Pearson, Henry Greenleaf. *The Life of John A. Andrew: Governor of Massachusetts, 1861–1865.* 2 vols. Boston: Houghton Mifflin, 1904.

Pease, William H., and Jane H. Pease. "Paternal Dilemmas: Emotion, Property, and Patrician Persistence in Jacksonian Boston." *New England Quarterly* 53 (June 1980): 147–67.

———. *The Web of Progress: Private Values and Public Spheres in Boston and Charleston, 1828–1843.* 1985; repr. Athens: University of Georgia Press, 1991.

Perkins, Bradford. *Prologue to War: England and the United States, 1805–1812.* Berkeley: University of California Press, 1961.

Persons, Charles E. "The Early History of Factory Legislation in Massachusetts: From 1825 to the Passage of the Ten Hour Law in 1874." In *Labor Laws and Their Enforcement,* ed. Susan M. Kingsbury, 1–129. New York: Longmans, Green, 1911.

Peterson, Merrill D. *The Great Triumvirate: Webster, Clay, and Calhoun.* New York: Oxford University Press, 1987.

———. *Olive Branch and Sword: The Compromise of 1833.* Baton Rouge: Louisiana State University Press, 1982.

Pinkney, Helen R. *Christopher Gore, Federalist of Massachusetts, 1758–1827.* Waltham, Mass.: Gore Place Society, 1969.

Potter, David. *The Impending Crisis, 1848–1861.* New York: Harper & Row, 1976.

Prince, Carl E., and Seth Taylor. "Daniel Webster, the Boston Associates, and the U.S. Government's Role in the Industrializing Process, 1815–1830." *Journal of the Early Republic* 2 (Fall 1982): 283–99.

Remini, Robert V. *Daniel Webster: The Man and His Time.* New York: W. W. Norton, 1997.

———. *Henry Clay.* New York: W. W. Norton, 1991.

———. *Martin Van Buren and the Making of the Democratic Party.* New York: Columbia University Press, 1959.

Rich, Robert. "'A Wilderness of Whigs': The Wealthy Men of Boston." *Journal of Social History* 4 (Spring 1971): 263–76.

Richards, Leonard L. *"Gentlemen of Property and Standing": Anti-Abolition Mobs in Jacksonian America.* New York: Oxford University Press, 1970.

———. "The Jacksonians and Slavery." In *Antislavery Reconsidered: New Perspectives on the Abolitionists,* ed. Lewis Perry and Michael Fellman, 99–118. Baton Rouge: Louisiana State University Press, 1979.

———. *The Life and Times of Congressman John Quincy Adams.* New York: Oxford University Press, 1986.

Roediger, David R., and Philip S. Foner, *Our Own Time: A History of American Labor and the Working Day.* London: Verso, 1989.

Rorabaugh, W. J. *The Craft Apprentice: From Franklin to the Machine Age in America.* New York: Oxford University Press, 1986.

Rose, Anne C. *Transcendentalism as a Social Movement, 1830–1850.* New Haven: Yale University Press, 1981.

Rothenberg, Winifred Barr. *From Market-Places to a Market Economy: The Transformation of Rural Massachusetts, 1750–1850.* Chicago: University of Chicago Press, 1992.

Salsbury, Stephen. *The State, the Investor, and the Railroad: The Boston & Albany, 1825–1867.* Cambridge: Harvard University Press, 1967.

Sanford, Charles L. "The Intellectual Origins and New-Worldliness of American Industry." *Journal of Economic History* 18 (March 1958): 1–16.

Schroeder, John H. *Mr. Polk's War: American Opposition and Dissent, 1846–1848.* Madison: University of Wisconsin Press, 1973.

Schwartz, Harold. *Samuel Gridley Howe: Social Reformer, 1801–1876.* Cambridge: Harvard University Press, 1956.

Scott, Donald N. *From Office to Profession: The New England Ministry, 1750–1850.* Philadelphia: University of Pennsylvania Press, 1978.

Seaburg, Carl, and Stanley Peterson. *Merchant Prince of Boston: Colonel T. H. Perkins, 1764–1854.* Cambridge: Harvard University Press, 1971.

Sellers, Charles. *The Market Revolution: Jacksonian America, 1815–1846.* New York: Oxford University Press, 1991.

Sewell, Richard H. *Ballots for Freedom: Antislavery Politics in the United States, 1837–1860.* 1976; repr. New York: W. W. Norton, 1980.

Shapiro, Samuel. "The Conservative Dilemma: The Massachusetts Constitutional Convention of 1853." *New England Quarterly* 33 (June 1960): 207–24.

———. *Richard Henry Dana, Jr., 1815–1882.* East Lansing: Michigan State University Press, 1961.

Sharp, James Roger. *American Politics in the Early Republic: The New Nation in Crisis.* New Haven: Yale University Press, 1993.

Sheidley, Harlow W. *Sectional Nationalism: Massachusetts Conservative Leaders and the Transformation of America, 1815–1836.* Boston: Northeastern University Press, 1998.

Shlakman, Vera. *Economic History of a Factory Town: A Study of Chicopee, Massachusetts.* 1936; repr. New York: Octagon Books, 1969.

Siracusa, Carl. *A Mechanical People: Perceptions of the Industrial Order in Massachusetts, 1815–1880.* Middletown, Conn.: Wesleyan University Press, 1979.

Smith, James Morton. *Freedom's Fetters: The Alien and Sedition Laws and American Civil Liberties.* Ithaca, N.Y.: Cornell University Press, 1956.

Spivak, Burton. *Jefferson's English Crisis: Commerce, Embargo, and the Republican Revolution.* Charlottesville: University Press of Virginia, 1979.

Stagg, J. C. A. *Mr. Madison's War: Politics, Diplomacy, and Warfare in the Early American Republic, 1783–1830.* Princeton, N.J.: Princeton University Press, 1983.

Stange, Douglas C. *Patterns of Antislavery among American Unitarians, 1831–1860.* Rutherford, N.J.: Fairleigh Dickinson University Press, 1977.

Stewart, James Brewer. *Wendell Phillips: Liberty's Hero.* Baton Rouge: Louisiana State University Press, 1986.

Stokes, Melvyn, and Stephen Conway, eds. *The Market Revolution in America: Social, Political, and Religious Expressions, 1800–1880.* Charlottesville: University Press of Virginia, 1996.

Story, Ronald. *The Forging of an Aristocracy: Harvard & the Boston Upper Class, 1800–1870.* Middletown, Conn.: Wesleyan University Press, 1980.

Thomas, John L. *The Liberator, William Lloyd Garrison: A Biography.* Boston: Little, Brown, 1963.

Thompson, Robert R. "John Quincy Adams, Apostate: 'Outrageous Federalist' to 'Republican Exile,' 1801–1809." *Journal of the Early Republic* 11 (Summer 1991): 161–83.

Thornton, Tamara Plakins. *Cultivating Gentlemen: The Meaning of Country Life among the Boston Elite, 1785–1860.* New Haven: Yale University Press, 1989.

Tomlins, Christopher L. *Law, Labor, and Ideology in the Early American Republic.* Cambridge: University of Cambridge Press, 1993.

Trefousse, Hans L. *Ben Butler: The South Called Him Beast!* New York: Twayne, 1957.

Tucker, Barbara M. *Samuel Slater and the Origins of the American Textile Industry, 1790–1860.* Ithaca, N.Y.: Cornell University Press, 1984.

Tyrrell, Ian R. *Sobering Up: From Temperance to Prohibition in Antebellum America, 1800–1860.* Westport, Conn.: Greenwood Press, 1979.

Van Tassel, David D. "Gentlemen of Property and Standing: Compromise Sentiment in Boston in 1850." *New England Quarterly* 23 (September 1950): 307–19.

Varg, Paul A. *New England and Foreign Relations, 1789–1850.* Hanover, N.H.: University Press of New England, 1983.

Von Frank, Albert J. *The Trials of Anthony Burns: Freedom and Slavery in Emerson's Boston.* Cambridge: Harvard University Press, 1998.

Ware, Caroline F. *The Early New England Cotton Manufacture: A Study in Industrial Beginnings.* Boston: Houghton Mifflin, 1931.

Ware, Edith Ellen. *Political Opinion in Massachusetts during the Civil War and Reconstruction.* New York: Columbia University Press, 1916.

Ware, Norman. *The Industrial Worker, 1840–1860: The Reaction of American Industrial Society to the Advance of the Industrial Revolution.* 1924; repr. Chicago: Quadrangle, 1964.

Warren, Charles. *Jacobin and Junto: or Early American Politics as Viewed in the Diary of Dr. Nathaniel Ames, 1758–1822.* 1931; repr. New York: Benjamin Blom, 1968.

Welch, Richard E., Jr. *Theodore Sedgwick, Federalist: A Political Portrait.* Middletown, Conn.: Wesleyan University Press, 1965.

White, Gerald T. *A History of the Massachusetts Hospital Life Insurance Company.* Cambridge: Harvard University Press, 1955.

Winthrop, Robert C., Jr. *A Memoir of Robert C. Winthrop.* Boston: Little, Brown, 1897.

Wright, Conrad Edick. *The Transformation of Charity in Postrevolutionary New England.* Boston: Northeastern University Press, 1992.

Yacovone, Donald. *Samuel Joseph May and the Dilemmas of the Liberal Persuasion, 1797–1871.* Philadelphia: Temple University Press, 1991.

Zemsky, Robert. *Merchants, Farmers, and River Gods: An Essay on Eighteenth-Century American Politics.* Boston: Gambit, 1971.

Zonderman, David A. *Aspirations and Anxieties: New England Workers and the Mechanized Factory System, 1815–1850.* New York: Oxford University Press, 1992.

DISSERTATIONS

Crocker, Matthew H. "'The Magic of the Many That Sets the World on Fire': Boston Elites and Urban Political Insurgents during the Early Nineteenth Century." Ph.D. diss., University of Massachusetts at Amherst, 1997.

Hall, Peter Dobkin. "Family Structure and Class Consolidation among the Boston Brahmins." Ph.D. diss., State University of New York at Stony Brook, 1973.

Haws, Robert James. "Massachusetts Whigs, 1833–1854." Ph.D. diss., University of Nebraska, 1973.

Kornblith, Gary John. "From Artisans to Businessmen: Master Mechanics in New England, 1789–1850." Ph.D. diss., Princeton University, 1983.

Rich, Robert Stanley. "Politics and Pedigrees: The Wealthy Men of Boston, 1798–1852." Ph.D. diss., University of California, Los Angeles, 1975.

Sheidley, Harlow Elizabeth Walker. "Sectional Nationalism: The Culture and Politics of the Massachusetts Conservative Elite, 1815–1836." Ph.D. diss., University of Connecticut, 1990.

Spalding, Robert Varnum. "The Boston Mercantile Community and the Promotion of the Textile Industry in New England, 1813–1860." Ph.D. diss., Yale University, 1963.

Voss-Hubbard, Mark. "Populism and Public Life: Antipartyism, the State, and the Politics of the 1850s in Connecticut, Massachusetts, and Pennsylvania." Ph.D. diss., University of Massachusetts at Amherst, 1997.

Index